Global Supply Chains in the Pharmaceutical Industry

Hamed Nozari
Islamic Azad University, Iran

Agnieszka Szmelter
University of Gdańsk, Poland

A volume in the Advances in Logistics, Operations, and Management Science (ALOMS) Book Series

IGI Global
DISSEMINATOR OF KNOWLEDGE

Published in the United States of America by
IGI Global
Business Science Reference (an imprint of IGI Global)
701 E. Chocolate Avenue
Hershey PA, USA 17033
Tel: 717-533-8845
Fax: 717-533-8661
E-mail: cust@igi-global.com
Web site: http://www.igi-global.com

Library of Congress Cataloging-in-Publication Data

Names: Nozari, Hamed, 1984- editor. | Szmelter, Agnieszka, 1989- editor.
Title: Global supply chains in the pharmaceutical industry / Hamed Nozari and Agnieszka Szmelter, editors.
Description: Hershey, PA : Business Science Reference, [2019]
Identifiers: LCCN 2017060406| ISBN 9781522559214 (hardcover) | ISBN 9781522559221 (ebook)
Subjects: LCSH: Pharmaceutical industry--Management. | Business logistics.
Classification: LCC HD9665.5 .G57 2019 | DDC 615.1068/7--dc23 LC record available at https://lccn.loc.gov/2017060406

This book is published in the IGI Global book series Advances in Logistics, Operations, and Management Science (ALOMS) (ISSN: 2327-350X; eISSN: 2327-3518)

British Cataloguing in Publication Data
A Cataloguing in Publication record for this book is available from the British Library.

Advances in Logistics, Operations, and Management Science (ALOMS) Book Series

ISSN:2327-350X
EISSN:2327-3518

Editor-in-Chief: John Wang, Montclair State University, USA

MISSION

Operations research and management science continue to influence business processes, administration, and management information systems, particularly in covering the application methods for decision-making processes. New case studies and applications on management science, operations management, social sciences, and other behavioral sciences have been incorporated into business and organizations real-world objectives.

The **Advances in Logistics, Operations, and Management Science** (ALOMS) Book Series provides a collection of reference publications on the current trends, applications, theories, and practices in the management science field. Providing relevant and current research, this series and its individual publications would be useful for academics, researchers, scholars, and practitioners interested in improving decision making models and business functions.

COVERAGE

- Political Science
- Operations management
- Finance
- Computing and information technologies
- Production management
- Information Management
- Services management
- Organizational Behavior
- Marketing engineering
- Risk Management

IGI Global is currently accepting manuscripts for publication within this series. To submit a proposal for a volume in this series, please contact our Acquisition Editors at Acquisitions@igi-global.com or visit: http://www.igi-global.com/publish/.

The Advances in Logistics, Operations, and Management Science (ALOMS) Book Series (ISSN 2327-350X) is published by IGI Global, 701 E. Chocolate Avenue, Hershey, PA 17033-1240, USA, www.igi-global.com. This series is composed of titles available for purchase individually; each title is edited to be contextually exclusive from any other title within the series. For pricing and ordering information please visit http://www.igi-global.com/book-series/advances-logistics-operations-management-science/37170. Postmaster: Send all address changes to above address.

Titles in this Series

For a list of additional titles in this series, please visit:
https://www.igi-global.com/book-series/advances-logistics-operations-management-science/37170

Operations Research for Military Organizations
Hakan Tozan (Istanbul Medipol University, Turkey) and Mumtaz Karatas (National Defense University, Turkey)
Information Science Reference • ©2019 • 445pp • H/C (ISBN: 9781522555131) • US $195.00

Cases on Quality Initiatives for Organizational Longevity
Archana Krishnan (PSG Institute of Management Coimbatore, India)
Business Science Reference • ©2018 • 449pp • H/C (ISBN: 9781522552888) • US $195.00

Enhancing Competitive Advantage With Dynamic Management and Engineering
Carolina Machado (University of Minho, Portugal) and J. Paulo Davim (University of Aveiro, Portugal)
Business Science Reference • ©2018 • 315pp • H/C (ISBN: 9781522553601) • US $195.00

Information Technology as a Facilitator of Social Processes in Project Management and...
Timothy C. Bagwell (Walden University, USA) Robert A. Cropf (Saint Louis University, USA) and Sheryl L. Foster-Gadkari (Strategic Impact, USA)
Business Science Reference • ©2018 • 217pp • H/C (ISBN: 9781522534716) • US $185.00

Handbook of Research on Cross-Cultural Business Education
Chandan Maheshkar (University of Indore, India) and Vinod Sharma (Christ Institute of Management, India)
Business Science Reference • ©2018 • 463pp • H/C (ISBN: 9781522537762) • US $235.00

Handbook of Research on Supply Chain Management for Sustainable Development
Ulas Akkucuk (Bogazici University, Turkey)
Business Science Reference • ©2018 • 439pp • H/C (ISBN: 9781522557579) • US $265.00

Globalization and Trade Integration in Developing Countries
Ahu Coşkun Özer (Marmara University, Turkey)
Business Science Reference • ©2018 • 320pp • H/C (ISBN: 9781522540328) • US $205.00

For an entire list of titles in this series, please visit:
https://www.igi-global.com/book-series/advances-logistics-operations-management-science/37170

IGI Global
DISSEMINATOR OF KNOWLEDGE

701 East Chocolate Avenue, Hershey, PA 17033, USA
Tel: 717-533-8845 x100 • Fax: 717-533-8661
E-Mail: cust@igi-global.com • www.igi-global.com

Editorial Advisory Board

Table of Contents

Detailed Table of Contents

Section 1
Logistics and Supply Chain Management

The first section contains the definitions of logistics, logistics support, supply chain, supply chain management, and descriptions of the basic functions of them. The section also indicates the role of the information systems in creating the success of supply chains.

The objective of this chapter is to create an introduction to all subsequent chapters of the book. This is a description of basics of logistics and logistics management used in every part of the supply chain, in every sector of the regional economies and the global economy. The primary research question to be answered is: What is the role of logistics in creation of the supply chain's success? The answer will allow for presenting logistics as a main element of supply chain management in the current global economic ecosystem. It will be a guideline for the readers about how to think about logistics support for all discussed functional areas of supply chain management mentioned in the following parts of the book.

Since their initiation—characterized by an unsophisticated structure—organizations declare the necessity to organize, coordinate, and manage resources. This necessity is emphasized through the appearance of emergent types of structure assorted with crossing boundaries strategies (strategic alliances, virtual enterprise, modular enterprise, and so forth). This paradigm shift has a prevailing effect on the "way of doing" within organizations and networks. The chapter aims to expose the theoretical approaches that explain the formation and the dynamics of the supply chain (Section 1). As a second step, the notion of the supply chain management (Section 2) and the supply chain performance. It also presents the impact of the IOS use on supply chain performance (Section 3).

Section 2
Global Pharmaceutical Industry

The section contains the description of the global pharmaceutical industry, megatrends and macrotrends in the global economy influencing its development, and many other issues allowing for the general analysis of the current state of this sector.

The pharmaceutical industry is seen as one of the most dynamic, volatile, and innovative parts of the global economic environment. It also has a big impact on the society and is an indicator of the healthcare systems' condition. Some changes have happened in the last decades, for example, shifting the production facilities to the developing countries, new market entries, or the new law changed the previously established and stable layout of market forces. The chapter aims at presenting the current situation of the global pharmaceutical industry including the main trends influencing the changes in this sector. Describing this part of the global market will ensure the right interpretation of the research results of the other parts of the book.

The pharmaceutical industry is trending in business decisions to demonstrate financial impact, influence on the behavior of consumers, governments, and businesses. This impact is beyond geographies and industries. It must be understood how a trend's impact will manifest itself in an actionable business planning horizon. Most of the pharmaceutical industries believe that global trends will shape business decisions over the next 5 to 10 years. Each management team in the pharmaceutical industry works on the global forces shaping their strategic context. The collisions approach is a systematic way to capture trends in strategy that enables your leadership team to rapidly combine multiple trends, facts, and perspectives to identify the "market-shaping force" that has the power to significantly shift spending and profit pools. This chapter discusses the effective competition in the pharmaceutical industry in the implementation of new technologies and trends to contribute to broader solutions.

Section 3
Primary and Support Processes in the Pharmaceutical Industry

This section presents the details of the production process (the primary process) in the pharmaceutical industry and the chosen functions of the support (logistics) process in this sector (product development, sales, and distribution).

The composite of the present pharmaceutical industry requires more effective medication improvement and generation. A product lifecycle (PLC) is the progression of stages from the product's production to the world until its last withdrawal from the market. Product lifecycle comprises various stages that a product must possess in its lifespan, for example, launching, growth, maturity, and decline stage. While each stage brings huge changes, a progression of procedures for the administration of product lifecycle is required. Product lifecycle management (PLM) is a precise, controlled idea for overseeing and creating products and product-related data. Enhanced patient consistency, income development, extended clinical advantages, and faster market dispatch are among the primary utilization of product lifecycle management. To create a viable and productive product lifecycle management program many qualities are viewed like promising start, vital arranging clear authority, supporting information and abilities, readiness for changing tenets of government and associations.

The most significant attribute of the pharmaceutical industry is its creations and advancements. The innovation of new drugs is necessary for improving the quality of human life and duration. Pharmaceutical drug development is a time-consuming, costly, and crucial process. The essential goal of drug development is to discover a dosage or dosage scale of a drug application that is both efficient in curing the desired disease and safe. Clinical trials including newly developed drugs that are directed in a progression of successive steps called stages to decide the security and efficacy of the new drug moreover the viability against the targeted diseases. There are four phases through which clinical trials are conducted. An investigational item can be assessed in more than one stage all the while in various clinical trials, and some clinical trials may cover two unique stages.

The most important stress related to the industrialized societies are diseases and health issues caused by taking medicines that are in unfavorable condition. The health issues caused due to the medications mainly depend on the quality of drugs. This is the main test confronted by any pharmaceutical organization wishing to guarantee its survival. The benefit in the pharmaceutical industries is higher. But now, the cost of the medicines is reduced as per the estimation is given by the government. Hence, pharmaceutical organizations now confront a moment of challenge to diminish costs through upgrading and enhancing their production methods. Based on the production process following in the pharmaceutical industries, the product quality can be varied and improved. This chapter prescribes the detailed information regarding the production practices that are followed in the pharmaceutical industries for the production of high-quality products.

Section 4
Supply Chain Management in the Pharmaceutical Industry

This section provides enhanced knowledge about supply chain management in the global pharmaceutical industry. It gives a detailed analysis of all functional areas related to the pharmaceutical supply chains including the newest solutions and current problems.

The pharmaceutical supply chain is presently a noteworthy research topic in process operations and administration. A lot of research has been embraced on office area and configuration, stock and circulation arranging, limit and generation arranging, and point-by-point planning. Just a little extent of this work straightforwardly addresses the issues confronted in the pharmaceutical division. The pharmaceutical industry is facing extraordinary difficulties caused by a maturing population, the expanding expense of medicinal services, the priority given by the governments to bring down the cost of medications, boundaries to a passage in developing markets, and the more extensive reception of non-specific medications. These are quite recently a portion of the many difficulties making weight on the overall revenue of pharmaceutical firms. Expanded expenses of R&D and a diminished number of affirmed sedates additionally demonstrates that the lion's share of prescription, which is anything but difficult to find, has just been found.

The pharmaceutical industry quite broadly encompasses a large and varied number of logistics and supply chain activities. The industry, as a whole, relies on some standard benchmarking indicators such as months of on-hand inventory and inventory turns; however, the existing metrics do not allow for idiosyncrasies of the industry or provide adequately detailed insight into the key factors that make a pharmaceutical supply chain excellence. Over 75% of the markup on pharmaceutical products takes place at the manufacturer. This causes inventory-carrying costs to increase dramatically once the distribution segments of the supply chain purchase the product. Wholesalers and large pharmacy chains suffer high carrying costs on the final product. Inside pharmaceutical supply chains, companies must also face issues of product expiration and limited shelf lives. Seasonal and short shelf life products such as flu vaccines leave companies without the opportunity to redistribute or reallocate product in order to meet demand.

The pharmaceutical industry is under severe pressure due to complex supply chains that are underutilized, inefficient, and ill-equipped to cope with the sort of products. The pharma supply chain must meet the demands of a fast-evolving marketplace and the shift from patient to an outcome to undergo a radical overhaul. Research and development (R&D) costs in the pharma industry are spiraling, development timelines are growing, and consumers are becoming increasingly knowledgeable about care options including drugs and treatment. The marketplace is fixed through the development cycle and increasing efficiency through rationalization or outsourcing of non-core activities. Recently, the pharma industry moved from the "one-size-fits-all" approach for the supply chain flexibility, responsiveness, and reliability. This chapter enables readers to understand the techniques for rapid commission and decommission new products and markets and alternate supply models, inventory tracking tools to eliminate counterfeiting and parallel-importing risks.

With traditional ERP systems, there is a lack of networking among suppliers, partners, and logistics providers. So, there is a need to have a holistic view of production and movement of goods from production to last mile delivery. The physical and digital supply chains need to be integrated to ensure secure supply chains that promote business excellence, collaboration among stakeholders, and reduce costs. The high-level view over their supply chains allows them to function better in a multi-channel world. It also helps them identify where to reduce stock without compromising customer service. Otherwise, it leads to a delay in delivery, counterfeit products, thefts, fraud, and cyberpiracy, which may lead to lawsuits and losing of brand image. The tacit function of supply chain management is to provide tracking of specific goods in the supply chain. So, it is imperative to leverage the blockchain technology stack to map multi-enterprise value networks and enable connected multi-modal networks.

The pharmaceutical supply chain is one of the most complex supply chains in the world. The primary objective of this chapter is to analyze the role of knowledge sharing barriers in supply chain performance. The chapter will explore significant knowledge sharing barriers that might deter the performance of a pharmaceutical supply chain. This chapter is expected to provide the twofold contribution to the academicians and practitioners. Firstly, it will socialize the importance of knowledge sharing barriers and the role they can play in deterring the performance of a pharmaceutical supply chain, and secondly, the prioritized ranking of the identified knowledge sharing barriers is expected to aid the policymakers and managers to understand the relative importance of the knowledge sharing barriers and design their knowledge management strategies accordingly.

Section 5
Pharmaceutical Supply Chain Characteristics: Case Studies

The last section contains a detailed description of the current issues in the pharmaceutical sector: one chapter about national issues and one from a company's perspective.

Corporate social responsibility policies have become an important management strategy in companies. This sector tries to respond to stakeholders' needs while developing socially responsible business activities and sustainable values. A sustainable supply chain is an integral part of CSR strategy in a pharmaceutical industry. Purchased goods and services have to present high standards and quality. As international companies have many suppliers and contractors, it is important to conduct and promote worked out values among all business partners. The aim of this chapter is to investigate the corporate social responsibility values of Polpharma Group. The chapter describes the long-term strategy of sustainability in Polpharma and the responsibilities of Polpharma in all business sectors. The most essential part will be the description of the process of sustainable supply chain formation. The chapter will describe the implementation of a code of conduct among suppliers. The case study in this chapter will be based on Polpharma, one of the largest Polish pharmaceutical companies.

The objective of this chapter is to analyze the collaboration networks of the Mexican pharmaceutical industry from an institutional approach. The pharmaceutical sector at a global level is characterized by a high dynamism in innovation and collaboration. One could say that the high value recorded by the industry is due to this. However, in Mexico, the lack of efficient institutions that ensure the appropriation of profits for investment in research within the industry is not perceived; this situation leads us to the next question, What are the dynamics of collaboration between pharmaceutical companies in Mexico? To answer this question, a database was created that identifies the alliances of the companies belonging to the Canifarma. Finally, a comparison of the number of registrations and patent applications between eight of these companies is made to measure the results of this situation.

Preface

INTRODUCTION

The global economy is a network of connections between different national economies, but also individual sectors. The proof of these strong relations was the reactions of individual ones to global, regional and local economic crises, which - as in the case of the last major crisis in 2007-2009 - significantly worsened their economic situation, forcing some companies even to declare bankruptcy.

Today's competitive advantage is not shaped by individual organizations, but by entire supply chains. Only the cooperation of suppliers of all chain tiers (especially 2nd Tier and 1st Tier suppliers), producers, wholesalers and retailers can provide an advantage over competitors. Therefore, the competitive struggle takes place between supply chains. Understanding this basis of functioning today's global business ecosystem allows for the design of chain structures (taking into account the use of appropriate technologies) so that, first and foremost, the information flow, then other resources, proceed efficiently, effectively and advantageously. The key to success is to understand that the information flow in today's supply chains is the primary one to the flow of other resources kinds (work, materials, money, capital).

The pharmaceutical industry has been described as one of the most innovative industries in the world. The reason for such a grading was the specificity of this sector - large expenditures on research and development, groundbreaking discoveries, inventing medicines for incurable diseases, etc. Also, it is influenced by a high level of quality management in industry, forcing supply chains to invest in the latest information technologies, a measurement of the quality of materials and finished products, transport and storage (especially in the case of cold chain management). That is why nobody is surprised today about the use of RFID or blockchain at a similar level to, for example, the one in the automotive industry, recognized for many years as the most innovative industry worldwide.

Nevertheless, there is easy-to-notice regionalization in this industry. It is divided into three parts: Big Pharma, Pharmerging and others. Big Pharma companies, originally from Western Europe, the USA and Japan, dictate the conditions of competition in the global market and are the best in research on primary drugs (brand drugs). Pharmaceutical companies in most cases do not have such significant amounts of money for business development, therefore they focus mainly on the development of generic medicines, also for their citizens, because generic drugs are usually cheaper. Other countries play a small role in shaping the global pharmaceutical sector.

Another reason to recognize that the pharmaceutical industry is unique is the fact that this industry shapes the state of the global society, especially the widely understood healthcare. The impact on public health in the pharmaceutical industry is undeniable. Therefore, it is subjected to a series of analyzes and criticisms, not only noticing its business but also its ethical character. This results in numerous reports and papers, mainly concerning: ethics in testing of substances and drugs on animals and people, ethics in the pricing of medicines for individual regional markets, dual patenting of medicines, generic drugs production, and finally - sustainable management, Corporate Social Responsibility (CSR), access to drugs of given brands in various parts of the world and charity activities. Therefore, this industry is particularly exposed to public dissatisfaction and criticism, which definitely inhibit the aspirations only to achieve high financial results. It is impossible to implement only business rules in this industry, but without including them, this industry could not carry out above all costly research in the framework of the drug development process. It should be mentioned that a very small number of research and experiments, and then testing of drugs, brings a positive result. Therefore, this industry has to be viewed holistically, trying to reconcile all the goals of all stakeholders, which seems to be a completely unachievable goal.

However, some of these goals can be implemented through logistics, focused primarily on providing the right resources at the right time, in the right place at the right acceptable cost. This is not usually the case, as is often mentioned in the literature, the provision of resources in the shortest time or at the lowest cost - it is about balancing all these goals to finally achieve the synergy effect, the overall best effect by combining them together. Supply chains will not avoid the necessity of solving classical logistic problems, such as make-or-buy (produce on their own or buy) as well as many conflicts of goals (tradeoffs) in different places of both single organizations and supply chains.

The basis for understanding logistics is understanding the specifics of the basic and logistic process, supporting. The basic process is usually the transformation of input resources (materials, knowledge and skills of employees, money, fixed assets) into output resources (finished product: good or service). The supporting process, referred to as the logistics process, includes everything that supports the implementation of the basic process: planning, forecasting, procurement, warehouse management, inventory management, sales and distribution, human resources management, information systems, etc. Understanding this foundation guarantees proper planning of logistics activities, also within the scope of supply chain management.

In view of the above considerations, the problems that many researchers and managers have been trying to solve for years remain valid, only the methods and tools for solving them are changing. However, despite their constant improvement, there are new conditions, variables that must be taken into account in these efforts, which compensate for the development of technology and make the same problems are insurmountable.

CAUSES OF PUBLISHING THE BOOK

Considering the above problems, and taking into account the small number of literature on global supply chains in the pharmaceutical industry, we decided together with the Publisher that we will try to create a book that will combine the logistics and the basic process dimension in the pharmaceutical industry.

The literature on supply chain management in the industry chosen by us is quite modest. Search engines of scientific literature currently point to about 200 articles similar to this topic (example EBSCOhost, 24/07/2018), but mainly focused on risk management in these chains, i.e. on a part of supply chain management (SCM), very important from the point of view of the need of cold chain management, but however, it is a partial subject that does not reflect the specifics of the entire SCM in the pharmaceutical industry. Also many studies concern outsourcing in the production processes of this sector, which in turn refers to the problem of make-or-buy.

In turn, EBSCOhost indicated three books on a similar topic (as at 24.07.2018), and Google Books on eight (the others referred to fragmentary topics, as well as scientific articles), so the publication of a book similar to ours has become, in our opinion, justified.

Numerous, dynamic changes have supported this need both in the pharmaceutical industry itself, which is a natural thing in highly innovative industries, but also in the field of changes in technologies used in logistics. Updating the literature in terms of their use is necessary because they are being developed implemented very quickly and information from 10 or 20 years ago is no longer valid.

These reasons led us to start a book design project that ended one year after it began. Now we can offer this book for the Readers.

ORGANIZATION OF THE BOOK

The book is organized into five sections and 14 chapters. A brief description of each of the chapters follows:

Section 1

Section 1 contains the definitions of logistics, logistics support, supply chain, supply chain management, and description of the basic functions of them. The section indicates also the role of the information systems in creating the success of supply chains

Chapter 1

Chapter 1 reviews and presents the basic definitions in the topic of the book. Global supply chains are mainly focused on optimizing their business processes and there is no alternative but to go towards logistics management. The chapter identifies the basic elements of logistics and their functions in the supply chain management. It also highlights the importance of logistics support system in supporting the primary (production) process, and – in this way - creating the success of the individual organization and the whole network, including the supply chain.

Chapter 2

Chapter 2 establishes the need for an information flow strategy and presents sample structures of this flow. The authors of this chapter contend that by investing in the development of the information systems, the organizations and supply chains can achieve better competitive advantage and improve their processes and the business itself.

Section 2

Section 2 contains the description of the global pharmaceutical industry, megatrends, and macrotrends in the global economy influencing its development, and many other issues allowing for the general analysis of the current state of this sector.

Chapter 3

Chapter 3 presents an analysis of the current state of the global pharmaceutical industry. It concerns in managing those supply chains and their characteristics, for example, sustainability and CSR activities. The author describes the pharmaceutical global ecosystem and mentions the biggest market players, their characteristics, but also global trends creating the broader context of the development of the pharmaceutical market.

Chapter 4

Chapter 4 takes theoretical and practical orientation and debates about the macroeconomic trends in the mentioned sector. It examines some challenges in supply chain operations as results of the global economic environment state. The overall aim of the chapter is to consider the issues related to launching new kinds of drugs, new ways of product procurement and distribution, but also embedding those into the global market changes.

Section 3

Section 3 presents the details of the production process (the primary process) in the pharmaceutical industry and the chosen functions of the support (logistics) process in this sector (product development, sales, and distribution).

Chapter 5

Chapter 5 reviews the whole product lifecycle and at the same time, it is the introduction to the subsequent chapters. It mentions the particular stages of developing, launching, producing and distributing the drug. The authors describe in detail each step of those processes and highlight the main milestones allowing to achieve the goal, which is launching a successful drug, what is the big challenge in the industry.

Chapter 6

Chapter 6 describes more in detail the drug development process. The author focuses on the processes of laboratory experiments and drug testing, also indicating the important issues of ethical testing policy. She also highlights the difficulties in developing an effective drug - very few experiments and tests are successful and allow the drug to be marketed.

Chapter 7

Chapter 7 addresses the issue of the primary process in the pharmaceutical supply chain, which is the production process, including, drug formulation, powder mixing, granulation, compression, hot melt extrusion etc., so very technical issues of the mentioned process. The author describes also the packaging as the crucial element of the production process, especially in the field of the quality management procedures.

Section 4

Section 4 provides the enhanced knowledge about the supply chain management in the global pharmaceutical industry. It allows for a detailed analysis of all functional areas related to the pharmaceutical supply chains including the newest solutions and current problems.

Chapter 8

Chapter 8 reviews issues surrounding pharmaceutical supply chain functioning. It mentions supply chain challenges, structures, organization, operation, fragmentation, and also the emerging field of the reverse logistics operations. The author describes also the future challenges influencing the strategies of global supply chains and possible future scenarios.

Chapter 9

Chapter 9 discusses in detail supply chain management practices, taking into consideration a high specifics level of the pharmaceutical industry. Those areas include customer service policy, forecasting, planning, procurement and distribution. The approach presented by the author is made on the process-based approach. The last part of the chapter highlights the risks in the current pharmaceutical supply chain management.

Chapter 10

Chapter 10 presents the best practices in the supply chain management, mentioned in the previous chapter. It presents all of the possible supply chain operations and describes the best solutions, also in cold chain management. This builds a set of the practices with high usefulness for managers.

Chapter 11

Chapter 11 describes in detail the similar topic to this mentioned in chapter 2, which is related to the information flow. The authors present the blockchain and

RFID technologies, their characteristics, a way of implementing, usefulness for the industry, including the pharmaceutical sector. They also provide a specification of the augmented reality environment, indicating the future challenges and possible development scenarios for the mentioned technologies.

Chapter 12

Chapter 12 addresses the issue of knowledge sharing in the global supply chains. The authors indicate the role of knowledge sharing systems in creating the supply chain success, including performance indicators. They present the wide approach to set, measure, interpret, correct, optimize and control the performance indicators in the field of knowledge sharing, very popular today, in the era of learning and self-learning organizations.

Section 5

Section 5 contains a detailed description of the current issues in the pharmaceutical sector: one about national and one about company's perspective

Chapter 13

Chapter 13 analyses a case study of one of the biggest pharmaceutical company in Poland and Europe – Polpharma. The author focuses her thoughts on the sustainability and Corporate Social Responsibility issues by analyzing the policy of this company from many perspectives (economic, social, environmental). This case study, very valuable for managers and CSR researches, provides many instructions helpful in the process of developing the company's strategy.

Chapter 14

Chapter 14 is also based on the case study, not on a single company, but the whole country. The authors describe the usefulness of the collaboration in creating a competitive advantage of the whole country's economy. They provide the theoretical and practical analysis of the Mexican pharmaceutical industry with taking into account the functioning of the global market players and their subsidiaries.

CONCLUSION

To conclude, this book was aimed to provide a wide range of topics and knowledge about the global pharmaceutical industry. This is the reason why we wanted to describe both general and detailed issues regarding this broad topic. We hope we succeeded, at least to some extent, and respond to this challenge by providing a valuable position on the market of scientific books.

I hope that this book will meet the expectations of dear Readers and will allow them to gain broad knowledge in the field of supply chain management in the pharmaceutical industry. With great apprehension, concerns, but also with hope, I give you this book counting on positive reception and constructive comments on the topics we have touched on.

Best regards,

Agnieszka Szmelter
University of Gdańsk, Poland

Acknowledgment

The editors would like to acknowledge the help of all the people involved in this project and, more specifically, to the authors and reviewers that took part in the review process. Without their support, this book would not have become a reality.

First, the editors would like to thank each one of the authors for their contributions. Our sincere gratitude goes to the chapter's authors who contributed their time and expertise to this book.

Second, the editors wish to acknowledge the valuable contributions of the reviewers and Editorial Advisory Board regarding the improvement of quality, coherence, and content presentation of chapters. Most of the authors also served as referees; we highly appreciate their double task.

Agnieszka Szmelter
University of Gdańsk, Poland

Hamed Nozari
Islamic Azad University, Iran

Section 1
Logistics and Supply Chain Management

The first section contains the definitions of logistics, logistics support, supply chain, supply chain management, and descriptions of the basic functions of them. The section also indicates the role of the information systems in creating the success of supply chains.

Chapter 1
Logistics Thinking:
The Basics of Logistics

Agnieszka Szmelter
University of Gdańsk, Poland

ABSTRACT

The objective of this chapter is to create an introduction to all subsequent chapters of the book. This is a description of basics of logistics and logistics management used in every part of the supply chain, in every sector of the regional economies and the global economy. The primary research question to be answered is: What is the role of logistics in creation of the supply chain's success? The answer will allow for presenting logistics as a main element of supply chain management in the current global economic ecosystem. It will be a guideline for the readers about how to think about logistics support for all discussed functional areas of supply chain management mentioned in the following parts of the book.

INTRODUCTION

Logistics is an area of economics and management very popular in the last few decades, mostly because of the growing awareness of managerial staff about the role of planning and control in creating the success of companies and supply chains. Therefore, many books and articles address problems related to logistics issues. However, because of that, logistics has different meanings and definitions, what is confusing when talking about particular functions of the company or supply chain management. The unification of the terms is necessary to make the analysis of business processes easier and to facilitate the communication between practitioners and research staff.

DOI: 10.4018/978-1-5225-5921-4.ch001

These problems formed the basis for the creation of this chapter. The Author hopes it will help to understand the role of particular functional areas to build the entire logistics support system in the presented sector as a whole, and in the individual organizations, which build the sector environment.

LOGISTICS THINKING

Logistics

Achieving the success on the market and improving the profitability of a given entity's business depends largely on the understanding that logistics is the strategic orientation of the company (Langley & Morice, 1982). Logistics in two ways is related to the company's strategy. First, the company implements a logistics strategy that obviously must be linked to other functional strategies of the entity (e.g. with a production, marketing and financial strategy) and a general strategy. Secondly, logistics is a part of the competitive strategy of the company and has a big impact on shaping its competitive advantage (Ciesielski, 1998).

Logistics in a Company

The task of the logistics process is to fulfill the support of the primary process within the logistics support system (Chaberek, 2014). Logistics provides the value for the customer (Chaberek, 2015) by implementing 5 logistics goals (5R): providing the right resources, in the right amount, in the right time, in the right place and at the right price (Chaberek, 2015). One can refer to the model of the added-value chain of M. Porter, in which this value is described as "an increase in value of goods as a result of a specific production process", i.e. deducting from the value of goods the costs of their production and sale (Begg, Fischer & Dornbusch, 2007). The sequence of activities performed by subsequent elements in the supply chain provides the added value to the end customer, both with his satisfaction, which can be related to the utility of the place and time in the logistics service model of Chaberek (see Figure 1). The customers buys the product in order to obtain certain benefits. A characteristic feature of logistics process is that it cannot exist without the primary process (production process) to be supported. Logistics process supports each phase of the production process and can (even should) be implemented by different organizational units, the elements of the supply chain or third parties through outsourcing (*make or buy* problem).

The main goal of every activities in logistics support system (LSS, see Figure 2) is advantageous purchase of resources, their effective use in order to produce certain goods or services and the effective selling of these products. These efficient use of resources aims at, first of all, minimizing material, time and technical losses.

Despite many efforts focused on achieving these objectives, wasting resources occurs. According to the Kaizen concept, there are several areas of it, as follows:

- Overproduction, and pursue to not to waste the capacities, in result – *trade-off* situation (using full capacities vs. Lower demand for goods or highly-floating one),
- Too big inventories, too high inventory values, resulting in the higher cost of the warehouse management and financial management, also the risk of aging or destruction,
- Correcting the errors and defects: the utilization or modification of the product already manufactured,
- Traffic: unnecessary and useless movement of workers which does not add value to the product,
- Processing: a two-way: machines overload or not using their capacity; wasting time and skills of employees,
- Waiting: time losses due to the bottlenecks in the processes, lack of fluent, smooth flow of resources,
- Transportation: the transport activities related to all other kinds of waste.

Figure 1. The primary process and the logistics process
Source: (Chaberek, 2002)

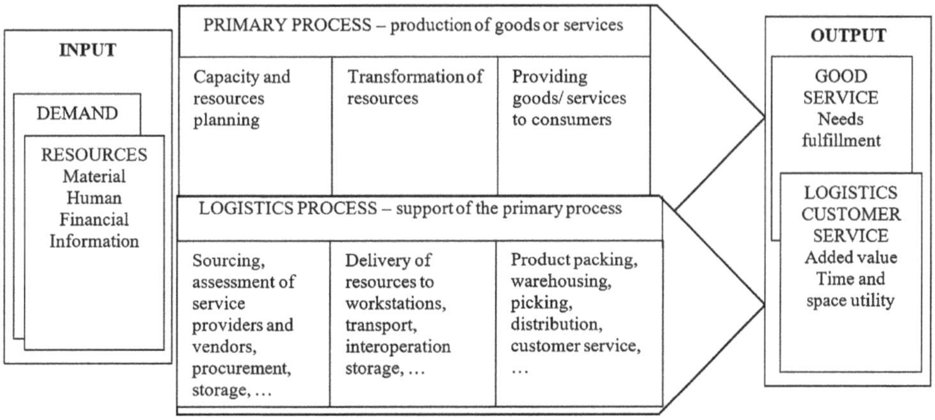

Figure 2. The logistics support system (LSS)
Source: (Chaberek, 2002)

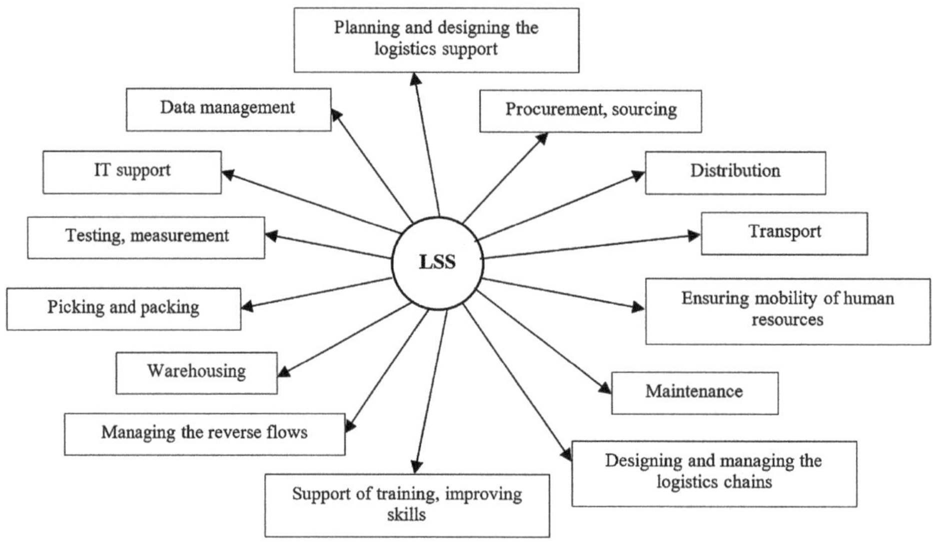

The logistics process can be fragmented, for example, due to the phase of the primary process it handles. Therefore, the logistics of the supply, production and distribution phases can be distinguished (Szmelter, 2012). Therefore, in the sphere of supply, logistics activities are based primarily on the assessment of potential suppliers, selection of purchase sources, making orders, accepting material and storing it. Support for the processing of resources into a finished product consists of delivering them to operational positions and handling of intermediates between them, also minimizing intermediate stocks. The logistics process in the distribution phase, in turn, includes packaging and storage of finished products, physical delivery to recipients and after-sales service. All of these activities are focused on providing the customer with a product that meets his requirements to ensure a high level of service and physical access to the good. The role of logistics is to eliminate from the processes the elements that do not create added value (this is a process of *reengineering*; Chaberek, 1999). The redesign of these processes is mostly aimed at minimizing costs and, above all, streamlining the process in order to obtain high-quality goods or services that meet customer requirements.

Logistics in a Supply Chain

Mentzer et al. (2001) pointed to the existence of more than 100 supply chain definitions. For the purpose of this study, the Author's one will be adopted here, based on those of Witkowski (1995, 2010), Christopher (1998), APICS (The Association for Operations Management, Association for Operational Management, (Lummus & Vokurka, 1999), Blaik (2001), Rutkowski (2004) and Jedliński (2015), that the supply chain is a network of interdependent and cooperating entities based on the principles of integration and coordination of resource flows based on the value chain of M. Porter, from the moment of creation or extraction of the resource to its consumption by the client (the final customer), also in the return flow, in order to achieve high efficiency and effectiveness of individual entities and the entire chain.

The functioning of supply chains can be seen as consisting of several layers for which the process of planning and implementing processes is carried out (see Figure 3). The corporation layer is the highest, most general layer consisting of all members of the supply chain, mainly reflecting business contacts between enterprises and the diversity of relationships and behaviors of these entities, i.e. meta- or macrologistic systems. The business layer presents the middle layer, i.e. micrologistic systems (individual organizations) - elements of each link in the supply chain (procurement, production, finance, sales, warehouse). The operational layer shows business processes implemented both in the unit and between the units. It can, therefore, be seen that the two higher layers are used to implement the system approach in logistics, and the lowest - to the process approach.

Various models of entities' integration have been described, among others by Blaik, Bruska, Kauf and Matwiejczuk (2013), as well as models of maturity and evolution of chains, among which are exchanged levels of evolution inside the enterprise (enterprise integration and corporate excellence) and outside (partner cooperation, cooperation in the value chain and full integration in the network). There are also many models of chains evolution, and for the purpose of this study, the model presented in Figure 4 was chosen.

Supply chain management is the management of the flow of resources, and thus the relations in the chain, so as to provide a certain value for the client at certain, possible lowest, acceptable costs. Its task is to maximize the synergy between its elements to achieve these goals. Supply chain management, chain strategy and individual entities' strategies should be coordinated and aligned to each other in order to effectively compete with the entire chain on the global market. In this respect, many tasks can be carried out, such as, for example, consolidation, restructuring of buyers, suppliers, competitors, sharing resources (including information), joint implementation of tasks (e.g. product development). Many factors that affect the nature of the activities and depend, inter alia, on from the scope of the supply chain, its size, industry specifics, etc. As part of the chain strategy, the nature of the relationship between the elements should be determined, which will affect communication, resource flows, etc. (Isaaksen & Kalsaas, 2009).

Figure 3. Logistic activities in three layers: supply chain, individual organization (business) and operational dimension
Source: (Ren, Ren, Chai, Liu & Tian, 2002)

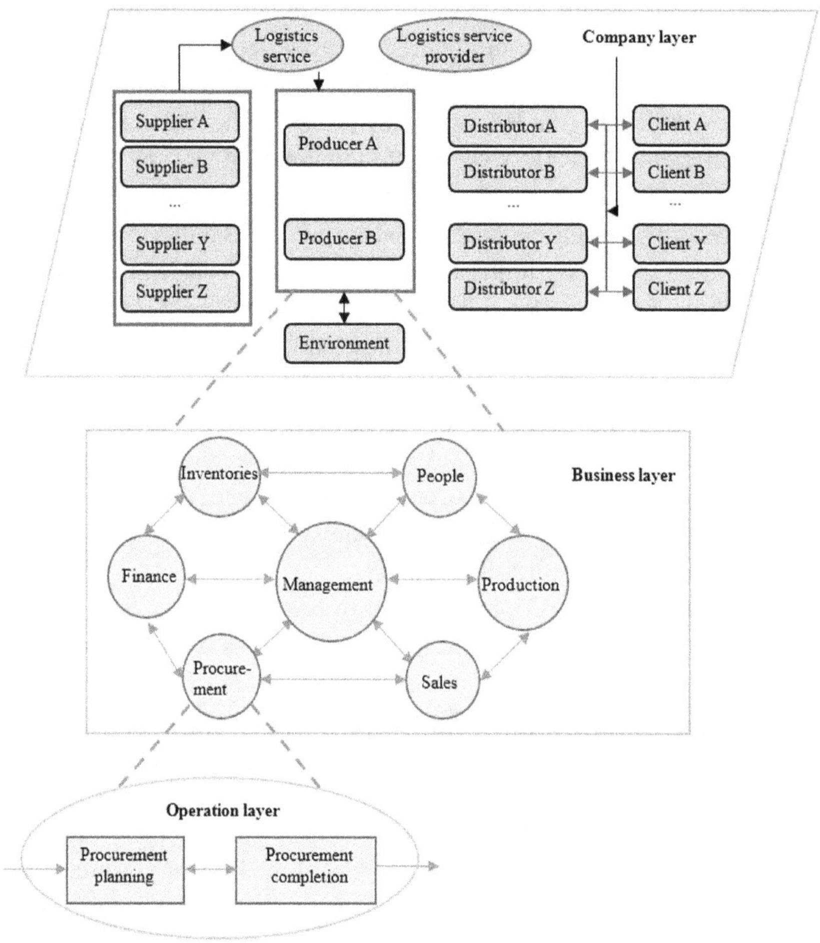

The functioning of the supply chain should be determined by three characteristics: flexibility, adaptability and resistance (Kramarz & Kramarz, 2013). Flexibility can be defined as the ability to restore the initial state after a disruption in the chain (deviations in planned flows of resources). It is particularly visible in unforeseen and crisis situations, such as economic crises. Adaptability is defined as the transition to a new state caused by long-term changes in the environment (e.g. structures and markets), which in the context of shaping logistic strategies are defined, among others, by megatrends (long-term trends). It is particularly visible when creating new needs or markets. In turn, resistance means reducing the negative effects of disturbances,

Figure 4. Typology of logistic networks
Źródło: (Wagenknecht, 2001)

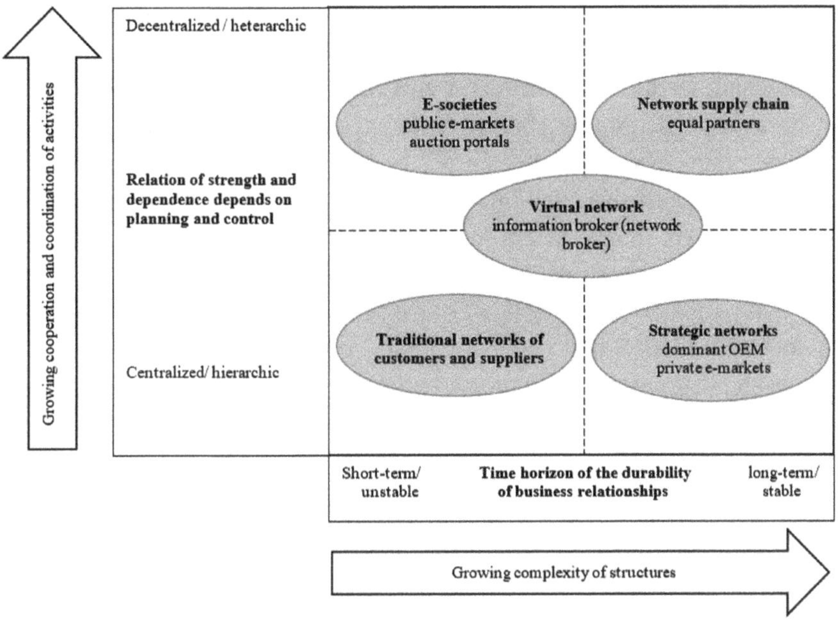

which can be achieved by providing flexibility as well as adaptability. These activities should be supported by the partnership and a vision of joint development in supply chains (Lee, 2007).

Supply chain links are connected by technical and technological, knowledge, social, administrative and legal (including capital) relations. Each of them must benefit the win-win in the long run, despite the often unfavorable conditions in the short term. According to Stadtler (2008), supply chain management is not the same as strategy, although it is an element of the supply chain strategy contributing to building its competitive position. Supply chain strategy is more than a product strategy (Borgstrom & Hertz, 2011). According to Borgstrom and Hertz (2011), supply chain organization is a determinant of the efficiency of material and product flow in the market and the efficiency of the chain itself. It is based on a set of resources that change over time (structure and quantity), therefore the adaptability of the strategy to market conditions is very important. Each supply chain should be seen as a set of opportunities to use resources (owned or future), such as (according to the eEPC notation) material, capital, human and information ones. Supply chain control is a process in which, based on defined requirements and expectations expressed in the form of business objectives, the supply chain is measured and evaluated to make decisions and implement corrective and preventive measures to increase the competitiveness of the goods and services provided.

The creation of global business networks resulted in the appearance of so-called ***orchestrators***. The orchestrators are entities that combine the functions of the supply chain leader, its coordinator and controller. It is they who set the main supply streams of the supply chain, create, at least in part, a short, medium and long-term strategy. They have to capture the differences between successive links of the chain, the enterprises that operate within them and create a whole from this diversity. Therefore, the orchestra must at least in part impose certain actions to individual participants of the chain so as to create the most coherent system of relations that will allow maximum use of the potential of the entire chain (Jedliński, 2009), not just its individual elements. Orchestrators within supply chains create decision centers (competence centers), which in turn dictate standards, methods and a plan to implement integration between entities, both in the information and economic sphere.

The orchestrator is responsible for determining the directions of development of the supply chain and for creating added value within its framework (Wasielewska-Marszałkowska, 2015). Therefore, it should manage, in addition to economic capital (tangible assets), also the intangible assets of this chain, including in particular (Rosińska-Bukowska, 2012):

- Structural capital:
    - Innovative capital (human resources, research and development activities),
    - Organizational capital (brand portfolio),
- Institutional capital (organizational culture).

The product, which goes to the final recipient, had to first pass the supply chain through the value chain system. Due to the fact that an entity operates in a chain or supply network, it does not just have to take care of its own value chain, but to analyze the chains of its predecessors and successors in the network. Moreover, individual value chains should be well integrated to connect to the value chain system, implement and coordinate efficient resource flows between the supply chain and supply chain elements.

The basis of all relations in the supply chains, logistic networks and companies was a logistics partnership. The concepts of managing the flow of resources (e.g. kaizen, ECR, just-in-time) determine the creation of a strategic logistics partnership that is based on two pillars. The first one concerns the elimination and reduction of business risk by sharing information, which significantly facilitates the implementation of the adopted strategy. In addition, you get the benefits of better inventory management, which goes to the cell that needs them at a particular moment. The second pillar concerns the elimination of activities that do not add value to products and which could be implemented by other entities. The chain coordinator can do it in many ways, dependent on the needs of the chain - remove intermediaries, change their role or introduce new ones (Ciesielski, 2002).

Logistics partnership, being an element of chains and logistics networks, is based on:

- Long-term building of long-lasting relationships,
- Strong connection with the environment (internal market, buyers, suppliers, potential employees, competitors, influential and opinion leaders),
- Portfolio management of buyers (analysis, changes, shaping attitudes),

In addition, this partnership is expanded in the logistics aspect by (Ciesielski, 2002):

- Cooperation in other areas than procurement, distribution and marketing,
- Strong operational integration, almost connecting enterprises into one organism,
- A common market strategy and subordination of individual goals to overarching goals (chain goals).

The effectiveness of the entire value creation chain is determined by the organization management concept, and globally, taking into account the complex chains in the automotive industry - management of the complexity of systems, including logistics systems. A variety of forms of cooperation between corporations should be described in this regard.

Logistics Strategy

The strategy can be defined by referring to its individual levels, variously presented in the literature (from two to four levels). The most popular interpretation presents two levels of enterprise strategy: global (general) strategy and partial (functional) strategies. Another, most extensive, divides strategies into: global (organization as a whole), strategy in relation to the industry in which it operates, functional and operational strategies. Another concept concerns the division into three types (levels) of the strategy: for organization (corporation) as a whole, each unit included in it and functional strategies implemented within the whole organization (eg marketing, production and logistics strategy).

According to Ciesielski (1998), there are three levels of the strategy (the same approach as presented in Figure 3):

- Of a company (transnational corporation)): in the area of choosing the products and markets,
- Of a production and trading unit (plant): in terms of a specific market or several markets (competitive strategy),
- Of functions implemented in the enterprise or functional areas operating within the enterprise or its unit (depending on the nature of these activities, for example, distinguish logistic, marketing, financial and other strategies).

In general, the goals of using logistic strategies can be reduced to two aims: lowering logistics costs and improving the management of available resources (Ciesielski, 2002). The company's logistics strategy should be adapted to the overall strategy (see Table 1). In the aspect of creating the entity's strategy, one can talk about logistics strategic decisions that later determine the creation of a logistic functional strategy (see Table 2).

According to Harrison and van Hoek (2010*)*, "a logistics strategy is a set of guidelines, drivers and well-established attitudes that help in the coordination of goals, plans and rules of conduct, but are strengthened as a result of conscious and unconscious behaviors manifested in the intra- and inter-organizational dimension. through partners making up the supply chain". For the purposes of the chapter, the author formulated her own definition: the logistic strategy is a set of long-term guidelines that help achieve 5W logistics goals in a single organization and the entire supply chain, to shape a competitive advantage at both levels, taking into account the objectives of the overall strategy and other functional strategies (marketing, financial, etc.) (Szmelter, 2017).

The logistics strategy should include basic information on the operations of the entity, like information on the location of warehouses, logistic centers, customer service levels, inventory control, cargo units, means of transport, outsourcing or lack of it, suppliers and recipients and their choice, IT solutions etc. The task of the logistics strategy is, inter alia, to develop the concept of integration of activities in geographically dispersed units that make up the supply chain. Harmonization of the strategy within the supply chain is necessary for its proper functioning, because it is easier to control companies with the same ones than with completely different priorities.

Planning in the supply chain should take place in the long-, medium- and short-term dimension and significantly differ in the case of mass-produced goods on the basis of MTS (Make-to-Stock) and customized or ordered in large quantities goods

Table 1. Logistics service in supranational strategies

Transnational Strategy	Preferences on the Service on Particular Markets	Service Capacities	Type of Market Logistics Services Portfolio	Way of Providing Resources
Global	Equal	Equal	Homogenous service implemented globally	Large sorting stations, a unified way of delivering resources
International	Similar	Similar	The largely homogenous, distinct way of implementation in individual markets	A network of central warehouses serving local markets
Multinational	Different	Different	Adapted to each market	Very diverse
Transnational	Different	Different (only in the case of some logistics activities)	The combination of homogeneous elements and service components tailored to the market	Diverse

Source: (Szymczak, 2004)

produced on the MTO (Make-to-Order) concept. In addition, in the case of both kinds of goods, product lifecycle planning is becoming more and more popular in accordance with the *cradle-to-cradle* approach, related to the closed loop supply chain management (CLSCM) concept.

In the face of the inseparable connection between the primary and logistics processes, it cannot be unambiguously determined whether there are specific factors only for the shaping of logistics strategy, without reference to other functional strategies. In other areas of activity, for example in financial accounting, these factors are relatively easy to be identified, because they are legal procedures, internal regulations, etc. It is equally easy to list the factors that make up the organization's legal strategy. On the other hand, logistic activity includes processes carried out in entities with different characteristics and thus affect to a certain extent all determinants shaping the general strategy. One can only speak about groups of factors that in a special way determine the creation of logistics strategies. These groups can be classified in relation to various criteria and reference systems. Factors that can influence the shaping of the logistics strategy build a diverse, heterogeneous, extensive set. Individual authors of studies on logistics in their works mentioned only some of them.

According to the concept of Baumgarten and Walter (2001), the beginning of the 21st century in logistics will dominate the trend of integration of value creation chains in the form of global networks. The ability to compete with others will be determined by properly created strategies for customer integration in value creation networks. Customer orientation will be stimulated mainly through innovation and service levels as well as sustained potential in these two areas. Integration of the value creation network will create strong value creation systems. At the same time, it will reduce the complexity of these systems, which will increase flexibility and speed up the response to changes in the environment. The initiative to create value will shift more and more towards the client. The new Internet communication channel will play a significant role in the creation of values as well as logistic strategies, which will influence the flow of information throughout the entire supply chain and result in many changes in the trade, like for example omnichannel logistics (Weiland, 2016).

Table 2. Logistics strategic decisions (parts of logistics strategy)

<table>
<tr><th>Group of Logistics Strategic Decisions</th><th>Individual Decision</th><th>Relation to Another Functional Strategy</th><th>Dimensions of Decision</th></tr>
<tr><td rowspan="4">Products and markets (logistics service)</td><td>Scope of logistics activities separately for each product and market</td><td>Marketing strategy</td><td rowspan="12">Relations with the external environment (suppliers, recipients, competitors)
Scope of logistics activity (products on the supply and sale markets covered by logistics service)
Scope of logistic activity (comparison of the area served logistically by the company with the area of activities outsourced to companies)</td></tr>
<tr><td>Scope of logistics system</td><td>Production strategy</td></tr>
<tr><td>Scope of outsourcing</td><td>Production strategy</td></tr>
<tr><td>Customer service standards</td><td>Marketing strategy</td></tr>
<tr><td rowspan="8">Internal structure</td><td>Logistic costs in relation to the level of customer service</td><td>Financial strategy</td></tr>
<tr><td>Logistic capital expenditures in relation to current logistics costs</td><td>Marketing strategy</td></tr>
<tr><td>Number of units</td><td>Production strategy</td></tr>
<tr><td>Location of units</td><td>Production strategy</td></tr>
<tr><td>Equipment in resources (including fixed assets and software)</td><td>Production strategy</td></tr>
<tr><td>Defining logistic services of own units</td><td>Production strategy</td></tr>
<tr><td>Defining inventory management rules</td><td>Production strategy</td></tr>
</table>

Source: own preparation based on Ciesielski, (1998)

The level of market service can be both the main differentiating element in the company's logistics strategy, support the main differentiating element or be one of the serial elements of the strategy. Market service is the ability of a given logistics system to meet customer needs in terms of reliability, communication and convenience. Reliability means, among others, punctuality and completeness of deliveries, correct circulation of documentation, etc. The time dimension of this reliability is not only timeliness in terms of deliveries, but also the speed of service, including the time of consideration of the guarantee. In a sense, reliability and time also involve communication, that is, providing full information to the client, the quality of communication, a small amount of interference in the flow of information, the speed of transfer. When determining the level of market service, the organization must, of course, analyze the offers of market competitors, as well as determine the logistic costs that the company is able to bear in this area.

The ongoing integration of supply chains within global networks has led to the emergence of the concept of Collaborative Planning, Forecasting and Replenishment (CPFR), consisting of synchronizing forecasts, risks, costs and profits from business partners' activities to improve efficiency whole chain. The basic element of this concept is joint planning of processes and decision making, which results in better coordination of activities within the chain and increasing its competitiveness (Thomé, Hollmann & do Carmo, 2014).

CHOSEN MEGATRENDS AFFECTING CONTEMPORARY LOGISTICS

Sustainable Supply Chain

Hentschel argues that logistics processes in global supply chains generate over 14% of global CO2 emission (Hentschel, 2012). Reducing such high level of logistics activity's side effects is a challenge for supply chain management in terms of implementing innovations in processes and products. Contemporary SCM concepts rely on sustainable (green, eco-efficient) supply chain model. This type of chain H. Brdulak defines as the environmentally friendly processing the resources to the extent that products can be maximally exploited without disturbing the environment (Brdulak 2012). Of course, this is also related to the reverse logistics and CLSCM. A combination of different innovations in many areas (processes, products, organization, technology etc.) occurs to reduce external costs and environmental negative impact. Objectives of building eco-efficiency of the supply chain is a long-term goal, and the green chains are not expected to change quickly. On the other hand, business relies on doing everything in a short time and achieving the goals as soon as possible.

Environmental Protection Agency created a guide „The Lean and Green Supply Chain: A Practical Guide for Materials Managers and Supply Chain Managers to Reduce Costs and Improve Environmental Performance" (EPA, 2000). According to this document, to create sustain (green) supply chain, chain leaders should (EPA, 2000):

- Identify environmental costs in a company (step: Identify Costs),
- Identify areas of company's activity, in which costs and environmental impact can be minimized (step: Determine Opportunities),
- Calculate benefits and profits from environmental actions (step: Calculate Benefits),
- Make decisions about its control and correction (step: Decide, Implement and Monitor).

The key to success can be tracking costs at the level of a single piece. That is why the whole system of flowing resources in the primary and reverse flow need to be designed, implemented and controlled (see Figure 5).

Growing Complexity and Popularity of Complexity Management

In today's global economy, changes are less predictable, more and more dynamic and rich in effects on many national economies because of their economic links. Companies are becoming complex as a result of the growth and implementation of increasingly complex business models. Consequently, the complexity of supply

Figure 5. Eco-efficiency in the supply chain
Source: (Burchart-Korol, Czaplicka-Kolarz, Witkowski, 2013).

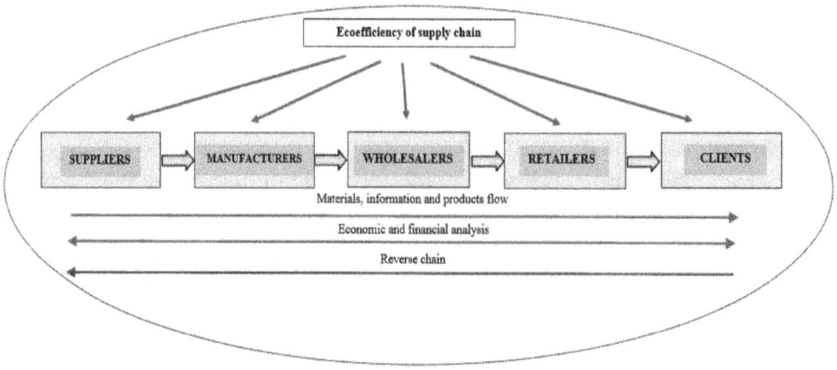

chains is growing, intensified by the globalization of operations. The increase in complexity is generally perceived as a necessity, but it has its limits. In practice, each system has a so-called critical complexity, the point beyond which it cannot develop further, unless its structure is not a subject to the necessary transformation.

Critical complexity quantifies the maximum amount of complexity that a given system is able to develop before its structure becomes loose or disintegrated. A company with a less complex structure will be better adapted to deal with situations of high uncertainty and will respond better to unexpected events (conflicts, crises, etc.). An organization with a very complex structure is also less profitable, more difficult to manage, and thus - less sustainable. Therefore, the management of complexity has become important in many industries.

No company operates in isolation, so the key to determining the company's condition lies in its interaction with the environment (business ecosystem). That is why in many cases companies' problems are external, not internal. For a number of them, the three main factors contributing the most to the complexity of these organizations were external. These were: volatility of the global macroeconomic situation, volatility of commodity prices and the condition of the sector in which the enterprise was operating. Internal factors had a much smaller impact on the global complexity of their business ecosystem, which did not exclude practical room for maneuver to reduce internal complexity (Marczyk, Czarnota & Gliński, 2014).

In the literature on the subject, there are no studies in which a universal definition of complexity would be constructed and this issue was presented comprehensively in relation to economic systems. The complexity of systems is a concept that is difficult to define due to its ambiguity and multidimensionality. Cz. Mesjasz (2014) defines the system as complex if it has a large number of elements that interact with each other. The complexity, according to him, is the inability to predict the behavior of the system, either by stochastic or deterministic methods. R. Baller (2008), in turn, specifies the complexity as the number of states that a given system can adopt.

The complexity of the system is generally described by its variability and diversity. It is understood in two ways:

- Static (diversity, number of variants),
- Dynamic (changeability).

The static dimension of complexity is its description at a given point in time (diversity), whereas the dynamic approach consists in considering this phenomenon in time (variability; Westphal, 2000). Taking into account two system features, which are the dynamics of changes and the diversity of system elements, simple, complicated and complex systems can be distinguished.

There are specific differences between complicated and complex systems. In a complicated system, individual elements, components and relations that exist between them can be isolated. The behavior of such a system can be known and predicted by observing the behavior of its constituent elements. This option is not available for complex systems. The value describing the complexity is the system variability, which is determined by the number of changes within this system in a given period of time.

In addition to the diversity of products, the structure of supply chains and the processes of internationalization of their activities have an impact on the development of the phenomenon of complexity. Increasing the number of elements included in the chains automatically increases the degree of complexity of relationships within the chain, compounded by trends related to the multidirectional flow of information. The processes that are implemented in the supply chains and networks are not very clear and chaotic, and the mentioned phenomena cause strengthening this effect over time.

Factors defining the complexity of logistic systems are presented in Figure 6. Complexity is determined by two dimensions of diversity: connectivity (diversity of relations) and variety (variety of elements, number of variants).

From the product point of view, they can be described as a variety of components (parts), and relationships between them. From the system point of view the diversity of companies should be taken into account, included in the supply network and connections (potential and the existing ones) between them. The diversity of relationships includes different types of relationships (because of their content) and their quantity, expressed with the density of links. The variety of elements contains a similar structure - the types of elements and their quantity.

Into the effects of complexity of logistics systems may be included effects of the occurrence of product variants diversity, which are mainly various costs. Managing the systems complexity means activities aimed at (Baller, 2008):

Figure 6. Diversity and connectivity as factors creating complexity
Source: (Szmelter, 2017).

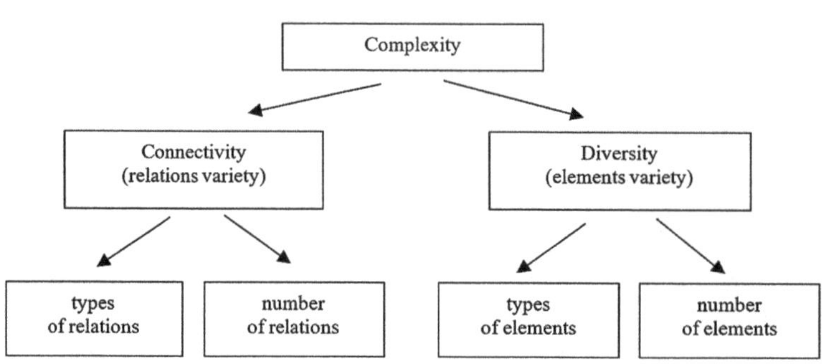

- Reducing the complexity,
- Mastering the complexity
- Avoiding the complexity.

A crucial element of the complexity management is the product variety management. For this purpose, companies should (Baller, 2008):

- Determine the optimal number of variants (one that will satisfy the needs of customers and at the same time will not cause low profitability of the product portfolio),
- Avoid product cannibalism,
- Prepare a valuation of variants procedure,
- Overcome information flow problems.

Development of the Information Logistics

Information as a Special Type of Resource

Since the task of logistics is to manage the flow of resources in logistic channels and chains, it should also be clarified what these resources are subject of flow and transformation in time and space. Resources are factors that are available in the desired forms and quantities, possessing features that foster the enterprise's objectives and are under the control of that enterprise (Chaberek, 2010). Their use in processes carried out in organizations should take place in a beneficial way (when their purchase will be made by the lowest possible costs with the acceptable quality), effective (when their use contributes to the objectives of the enterprise) and efficient (when to achieve these goals they use as little as possible).

The task of logistic systems is therefore to create appropriate conditions for the implementation of the resource flow. This is not only about providing the necessary equipment for the implementation of processes, but also about providing the right organizational solutions. Due to the increased complexity of modern logistics processes and systems, organizational and technical activities are also increasingly complex, which determines the emergence of new solutions, largely related to electronics and information technologies.

The information is described by a number of features, thanks to which it is easy to understand its specificity as a resource subjected to the process of flow in economic systems (Szmelter, 2012). First of all, it is immaterial and therefore a carrier is required, thanks to which it is possible to perform operations related to its flow. It is characterized by mobility (it can be moved in time and space) and inexhaustibility (it does not wear out or breaks down). Sharing information does not contribute to its loss. It is durable, easy to duplicate. It may be outdated. Ways of reaching it are often limited, which contributes to the asymmetry of information - uneven access to it. It is characterized by both objectivity and subjectivity (the same message can be interpreted differently by different recipients; Grudzień, 2012). In addition, interpreting much information at the same time results in greater value for the organization than analyzing them separately, which is described by synergy (Mańkowski, 2009; Szmelter, 2014). This phenomenon, ubiquitous in logistics and information technology, has a positive impact on making the right business decisions.

Information - due to the fact that it is one of the main types of resources - is subject to the same processes as the others, even though it is immaterial. Therefore, one can talk about the logistics service of information flow in the sphere of supply, production and distribution. The flow of information is related to the following processes:

- Acquiring information,
- Generating information,
- Information storage,
- Information processing,
- Using information,
- Sending information,
- Sales of information.

Information Supply System

The growing importance of information in the activities of modern organizations has led to the need to develop new logistics solutions. Over time, a separate area of knowledge has developed - logistics management information. This field deals with the flow of information in various processes taking place in the logistics system (enterprise, supply chain), from demand forecasting, through production planning, distribution of goods, provision of services, to recycling, utilization and redevelopment processes. The *information logistics system* (information supply system) includes all information processes in the organization, both those taking place within it, as well as processes carried out jointly with other entities from the outside.

The main task of the system is to provide the right information (information resource), in the right place (right person), at the right time (in a timely manner), in the right amount (avoiding excess and redundancy of information), about the right quality (reliability of information), and at the right cost (cost of obtaining, processing and sending information). The set of information provided by logistic support allows the right persons to make the right decisions (the best decisions from a set of possible decisions).

Information logistics deals with the flow of information in various processes taking place in the enterprise, from forecasting demand, through production planning, to the distribution of goods and services. Information, passing through various organizational units within the organization and by the cells of various organizations in the supply chain, ultimately in the same or modified form in which they were originally created, should reach the right person.

It would be impossible to fulfill the tasks of information logistics, if not for IT solutions that support the logistics service of the information flow process. In the supply chains, three stages of computerization can be distinguished:

- Organizational information systems,
- Inter-organizational information systems,
- Information systems of supply chains.

Logistics meets two basic functions in building management information systems: creative and integrating. The first one relates to organizational activities, and more precisely to the future users of the system, what information should be entered into it and what final result they are interested in (what should be the final content and form of the information provided). You should also determine the availability of information for individual users of the system and the frequency with which information is to be provided (regularly or only on request). The integrating function, in turn, is to find a balance between the quality of information supply, the actual needs of the entity and the costs of all activities related to the flow of information.

Information supply systems process data into information. Submitting data to various transformations, the nature of which is determined by the needs of the final recipient, results in the creation of information passed on to the recipient. Data and information contribute to the acquisition and expansion of knowledge, including logistical knowledge, which is necessary to implement the decision-making process. From an economic point of view, information-related processes involve costs, valuation of this information, demand for it, its supply, value, physical and legal availability, which again confirms the resource nature of information.

The information supply system connects individual organizational units, located in various places in the organizational structure of the entity. These connections exist both within the organization (between the cells that operate in it), as well as outside (between the cells of the organization and the cells of other entities or other elements of the external environment). This system is a network of connections between the points of sending a message containing information and collection points

In some studies, one can meet the concept of *information metabolism*. There are enterprises, especially information and financial agencies, which must have it at a higher level than others because of the need to constantly update data and compete with market rivals to provide information to viewers or clients as the first on the market (Jagersma, 2011).

IT systems are an integral part of the information supply system and are designed to handle economic processes, including logistics. Information systems, including IT, have given rise to major changes in the management of material resources at the micro, meta and macro scale. Without IT support, it would not be possible to achieve the goals of logistics, that is, to provide the right resources, in the right quantity, with the right quality, at the right time, in the right place and at the right price. IT tools that support the flow of information, accompanying or not accompanying the flow of goods, submit data and information to various types of operations, which at the same time make them the tools of the enterprise information supply system.

FUTURE RESEARCH DIRECTIONS

The basics of logistics are unchangeable. Always the logistics process will support the primary one thanks to the functioning of the logistics support system. There is a necessity of unify the approaches of different researchers to understand logistics activities always in the same way. Without it, further research on logistics development will be not clear.

Future research should be focused on the implementation of logistics in particular areas and sectors taking into account current market changes, because there are many phenomena in the global economy and every of them has its individual character and dynamics. Meshing them causes a unique ecosystem with unique requirements at a certain moment in time, but different in various sectors. What is more, there are also areas of logistics developing faster than other ones, for example the information logistics. These and other problems should be addressed in future research.

CONCLUSION

Logistics concerns every human activity, both business and non-business. Its essence is to control the processes of resource flow within the organization and between it and other organizations in the channels and logistic chains. These flows should be integrated in time and space to achieve acceptable and low costs and at the same time ensure the highest possible level of customer service, both internal and external. Flows of all resources should be fully coordinated, which means the integration of the activities of many entities, at many levels of management. As a result, the desired level of process optimization can be achieved.

ACKNOWLEDGMENT

This research was supported by the University of Gdańsk within the preparing the Author's doctoral thesis "Determinants of shaping logistics strategies in global automotive industry".

REFERENCES

Baller, R. (2008). *Komplexitätsmanagement logistischer Prozesse. Studienarbeit an der Dresden International University MBA in Logistics Management vorgelegt von Lehrstuhl für BWL.* Ingolstadt: Verlag fuer oekonomische Texte.

Baumgarten, H., & Walter, S. (2011). Trends und Strategien in der Logistik. In H. Baumgarten, H. Wiendahl, & J. Zentes (Eds.), *Logistikmanagement. Strategien-Konzepte,-Praxisbeispiele* (pp. 13–21). Berlin: Springer.

Begg, D., Fischer, S., & Dornbusch, R. (2007). *Makroekonomia*. Warszawa: PWE.

Blaik, P. (2001). *Logistyka. Koncepcja zintegrowanego zarządzania*. Warszawa: PWE.

Blaik, P., Bruska, A., Kauf, S., & Matwiejczuk, R. (2013). *Logistyka w systemie zarządzania przedsiębiorstwem*. Warszawa: PWE.

Borgstrom, B., & Hertz, S. (2011). Supply Chain Strategies: Changes in Customer Order-Based Production. *Journal of Business Logistics*, *32*(4), 361–373. doi:10.1111/j.0000-0000.2011.01031.x

Brdulak, H. (Ed.). (2012). *Logistyka przyszłości*. Warszawa: PWE.

Burchart-Korol, D., Czaplicka-Kolarz, K., & Witkowski, K. (2013). Metody oceny ekoefektywności w zarządzaniu łańcuchem dostaw. *Logistyka*, *5*, 258–263.

Chaberek, M. (1999). Logistyka - dawne i współczesne płaszczyzny jej praktycznego stosowania. *Pieniądze i Więź*, *3*, 140–145.

Chaberek, M. (2002). *Makro-i mikroekonomiczne aspekty wsparcia logistycznego*. Gdańsk: Wyd. UG.

Chaberek, M. (2010). Praktyczne i teoretyczne aspekty kontaminacji i atomizacji logistyki i informatyki ekonomicznej. In Informatyczne narzędzia procesów logistycznych (pp. 13-24). Warszawa: Wyd. CeDeWu.

Chaberek, M. (2014). Theoretical, regulatory and practical implications of logistics. *LogForum*, *10*(1), 3–12.

Chaberek, M. (2015). Logistyczne aspekty bezpieczeństwa. *Zeszyty Naukowe Uniwersytetu Gdańskiego. Ekonomika Transportu i Logistyka, 56*, 21–36.

Christopher, M. (1998). *Logistics and supply chain management: Strategies for reducing costs and improving service*. London: Financial Times - Prentice Hall.

Ciesielski, M. (1998). *Strategie logistyczne przedsiębiorstw*. Poznań: Wyd. AE w Poznaniu.

Ciesielski, M. (Ed.). (2002). *Sieci logistyczne*. Poznań: Wyd. AE w Poznaniu.

EPA. (2000). *The Lean and Green Supply Chain: A Practical Guide for Materials Managers and Supply Chain Managers to Reduce Costs and Improve Environmental Performance*. Retrieved from: https://www.epa.gov/p2/lean-and-green-supply-chain-practical-guide-materials-managers-and-supply-chain-managers-reduce

Grudzień, Ł. (2012). Koncepcja oceny jakości informacji o procesach w systemach zarządzania. In R. Knosala (Ed.), *Materiały XV Konferencji Innowacje w zarządzaniu i inżynierii produkcji* (pp. 633–644). Opole: Wyd. AE w Opolu.

Harrison, A., & van Hoek, R. (2010). *Zarządzanie logistyką*. Warszawa: PWE.

Hentschel, B. (2012). Green Logistics – a call for sustainability in logistics chains. *Logistyka, 6*, 15–17.

Isaksen, A., & Kalsaas, B. T. (2009). Suppliers and Strategies for Upgrading in Global Production Networks: The Case of a Supplier to the Global Automotive Industry in a High-cost Location. *European Planning Studies, 17*(4), 569–585. doi:10.1080/09654310802682131

Jagersma, P. K. (2011). Competitive information logistics. *Business Strategy Series, 12*(3), 136–145. doi:10.1108/17515631111130103

Jedliński, M. (2009). In pursuit of the essence of logistic potential of an enterprise. *LogForum, 5*(8), 1–7.

Jedliński, M. (2015). Dynamic logistics strategies in the company logistics potential management. *Russian Journal of Logistics and Transport Management, 2*(1), 3–10. doi:10.20295/2313-7002-2015-1-3-10

Kramarz, W., & Kramarz, M. (2013). Wspomaganie sterowania przepływami materiałowymi w sieciowych łańcuchach dostaw - zakłócenia i odporność. *Logistyka, 5*, 315–319.

Langley, C. J. Jr, & Morice, W. D. (1982). Strategies for Logistics Management: Reactions to a Changing Environment. *Journal of Business Logistics, 3*(1), 1–16.

Lee, H. L. (2007). Sekret najbardziej efektywnych łańcuchów dostaw. In *Zarządzanie łańcuchem dostaw* (pp. 99–108). Gliwice: Helion.

Lummus, R. R., & Vokurka, R. J. (1999). Defining supply chain management: A historical perspective and practical guidelines. *Business Process Management Journal*, *6*(2), 11–17.

Mańkowski, C. (n.d.). *Synergia w logistyce*. Gdańsk: Wyd. UG.

Marczyk, J., Czarnota, J., & Gliński, J. (2014). *Trend: Wzrost złożoności jako sygnał ostrzegawczy*. Retrieved from: https://www.hbrp.pl/b/trend-wzrost-zlozonosci-jako-sygnal-ostrzegawczy/flU42RBp

Mentzer, J. T., DeWitt, W., Keebler, J. S., Min, S., Nix, N. W., Smith, C. D., & Zacharia, Z. G. (2001). Defining supply chain management. *Journal of Business Logistics*, *22*(2), 1–25. doi:10.1002/j.2158-1592.2001.tb00001.x

Mesjasz, C. (2014). Zalety i wady koncepcji złożoności systemów organizacyjnych. In Współczesne kierunki rozwoju nauk o zarządzaniu w kontekście dokonań naukowych Profesora Adama Stabryły (pp. 129-150). Kraków: Mfiles.pl.

Ren, C., Ren, S., Chai, Y., Liu, Y., & Tian, C. (2002). Modeling agile supply chain dynamics: A complex adaptive system perspective. In *Proceedings of the IEEE International Conference on Systems, Man and Cybernetics* (vol. 3, pp. 1-6). IEEE.

Rosińska-Bukowska, M. (2012). *Rozwój globalnych sieci biznesowych jako strategia konkurencyjna korporacji transnarodowych*. Łódź: Wyd. UŁ.

Rutkowski, K. (2004). Zarządzanie łańcuchem dostaw – próba sprecyzowania terminu i określenia związków z logistyką. *Gospodarka Materiałowa i Logistyka*, *12*, 2–8.

Stadtler, H. (2008). Supply Chain Management - An Overview. In H. Stadtler & C. Kilger (Eds.), *Supply Chain Management and Advanced Planning. Concepts, Models, Software and Case Studies* (4th ed.; pp. 3–28). Berlin: Springer.

Szmelter, A. (2012). Wykorzystanie koncepcji Six Sigma w logistyce zaopatrzenia. *Roczniki Naukowe Wyższej Szkoły Bankowej w Toruniu*, *11*(11), 391–402.

Szmelter, A. (2014). *Synergy phenomenon in supply logistics*. Saarbrücken: LAP Lambert Academic Publishing.

Szmelter, A. (2017). *Determinanty kształtowania strategii logistycznych w światowym przemyśle motoryzacyjnym* (Unpublished doctoral dissertation). University of Gdańsk, Sopot, Poland.

Szymczak, M. (2004). *Logistyka w procesie internacjonalizacji przedsiębiorstw*. Poznań: Wyd. AE w Poznaniu.

Thomé, A. M. T., Hollmann, R. L., & do Carmo, L. S. (2014). Research synthesis in collaborative planning forecast and replenishment. *Industrial Management & Data Systems*, *114*(6), 949–965. doi:10.1108/IMDS-03-2014-0085

Wagenknecht, C. (2001). *Logistik - Planung und Steuerung von umfassenden Geschäftsprozessen*. Retrieved from: http://www.uni-kl.de/MISP/vortrag_wagenknecht.pdf

Wasielewska-Marszałkowska, I. (2015). Rozwój oferty usług i zadań usługodawców logistycznych i jego wpływ na zarzadzanie współczesnymi łańcuchami dostaw. *Zeszyty Naukowe Uniwersytetu Gdańskiego. Ekonomika Transportu i Logistyka*, *56*, 177–190.

Weiland, D. (2016). Omnichannel as a new challenge for logistics. *Torun Business Review*, *15*(4), 69–78.

Westphal, R. (2000). Komplexitätsmanagement in der Produktionslogistik. *Diskussionsbeiträge aus dem Institut für Wirtschaft und Verkehr*, *4*, 1–61.

Witkowski, J. (1995). *Strategia logistyczna przedsiębiorstw przemysłowych*. Wrocław: Wyd. AE we Wrocławiu.

Witkowski, J. (2010). *Zarządzanie łańcuchem dostaw. Koncepcje, procedury, doświadczenia*. Warszawa: PWE.

ADDITIONAL READING

Brabazon, P. G., & MacCarthy, B. (2004). Giving customers the car they want. *Manufacturing Engineer*, *83*(1), 1–2. doi:10.1049/me:20040105

Brettel, M., Friederichsen, N., Keller, M., & Rosenberg, M. (2014). How virtualization, decentralization and network building change the manufacturing landscape: An Industry 4.0 Perspective. *International Journal of Science. Engineering and Technology*, *8*(1), 1–8.

Brown, A., Amundson, J., & Badurdeen, F. (2014). Sustainable value stream mapping (Sus-VSM) in different manufacturing system configurations: Application case studies. *Journal of Cleaner Production*, *85*, 164–179. doi:10.1016/j.jclepro.2014.05.101

Clemons, E. K. (2008). How information changes consumer behavior and how consumer behavior determines corporate strategy. *Journal of Management Information Systems*, *25*(2), 13–40. doi:10.2753/MIS0742-1222250202

Fleischmann, B., Meyr, H., & Wagner, M. (2008). Advanced Planning. In H. Stadtler & C. Kilger (Eds.), *Supply Chain Management and Advanced Planning. Concepts, Models, Software and Case Studies* (4th ed., pp. 71–95). Berlin, Heidelberg: Springer.

Fredriksson, P., & Gadde, L. E. (2005). Flexibility and rigidity in customization and build- to-order production. *Industrial Marketing Management*, *34*(7), 695–705. doi:10.1016/j.indmarman.2005.05.010

Mason-Jones, R., & Towill, D. R. (1999). Using the information decoupling point to improve supply chain performance. *International Journal of Logistics Management*, *10*(2), 13–26. doi:10.1108/09574099910805969

Phillips, L. W., Chang, D. R., & Buzzell, R. D. (1983). Product quality, cost position and business performance: A test of some key hypotheses. *Journal of Marketing*, *47*(2), 26–43. doi:10.2307/1251491

Weaver, W. (1948). Science and Complexity. *American Scientist*, *36*(4), 536–545. PMID:18882675

Zinn, W., & Levy, M. (1988). Speculative inventory management: A total channel perspective. *International Journal of Physical Distribution & Materials Management*, *18*(5), 34–39. doi:10.1108/eb014702

KEY TERMS AND DEFINITIONS

Closed-Loop SCM: Supply chain management concept based on the assumption that both primary and reverse flows should be an object of logistics activities and the reverse flow can be a source of resources.

Cradle-to-Cradle Concept: A concept of using end-of-life products to re-process them or disassemble to recover raw materials or parts.

eEPC Notation: Extended event-driven process chain notation. A business process management notation created by A.W. Scheer to map, simulate, and optimize business processes.

Make-or-Buy: A situation when the organization has to decide if order goods or services or make them on its own.

Megatrends: Long-term trends in the global economy.

Primary Process: Process of production of a good or service.

Secondary Process: Logistics process supporting the primary process.

Trade-Off: A situation when an optimization or lowering the cost of operations in one functional area result in growing costs in other area. An example can be lower inventories but more frequent deliveries.

Chapter 2
Supply Chain and Inter-Organizational Information Systems Role

Tharwa Najar
University of Mannouba, Tunisia

Mokhtar Amami
MIS and Supply Chain Business Administration RMC, Canada

ABSTRACT

Since their initiation—characterized by an unsophisticated structure—organizations declare the necessity to organize, coordinate, and manage resources. This necessity is emphasized through the appearance of emergent types of structure assorted with crossing boundaries strategies (strategic alliances, virtual enterprise, modular enterprise, and so forth). This paradigm shift has a prevailing effect on the "way of doing" within organizations and networks. The chapter aims to expose the theoretical approaches that explain the formation and the dynamics of the supply chain (Section 1). As a second step, the notion of the supply chain management (Section 2) and the supply chain performance. It also presents the impact of the IOS use on supply chain performance (Section 3).

DOI: 10.4018/978-1-5225-5921-4.ch002

INTRODUCTION

Throughout the last decade, there has been an exponential increase of professional and academic articles over the nature and importance of supply chain strategies. Therefore, literature represents multiple perspectives and approaches focusing on today's supply chain visions (Lambert & Cooper, 2000; Macpherson, 2001; Tan, 2001; Otto & Kotzab, 2003; Holweg et al.,2005; Ketchen & Hult, 2007).

Traditionally, supply chain management has been viewed as a process for transferring materials and goods. The focus on strategic supply chain management has changed the traditional supply chain vision. Early Marketing academics conceptualized key factors for why and how channels are created and structured by identifying who should be a member of the channel and describing the need for channel coordination and drawing actual marketing channel (Lambert & Cooper, 2000). However, they did not build the contributions of suppliers' involvement and all processes of the whole supply chain. More recently, other academics (eg; La Forme et al., 2007; Angerhofer & Angelides, 2006) introduced the notion of collaborative supply chain in which collaboration is defined as a way by which all companies in a supply chain are actively working together towards common objectives, and is characterized by sharing information, knowledge, risks and profits. Based on the agency theory, a business relationship is composed of a principal and an agent engaged in a cooperative relationship. Even though that they have different goals and attitudes toward risk, their behavior is complimentary. In supply chains, this behavior warranties complete information symmetry between units. Under these conditions, the problems of opportunism and interest conflict are uncovered. A contract is considered as a mean of controlling the relationship, depending on the contract is a behavior-based or outcome-based. The foundation of the relation principal-agent is the compromise between the cost of measuring behavior and the cost of measuring outcomes and transferring risk to the agent (Eisenhardt, 1989).

Many forms of controlling are undertaking to align the interests of the agent in solidarity with those of the principal, such as piece rates, profit sharing, efficiency wages, performance measurement (including financial statements), the agent posting a bond, or fear of firing. With the emphasis on relational aspects, more behavioral mechanisms appeared. This idea is supported by the Social Exchange Theory focusing on the interactive relationships between partners and considers material as well as non-material exchanges. In addition, Social Network Analysis can be considered as a suitable method to explain the dynamics of the interactions between the actors in the supply chain. It joins the systems approach of supply chains. In the same vein, Ketchen and Hult (2007) discussed the concept of "best value supply chains" as an emergent vision of supply chain including the above confirmations. They specified it as chains that are most likely to prosper within today's competitive global landscape. Furthermore, they illustrated the difference between the two visions on the basis of several theoretical references (see Table 1).

SUPPLY CHAIN MANAGEMENT CONCEPT

Interest in supply chain and its management, both in the industry and in academia, has grown rapidly over the past years and continues to grow. Hence, several studies have been concentrated on supply chain concepts, strategies and models.

In the following section, the importance of the concept of supply chain and supply chain management in encompassing economic challenges is presented. In other words, the authors attempt to specify definitions and key concepts related to the issues of supply chain and supply chain management.

Table 1. Theoretical perspectives to distinguish the best value and traditional supply chains

Theoretical Perspective	Best Value Supply Chain	Traditional Supply Chain
Transaction cost economics	Focus on total costs, not just transaction costs, as the basis of "make or buy" decisions Short-term costs play a secondary role if the potential for long-term, trusting relationships exists	Focus on transaction costs as the basis of "make or buy" decisions Opportunism undermines trust; short-term costs are a primary consideration
Resource dependence theory	Supply chain members recognize that dependence can create forbearing and trust.	Each member tries to avoid becoming dependent on others and tries to make others dependent on him.
Network theory	A blend of strong and weak ties that matches supply chain needs is created in order to maximize supply chain performance.	Strong and weak ties formed on a case-by-case basis rather than strategically
Social capital theory	Shared goals, values, and experiences create shared sensemaking and improved performance.	A mix of shared and firm-level goals, values, and experiences circumscribe (limit) sensemaking and limit performance
Strategic choice	Strategic decisions made with concern for the chain as the primary driver. This "strategic supply chain management " open the door to unique blended strategies that transcend the firm	Strategic decisions made with concern for the firm as the primary driver. This approach constrains firms to using a generic strategy such as prospector or low cost leader
Resource-based view/ knowledge-based view	Assume that unique resources exist at the supply chain level and that supply chains can be inimitable competitive weapons	Assume that unique resources reside within firms. Supply chain management is thus a tool to complement these resources

Source: (Ketchen & Hult, 2007)

Supply Chain Management

Supply Chain

The concept of the supply chain has attracted the attention of many academics. A significant number of academics attempted to deal with the dimensions of the concept and suggested different definitions (see Table 2).

Otto and Kotzab, (2003) argued the relevance of comparing supply chains concept based on six different perspectives: system dynamics, operations research, logistics, marketing organizations and strategy perspectives. Basically, they characterized the supply chain (SC) as follows:

- **System Dynamics Perspective:** SC is viewed as a chain of consecutive, sequentially interdependent local transaction systems.
- **Operations Research Perspective:** SC is viewed as a configurable and flow-programmable resource network, which has the function of moving material objects from the sources of production to the final customers, thereby adhering to various restrictions.
- **Logistics Perspective:** SC is understood as a set of business processes, in which management purposes are compared to generic business process models.

Table 2. Supply chain Definitions

Definition	Authors
A supply chain may be defined as an integrated process wherein a number of various business entities (i.e., suppliers, manufacturers, distributors, and retailers) work together in an effort to: (1) acquire raw materials, (2) convert these raw materials into specified final products, and (3) deliver these final products to retailers.	Beamon, 1998
A supply chain is a network of organizations that are involved, through upstream and downstream linkages, in the different processes and activities that produce value in the form of products and services in the hands of the ultimate customer"	Christopher, 1998
A supply chain is defined as the group of organizations involved in the design, manufacture, distribution and retail of a specific product group	Holland, 1995
A supply chain is a network of facilities that performs the functions of procurement of material, the transformation of material to intermediate and finished products, and distribution of finished products to customers.	Lee & Billington, 1993
A supply chain consisted of a network of facilities linked by material flow from suppliers through production to end consumers and an information flow throughout the network.	Petrovic et al.,1998

Source: (sources mentioned in the table)

- **Marketing Perspective:** Outputs of the SC are primarily costs and customer services. The dictum (saying) of all activities is "customer orientation".
- **Organization Perspective:** SC appears as a set of inter-organizational relationships. The relationships can occur in different forms (chain net, vertical, horizontal…).
- **Strategy Perspective:** SC doesn't consist of companies, processes or value creation or value creation steps any longer, but instead of competencies and profits. Companies possess resources, which need to be connected properly to produce competitive products.

Academics and practitioners, individually, have primarily investigated the various processes of the supply chain. Recently, increasing attention has been paid to the performance, design, and analysis of the supply chain as a whole. As far as this issue is concerned, S-Levi et al.(2002) have widely discussed the *systems approach* to supply chain management. This chapter is aimed to illustrate confirmations above by Christopher's definition (1998) which focuses on interconnections between upstream and downstream channel units. Indeed, he defines supply chain as "a network of organizations that are involved, through upstream and downstream linkages, in the different processes and activities that produce value in the form of products and services in the hands of the ultimate customer".It's important to assert that the concept of supply chain emphasizes the major role of information in inter-organizational connectedness. That is what explains the existence of information flow associated with the physical flow of materials and products (Siau & Tian, 2004) (See Exhibit 1). In fact, a supply chain is typically characterized by a forward flow of materials and a backward flow of information (Sarimveis et al.,2008).

This statement is confirmed by Nurmilaakso's (2007) definition stipulating that a supply chain is a bidirectional flow of information, products and money between the initial suppliers and final customers through different organizations. Thus, we claim that literature draws definitions focusing on multiple businesses and relationships being established between partners (Hagelaar & Van der Vorst, 2001; Macpherson, 2001) rather than supply chain processes.

Supply Chain Management (SCM)

Although the word "supply chain management" has been used since the 80s by the scholar and commercial press, confusion is still persisting concerning its signification (Tan, 2001). Literature suggests a considerable number of SCM definitions but it is interesting to claim that there's no explicit and clear description of SCM or of its activities.

Based on the analysis of existing studies, Tan (2001) distinguished three main streams describing the supply chain management. The first stream is related to the supply and purchasing perspective which is synonymous with the supplier basis integration that evolves from the traditional purchasing and supply management functions. The second stream concerns the transportation and logistics perspective of the merchants which emphasizes location and logistics issues more often than transformation. According to this perspective, the supply chain management incorporates logistics focus into the strategic decision of the business. About this issue, Lambert and Cooper (2000) claimed that SCM was viewed as logistics outside the firm to include customers and suppliers. Moreover, they associated the confusion between logistics and supply chain management with the idea that logistics is a functional silo within organizations and is also a bigger concept that deals with the management of material and information flow across the supply chain.

The last stream focuses on a unified and integrated SCM strategy. The goal of the integrated supply chain strategy is to create manufacturing processes and logistics functions seamlessly across the supply chain as an effective competitive weapon that cannot easily be duplicated by competitors.

SCM Functions

SCM appears to treat all organizations within the value chain as a unified "virtual business" entity (Tan, 2001). It is a process of activities and functions ensuring competitiveness (Siau & Tian, 2004). In fact, a successful SCM requires a change from individual functions to integrating activities into key supply chain processes (Lambert & Cooper, 2000). Most often, we talk about supply chain management practices, which have been defined as a set of activities undertaken in an organization to promote effective management of its supply chain (Li et al.,2005). Moreover, the process can be viewed as a structure of activities designed to act with a focus on end consumers and on the dynamic management of flows involving products, information, cash knowledge, and ideas (Lambert & Cooper, 2000). Literature does not offer a unified framework exposing the main processes or practices of supply chain management. Indeed, many studies did some effort to address various but interesting aspects of SCM practices. Each classification describes SCM practices from a variety of different perspectives with a common goal of ultimately improving organizational performance. As a consequence, literature is likely to be rich concerning the main SCM activities and functions which are related to SC processes (see Table 3).

Some cases can illustrate the ideas mentioned above. Angerhofer and Angelides (2006) argued that the performance of supply chain processes (Plan, source, make and deliver) influences the performance of the whole collaborative supply chain. Yeung et al.(2008) identified in their framework three processes to operations performance:

Table 3. Supply Chain Management activities and functions

Activities and Processes	Authors
Consumer relation marketing, client services marketing, demand management, order achievement, production flow management, product procurement development and commercialization.	Ellram & Cooper, 2000
Distribution network configuration, inventory control, supply contracts, distribution strategy, supply chain integration and strategic partnering, outsourcing and procurement strategies, product design information technology and decision support systems and customer value creation.	Levi et al.,2002
Planning, product design and development, sourcing, manufacturing, fabrication, assembly, transportation, warehousing, distribution and post-delivery customer support.	Tan, 2001
Supply chain activities covered include production and delivery strategy, inventory, forecasting, and enterprise software, as well as integration aspects related to interaction and communications with customers and suppliers.	Robb et al.,2008
SC functions can be viewed in ten processes; customer-driven supply chain, demand driven sales planning, transport and distribution, lean manufacturing, supplier collaboration, supply logistics, integrated supply chain management, reverse logistics, product design and product development and product evolution.	La Forme et al.,2007

Source: (sources mentioned in the table)

Strategic Planning process/Organizing (Sourcing planning, Manufacturing planning and Delivering planning) and operational process controlling (Sourcing, Manufacturing and delivering). Moon et al.(2008) added another process- the scheduling process. From the same perspective, Beamon (1998) revealed two basic integrated processes: (1) the production planning and inventory control process, and (2) the distribution and logistics process.

Levi et al.(2002) and Gunasekaran et al.,(2004) revealed three levels of SCM: strategic, tactical and operational. More precisely, the supply chain management involves a variety of processes that emphasize the importance of relationships management (whether with the consumers or the partners). Lambert and Cooper (2000), for example, identified eight processes: customer relationship management, customer service management, demand management, order fulfillment, manufacturing flow management, supplier relationship management, product development and commercialization, and returns management. Guided with the 21st century logistics framework, Closs and Mollenkopf (2004) identified three basic supply chain management processes: behavioral process (relationship), planning and control process (measurement, technology and planning) and operational process (material). Li et al.(2005) validates six dimensions of SCM practices: strategic supplier partnership, customer relationship, information sharing, information quality, internal lean practices, and postponement.

Li et al.(2008) used a multidimensional approach to characterize SCM practices: strategic supplier partnership, customer relationship, level of information sharing, quality of information sharing and postponement.

All those activities are supported by a continuous information flow all over the procurement, production and distribution channel. In their study on reverse supply chains and based on supply chain literature, De la Fuente et al.(2008) distinguished eight general supply chain management processes.

SCM: Towards a Relational SCM

As a relatively complex concept, the notion of supply chain management can become clearer and richer if examined from a variety of important theoretical perspectives. Thus, this sub-section aims to discuss the supply chain management issue within a theoretical point of view. For this purpose, several theories are set up to justify the supply chain management evolution, namely the transaction cost theory, the strategy theory, the culture and change theory, the resource dependence theory and the network theory.

The decision to outsource business processes and create a supply chain outside the organization clearly requires an economic assessment (Macpherson, 2001). The decision is based on a transaction costs approach where there is an examination of the comparative costs of planning, adapting and monitoring task completion under alternative governance structures (Williamson, 1981). Williamson's analysis specifies the key dimensions of the transaction cost, namely the uncertainty and the asset specificity, which vary governance structure. Based on the assumption of the variability of human behavior (source of uncertainty), formal and informal contracts are likely to reduce risk opportunism and uncertainty (Ring & Van de Ven, 1994). When specificity and uncertainty are high, a more relational and long-term contract inside the firm will be the most likely governance structure (Williamson, 1981).

From a strategic point of view, the supply chain management is considered as an essential component of long-term business competitiveness. In other words, SCM is the length of time and the level of trust, development, communication, effort and integration that create the unique quality of relationship (Macpherson, 2001). In addition, the strategy theories highlight the importance of core relational competences in establishing an effective SCM. Furthermore, based on a strategic choice theory, Ketchen and Hult (2007) asserted that strategic decisions are made with concern for the chain as the primary driver. This strategic supply chain management opens the door to the adoption of strategies that foster agility and adaptability within supply chains.

SUPPLY CHAIN PERFORMANCE, IOS AND IOR

The external environment is becoming the next frontier of performance measurement. In the following years, there is an expectation to focus on inter-organizational metrics such as supply chain performance measurement (Folan & Browne, 2005). Thus, the concept of supply chain performance has taken new dimensions. In fact, the role of supply chain measures and metrics in the success of an organization cannot be overstated because they affect strategic, tactical and operational planning and control (Gunasekaran et al., 2004). Thus, many academics are interested in establishing a unified basis to supply chain performance assessment (Otto & Kotzab, 2003; Gunasekaran et al.,2004; Chang et al., 2007; Agarwal et al.,2006). Nowadays, we are talking about systems of performance metrics (such as; balanced scorecard system or business process reengineering performance measurement system) rather than recommendations (Folan & Browne, 2005; Angerhofer & Angelides, 2006).

Supply Chain Performance

When all strategic organizations in the value chain integrate and act as a single unified entity, performance is enhanced throughout the system of suppliers (Tan, 2001). Therefore, the concept of supply chain performance has a tight link with the supply chain management functions. We argue that the determinants of performance are aligned with the major objectives of SCM. Consequently, three levels related to the performance of the supply chain are distinguished.

The first level deals with the financial advantages, which are the result of the following factors: a reduction of cost associated with high level of stock, expedition, and exploitation cost; cost advantages compared with competitors; and a beneficial margin due to the reduced production cost. The second level reflects the enhancement of operational activities: reduced life cycles, lower stock level, less over-stocking, reduced inventory returns, and higher productivity. The third level tackles the customer's services: reliable delivery and immediate response to changes.

This classification is not unique since the literature suggests other notions associated with supply chain performance. For instance, the notions of flexibility, responsiveness and competitive versatility can be mentioned. In fact, flexibility is considered among the critical factors which procure competitive advantages (Gunasekaran et al.,2004). This was confirmed by the work of Lohman et al.(2004) in an attempt to characterize relevant aspects of performance. They presented three main perspectives: resources, output and flexibility (see Table 4).

Table 4. Relevant aspects of performance

Perspective	Description
Resources	Expenses (e.g. distribution costs, inventory-related costs, service costs) Assets (e.g. inventory carrying costs)
Output	Financial (e.g. sales, profit, return on investment) Time (e.g. customer response time, delivery lead time, on-time deliveries, fill rate) Quality (e.g. reliability, shipping errors, customer complaints)
Flexibility	Volume flexibility (ability to respond to changes in demand) Delivery flexibility (ability to respond quickly to tight delivery requests) Mix flexibility (ability to respond to changes in the mix of products demand) New product (and modified product) flexibility (ability to respond to demand for new products)

Source: (Lohman et al.,2004)

Malone (1988) characterizes organizational performance with three dimensions, namely production, coordination and flexibility. Levi et al.(2002) associate supply chain performance with four perspectives: reliability, reactivity, costs and resources usage. Chang et al.(2007) mentioned five supply chain performance attributes: R&D (Design, technique, Odds, Customization, Innovation), Cost (Price, Quantity, Discount, Decrement, Rush), Quality (Import, On-line, Reliability, Stability), Service (Delivery, Accuracy, Assurance, Stockout), and Response (Regular, Emergency, Volume, Specification, Modification). Moreover, Otto and Kotzab (2003) derived the goals of supply chain management from six perspectives and described standard problems, solutions and performance metrics. Gunasekaran et al.(2004) distinguish six determinants of performance, namely; order planning and production level improvement, delivery time and procurement improvement, customer's satisfaction improvement, and logistics cost reduction.

Chen and Paulraj (2004) distinguished between the supplier performance and the buyer performance to cover the supply chain performance concept. Accordingly, the supplier performance was measured in terms of quality, cost, flexibility, delivery and prompt response. However, the buyer performance was measured in term of market share, return on investment, present value of the firm, firm's net income, and after-sales profit.

Furthermore, Verma and Pullman (1998) ranked the importance of the supplier attributes of quality, on-time delivery, cost, lead-time and flexibility. Wang et al.(2006) attributed five factors influencing the supply and the supplier selection performance: R &D, cost, quality, service and response. Similarly, Tracey and Tan (2001) developed some supplier selection criteria, including quality, delivery, reliability, performance and price, and assessed the customer's satisfaction based on price, quality, variety and delivery.

Performance Measurement System (PMS)

The identification of supply chain performance determinants is considered as the first step to elaborate performance management. Measures selection is imprecise and quite difficult due to the subjectivity of selection criteria. Furthermore, non-financial measures and qualitative words of performance evaluation, (for instance; good, very good, middle…) could not give a clear definition of the firm position among competitors (Beamon, 1999). Hence, new considerations have to be established to refine performance metrics (as financial measures). Accordingly, academics have attempted to institute different recommendations and systems to encompass restrictions of the existing literature (Folan & Browne, 2005). The following section discusses the metrics of supply chain performance and provides some selective examples.

Many organizations have not succeeded in maximizing their supply chain's potential because they have failed to elaborate the performance measures and metrics needed to integrate their supply chain to maximize effectiveness and efficiency (Gunasekaran et al.,2004). Thus performance measures development has recently occupied the attention of academics (Otto & Kotzab, 2003; Folan & Browne, 2005; Agarwal et al.,2006; La Forme et al.,2007; Gaiardelli et al.,2007; Berrah & Clivillé, 2007; De la Fuente et al.,2008). In fact, among the most subtle fields in the measurement of the performance is the development of performance evaluation systems as opposed to specific measures (financial and non-financial measures) (Levi et al.,2000). A measurement system should facilitate the assignment of metrics to where they would be most appropriate. Furthermore, selected metrics should reflect a balance between financial and non- financial measures that can be related to strategic, tactical and operational levels of decision making and control (Gunasekaran et al.,2004; Angerhofer & Angelides, 2006). Performance studies and models were created in order to facilitate the measurement of organizational goals fulfillment and to allow the assessment of used strategy and techniques effectiveness.

Several questions must be asked in this respect: What will be measured? How can one integrate various individual measurements in this system of measurement? How much time is needed for measurements? How and when measurements will be evaluated? Another challenge related to the elaboration of these systems is the flexibility with supply chain objectives. Indeed, Gunasekaran et al.(2004) argued that measurement should be understandable by all supply chain members and should not offer the possibility of manipulations. As a consequence, various frameworks were developed to discuss the concept of such measurement systems (Neely et al.,1995; Folan & Browne, 2005). Moreover, literature dealing with measurement systems seems to be rich by introducing notions such as supply chain processes, collaboration and performance metrics (La Forme et al.,2007).

The initial building blocks of all performance measurement initiatives (frameworks or systems) is termed Performance Measurement (PM) recommendations. It is important to reveal that each PM system includes two frameworks, one is structural (typology of performance measure management), and the other is procedural (step by step process). It is, on the whole, the principle of most systems of measurement (Folan & Browne, 2005).

The recommendations mentioned can be divided into two areas: recommendations for performance measures and recommendations and issues for PM framework and system design. Once the series of recommendations are collected, they are used as a background for the framework development. A framework refers to the active employment of particular sets of measurement recommendations.

The well-known example of the *balanced scorecard system* of performance measurement can be mentioned. On the structural level, this approach admits four recommendations prospects: financial prospects, prospects related to the customer, prospects related to the internal businesses and prospects related to the development and the training.

With regard to the procedural level, Kaplan and Norton (1996) developed a set of stages through which, an organization can create its own system of measurement in coherence with its strategies. The stages are categorized as follows:

1. Translating the vision which is concerned with the clarification and the elaboration of a consensus on the strategic vision of the supply chain.
2. Communication and linking. It is the process which enables managers to communicate their strategy within supply chain units and connect links with individual and departmental objectives.
3. Businesses planning. It is the process enabling organizations to integrate their businesses and financial plans.
4. Feedback and learning. It gives organizations the capability for strategic learning. Hence, existing processes predict whether individual or departmental financial goals have been achieved.

Inter-Organizational PMS

Recently, studies on supply chain performance measurement have gained a widespread interest in the field of performance measurement (Gaiardelli et al.,2007; Berrah & Clivillé, 2007; De la Fuente et al.,2008).

Moreover, the emphasis was basically addressed to the inter-organizational performance measurement required to build inter-organizational PM systems (Folan & Browne, 2005).

If only based on traditional logistics performance measures (order fill rates, error rates, inventory costs…), systems could not answer a number of wide range questions such as: How effective are the firms in the supply chain interaction? How flexible is the entire supply chain in responding to requests for customized packages, orders and products? (Folan & Browne, 2005). Hence, a combination of intra- and inter-organizational (and financial and non-financial measures) performance measurement systems could encompass the overall supply chain aspects (see Figure 1).

Dealing with the concept of the collaborative supply chain, La Forme et al.(2007) identified a set of performance indicators aiming at underlining collaborative practices impacts. They revealed at first step perspectives (flexibility, reactivity, quality, resources utilization, and shorter and controlled delays) and then related measures. Moreover, Gaiardelli et al.(2007) extended their research to define a structured business performance measurement system for the after-sales business. Then, they set up a multi-attribute set of measures needs designed consistently at every level of the supply chain.

The establishment of a strict measurement system is the first step towards the supply chain evaluation performance. The selection of evaluation metrics is likely to be a critical phase to the measurement success.

In order to study the existing performance measures in the literature, academics classified them into categories. For instance, Neely et al.(1995) and Agarwal et al.,(2006) revealed four categories: quality, time, flexibility, and cost. This categorization is a useful tool for the analysis of systems. A model can be developed to improve a characteristic of a system such as time. The model can then compare the manufacturing lead time by the change of the system configuration. Thus, comparison and analysis can be carried out between measurements of the same category, so that the choice of measurement of the performance in this category can be made easier (Beamon, 1999).

Jammernegg and Reiner (2007) measured the supply chain performance improvement by the reduced total costs (transport, inventory carrying and resources), as well as the improved customer service (delivery performance). Ayadi (2004) distinguished four categories of supply chain performance: operational effectiveness, strategic efficiency, organizational effectiveness and costs of management. Metrics are as follows: the respect of orders delay, the improvements in the consumers' services, and the improvement of the communication with the partners and the reduction of telecommunication costs… Otto and Kotzab (2003) identified supply chain performance metrics according to six perspectives. (see Table 5).

Figure 1. The evolution of supply chain performance measurement
Source: (Folan & Browne, 2005)

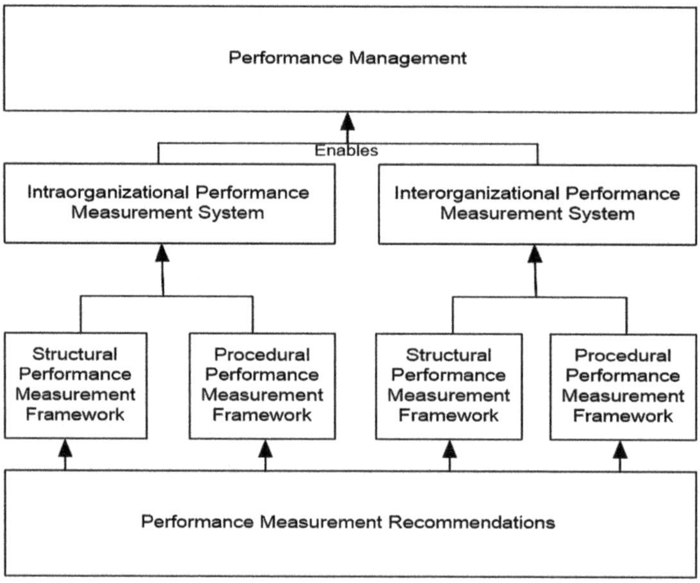

Table 5. Supply chain performance metrics

Perspectives	Performance Metrics
System dynamic	Capacity utilization, cumulative inventory level, stock-outs, time lags, time to adapt.
Operations Research	Logistics costs per unit, service level, time to deliver
Logistics	Integration, lead times, order cycle time, inventory level, flexibility
Marketing	Customer satisfaction, distribution costs per unit, market share/ channel costs
Organization	Transaction costs, time to network, flexibility, a density of relationships
Strategy	Time to network, time to market

Source: (Otto & Kotzab, 2003)

Furthermore, based on SCM activities or processes (Plan, Source, make and deliver), Gunasekaran et al.(2004) identified supply chain performance metrics. The table (see Table 6) recapitulates the different levels (strategic, tactical and operational) adopted to categorize evaluation metrics.

Table 6. Supply chain performance metrics framework

Processes	Strategic	Tactical	Operational
Plan	Level of customer perceived value of the product, aariances against budget, order lead time, information processing ratio, total cycle time, total cash flow time, product development cycle time	Customer query time, product development cycle time, the accuracy of forecasting techniques, planning process cycle time, order entry methods, human resource productivity	Order entry methods, human resource productivity
Source	Decisions outcomes, returns on investments	SupplierdDelivery performance, supplier lead-time against industry norm, supplier pricing against the market, the efficiency of purchase order cycle time, efficiency of each flow method, supplier booking in procedures	Efficiency of purchase order cycle time, supplier pricing against market
Make/ Assemble	Range of products and services	Percentage of defects, cost per operation hour, capacity utilization of economic order quantity	Percentage of defects, cost per operation hour, human resource productivity index
Deliver	Flexibility of service system to meet customer needs, the effectiveness of enterprise distribution planning schedule	Flexibility of service system to meet customer needs, the effectiveness of enterprise distribution planning schedule, the effectiveness of delivery invoice methods, percentage of finished goods in transit, delivery reliability performance	Quality of delivered goods, on-time delivery of goods, the effectiveness of delivery invoice methods,the number of faultless delivery notes invoiced, the percentage of urgent deliveries, information richness in carrying out delivery, delivery reliability performance.

Source: (Gunasekaran et al.,2004)

INTER-ORGANIZATIONAL INFORMATION SYSTEMS, IORS AND SUPPLY CHAIN PERFORMANCE

The usage of inter-organizational information systems is explained most of time by the influence of dominant organizations on dependent ones (Cunningham & Tynan, 1993, Benjamin et al.,1990; Meier, 1995; Trkman et al.,2010). However, some academics flash on the motivation of organizations to adopt IOS to yield competitive advantages. Whatever IOS adoption targets, the literature demonstrates their outcomes especially in term of cost, capacity and communication quality (Bakos & Treacy, 1986).

Nonetheless, there exists a great deal of controversy about the direct impact of Information Technology on firm performance (Cokky & Martin, 2004) and competitive advantages (Powell & Dent Micallef, 1997). While some authors have reported positive impacts, others have reported negative or no impacts (Mukhopadhyay et al.,1995; Kumar & Van Dissel, 1996; Boonstra & Vries, 2005).

Researchers have studied various IS capabilities either in its operational or strategic aspects (Bakos & Treacy, 1985; Amami & Brimberg, 2003; Srinivasan et al.,1994; Cunningham & Tynan, 1993; Holland, 1995; Mc Laren et al.,2004).

Besides, there has been a considerable debate about the effect of IOSs on the creation and sustainability of competitive advantages (Johnston & Vitale, 1988; Meier, 1995; Powell & Dent-Micallef, 1997). Different conclusions have been reached especially concerning the improvement of inter-organizational coordination (Hart & Saunders, 1997; Cunningham & Tynan, 1993; Srinvasan et al.,1994; Kumar & van Dissel, 1996; Subramani, 2003), the creation of external opportunities of commercialization (Iacovou et al.,1995) and quality differentiation which add value for the customer (Nault & Dexter, 1995). Aside, debates revealed the conditional influence of IOS usage on firm performance differences (Barney & Arikan, 2001; Wade & Huland, 2004; Barney, 1991). The issue of the impact of inter-organizational information systems on performance and mainly on financial returns has gained a wide interest (Mukhopadhyay et al.,1995; Riggins et al.,1994; Massetti & Zmud, 1996; Riggins et al.,1994; Srinivasan et al.,1994; Iacovou et al.,1995).

The improvement of performance has been treated in several points of view; for instance; in term of short production time, reduced inventory level (Sawaya, 2002; Iacovou et al.,1995), less coordination cost (Clemons et al.,1993) and reduced product life cycle (Wenna, 2002).

Levi et al.,(2002) distinguished IOS functionalities, namely; SC members information collection and enabled collaboration access and analysis information. That's what effectively gives to the IOS adoption an overriding role in supporting the supply chain management functions (Levi et al.,2002; Ruppel, 2004). Among most cited IOS use advantage is the integration of channel units. In fact, the use of IT in the supply chain can be seen as a driving force for bridging a gap between the actual and potential pattern of integrative logistics operations (Gunnarsson & Jonsson, 2003).

The integration is usually supported by Information Technologies (Grean & Shaw, 2000; Lee & Whang, 2001), in particular by IOS (Parekh, 2001; Lu et al.,2005). About this issue, Benjamin et al.,(1986) introduce the term of "electronic integration" taking advantage of it "when a supplier and a procurer use information technology to create joint, interpenetrating processes at the interface between value-added stages". Zaheer and Venkatraman (1994) refers to electronic integration as "a form of vertical quasi-integration achieved through the deployment of dedicated computers and communication systems between relevant actors in the adjacent stages of the value chain". In addition, Barki and Pinsonneault (2003) define the construct of organizational integration as "the responsiveness of the distinct processes and technologies of the entire value chain of an organization". They advance that information technologies enable large scale integration and heighten competition to integrated chains.

Obviously, electronic integration is the most cited advantages of IOS use within supply chains. IOS support main role of SCM in integrating upstream and downstream units of the chain. Basically, IOS role in successful integration is catalyzed by customer-supplier connection (Warkentin et al.,2001; Khawaja et al.,2005) and real-time supplier's reaction to changes. In fact, Bakos and Treacy (1986) suggest that IOS allow firms to integrate their information-related activities without disturbing the legal boundaries of entities concerned. EDI application is viewed as the most used technology for the integration of SC (Sakaguchi et al.,2002). However, we previously distinguished between the intra- and inter-organizational integration and their related IOS. The present subsection will propose some models that focus on the electronic integration process and enabled-technologies.

IOS Impact and IORs Attributes

Kumar et al.,(1998) assert that the explanation of IOS role and outcomes within organizations shouldn't be discussed only with technical-economic and socio-political perspectives focusing on the need for a complementary perspective. Hence, they propose a perspective emphasizing collaboration and cooperation as the key to understanding interaction processes. This perspective introduces the *third rationality of information systems in which trust, social capital, and collaborative relationships become the key concepts for interpretation*. This problematic issue has been uncovered by several studies such as Williams (1997) who claims that advances in the use of inter-organizational information systems entail greater interdependence between organizations. Obviously, he adds that the advantages of IOS depend more on trust and cooperation between organizations. In addition, Lee and Lim (2003) ascertain that successful partnerships tend to show some behavioral characteristics (e.g., commitment and trust) that help guide the flow and the complex interchange of information between partners, which in turn promote the use of IOS. Hu and Sheu (2005) characterize channel climate by two factors; mutual trust and relationship continuity.

Reasoning alike, Hart and Saunders (1997) reveal that trust plays an important role in EDI use for two reasons; (1) it encourages firms to make investments necessary for electronic information exchange and (2) it discourages opportunistic behavior that would clearly reduce the opportunity for greater information sharing over time. At the same vein, Powell and Dent-Micallef (1997) advance that electronic data interchange system that only marginally improves performance under ordinary conditions, but produces sustainable advantages when combined with preexisting supplier trust. Meier (1995) who claims that IORs management is a key guaranty of IOS implementation success has advanced the same statement. Amami and Brimberg (2004) add the construct of cooperation with trust as leveraging factors of Web-based IOS use. Also, Hart and Saunders (1997) claim that inter-firm relations, particularly trust, will gain preeminent importance in the management of electronic linkages (enabled by electronic data interchange). In addition, Williams (1997) advances that IORs varying characteristics are likely to affect the breadth and the depth of effective IOS use between organizations.

Aside, Subramani (2003) studied the issue of the impact of information systems use within supply chain relationships. He found, from 131 suppliers using a *Supply Chain Management Systems* (SCMS) implemented by one large retailer support, that relationship-specific intangible investments play a mediating role linking SCMS use to benefits. Moreover, Srinivasan et al.(1994) reveal that operational complexity moderate IOS use impact. Also, Barki and Pinsonneault (2003) suggest the influencing role of task complexity on organizational integration which is considered among main advantages of IOS use. They assign a specific coordination mechanism for each type of complexity. Also, Fang et al.,(2008) advances that information technology adoption and relationship activities lead to effective inter-organizational changes and focuses on the moderating effect of partner characteristics.

Clemons and Row (1993) advance that bargaining power could influence IOS use. They demonstrate the critic role of long-term cooperative relationships on IT use in the context of outsourcing activity. In addition, Cunningham and Tynan (1993) claim that effective exploitation of IT-supported IORs is emphasized by the focus on partners relationships nature. Zaheer and Vankatraman (1994) found general support for the importance of two constructs; asset specificity and trust, in explaining the degree of electronic integration which is considered among the most important advantages of IOS use. All these discussed issues are presented in the table (see Table 7).

CONCLUSION

Interdependencies create the necessity to manage and control the performance. That's what explains the focus on strategic supply chain management as a process covering efficiencies issues and global chain performance lift. Regarding its definition "grouped into three major categories: 1) The management of the flow of goods from

Table 7. Main IOS impact Problematic

Main Issue	IOS Related Problematic	IOS Impact	Authors
IOS Adoption and Use	The role of power and trust in adopting and using EDI in dyadic buyer-supplier relationships. When EDI adoption is viewed as an opportunity, this could improve inter-organizational relations in terms of coordination level and organizational changes support.	Improve Inter-organizational coordination	Hart & Saunders 1997; Soliman & Janz, 2004
	Small firm EDI adoption is influenced by a set of factors. EDI-capable firm is due to external pressure, especially from trading partners	EDI is used to create for small firms external opportunities with potential trade partners	Iacovou et al.,1995
	Linking IOS usage literature with the nature of inter-organizational business communications (Buyer-seller relationships). The analysis of the nature of buyer-seller relationships can provide valuable insights into the use of IT in an inter-organizational context.	Affect the various aspects of inter-organizational relationships, Closer buyer-seller relationship	Cunningham & Tynan, 1993; Subramani, 2003
IOS Impact	The identification of IOS typologies (is IOS a competitive advantage or a strategic necessity?) could justify the importance of relationships management in establishing and managing successful inter-organizational information systems.	Competitive advantages realized from the use of IOS. Impact on organizational boundaries and flexibility.	Meier, 1995; Johnston & Vitale, 1988; Powell & Dent-Micallef, 1997
	IOS enables the transition from interfirm competition to cooperation. However, long-term relationships, if not nurtured, can degenerate into conflict.	Sustainable collaboration moderated by conflict resolution	Kumar & Van Dissel, 1996
	The impact of IOSs on the management and the structure of a product-market supply chain.	A managerial perspective of the impact of IOS on firm competition	Holland, 1995
	Impact of IOS on the organizational capabilities of the supply chain (operational efficiency, operational flexibility, internal/external planning and analysis)	–	Mc Laren et al.,2004
	The importance of the deployment of information systems (vertical information integration) to coordinate JIT (just in time) material flows.	Impact on the coordination level. EDI can significantly enhance the benefit of JIT systems.	Srinvasan et al.,1994
	Analyzing the business value added by the use of EDI technology. The impact of the use of the EDI technology on the financial returns from improved information exchanges.	Impact of improved information exchanges on performance	Mukhopadhyay et al.,1995; Riggins & al., 1994; Massetti & Zmud, 1996
	It evaluates the extent to which the added value to customers from a supplier's application of information technology (inter-organizational systems) is manifested through premium prices of a traded good.	The main role of information technology is differentiation quality which could influence prices and then added value	Nault & Dexter, 1995
	The study considers the effect of IOSs on the structure of market networks. How can IOSs blend relationships structures to intermediate forms?	IOSs support mixed mode network structures to coordinate economic activity with trading partners. IOSs combine market and hierarchy elements simultaneously	Holland & Lockett (1997)

Source: (sources mentioned in the table).

supplier to final user; 2) The system-wide coordination of product and information flows; and 3) The development of relationships and the integration of all activities that provide customer value throughout the distribution channel. (Giunipero & de Brand, 1996); the supply chain management has been viewed as one of the most powerful operation paradigms for improving organizational competitiveness in manufacturing and services.

Since the concept of supply chain emphasizes the major role of information in inter-organizational connectedness, the problems of transparency and complete informational integration along the chain still existing, particularly when the network covers a great number of organizations. Academics investigated those issues and attempted to resolve the problem of integration and SCM process by the implementation of coordination mechanisms. Information technology is a perfect mean to promote IORs and either supply chain strategy.

REFERENCES

Akbar, Z. (1994). Determinants of Electronic Integration in the Insurance Industry: An Empirical Test. *Management Science*, *40*(5), 549–566. doi:10.1287/mnsc.40.5.549

Amami, M., & Brimberg, J. (2004). *Technology Diffusion: The role of Web Systems, Environment and Organizational Factors*. AIM.

Anderson, D. L., & Lee Hau, L. (2001). New Supply Chain Business Models – The Opportunities and Challenges. *The ASCET Project.*.

Andreas & Kotzab. (2003). Does supply chain management really pay? Six perspectives to measure the performance of managing a supply chain. *European Journal of Operational Research*, *144*, 306–320.

Angerhofer, J., & Angelides Marios, C. (2006). A model and a performance measurement system for collaborative supply chains Bernhard. *Decision Support Systems*, *42*(1), 283–301. doi:10.1016/j.dss.2004.12.005

Ashish, A., & Shankar, R. (2006). Modeling the metrics of lean, agile and agile supply chain: An ANP-based approach. *European Journal of Operational Research*, *173*(1), 211–225. doi:10.1016/j.ejor.2004.12.005

Bakos, J. Y., & Treacy, E. T. (1986, June). Information technology and corporate strategy; A research perspective. *Management Information Systems Quarterly*, *10*(2), 107–119. doi:10.2307/249029

Barki, H., & Pinsonneault, A. (2003). *The Construct of Organizational Integration: A Research Framework and Its Application to Enterprise Systems Research*. Cahier du Geris no 03-04 Février.

Barney Jay, B. (2001). Resource-based theories of competitive advantage: A ten year retrospective on the resource-based view. *Journal of Management*, *27*(6), 643–650. doi:10.1177/014920630102700602

Barney Jay, B., & Arikan Asli, M. (2001). The Resource-based View: Origins and Implications. *Strategic Management Journal*.

Beamon Benita, M. (1998). Supply Chain Design and Analysis: Models and Methods. *International Journal of Production Economics*, *55*(3), 281–294. doi:10.1016/S0925-5273(98)00079-6

Benjamin, R. I., de Long, D. W., & Morton, M. S. (1990). Electronic data interchange: How much competitive advantage? *Long Range Planning*, *23*(1), 29–40. doi:10.1016/0024-6301(90)90005-O

Boonstra, A., & de Vries, J. (2005). Analyzing inter-organizational systems from a power and interest perspective. *International Journal of Information Management*, *25*(6), 485–501. doi:10.1016/j.ijinfomgt.2005.08.006

Brenda, M., & Zmud, R. W. (1996). Measuring the Extent of EDI Usage in Complex Organizations: Strategies and Illustrative Examples. *Management Information Systems Quarterly*, *20*(3), 331–345. doi:10.2307/249659

Chang, S.-L., Reay-Chen, W., & Shih-Yuan, W. (2007). Applying a direct multi-granularity linguistic and strategy-oriented aggregation approach on the assessment of supply performance. *European Journal of Operational Research*, *177*(2), 1013–1025. doi:10.1016/j.ejor.2006.01.032

Chen, I. J., & Antony, P. (2004). Towards a theory of supply chain management: The constructs and measurements. *Journal of Operations Management*, *22*(2), 119–150. doi:10.1016/j.jom.2003.12.007

Chiung, M., Hae, L. Y., & Seok, J. C. (2008). Integrated process planning and scheduling in a supply chain. *Computers & Industrial Engineering*, *54*(4), 1048–1061. doi:10.1016/j.cie.2007.06.018

Choon. (2001). A framework of supply chain management literature. *European Journal of Purchasing & Supply Management, 7*, 39-48.

Chow, W. S., Madu, C. N., Kuei, C.-H., Lu, M. H., Lin, C., & Tseng, H. (2008). Supply chain management in the US and Taiwan: An empirical study. *The International Journal of Management Science Omega, 36*(5), 665–679. doi:10.1016/j.omega.2006.01.001

Christopher, M. (1998). *Logistics and Supply Chain Management: Strategies for reducing cost and improving service*. London: Financial Times Pitman Publishing.

Clemens, L., Leonard, F., & Marc, W. (2004). Designing a performance measurement system: A case study. *European Journal of Operational Research, 156*(2), 267–286. doi:10.1016/S0377-2217(02)00918-9

Clemons & Row. (1991). Sustaining IT Advantage: The Role of Structural Differences. *MIS Quarterly, 15*(3), 275-292.

Closs , & Mollenkopf, . (2004). A global supply chain framework. *Industrial Marketing Management, 33*(1), 37–44. doi:10.1016/j.indmarman.2003.08.008

Cokky, H., & Smits, M. (2004). *A resource based and real options perspective on IT infrastructure investments aiming for strategic flexibility*. Center for Research on Information Systems Management.

Cunningham, C., & Tynan, C. (1993). Electronic Trading, Inter-organizational Systems and the nature of Buyer-seller Relationships: The need for a network Perspective. *International Journal of Information Management, 13*(1), 3–28. doi:10.1016/0268-4012(93)90044-5

De la Fuente, M., Ros, L., & Cardós, M. (2008). Integrating Forward and Reverse Supply Chains: Application to a metal-mechanic company. *International Journal of Production Economics, 111*(2), 782–792. doi:10.1016/j.ijpe.2007.03.019

France-Anne Gruat, L. F., & Vale'rie Botta, G. (2007). A framework to analyse collaborative performance. *Computers in Industry, 58*(7), 687–697. doi:10.1016/j.compind.2007.05.007

Giunipero, L. C., & Brand, R. R. (1996). Purchasing's role in supply chain management. *International Journal of Logistics Management, 7*(1), 29–38. doi:10.1108/09574099610805412

Grean & Shaw. (2000). *Supply-Chain Integration through Information Sharing: Channel Partnership between Wal-Mart and Procter & Gamble*. Center for IT and e-Business Management, University of Illinois at Urbana-Champaign.

Gunasekaran, A., Patel, C., & McGaughey Ronald, E. (2004). A framework for supply chain performance measurement. *International Journal of Production Economics, 87*(3), 333–347. doi:10.1016/j.ijpe.2003.08.003

Gunnarsson, C., & Jonsson, S. (2003). Charge the relationships and gain loyalty effects: Turning the supply link alert to IT opportunities. *European Journal of Operational Research, 144*(2), 257–269. doi:10.1016/S0377-2217(02)00392-2

Hagelaar G., &Van Der Vorst J. (2001). *Environmental Supply Chain Management: using Life Cycle Assessment to structure supply chains.* Paper IAMA, Sydney, Australia.

Haralambos, S., Panagiotis, P., Tarantilis, C. D., & Kiranoudis, C. T. (2008). Dynamic modeling and control of supply chain systems: A review. *Computers & Operations Research, 35*(11), 3530–3561. doi:10.1016/j.cor.2007.01.017

Holland, C. P. (1995). Cooperative supply chain management: The impact of inter-organizational information systems. *The Journal of Strategic Information Systems, 4*(2), 117–133. doi:10.1016/0963-8687(95)80020-Q

Holland, C. P., & Geoffrey, L. A. (1997). Mixed Mode Network Structures: The Strategic Use of Electronic Communication by Organizations. *Organization Science, 8*(5), 475–48. doi:10.1287/orsc.8.5.475

Holweg, M., Disney, S., Holmstrom, J., & Smaros, J. (2005). Supply Chain Collaboration: Making Sense Of The Strategy Continuum. *European Management Journal, 23*(2), 170–181. doi:10.1016/j.emj.2005.02.008

Hong Ilyoo, B. (2002). A new framework for inter-organizational systems based on the linkage of participants' roles. *Information & Management, 39*(4), 261-270.

Iacovou, C. L., Benbasat, I., & Dexter, A. S. (1995). Electronic Data Interchange and Small Organizations: Adoption and Impact of Technology. *Management Information Systems Quarterly, 19*(4), 465–485. doi:10.2307/249629

Inkpen, A. C., & Julian, B. (1994). International Joint Ventures and Performance: An Inter-organizational Perspective. *International Business Review, 3*(3), 201–217. doi:10.1016/0969-5931(94)90002-7

Kaplan & Duchon. (1988). Combining qualitative and quantitative methods in information systems research: A case study. *Management Information Systems Quarterly*, 571–586.

Ketchen Jr David, J., Hult, G., & Tomas, M. (2007). Bridging organization theory and supply chain management: The case of best value supply chains. *Journal of Operations Management*, *25*(2), 573–580. doi:10.1016/j.jom.2006.05.010

Khawaja, S. A., Malhotra, M., & Grover, V. (2005). Examining the Impact of Inter-organizational Systems on Process Efficiency and Sourcing Leverage in Buyer-Supplier Dyads. *Decision Sciences*, *36*(3), 365.

Kumar, K., & van Dissel, H. G. (1996). Sustainable collaboration: Managing Conflict and cooperation in inter-organizational Systems. *Management Information Systems Quarterly*, *20*(3), 279–300. doi:10.2307/249657

Lai, K., Ngai, E. W. T., & Cheng, T. C. E. (2002). Measures for evaluating supply chain performance in transport logistics. *Transportation Research Part E, Logistics and Transportation Review*, *38*(6), 439–456. doi:10.1016/S1366-5545(02)00019-4

Lambert Douglas, M., & Cooper Martha, C. (2000). Issues in Supply Chain Management. *Industrial Marketing Management*, *29*(1), 65–83. doi:10.1016/S0019-8501(99)00113-3

Lamia, B., & Vincent, C. (2007). Towards an aggregation performance measurement system model in a supply chain context. *Computers in Industry*, *58*(7), 709–719. doi:10.1016/j.compind.2007.05.012

Lee, H., & Whang, S. (2001). *E-business and Supply Chain Integration*. Stanford Global Supply Chain Management Forum, SGSCMF-W2-2001.

Lee, H. L., & Billington, C. (1992). Supply Chain Management: Pitfalls and Opportunities. *Sloan Management Review*, *33*(Spring), 65–73.

Levi, Kaminsky, & Levi. (2002). Designing and managing the supply chain, Concepts, strategies and Case studies (2nd ed.). McGraw-Hill/Irwin.

Li, S., Ragu-Nathan, B., Ragu-Nathan, T. S., & Subba Rao, S. (2006). The impact of supply chain management practices on competitive advantage and organizational performance. *Omega*, *34*(2), 107–124. doi:10.1016/j.omega.2004.08.002

Li, S., Rao, S., Ragunathan, T., & Ragunathan, B. (2005). Development and validation of a measurement instrument for studying supply chain management practices. *Journal of Operations Management*, *23*(6), 618–641. doi:10.1016/j.jom.2005.01.002

Longest & Young. (2000). *Health care management*. New York: Delmar.

Lu, X.-H., Huang, L.-H., & Heng, M. S. H. (2005). Critical success factors of inter-organizational information systems; A case study of Cisco and Xiao Tong in China. *Information & Management*.

Macpherson, A. (2001). *Corporate directions in supply chain management: Implications for SME competences and inter-organizational relations*. working paper022.

Malone Thomas, W. (1988). What is Coordination Theory? *National Science Foundation Coordination Theory Workshop*.

Malone, Thomas, & Yates. (1986). *Electronic Markets and Electronic Hierarchies: Effects of Information Technology on Market Structures and Corporate Strategies*. Center for Information Systems Research.

McLaren, T. S., Head, M. M., & Yuan, Y. (2004). Supply chain management information systems capabilities. An exploratory study of electronics manufacturers. *Information Systems and e-Business Management*, *2*(2), 207–222. doi:10.100710257-004-0035-5

Meier, J. (1995). The importance of relationship management in establishing successful inter-organizational systems. *Journal of Strategic Information Systems*, *4*(2), 135-148.

Michael, W., & Hulland, J. (2004). Review: The Resource-Based View And Information Systems Research: Review, Extension, And Suggestions For Future Research. *Management Information Systems Quarterly*, *28*(1), 107–142. doi:10.2307/25148626

Nault Barrie, R., & Dexter Albert, S. (1995). Added Value and Pricing with Information Technology. *Management Information Systems Quarterly*, *19*(4), 449–464. doi:10.2307/249628

Neely, A., Adams, C., & Kennerley, M. (1995). *The Performance Prism: The Scorecard for Measuring and Managing Business Success*. Financial Times Prentice Hall.

Nurmilaakso, J.-M. (2007). Adoption of e-business functions and migration from EDI-based toXML-based e-business frameworks in supply chain integration. *International Journal of Production Economics*.

Nurmilaakso, J. M., & Kotinurmi, P. (2004). A review of XML based supply chain integration. *Production Planning and Control*, *15*(6), 608–621. doi:10.1080/0953 7280412331283937

Paolo, G., Nicola, S., & Lucrezia, S. (2007). Performance measurement of the after-sales service network—Evidence from the automotive industry. *Computers in Industry*, *58*(7), 698–708. doi:10.1016/j.compind.2007.05.008

Parekh. (2001). *It's Not Just About Software: A Holistic View on Supply Chain Management in the Connected Economy*. Plan Central Inc.

Paul, F., & Jim, B. (2005). A review of performance measurement: Towards performance management. *Computers in Industry*, *56*(7), 663–680. doi:10.1016/j.compind.2005.03.001

Petkov, V., Petkova, O., Andrew, T., & Nepal, T. (2007). Mixing Multiple Criteria Decision Making with soft systems thinking techniques for decision support in complex situations. *Decision Support Systems*, *43*(4), 1615–1629. doi:10.1016/j.dss.2006.03.006

Pfeffer, J., & Salanick, G. R. (1978). *The External Control of Organizations: A Resource-dependence Perspective*. New York: Harper & Row.

Powell, T. C., & Dent-Micallef, A. (1997). Information Technology as Competitive Advantage: The Role of Human, Business, and Technology Resources. *Strategic Management Journal*, *18*(5), 375–405. doi:10.1002/(SICI)1097-0266(199705)18:5<375::AID-SMJ876>3.0.CO;2-7

Riggins, F. J., Kriebel, C. H., & Mukhopadhyay, T. (1994). The Growth of Inter-organizational Systems in the Presence of Network Externalities. *Management Science*, *40*(8), 984–998. doi:10.1287/mnsc.40.8.984

Robb David, J. (2008). Supply chain and operations practice and performance in Chinese furniture manufacturing. *International Journal of Production Economics*, *112*(2), 683–699. doi:10.1016/j.ijpe.2007.04.011

Ruppel, C. (2004). An information systems perspective of supply chain tool compatibility: The roles of technology fit and relationships. *Business Process Management Journal*, *10*(3), 311–324. doi:10.1108/14637150410539713

Russell, J. H., & Vitale, M. R. (1988). Creating Competitive Advantage with Inter-organizational Information Systems. *Management Information Systems Quarterly*, *12*(2), 153–165. doi:10.2307/248839

Sangjae, L., & Gun, L. G. (2003). The impact of partnership attributes on EDI implementation success. *Information & Management*, *42*, 503–516.

Shapiro, J. F. (2001). *Beyond Supply Chain Optimization to Enterprise Optimization*. Enterprise Optimization, Academic Research.

Shih-Yuan, W., Chang, S.-L., & Wang, R.-C. (2006). Assessment of supplier performance based on product-development strategy by applying multi-granularity linguistic term sets. *Omega*.

Shyh-Rong, F., Jyh-Jeng, W., Shih-Chieh, F., Chang, Y.-S., & Chao, P.-W. (2008). Generating effective inter-organizational change: A relational approach. *Industrial Marketing Management*, *37*(8), 977–991. doi:10.1016/j.indmarman.2007.08.004

Siau, K., & Tian, Y. (2004). Supply chains integration: Architecture and enabling technologies. *The Journal of Computer Information Systems*, *44*(3), 67.

Smith, R., & Van De Ven, A. H. (1992). Structuring Cooperative Relationships between Organizations. *Strategic Management Journal*, *13*(7), 483–498. doi:10.1002mj.4250130702

So Young, S., & Michael, L. (2008). The effect of forecasting and information sharing in SCM, for multi-generation products. *European Journal of Operational Research*, *186*(1), 276–287. doi:10.1016/j.ejor.2007.01.034

Soliman, K. S., & Janz, B. D. (2004). An exploratory study to identify the critical factors affecting the decision to establish Internet-based inter-organizational information systems. *Information & Management*, *41*(6), 697–706. doi:10.1016/j.im.2003.06.001

Srinivasan, K., Kekre, S., & Mukhopadhyay, T. (1994). Impact of Electronic Data Interchange Technology on JIT Shipments. *Management Science*, *40*(10), 1291–1304. doi:10.1287/mnsc.40.10.1291

Subramani Mani, R. (2003, September). How suppliers benefit from IT use in supply chain relationships? *MIS Quarterly*.

Thomas Douglas, J., & Griffin Paul, M. (1996). Invited Review Coordinated supply chain management. *European Journal of Operational Research*, *94*(1), 1–15. doi:10.1016/0377-2217(96)00098-7

Toru, S., Clay, D. C., & Nicovich Stefan, G. (2002). Development of an integrated supply chain model. *Eighth Americas Conference on Information Systems*.

Tracey, M., & Tan, C. L. (2001). Empirical analysis of supplier selection and involvement, customer satisfaction, and firm performance. *Supply Chain Management*, *6*(3–4), 174–188. doi:10.1108/EUM0000000005709

Trevor, W. (1997). Strategic Information systems Interorganisational Information Systems: Issues affecting interorganisational cooperation. *The Journal of Strategic Information Systems*, *6*(3), 231–250. doi:10.1016/S0963-8687(97)00018-8

Tridas, M., Sunder, K., & Suresh, K. (1995). Business Value of Information Technology: A Study of Electronic Data Interchange. *Management Information Systems Quarterly*, *19*(2), 137–156. doi:10.2307/249685

Trkman, P., McCormack, K., de Oliveira, M. P. V., & Ladeira, M. B. (2010). The impact of business analytics on supply chain performance. *Decision Support Systems*, *49*(3), 318–327. doi:10.1016/j.dss.2010.03.007

Tung-Lai, H., & Jiuh-Biing, S. (2005). Relationships of channel power, noncoercive influence strategies, climate, and solidarity: A real case study of the Taiwanese PDA industry. *Industrial Marketing Management*, *34*(5), 447–461. doi:10.1016/j.indmarman.2004.10.005

Verma, R., & Pullman, M. E. (1998). An analysis of the supplier selection process. *Omega*, *26*(6), 739–750. doi:10.1016/S0305-0483(98)00023-1

Warkentin, Sugumaran, & Bapna. (2001). E-knowledge networks for inter-organizational collaborative e-business. *Logistics Information Management*, *14*(1-2), 149-162.

Wenna. (2002). *The transforming power of Business to Business Electronic Business.* Next Generation Business Publishing.

Werner, J., & Gerald, R. (2007). Performance improvement of supply chain processes by coordinated inventory and capacity management. *International Journal of Production Economics*, *108*(1-2), 183–190. doi:10.1016/j.ijpe.2006.12.047

Williamson Oliver, E. (1981). The economics of organization: The transaction cost approach. *American Journal of Sociology*, *87*(3), 548–577. doi:10.1086/227496

Yannis & Erik. (1992). *When Quality Matters: Information Technology And Buyer-Supplier Relationships.* Center for Coordination Science Technical Report.

Yeung, Lo, Yeung, & Cheng. (2008). Specific customer knowledge and operational performance in apparel manufacturing. *International Journal of Production Economics.*

KEY TERMS AND DEFINITIONS

EDI: "The computer-based exchange of standardized business documents which improve interorganizational coordination by reducing time lags associated with document delivery and internal information processing, among other things."

Information Technologies Are "a set of devices that store: process and communicate information. They are organized in a way they can perform a set of tasks". A system is "a collection of objects, such as people, resources; concepts and procedures intended to perform an identifiable function or serve a goal". Hence, the combination of many technologies creates information systems which are "a set of information, information technologies, people and work design practices organized to accomplish goals."

Interorganizational Information System: (IOS): Are systems based on information technology that cross organizational boundaries.

Interorganizational Relationships: Are interconnections between entities within a B2B environment.

Performance of the Supply Chain: Is related to the effectiveness of supply chain management functions. It has financial, operational and customers services levels to be assessed.

Supply Chain: Is an integrated process for the aim to deliver products or services to the final clients.

Transaction Cost: A transactions cost is any activity which is engaged in to satisfy each party to an exchange that the value given and received is in accord with his or her expectations.

Section 2
Global Pharmaceutical Industry

The section contains the description of the global pharmaceutical industry, megatrends and macrotrends in the global economy influencing its development, and many other issues allowing for the general analysis of the current state of this sector.

Chapter 3 Global Pharmaceutical Industry: Characteristics and Trends

Agnieszka Szmelter
University of Gdańsk, Poland

ABSTRACT

The pharmaceutical industry is seen as one of the most dynamic, volatile, and innovative parts of the global economic environment. It also has a big impact on the society and is an indicator of the healthcare systems' condition. Some changes have happened in the last decades, for example, shifting the production facilities to the developing countries, new market entries, or the new law changed the previously established and stable layout of market forces. The chapter aims at presenting the current situation of the global pharmaceutical industry including the main trends influencing the changes in this sector. Describing this part of the global market will ensure the right interpretation of the research results of the other parts of the book.

INTRODUCTION

The global economy is constantly changing. There are some long-term trends (megatrends) affecting the global ecosystem, the network of market forces and competitive advantages of every company. Some of the sectors are more innovative than others because of their core business specifics. These are automotive, chemical, IT and pharmaceutical industry. They guide other branches how to be not only innovative. but profitable, responsible, and sustainable companies. The scope of the

DOI: 10.4018/978-1-5225-5921-4.ch003

global players' supply chains operations force those big companies to better plan, perform and control their processes.

The global economic environment is changing also in the pharmaceutical industry and the aforementioned megatrends, for example, relocation of business entities, is related to those changes. The aging population and growing purchasing power of emerging countries and Eastern societies cause the new range of needs in particular regions for both original (brand) and generic drugs. Many companies made their decisions to relocate production facilities to countries with lower operation costs, especially with the qualified and not expensive workforce. There are some shifts not only in the area of the production operations, but also in research and development (Epstein, 2007).

The technological improvement is also visible in the pharma sector. New drugs require a huge financial involvement of many parties and now some of the R&D processes are carried out by third parties. All those phenomena are building the new pharmaceutical industry, so different from the well-known model established in the 1980s and 1990s.

Because of the complicated situation in the pharmaceutical industry and a wide range of the variables influencing its state, the current characteristics and trends are not known well yet. Therefore, the primary aim of the study is to present the current situation of the global pharmaceutical industry, to highlight the trends, barriers, problems and guidelines for this sector development. The structure of the paper is as follows. Firstly, the research approach is described to highlight the path to analyze materials and formulate conclusions. Then, research results are presented. In the next section, the Autor describes the research limitations, discusses the results and identify the future research directions. The last section consists general conclusions. The chapter content is supported by an appendix presenting the research data obtained from many sources.

RESEARCH METHODS

Descriptive Statistics and Data Interpretation

According to the main objective of this chapter, which is describing the current state and trends in the pharmaceutical industry, only the simple forms of data presentation and analysis were applied, such as structure and dynamics indicators (see Research results section).

Literature Review Procedure

The research in this chapter is a basic research. Therefore, the literature review procedure of Denyer and Tranfield (2009) (see Table 1) was chosen as, in the opinion of the Author, the best one to achieve the mentioned goal. A modified procedure is used to explain phenomena, mostly in socio-economic research areas. It allows for state-of-the-art analysis. This standardized research procedure makes research in this paper transparent, replicable, exclusive, aggregative and heuristic. The full size of the literature review observation sheet was too big to be published in the Appendix, that is why the Author decided to include only the main results.

Firstly, 6 literature search engines were chosen according to their range and scope (DOAJ, EBSCOhost, Google Scholar, Infona, MEDLINE, Web of Science). After this step, the Boolean Logic was used to identify the literature to further analysis. The inclusion criteria were (see Table 2):

- "Pharmaceutical" in title, "global" in title or abstract, "logistics" in the text,
- Area: economics, business and management,
- Full-text records for reviewed articles,
- Publication year: from 2010.

The next step in the procedure was to verify the abstracts. Then duplicated records were eliminated and the Author obtained 87 articles for the content review. This step contained topic control and assessing the level of corresponding to the main area and aim of this chapter. Finally, 41 papers about the pharmaceutical industry were selected to be mentioned in the Results section and in the Appendix (see Table 4).

Table 1. Research procedure

Phase	Stage
I	1. Determining the study purpose
II	1. Determining basic literature (searching in search engines)
	2. Selection of publications for further analysis
	3. Preparing publications database
III	1. Bibliometric analysis
	2. Content (text) analysis
IV	1. Preparing a report (research results)

Source: own preparation

Table 2. The process of literature database creation

Search Criteria	Search Engine					
	DOAJ	EBSCOhost	Google Scholar	Infona	MEDLINE	Web of Science
"pharmaceutical" TI, "global" TI or AB, "logistics" TX, area: economics and management, publication year: 2010 and later, full-text	3	54	27	12	2	20
After abstracts verification	3	45	23	9	2	24
After removing duplicates	87					
After text analysis	41					

Source: own preparation

RESEARCH RESULTS

Because the results from the two research procedures applied were similar and related to the same research problems and topics, the Author decided to merge them and place within one section.

General Situation in the Global Pharmaceutical Industry

Generally, the whole global pharmaceutical industry can be divided into three parts. First is the part dominated by the well-known, established brands, which are companies from the USA, Europe and Japan. Despite the many changes in the global ecosystem, this is still true that the Western countries dominated the global pharmaceutical industry (see Table 3). The pharmaceutical enterprises from those countries are jointly called by researchers and practitioners as the Western Big Pharma or Big Pharma (Tempest, 2010). The expenditures for the medicines in those countries also are higher than in developing ones. According to Tempest (2010), in 2010 88% of the world's drugs were consumed by only 18% of the population, so the remaining 82% of world's population has an access to 12% of drugs. The global market was worth 1,43 billion USD until 2020. The second group build the emerging economies (China, India and others) called jointly as Pharmerging, which are focused now on developing the pharmaceutical market, gain the foreign direct investments and support the national industry (de Castro, 2011; Rehman, Rashid, Ashfaq, Saif & Ahmad, 2015). The remaining world countries create the third group.

According to the Statista Group, the global consumption value will increase from 887 bln USD in 2010, trough 1135 bln USD in 2016 to 1430 bln USD in 2020 (Statista, 2017). According to the Torreya Bank (an investment bank for life sciences), the pharmaceutical sector will triple in size in the next 40-50 years (Torreya, 2017). The total global revenues of the ethical pharmaceutical sector are now about 1,1 trillion USD.

Supply

The IFPMA 2017 paper reported that developing the new medicine takes 10-15 years, and there is a very low success ratio in R&D in the pharmaceutical area. Now pharmaceutical companies work on over 1900 cancer drugs, 200 HIV/AIDS, 1300 neurology ones, 1200 for infection diseases (IFPMA, 2017).

There is a big amount of publications about the Indian (ranked as the 13th market in the world; Reddy, Rao, 2014) and Chinese (ranked as the second) pharmaceutical industry. Those markets are promising, especially for generic drugs (Chui, 2009), which have the same active pharmaceutical ingredient like the brand, patented product. Nevertheless, there is a way for keeping the drug prices high, namely the secondary patenting. In that way, even if there is nothing new in the drug, a producer can prolong the time of the legal protection and dictate the prices (Sampat & Shalden, 2017). In the future, the industry will face such challenges like aging society, strict cost control, a growth of the rare disease drugs and the emerging markets, especially China and India (Duperon & Cinar, 2010; Reddy & Rao, 2014).

Nevertheless, despite numerous publications about the emerging economies (Horner, 2016), highly important for the global economic ecosystem, still, Western Big Pharma is the most important part of the sector.

Most of the largest pharmaceutical companies are from so-called Western countries, especially from the US (Appendix, see Table 3), what is natural if this market has over 40% of the global market share. Almost every big corporation in the chosen sector has its origin in America. Then, few other may be mentioned, located in Japan, Germany, Switzerland, and the United Kingdom. In the group of the identified brands ranked in the international and global databases with use of different indices, only 5 of them were from China and 2 from India. The biggest companies today in China are Yangtze Rivr Pharma, Hengrui, CR Pharma Rx Segment, Qilu Pharma and Kangmei Pharma. In India, the market (among the share of the western companies) is dominated by Lupin and Sun Pharma.

However, there is also the other side of this problem. Those Big Pharma companies, even if have their headquarters in the Western countries, locate their sites, production plants and R&D facilities in other countries, especially in Asia. Therefore, often appearing voices about the role of the emerging markets in shaping global pharmaceutical industry can be right and cannot be ignored. Emerging economies try to enter the global market with the offer for people less privileged to have an access to drugs. Especially, the problems are visible for many years in Africa and South-East Asia. However, the situation is changing. The emerging economies are responsible for over 50% of pharma growth in 2009 (in 2001 only 7%). China's market has grown six times from 2004 to 2017, so even if the pace of growth will be lower every year, this market has a huge potential to grow rapidly and be one of the biggest worldwide (today it is the second after the US market) (Spigarelli & Wei, 2012; Hollinshead; 2017).

There are many dimensions companies are assessed by different research and consulting agencies. The most popular seem to be Forbes ranking of the biggest companies in the world (here presented: Forbes 2000). The Author, to make the results more dispassionate against the one chosen ranking, decided to include more, like Top 50 Global Pharma Companies and Top 10 Pharma Brands. As can be seen, some brands are ranked higher than others. They are Allergan, Amden, AstraZeneca, Eli Lilly, GlaxoSmithKline, Merck, Novartis, Takeda and many others. The more rankings include a brand, the more objective the general assessment. Those research results could be of course, interpreted in other ways, the Author decided to include other indices in the analysis, referring to other areas like sustainability and access to drugs.

Kesic (2011) mentioned the future trends the pharmaceutical companies will face in the future, as follows:

- Increased globalization,
- Increased competitiveness and change in its character,
- Low number of brand new products, despite increased investments into r&d,
- Increased importance of legal, regulatory issues,
- Fast consolidation and concentration of the world pharmaceutical industry (m&a),
- Increased importance of marketing management,
- Development of new therapeutic fields and technologies (biotechnology, pharmacogenomics),
- Ageing of the world population,
- Rapid development of world generic markets.

Demand

The World Drug Report 2017 stated that the 5% of the world's population is responsible for the 50% of drug consumption (UNODC, 2017). This is a description of the American society. Nevertheless, other countries note big volumes of sales.

These are Switzerland, Japan, Canada and Germany. There are no available data about the consumption per one citizen, but they could be similar to the presented one. The OECD countries together are responsible for over 80% of the global drug consumption (see Figure 1 and Galović, 2015). The United States are the biggest consumer of drugs, and also, the biggest market players are from the US. According to the World Report, the American society has a share of 41% of medicines consumption. Pharmerging countries will have 25% of it until 2020, now they have nearly 20% (UNODC, 2017).

There are two major problems when talking about medicines. The first one is the overuse of them and drug addiction. The mentioned Report shows that 28 million of healthy life years were lost because of the drug use and 17 million because of the drug use disorders and resulted in disabilities and premature death (UNODC, 2017). The second problem is the lack of availability of drugs in some world regions, especially in the developing or poor countries. The unavailability of medicines is caused not only by the economic problems but political ones (wars), which multiply the deaths in the conflicted regions (Grover, Citro, Mankad & Lander, 2012). One of the indices placed in the table 3 in the Appendix is The Access to Medicine Index, published by The Access to Medicine Foundation. According to this ranking, the best access to the medicines (among previously identified companies form the Forbes 2000) provide AbbVie, AstraZeneca, Gilead Sciences, GlaxoSmithKline (the leader), Johnson&Johnson (the second place), Merck, Novartis (the third place) and Novo-Nordisk.

Strategies

Companies in pharma can choose or combine strategies based on generic strategy, developing world strategy or outsource strategy (Hodgon & Hoque, 2017). The most of the identified and analyzed papers were about the pharmaceutical market strategies in the emerging economies, which are mainly focused on the generic strategy. Therefore, it is hard to define, what is real main strategy in the pharmaceutical industry. Few sources indicate that developing world strategy and outsourcing strategy are characteristics for the Big Pharma, and the generic strategy -for Pharmerging.

The top generic producers worldwide reported by the PoliticIndia in 2015 were Teva (Israel), Sandoz (originally from Switzerland, today a part of Novartis), and Mylan (United States) with the following - Watson (United States, today: Actavis), Hospira (United States) and Stada Arzneimittel (Germany) (PoliticIndia Research, 2015). The worlds generic sector is dominated by 17 largest global companies (45% value share) followed by ca. 280 smaller companies (so-called speciality pharma with 23% share). Generics market shares the value of 11%, China pharma – 10%, Japan pharma – 6%. Biotechnology in the development stage has 3% and both

Figure 1. Expenditure on retail pharmaceuticals per capita, 2015 (or nearest year)
Source: OECD, 2017

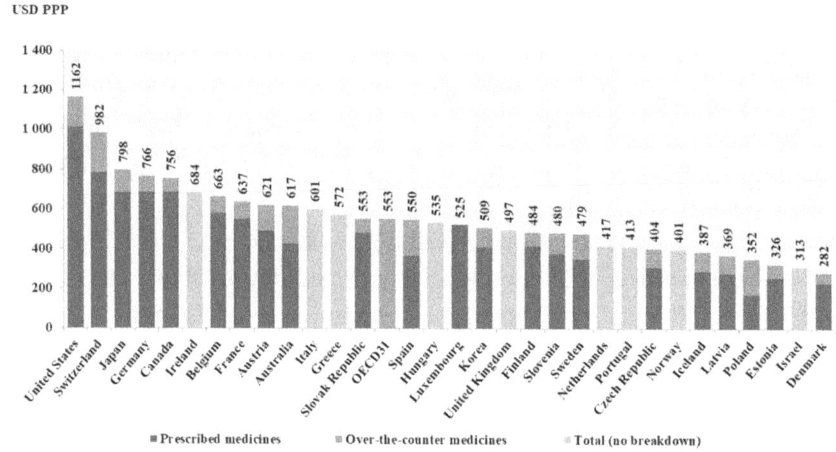

Korean and Animal Health market – 1%. This information about the supply market side is true combining with the consumption (demand) side (see Figure 2), because the mentioned western countries are also the main customers of those products.

Strategies in the mentioned industry are also similar to those in other sectors like IT or automotive. There is a megatrend of the capital concentration, observable for many years (Anwar, 2008; Kesic, 2011; Shijaku, Larraza-Kintana & Urtasun-Alonso, 2016). The pharmaceutical industry also fits in this one. For the last two

Figure 2. Share of generics in the total pharmaceutical market, 2015 (or nearest year)
Source: OECD, 2017

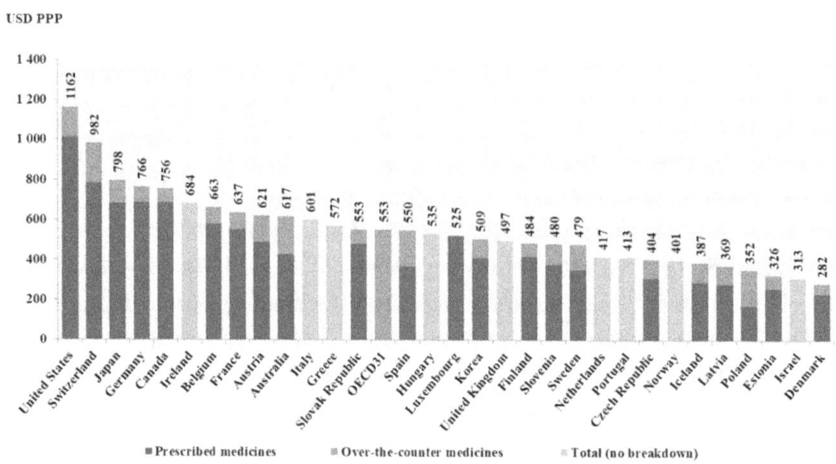

decades, especially in the time of or soon after the economic crises, many mergers and acquisitions were observed. The best one seems to be this between Genentech and Roche and result of this is a good pace in patenting new solutions, contrary to the rest of Western companies (the total number of the new-patented medicines is decreasing for a couple of years). Still, if talk about the biggest companies in the pharmaceutical industry, most of them are American (see Table 3, Appendix). Those and other but similar kinds of collaboration (joint ventures, local partnerships, knowledge sharing, access to marketing channels) are promising.

One of the subsequent topics in the pharmaceutical industry is a trend of outsourcing the medical research in the process of the drug development (Adobor, 2012; Srivastava, 2016). This relocation of the industry production to the Asian countries has an impact on the environment, so additional CSR actions should be planned and provided to avoid the negative impact or overuse (Rehman et al., 2015).

Current Issues

CSR

For over 20 years numerous foundations and other non-government organizations call for the implementation of solutions for less-privileged societies. One of the directions of the corporation's and smaller companies' actions is the Corporate Social Responsibility area. Understanding the CSR is still evolving, but almost everyone knows the approach of three dimensions of the CSR: economic, social and environmental one (aus der Beek et al., 2016). Those kinds of actions are especially necessary in the case of the pharmaceutical industry because it is strictly related to saving people's lives.

The global pharmaceutical companies are involved in many public health programs (Sturchio, 2008), they start new foundations and donate, for example, access to drugs in chosen parts of the world, take care about the lowering children mortality and run the maternal health care programs. For example, all the healthcare programs regarding drugs and vaccines against malaria saved lives over 1 million African children (aus der Beek et al., 2016).

From the economical point of view, a good solution can be PPP - public-private partnerships (Witty, 2011), joining the forces against some diseases. This is not only medicines dispensation (which is the core business operations of the industry), but medical training and disease prevention campaigns.

New financing and pricing models and international commitments (for example the Advanced Market Commitment), including tax exemptions and brakes encourage the private sector to invest in research and development (Witty, 2011). Such cooperation is focused on, among others, spurring basic research, widening the access to medicines, building the infrastructure, transferring the technology (Dunlap-Hinkler, Kotabe & Mudambi, 2010; Guler & Nerkar, 2012; Hu, Scherngell, Man, Wang & Kim, 2014; Daems, Maes, Mehra, Carroll & Thomas, 2014). Those kinds of operations need special planning and control procedures. It needs the support of the primary processes, so logistics problems solving (transportation, distribution, planning the operations, sourcing, needs analysis etc.), therefore the mathematical and IT solutions are needed to address specific needs of this part of the market (Sturchio, 2008).

Corporate Social Responsibility is still growing (Droppert & Bennet, 2015), and new activities are included in CSR strategies in pharma sector. Among those the most popular studied by Droppert and Bennet (2015) are donations, price differentiation (Verniers, Stremersch & Croux, 2011; Park et al., 2016) and special licensing for resource-poor countries, increasing product distribution capacity, supply chain support, mHealth initiatives, healthcare campaigns, employee placement programs and targeted research and development (addressing health care issues of developing and poor countries) (Toma & Marinescu, 2012). Of course, there are many benefits those firms gain during implementing their CSR strategies (Shaw & Whitney, 2016). Those have reputational and competitive character. There are few well-known sustainability indices which are used to measure the sustainability of companies in economics, environmental and social dimension.

There are two main sustainability indices (Global 100 Most Sustainable Corporations and Dow Jones Sustainability Index, see Table 3) and one about ethics in the business operations (Covalence Ethical Ranking, 2009). Firstly, only some of the identified biggest market players were ranked in those ratings. Secondly, it is easy to notice that some of them are especially active in the mentioned area. Those are Abbott Laboratories, AbbVie, AstraZeneca, Bayer, Boehringer Ingelheim, Bristol Myers, CIGNA Group, Daiichi Sankyo, Eli Lilly, GlaxoSmithKline (the leader), Johnson&Johnson, Medtronic, Merck, Novartis (the second leader), Pfizer, Roche Holding, Sanofi, Takeda.

SCM

Pharmaceutical supply chains are specific because of the characteristic of the products sold and also the law issues multiple in the sector and different in many countries. That is why when talking about the global pharma industry corporations, supply chain planning in those companies is described as very complex (more than complicated). There are many mathematical and statistic models supporting supply chain planning in this industry although it has to be clearly stated that there are many uncontrolled variables in the process of the analysis (Sousa et al., 2011; Susarla & Karimi, 2012; Mousazadeh, Torabi & Zahiri, 2015). Friemann and Schönsleben (2013) presented the findings for logistics in supply chain management. According to their work, pharmaceutical logistics should be benchmarked to some extent on the automotive industry and shift some operations to the third parties according to outsourcing strategy (and offshoring; see Graya, Roth & Leiblein, 2011). Among those solutions can be mentioned lean management, VMI, collaboration with suppliers and data transparency (Friemann & Schönsleben, 2013).

An essential part of the supply chain management in this sector is cold chain management. This flow management regarding temperature-sensitive pharmaceuticals. Cold chain management is addressed by many legal and less formal guidelines, for example, those created by World Health Organization, International Conference on Harmonization, Food and Drug Administration, United States Pharmacopeia, Health Canada, and the European Union (Bishara, 2006).

Cold chain management requires a longer time for planning and execution and also because of the more volatile demand. In logistics, the emerging economies will be more important in the future, but they create barriers because of the growing number of legal local regulations (Sampata & Shadlen, 2017). A comprehensive description of the legal issues in the chosen industry is made by Grosse (2013).

Also, like in other sectors, in pharma especially important will be reliability, responsiveness, flexibility, costs and asset management. Customer service level, logistics costs and inventory metrics will affect logistics performance in global supply chains (Harrington, Phillips & Singh Srai, 2017; Teker, 2017).

FUTURE RESEARCH DIRECTIONS

The global pharmaceutical industry is highly dynamic and innovative. It is one of the main sectors defining directions of the economic and technological development. Life sciences will be a major motor of the future growth, but its characteristics, specifics and shape are unknown. Predictions are not precise, so the complex forecasts should be made, taking into account many variables, based on current trends, established and emerging ones.

There are many areas should be discussed in the future in the field of innovation and growth in the pharmaceutical industry (Abraham, 2009), for example peptide therapeutics, control of inflammation, nucleic acid therapeutics, cell therapy, implantables and electroceuticals (like sensors) therapeutics. The pharmaceutical sector is very differentiated and dispersed, as are the known and unknown diseases. That is the reason for the further social, biological, medical, chemical and economical research. What is more, the problem with the drug addiction and unavailability should be addressed not only by the researchers but countries and international organizations. Despite improvements made, the situation in poor countries is still tragic.

There are also many logistics problems needed to be addressed in the future, but very universal in their nature, like procurement strategies, distribution networks and inventory and warehouse management (Friemann & Schönsleben, 2016). Nevertheless, despite their seemingly universal character, the specifics of the drugs and medicines dictates the way of transportation and warehousing, so the pharmaceutical inidustry problems in this area can be different from those reported by other sectors.

CONCLUSION

The current situation in the global pharmaceutical market is very complex, especially because of the growing position of the emerging economies (Nugraha, 2007). The traditional, established balance of power has been changing and it seems the new market players can dominate in some sector parts, for example, production of generics or outsourcing of the R&D operations. Undoubtedly, there is a decrease in new patents, and there are some serious problems with the legal issues in this industry, for example, the secondary patenting. What is more, when talking about the consumption, there are problems of overuse and lack of access to medicines. Those and many other problems should be addressed in future activities of governments, companies and academics.

REFERENCES

Abraham, J. (2009). Global health challenges in the pharmaceutical world. *Health Economics, Policy, and Law*, *4*(01), 115–127. doi:10.1017/S174413310800457X PMID:19099620

Adobor, H. (2012). Ethical Issues in Outsourcing: The Case of Contract Medical Research and the Global Pharmaceutical Industry. *Journal of Business Ethics*, *105*(2), 239–255. doi:10.100710551-011-0964-0

aus der Beek, T., Weber, F. A., Bergmann, A., Hickmann, S., Ebert, I., Hein, A., & Küster, A. (2016). Pharmaceuticals in the environment—global occurrences and perspectives. *Environmental Toxicology and Chemistry*, *35*(4), 823–835. doi:10.1002/etc.3339 PMID:26666847

Daems, R., Maes, E., Mehra, M., Carroll, B., & Thomas, A. (2014). MD3, Pharmaceutical Portfolio Management: Global Disease Burden and Corporate Performance Metrics. *Value in Health*, *17*(6), 732–738. doi:10.1016/j.jval.2014.07.005 PMID:25236997 de Castro, L. A. B. (2011). Partnering Brazilian biotech with the global pharmaceutical industry. *Nature Biotechnology*, *29*(3), 210–211. doi:10.1038/nbt.1801 PMID:21390019

Droppert, H., & Bennett, S. (2015). Corporate social responsibility in global health: An exploratory study of multinational pharmaceutical firms. *Globalization and Health*, *11*(15), 1–8. PMID:25886175

Dunlap-Hinkler, D., Kotabe, M., & Mudambi, R. (2010). A story of breakthrough versus Incremental innovation: Corporate entrepreneurship in the global pharmaceutical industry. *Strategic Entrepreneurship Journal*, *4*(2), 106–127. doi:10.1002ej.86

Duperon, W. O., & Cinar, E. M. (2010). Global Competition Versus Regional Interests: FDI and Pharmaceuticals in India. *Journal of International Commercial Law and Technology*, *5*(4), 181–200.

Friemann, F., & Schönsleben, P. (2013). *Global Logistics Excellence and Best Practices in Pharma: Results from an interview series with 11 large, multinational pharmaceutical companies*. Retrieved from: https://www.research-collection.ethz.ch/

Friemann, F., & Schönsleben, P. (2016). Reducing Global Supply Chain Risk Exposure of Pharmaceutical Companies by Further Incorporating Warehouse Capacity Planning into the Strategic Supply Chain Planning Process. *Journal of Pharmaceutical Innovation*, *11*(2), 162–176. doi:10.100712247-016-9249-6

Galović, T. (2015). The international competitiveness of the pharmaceutical industry within 21 OECD countries. *Ekonomski Vjesnik*, *28*(1), 225–241.

Gray, J. V., Roth, A. V., & Leiblein, M. J. (2011). Quality risk in offshore manufacturing: Evidence from the pharmaceutical industry. *Journal of Operations Management*, *29*(7-8), 737–752. doi:10.1016/j.jom.2011.06.004

Grosse, A. (2013). *Pharmaceutical Patents, Global Health and the TRIPS Agreement* (Unpublished seminar paper). University of Vienna, Austria.

Grover, A., Citro, B., Mankad, M., & Lander, F. (2012). Pharmaceutical companies and global lack of access to medicines: Strengthening accountability under the right to health. *The Journal of Law, Medicine & Ethics*, *40*(2), 234–250. doi:10.1111/j.1748-720X.2012.00661.x PMID:22789043

Guler, I., & Nerkar, A. (2012). The impact of global and local cohesion on innovation in the pharmaceutical industry. *Strategic Management Journal*, *33*(5), 535–549. doi:10.1002mj.957

Harrington, T. S., Phillips, M. A., & Singh Srai, J. (2017). Reconfiguring global pharmaceutical value networks through targeted technology interventions. *International Journal of Production Research, 55*(5), 1471–1487. doi:10.1080/00207543.2016.1221541

Hodgon, V. M., & Hoque, M. E. (2017). The growth strategies of a global pharmaceutical company: a case study of Aspen Pharmacare Holdings Limited. *Problems and Perspectives in Management, 15*(1), 248-259.

Hollinshead, G. (2017). The tortuous ascent of global value chains – the case of pharmaceutical R&D in China. *Critical Perspectives on International Business, 13*(3), 244–262. doi:10.1108/cpoib-09-2016-0032

Horner, R. (2016). Pharmaceuticals and the Global South: A Healthy Challenge for Development Theory? *Geography Compass, 10*(9), 363–377. doi:10.1111/gec3.12277

Hu, Y., Scherngell, T., Man, S. N., & Wang, Y. (2013). Is the United States Still Dominant in the Global Pharmaceutical Innovation Network? *PLOS ONE, 8*(11), e77247, 1-7.

Kesic, D. (2011). Pharmaceutical Industry in Strategic Development. *International Journal of Economics and Research, 2*(6), 29–37.

Kim, H. R. (2014, January). Formulation of a Success Model in Pharmaceutical R&D: Efficient Innovation Model. *SAGE Open*, 1–9.

Mousazadeh, M., Torabi, S. A., & Zahiri, B. (2015). A robust possibilistic programming approach for pharmaceutical supply chain network design. *Computers & Chemical Engineering, 82*, 115–128. doi:10.1016/j.compchemeng.2015.06.008

Nugraha, A. S. (2007). Global pharmaceutical industries, drugs exploration and patenting: Impact on developing countries. *Pharmaceutical Journal of Indonesia, 5*(2), 1–8.

OECDC. (2017). *World Drug Report 2017*. Retrieved from: https://www.unodc.org/wdr2017/index.html

Park, Y., Goto, D., Yang, K. F., Downton, K., Lecomte, P., Olson, M., & Mullins, C. D. (2016). A Literature Review of Factors Affecting Price and Competition in the Global Pharmaceutical Market. Value in Health. *The Journal of The International Society for Pharmacoeconomics and Outcomes Research, 19*(3), A265.

PoliticIndia Research. (2015). *Market analysis of global pharmaceutical industries and trend estimation*. Report Sample. Retrieved from: http://www.politicindia.com/reports.php?rid=13

Reddy, J., & Rao, M. (2014). Opportunities for Indian pharmaceutical companies in the era of globalization. *Journal of Global Trends in Pharmaceutical Sciences*, *5*(2), 1567–1575.

Rehman, M. S. U., Rashid, N., Ashfaq, M., Saif, A., Ahmad, N., & Han, J.-I. (2015). Global risk of pharmaceutical contamination from highly populated developing countries. *Chemosphere*, *138*, 1045–1055. doi:10.1016/j.chemosphere.2013.02.036 PMID:23535471

Sampata, B. N., & Shadlen, K. C. (2017). Secondary pharmaceutical patenting: A global perspective. *Research Policy*, *46*(3), 693–707. doi:10.1016/j.respol.2017.01.005

Shaw, B., & Whitney, P. (2016). Ethics and compliance in global pharmaceutical industry marketing and promotion: The role of the IFPMA and self-regulation. *Pharmaceuticals Policy and Law*, *18*(1-4), 199–206. doi:10.3233/PPL-160443

Shijaku, R., Larraza-Kintana, M., & Urtasun-Alonso, A. (2016). Organizational dynamic embeddedness and external shocks: The impact of financial and recession crises in strategic networks of the global pharmaceutical industry. *Complexity*, *21*(S1), 602–621. doi:10.1002/cplx.21776

Sousa, R. T., Liu, S., Papageorgiou, L. G., & Shah, N. (2011). Global supply chain planning for pharmaceuticals. *Chemical Engineering Research & Design*, *89*(11), 2396–2409. doi:10.1016/j.cherd.2011.04.005

Spigarelli, F., & Wei, H. (2012). *The rising Chinese pharmaceutical industry: local champions vs global players*. c.MET Working paper 06/2012.

Srivastava, R. (2016). How Indian Pharmaceutical Companies Are Building Global Brands: The Case of the Himalaya Herbal Brand. *Thunderbird International Business Review*, *58*(5), 399–410. doi:10.1002/tie.21827

Statista. (2017). *Medicine Spending Worldwide*. Retrieved from: https://www.statista.com/statistics/280572/medicine-spending-worldwide/

Susarla, N., & Karimi, I. A. (2012). Integrated supply chain planning for multinational pharmaceutical enterprises. *Computers & Chemical Engineering*, *42*, 168–177. doi:10.1016/j.compchemeng.2012.03.002

Teker, S. C. (2017). The Implementation of Analytic Hierarchy Process in Pharmaceutical Industry for Selection Process of 3rd Party Logistics Service Provider. *Öneri, 12*(48), 107-124.

Tempest, B. (2010). A structural change in the global pharmaceutical marketplace. *Journal of Genetic Medicine*, *7*, 113–117.

Toma, S.-G., & Marinescu, P. (2012). Business Models Based on Corporate Social Responsibility: The Case of Global Pharmaceutical Companies. Ovidius University Annals. *Economics Sciences Series*, *XII*(1), 1221–1225.

Torreya. (2017). *Global Pharma Industry Study*. Retrieved from: https://torreya.com/publications/torreya_global_pharma_industry_study_october2017.pdf

Verniers, I., Stremersch, S., & Croux, C. (2011). The global entry of new pharmaceuticals: A joint investigation of launch window and price. *International Journal of Research in Marketing*, *28*(4), 295–308. doi:10.1016/j.ijresmar.2011.05.008

Witty, A. (2011). New Strategies For Innovation In Global Health: A Pharmaceutical Industry Perspective. *Health Affairs*, *30*(1), 118–126. doi:10.1377/hlthaff.2010.0933 PMID:21209447

ADDITIONAL READING

Amaro, A. C. S., & Barbosa-Póvoa, A. P. F. D. Industrial Supply Chains With Reverse Flows. (2008, November). A Real Pharmaceutical Case Study. *Computers & Chemical Engineering*, *32*(11), 2606–2625. doi:10.1016/j.compchemeng.2008.03.006

Blanc, L. (2015). The European Pharmaceutical Industry in a Global Economy: What drives EU exports of pharmaceuticals? *Bruges European Economic Research Papers*, *31*, 38.

Chaudhuri, S., Goldberg, P. K., & Jia, P. (2006). Estimating the Effects of Global Patent Protection in Pharmaceuticals: A Case Study of Quinolones in India. [PubMed]. *The American Economic Review*, *96*(December), 1477–1514. doi:10.1257/aer.96.5.1477 PMID:29135209

Greve, J. (2008). Healthcare in developing countries and the role of business: A global governance framework to enhance the accountability of pharmaceutical companies. *Corporate Governance: The International Journal of Business in Society*, *8*(4), 490–505. doi:10.1108/14720700810899220

Haakonsson, S. J. (2009). The Changing Governance Structures of the Global Pharmaceutical Value Chain. *Competition & Change*, *13*(1), 75–95. doi:10.1179/102452909X390574

Jadhav, V. M., Gholve, S. B., & Kadam, V. J. (2009). Validation of Cold Chain Products – An Essential Need for Global Pharmaceutical Supply Chain. *International Journal of Pharm Tech Research*, *1*(2), 358–359.

Mascarenhas, O. A., Kesavan, R., & Bernacchi, M. (2005). Global Marketing of Lifesaving Drugs: An Analogical Model. *Journal of Consumer Marketing*, *22*(7), 404–411. doi:10.1108/07363760510631147

Velásquez, G. (2012). Rethinking the R&D Model for Pharmaceutical Products: A Binding Global Convention. *Policy Brief*, *8*, 1–5.

KEY TERMS AND DEFINITIONS

Big Pharma: A group of the largest pharmaceutical companies, which have their origin in so-called Western countries, especially in USA, Western Europe, and Japan.

Cold Chain Management: Management of the flow of temperature-sensitive pharmaceuticals.

Corporate Social Responsibility: A type of international private business self-regulation aimed at taking care of the society and environment and minimizing or reducing a negative impact of the company on them.

Generic Drug: Equivalent to a brand-name product but not having a brand name. It contains the same active pharmaceutical ingredient as the original (brand) drug, mostly also the same dosage, strength, route of administration, quality, performance, and intended use.

Pharmerging: A group of countries having low position on the pharmaceutical market, but having a speed pace of growth. Those are China and India, in lower extent Brazil, South Africa, and other countries.

Public-Private Partnership (PPP): A (usually long-term) cooperative arrangement between two or more public and private sectors/companies to carry out a project, a set of projects.

Supply Chain Management: A concept of managing the flow of resources in the supply chain containing suppliers, producers, distributors, intermediaries, wholesalers, retailers, third or fourth party logistics (3PL, 4PL).

APPENDIX

Table 3. Global pharmaceutical companies and their rankings

Ranking	Forbes 2000 - 2017 Edition						Top 50 Global Pharma Companies 2018	Top 10 Pharma Brands	Change the World 2017	Global 100 Most Sustainable Corporations 2018	Covalence Ethical Ranking 2009	The Access to Medicine Index 2016	Dow Jones Sustaina-bility Index 2017
Company	Rank	Country	Sales	Profits	Assets	Market Value	Rank	Rank	Rank	Rank	Rank	Rank	Status
Abbott Laboratories	#242	United States	$20.9 B	$1.4 B	$55 B	$75.7 B	#35				#5		G
AbbVie	#143	United States	$25.6 B	$5.9 B	$66.1 B	$104.5 B	#9					#9	G
Actelion	#1144	Switzerland	$2.5 B	$707 M	$2.1 B	$30.5 B	#46						
Aetna	#160	United States	$63.2 B	$2.3 B	$69.1 B	$45.1 B					#12		
Alexion Pharmaceuticals	#1235	United States	$3 B	$394 M	$13.3 B	$26 B	#41						
Alfresa Holdings	#1381	Japan	$23.5 B	$306 M	$11.3 B	$4 B							
Allergan	#149	Ireland	$15 B	$15 B	$129 B	$80.1 B	#12			#20			
AmerisourceBergen	#315	United States	$148.3 B	$1.3 B	$33.9 B	$19 B							
Amgen	#131	United States	$22.7 B	$7.7 B	$77.6 B	$120.3 B	#10	#6			#25		
Aspen Pharmacare Holdings	-	South Africa					#47						
Astellas Pharma	#528	Japan	$12.1 B	$1.9 B	$15.9 B	$28 B	#21				#28	#20	
AstraZeneca	#176	United Kingdom	$23 B	$3.7 B	$62.5 B	$75.2 B	#11	#9		#34	#8	#7	S
Baxter International	#520	United States	$10.2 B	$4.9 B	$15.5 B	$28.6 B					#11		-
Bayer	#89	Germany	$51.8 B	$5 B	$90.1 B	$94.4 B	#16					#12	S
Beckton-Dickinson	#346	United States	$12.4 B	$1.3 B	$24.3 B	$39.2 B					#16		
Biogen	#372	United States	$10.5 B	$3.7 B	$22.9 B	$58 B	#24						S,IM
Boehringer Ingelheim	-	Germany					#18				#6	#16	
Boston Scientific	#848	United States	$8.4 B	$347 M	$18.1 B	$33.7 B					#24		

continued on following page

Table 3. Continued

Ranking	Forbes 2000 - 2017 Edition						Top 50 Global Pharma Companies 2018	Top 10 Pharma Brands	Change the World 2017	Global 100 Most Sustainable Corporations 2018	Covalence Ethical Ranking 2009	The Access to Medicine Index 2016	Dow Jones Sustainability Index 2017
Company	Rank	Country	Sales	Profits	Assets	Market Value	Rank	Rank	Rank	Rank	Rank	Rank	Status
Bristol-Myers Squibb	#234	United States	$19.4 B	$4.5 B	$33.7 B	$88 B	#14				#2	#13	-
Cardinal Health	#281	United States	$127.2 B	$1.4 B	$35 B	$26 B							IM
Celgene	#346	United States	$127.2 B	$1.4 B	$35 B	$26 B	#20						
China Resources Pharmaceutical Group	#1029	Hong Kong	$20.2 B	$364 M	$17.3 B	$7.3 B							
Chugai Pharmaceutical	-	Japan					#37						
CIGNA Group	#209	United States	$39.7 B	$1.9 B	$60.3 B	$39 B					#22		G
CSL	-	United States					#26						
Daiichi Sankyo	#839	Japan	$8.9 B	$550 M	$17 B	$15.5 B	#25				#19	#18	S
Dainippon Sumitomo Pharma	-	Japan					#40						
Eisai	#1304	Japan	$4.9 B	$507 M	$8.9 B	$14.9 B	#31					#11	-
Eli Lilly	#221	United States	$21.2 B	$2.7 B	$38.8 B	$94.1 B	#15			#37	#13	#17	
Endo Health Pharmaceuticals	-	United States					#33						
Ferring Pharmaceuticals	-	Switzerland					#50						
Fresenius	#228	Germany	$32.2 B	$1.8 B	$49 B	$43.9 B	#36						
Genentech	-	United States									#23		
Gilead Sciences	#134	United States	$30.3 B	$13.5 B	$57 B	$87 B	#7	#7				#8	

continued on following page

Table 3. Continued

Ranking	Forbes 2000 - 2017 Edition						Top 50 Global Pharma Companies 2018	Top 10 Pharma Brands	Change the World 2017	Global 100 Most Sustainable Corporations 2018	Covalence Ethical Ranking 2009	The Access to Medicine Index 2016	Dow Jones Sustainability Index 2017
Company	Rank	Country	Sales	Profits	Assets	Market Value	Rank	Rank	Rank	Rank	Rank	Rank	Status
GlaxoSmithKline	#195	United Kingdom	$37.6 B	$1.2 B	$73 B	$99.8 B	#8	#10		#53	#1	#1	G
Grifols	#1191	Spain	$4.5 B	$603 M	$10.7 B	$16.8 B	#38						
Janssen	-	United States	a company of Johnson&Johnson					#4					
Jazz Pharmaceuticals	#1902	Ireland	$1.5 B	$389 M	$4.8 B	$9.2 B							
Jiangsu Hengrui Medicine	#1497	China	$1.6 B	$390 M	$2.1 B	$18.7 B							
Johnson&Johnson	#32	United States	$71.9 B	$16.4 B	$141.2 B	$338.6 B	#6		#9	#92	#7	#2	
Kangmei Pharmaceutical	#1487	China	$3.2 B	$496 M	$7.9 B	$13.4 B							
Kyowa Hakko Kirin	-	Japan					#48						
Les Laboratoires Servier	-	France					#32						
Lupin	#1717	India	$2.5 B	$444 M	$3.6 B	$9.9 B	#45						
Mallinckrodt Pharmaceuticals	-	United Kingdom					#42						
McKesson	#188	United States	$196.5 B	$2 B	$57.9 B	$30.5 B							
Medco Health Solutions	-	United States									#21		
Medipal Holdings	#1299	Japan	$28.2 B	$296 M	$13.5 B	$3.7 B							
Medtronic	#116	Ireland	$29.4 B	$4 B	$97.6 B	$110 B					#26		IM
Menarini	-	Italy					#43						

continued on following page

Table 3. Continued

Ranking	Forbes 2000 - 2017 Edition						Top 50 Global Pharma Companies 2018	Top 10 Pharma Brands	Change the World 2017	Global 100 Most Sustainable Corporations 2018	Covalence Ethical Ranking 2009	The Access to Medicine Index 2016	Dow Jones Sustaina-bility Index 2017
Company	Rank	Country	Sales	Profits	Assets	Market Value	Rank	Rank	Rank	Rank	Rank	Rank	Status
Merck	#100	United States	$39.6 B	$3.9 B	$95.4 B	$173.3 B	#4	#3		#13	#17	#5	
Merck	#288	Germany	$16.6 B	$1.8 B	$41.1 B	$49.1 B	#27					#4	
Mitsubishi Tanabe Pharma	-	Japan					#44						
Mylan	#640	United Kingdom	$11.1 B	$480 M	$34.7 B	$21.2 B	#23						
Novartis	#61	Switzerland	$48.5 B	$6.7 B	$130.4 B	$193.2 B	#2	#5	#4	#64	#3	#3	S
Novo Nordisk	#375	Denmark	$16.6 B	$5.6 B	$13.8 B	$88.2 B	#17	#8			#9	#10	B
ONO Pharmaceutical	#1595	Japan	$2.2 B	$444 M	$5 B	$12.3 B	#49						
Otsuka Holding	#578	Japan	$11 B	$852 M	$22.7 B	$25.1 B	#29						
Perrigo	#1428	Ireland	$5.6 B	$-1.5 B	$17.5 B	$9.9 B							
Pfizer	#47	United States	$52.8 B	$7.1 B	$171.6 B	$203.1 B	#1	#1			#15	#14	
QuintilesIMS	#1076	United States	$6.9 B	$115 M	$21.2 B	$18.7 B							
Regeneron Pharmaceuticals	#987	United States	$4.9 B	$880 M	$7 B	$40.4 B	#39						
Roche Holding	#79	Switzerland	$51.3 B	$9.7 B	$75.6 B	$219.3 B	#3	#2			#4	#19	G
Sanofi	#88	France	$37.4 B	$5.2 B	$110.4 B	$116.1 B	#5			#22	#14	#6	B
Schering-Plough		United States									#30		
Shanghai Fosun Pharmaceutical (group)	#1766	China	$2.2 B	$423 M	$6.3 B	$9.8 B							

continued on following page

Table 3. Continued

Ranking	Forbes 2000 - 2017 Edition						Top 50 Global Pharma Companies 2018	Top 10 Pharma Brands	Change the World 2017	Global 100 Most Sustainable Corporations 2018	Covalence Ethical Ranking 2009	The Access to Medicine Index 2016	Dow Jones Sustaina-bility Index 2017
Company	Rank	Country	Sales	Profits	Assets	Market Value	Rank	Rank	Rank	Rank	Rank	Rank	Status
Shionogi	#1219	Japan	$3.1 B	$852 M	$5.5 B	$17.4 B							
Shire	#562	Ireland	$11.6 B	$342 M	$67 B	$51.3 B	#22						
Sinopharm Group	#581	China	$38.9 B	$701 M	$22.7 B	$12.7 B							
Sun Pharma Industries	#1023	India	$4.6 B	$1.1 B	$9.1 B	$24.9 B	#30						
Suzuken	#1585	Japan	$20.1 B	$244 M	$10.6 B	$3.2 B							
Takeda Pharmaceutical	#348	Japan	$15.9 B	$1.2 B	$35.5 B	$36.9 B	#19			#44	#18	#15	-
Teva Pharmaceutical	#485	Israel	$21.9 B	$337 M	$92.9 B	$32.4 B	#13						
Toho Holdings	#1903	Japan	$11.8 B	$199 M	$5.6 B	$1.6 B							
UCB	#1212	Belgium	$4.6 B	$601 M	$10.8 B	$14.6 B	#34			#4			
United Health Group		United States									#10		
Valeant Pharmaceuticals	#1248	Canada	$9.7 B	$-2.4 B	$43.5 B	$3.3 B	#28						
WellPoint	-	Canada									#20		
Yunnan Baiyao Group	#1548	China	$3.4 B	$457 M	$3.4 B	$13.1 B							
Zimmer Biomet	#887	United States	$7.7 B	$300 M	$26.7 B	$24.1 B					#27		
Zoetis	#1047	United States	$4.9 B	$821 M	$7.6 B	$25.8 B							

(Data source: own preparation based on: forbes.com; pharmexec.com; interbrandhealth.com; fortune.com; corporateknights.co; covalence.ch; accesstomedicineindex.org).

Table 4. Literature review results (grouped by the main area of research topic)

Source	Pub. Year	Main Research Problem/Topic	Country/ Countries	Main Research Method	Results	Main Area
Grover,Citro, Mankad, & Lander	2012	Analysis of the access to the drugs	None	Document and literature review	Millions of people lack access to life-saving drugs because they are too expensive or because they do not exist at all. Mechanisms of charity activities of the corporations are ineffective and need to be improved.	ACCESS
Sturchio	2008	Public health programs led by pharma companies and their impact on changing the public health problems	USA (only chosen company)	Document review, viewpoint (expert)	Review of PPP initiatives – a synergy between public and private organizations to address the current problems of the healthcare worldwide	CSR
Witty	2011	CSR and private-public cooperation in the industry	None	Document and literature review	In close cooperation with the international public health community, industry stands ready to create and effectively deliver products of value to all patients throughout the world	CSR
Adobor	2012	The outsourcing of medical research in drug development	None	Document and literature review	There is a need to create more specific law in the clinical research destination countries, enabling the control of the trials and compatible with the Helsinki Declaration. There is no enough control of the clinical research, which has been shifted from Western to the Eastern countries.	CSR
Toma & Marinescu	2012	Business models of CSR in the global pharma market	USA (only one us company)	Documents and literature review	The big pharma has made tremendous contributions to human well-being and the business models based on CSR are increasingly implemented in the global pharmaceutical industry	CSR
Droppert & Bennett	2015	CSR strategies - factors	None	Public data analysis, interview (purposive selection)	CSR differed for each firm., primary factors that motivated csr engagement were: reputational benefits, recruitment and employee satisfaction, better rankings in sustainability indices, entrance into new markets, long-term economic returns, and improved population health. In terms of CSR strategy, firms were at different points on a spectrum ranging from philanthropic donations to integrated systemic shared value business models.	CSR

continued on following page

Table 4. Continued

Source	Pub. Year	Main Research Problem/Topic	Country/ Countries	Main Research Method	Results	Main Area
Aus der Beek et al.	2016	An up-to-date review of the current state of knowledge on the global relevance and prevailing concentrations of pharmaceuticals in the environment	None (but regional differentiation)	Literature review and metaanalysis	Measured Environmental Concentrations have become increasingly available in emerging and developing countries. In a number of countries, certain pharmaceuticals are detected in surface waters, suggesting that adverse ecotoxicological effects might be possible at hot spots downstream of urban sewage discharge in densely populated areas. There is only a partial overlap of the pharmaceutical substances detected globally: different pharmaceutical groups have been the focus of monitoring campaigns in different UN regions, such as antibiotics in Asia and estrogens in Africa. Fourth, urban wastewater discharge is the dominant emission pathway, but discharges from manufacturing, hospitals, animal husbandry, and aquaculture facilities are important locally. The publicly available data on national pharmaceutical consumption is currently not sufficiently detailed for a comprehensive regional analysis of environmentally relevant pharmaceuticals.	CSR
Shaw & Whitney	2016	Role of the international federation of pharmaceutical manufacturers and association in the creation of ethics in the pharmaceutical industry	None	Document and literature review	The activities of the IFPMA and its member associations and companies are an example of the broader trend towards greater business ethical frameworks in the pharmaceutical industry	CSR
Galović	2015	Pharmaceutical industry in 21 OECD countries between 2004 and 2009	21 OECD countries	Statistical analysis	When it comes to the OECD, intra-industry trade of pharmaceuticals, older European member states got higher scores, most highly developed countries have preconditions for improvement, of international competitiveness and development of revealed comparative advantages, while other countries have smaller possibilities for reaching this scenario.	GENERAL
Politicindia Research	2015	Characteristics of the global pharmaceutical industry	None	Document and literature analysis	-	GENERAL

continued on following page

Table 4. Continued

Source	Pub. Year	Main Research Problem/Topic	Country/ Countries	Main Research Method	Results	Main Area
Hodgon & Hoque	2017	Growth strategy in the pharmaceutical industry	South Africa (only one company)	Document and literature analysis	A number of growth strategies include a) organic growth, b) inorganic growth, in the form of carefully planned and well-executed acquisitions, aligned to the group strategy, c) extending territorial coverage through global expansion, particularly into emerging pharmaceutical countries, and d) ongoing investment in production capabilities as a means of achieving a strategic advantage .	GENERAL
Dunlap, Hinkler, Kotabe & Mudambi	2010	Corporate entrepreneurship, innovations and breakthroughs	USA	Conceptual model, statistical analysis	Products that emerge from joint ventures and alliances are more likely to be breakthroughs	INNOVATIONS
Guler & Nerkar	2012	Intraorganizational networks and cohesion within an organization	None	Statistical analysis	Local cohesion has a positive impact on the innovative performance of a firm, and global cohesion has a negative impact.	INNOVATIONS
Hu. Scherngell, Man, Wang	2013	The role of the US companies in innovations	USA	Statistical method	The USA still dominates in the global pharmaceutical innovation network, however, it shows a slightly decreasing prominence in the networks of either total new drugs or NME drugs in the time period 2006–2010	INNOVATIONS
Daems, Maes, Mehra, Carroll & Thomas	2014	The relationship between business and social parameters associated with pharmaceutical innovation in three distinct disease areas	None	Case study, econometric method	The framework that can assist innovation-driven biopharmaceutical companies as they strive to meet the medical needs of patients	INNOVATIONS
Kim	2014	Building the Efficient Innovation Model for the industry	None	Document and literature review	The important relationship between managerial capabilities, strategies, and innovation (an industrial success model).	INNOVATIONS
Hollinshead	2017	Exploring the micro-political complexities of operating over institutional distance in a modern international enterprise in R&D in China in the pharmaceutical industry	China	Interview	In the context of an enterprise intent on innovation, motivational logics in the context of an enterprise intent on innovation, motivational logics themselves emanate from the embedded positions of diverse organizational actors, in turn bringing to the fore issues of power, resistance, ethnicity and language, themselves emanate from the embedded positions of diverse organizational actors, in turn bringing to the fore issues of power, resistance, ethnicity and language.	INNOVATIONS

continued on following page

Table 4. Continued

Source	Pub. Year	Main Research Problem/Topic	Country/ Countries	Main Research Method	Results	Main Area
Grosse	2013	Legal issues in the pharma industry (TRIPS agreement)	None	Document and literature review	Substantive TRIPS provisions lack clarity because they represent compromise formulations resulting from multilateral negotiations	LAW
Sampata & Shadlen	2017	Secondary patenting	None	Statistical analysis	Cross-national grant rates for secondary patents, despite the harmonization aimed for by the TRIPS. Secondary patenting is identified as a global problem.	LAW, ETHICS
Anwar	2008	Mergers in the pharmaceutical industry	France	Case study	Mergers can provide many benefits despite the barriers of growth they cause (for example the need to reorganize the organization).	MERGERS
Kesic	2011	Characteristics of the global pharmaceutical industry, especially whether a marketing management plays an important role in the operational and strategic performance	None	Document and literature review, survey	Capital concentration is a part of the strategy of companies and is linked to the market changes, also R&D activities. Marketing is one of the most important strategic orientation of the companies.	MERGERS
Shijaku, Larraza-Kintana & Urtasun-Alonso	2016	Situation of the pharmaceutical industry network during and after the economic crisis	None	Statistical analysis	Smaller companies were more endangered with the financial problems than bigger ones. Mergers significantly changed the centrality of the networks	MERGERS
Chui	2009	Generics market in China	China	Document review, viewpoint (expert)	The Chinese market is very good (and will be still in the next years) for both domestic and foreign generic drugs makers. It will be strenghtened by the process of ageing the Chinese society and growing number of city habitants and their lifestyle and health problems. The society cannot afford buying original brand drugs, so will buy generics.	PHARMERGING
Duperon & Cinar	2010	Description of the Indian pharmaceutical market	India	Document and literature review	India is a large market with the high potential to produce drugs to the domestic and patent-honouring countries and for drug trials.	PHARMERGING
De Castro	2011	Characteristics of the Brazilian pharmaceutical industry	Brazil	Expert voice	Brazilian industry, because of the multiple government actions, is able to develop innovative drugs	PHARMERGING
Spigarelli & Wei	2012	Main features and challenges of the Chinese pharmaceutical industry	China	Document and literature review	Chinese market seems to be evolving into a highly competitive marketplace, where Chinese firms are training not only to keep market shares compared to western firm, but also to conquer an active and strategic position in the global value chain of the global pharmaceutical market.	PHARMERGING

continued on following page

Table 4. Continued

Source	Pub. Year	Main Research Problem/Topic	Country/ Countries	Main Research Method	Results	Main Area
Nugraha	2014	The impact of global trends on the pharmaceutical industry in developing countries	None	Literature review	Multinational companies have not played significant roles in the development of global pharmaceutical industries yet, even though they have set up partnerships programs. They exploit the markets and people as a trials subjects.	PHARMERGING
Reddy & Rao	2014	Characteristics of the Indian pharmaceutical industry	India	Literature review	Indian pharmaceutical industry has a lot of potentials, but makes no significant development and need to be more innovative	PHARMERGING
Rehman, Rashid, Ashfaq, Saif & Ahmad	2015	The impact of the industrial relocation on the environment	China, bangladesh, Pakistan, India	Literature review	There are many threads for the studied countries in environmental issues regarding the production in the pharmaceutical industry. The worst situation in this regard is in Bangladesh, India and Pakistan, better in China, where the awareness is higher.	PHARMERGING
Horner	2016	The situation of the global South in the pharmaceutical industry	None (region: global South)	Document and literature review	The situation of the global South is changing but still, the pharmaceutical industry in the southern countries is poor. There are complementaries between industry and health.	PHARMERGING
Srivastava	2016	Building global brands of the Indian pharmaceutical industry	India	Interview	For herbal brand marketing, an emphasis on results, response time, and lower side effects with improved quality of life are the right approach. Franchising is the right approach to build the competitive advantage in the industry.	PHARMERGING
Verniers, Stremersch & Croux	2011	Launch of the new product: launch prices, launch windows	50 chosen countries	Statistical analysis (modeling)	The fastest launch occurs when the launch price is high, the highest launch price occurs at a launch window of 85 months. The health regulator acts strategically in that the extent to which it delays the launch of a new drug increases with the price of the new drug. Overall, regulation increases the launch window, except for patent protection. Surprisingly, the regulation does not directly impact launch price.	PRICE
Park, Goto et al.	2016	Price and competition	EU and Canada	Literature review	The impact of market and regulatory factors on price and competition may vary across countries, a complex analysis of the market and regulatory factors and long-term cost-effectiveness of pharmaceutical products is needed to better inform decision-makers about the impact on the society.	PRICE

continued on following page

Table 4. Continued

Source	Pub. Year	Main Research Problem/Topic	Country/ Countries	Main Research Method	Results	Main Area
Bishara	2006	Cold chain management	None	Document review, viewpoint (expert)	There are many guidelines for cold chain management. Due to the presence of multiple uncontrolled variables in the distribution process, developing an appropriate monitoring program is essential.	SCM
Graya, Roth, Leiblein	2011	Quality risk of offshore manufacturing in the pharma industry	USA and Puerto Rico	Statistical analysis	Puerto Rican plants operate with a significantly higher quality risk than matching plants operated by the same firm located in the mainland u.s., on average. The study highlights the need for the food and drug administration (FDA)) to continue to intensify its inspection focus on international manufacturing.	SCM
Sousa, Liu, Papageorgiou & Shah	2011	Optimizing the global supply chain planning	None	Statistical analysis	A ready-to-use model of optimizing the flows in supply chains.	SCM
Susarla & Karimi	2012	Supply chain planning	None	Statistical analysis	A simple MILP-LP model for multiperiod enterprise-wide planning in a multi-site, multi-echelon, and global network of a pharmaceutical company; the model integrates procurement, production, and distribution along with the effects of international tax ifferentials, inventory holding costs, material shelf-lives, waste treatment/disposal, and other real-life factors on the after-tax profit of the company	SCM
Friemann, Schönsleben	2013	Best practices in logistics in global pharmaceutical industry	None	Interview	The biggest limitations in storage capacities are encountered in the distribution centers. Emerging markets will become more relevant in future and the majority of the companies is already locally operating in some of them.	SCM
Mousazadeh, Torabi & Zahiri	2015	Supply chain planning (mostly production and distribution)	None	Statistical analysis	The model helps to make several decisions - for example opening of pharmaceutical manufacturing/distribution centers (mod-term planning, tactical decisions)	SCM
Harrington, Phillips & Singh Srai	2017	Categorization of advanced manufacturing technology (amt) to make shift form make-to-stock strategy into the make-to-order strategy	United Kingdom	Mixed: expert input and case study	A framework for categorization of the amt; the shift from MTS (make-to-stock) to MTO (make-to-order) is necessary but there are many obstacles to implement it everywhere.	SCM

continued on following page

Table 4. Continued

Source	Pub. Year	Main Research Problem/Topic	Country/ Countries	Main Research Method	Results	Main Area
Teker	2017	Selection process of the Third Party Logistics Provider	None	Statistical analysis	Experience, risk amanagement and relationship referring to trust, reliability and compatibility are the most important criteria in the mentioned process	SCM

(Data source: research papers presented above.)

Chapter 4
Global Macrotrends in Pharmaceutical Industry

Suganya S.
SSN College of Engineering, India

ABSTRACT

The pharmaceutical industry is trending in business decisions to demonstrate financial impact, influence on the behavior of consumers, governments, and businesses. This impact is beyond geographies and industries. It must be understood how a trend's impact will manifest itself in an actionable business planning horizon. Most of the pharmaceutical industries believe that global trends will shape business decisions over the next 5 to 10 years. Each management team in the pharmaceutical industry works on the global forces shaping their strategic context. The collisions approach is a systematic way to capture trends in strategy that enables your leadership team to rapidly combine multiple trends, facts, and perspectives to identify the "market-shaping force" that has the power to significantly shift spending and profit pools. This chapter discusses the effective competition in the pharmaceutical industry in the implementation of new technologies and trends to contribute to broader solutions.

INTRODUCTION

Global macro trends in the pharmaceutical industry remain front and center this year. Here the increased consolidation of providers meets the bigger regulators that weigh the pros and cons of the proposed deals between bigger pharma industrialists. Provider systems are joining forces and snapping up private practices. Overall, consolidation in the healthcare and pharmaceutical industries is likely to continue, because smaller companies will need to increase their negotiating power when

DOI: 10.4018/978-1-5225-5921-4.ch004

competing with their new larger rivals. The apparent forces in pharmaceutical industries create new investment opportunities, mitigate risks, stress-test an existing strategy, or craft a new strategic direction. Strategy Analytics Center (STAC) is a creative approach that helps leaders make sense of internal and external data on corporate performance, macroeconomic changes, and global and local trends so that executives can develop more robust strategies for creating value, identifying business opportunities, and pursuing growth. In such cases, industrialists can convert complexity into opportunity by designing plans, innovations, rethinking their strategies in the context of these forces.

STRATEGIC MANAGEMENT

In this section, the examination of the present and future environment elements of an organization or industry is made where objectives are formulated, implemented, achieved, and evaluated. The factors are used to determine the macrotrends as follows.

Drug Pricing

Pricing pressures around the world and unanswered value gaps to differentiate new medicines add to the potential for healthcare system bankruptcy as it currently exists, because medical care inflation continues to be unchecked. It reforms the market changes that impact device and drug manufacturers.

Pricing is one of the major reasons for the growth of biologics that continue to dominate the pharmaceutical news in the coming years. Charging high prices for pharmaceutical products may gain money to be used in the research and development of new drugs. National and international funding agencies have been spent fund on drugs that mean less money for other healthcare or nonhealthcare services. The Centers for Medicare & Medicaid Services (CMS) (www.mce.eu) reimburse the money that market shareholders fix to control the costs of drugs. The pricing pressure on providers, hospitals, and health systems affects the patients to get medications they need. How the drug choices and value delivered is yet paid attention by the public and private players. Such pressure on biologic drugs makes manufacturers rethink the business model. Much drug foundation financially encourages pharma industries to develop a drug for deadly diseases as personalized treatments continue to drive biopharmaceutical innovation.

Pharmaceutical manufacturing trends also meet with the real market challenges of flexible biologic drugs, closer partnerships between the pharmaceutical industry and regulators. It results in the novel concepts to be implemented faster with existing talents that are influencing biopharmaceutical trends to meet the drug availability demands.

Network

Provider network offers knowledge for patients to choose a network for health plans. Increasing healthcare costs continue to outpace inflation, creating greater incentives for insurers to offer plans with high deductibles and narrow networks. The consumer questions the access quality of the narrow network. Medicare Advantage plans provide the adequate knowledge on proper fee (Pharma Outlook, 2017).

Employers

Market trends collide, and employers have become concerned about their ability to continuously offer health benefits that will maintain a healthy, productive workforce. The employees must be able to analyze the benefits that are viable to offer health coverage, especially when employers are faced with uncertain insurance premiums. Consumer-directed health plans, in which employers are considering, include offering health plans with increasing employee cost-sharing and offering employees a defined contribution to purchase their own coverage.

Specialty Drugs

Employers have been experiencing effective ways to manage the rising cost of specialty drugs. Utilization restrictions for specialty prescription drugs, including prior authorization or limiting quantities based on clinical evidence is expected by the National Employer Initiative (NEI) on Biologics & Specialty Drugs (A Report on Healthcare, 2014).

Education Gaps

Gap across all stakeholders, including regulators, drug manufacturers, payers, patients, and employers as plan sponsors continue to face knowledge gaps regarding healthcare, along with the challenges facing each other. Awareness programs let stakeholders realize the education gap exists in developing products. Mobile device tools are one of the best approaches taken healthcare societies to know the cost of their treatment and can obtain the healthcare services that address their needs.

Value

Transparency apps are welcome as a quality tools for health planning of a patient and reporting the performance of healthcare. From the report generated from apps, a patient's healthcare decision can become better.

Rising Customer Expectations

The commercial environment is getting harsher, as healthcare payers impose new cost constraints on healthcare providers and scrutinize the value medicines offer much more carefully. They want new therapies that are clinically and economically better than the existing alternatives, together with hard, real-world outcomes data to back any claims about a medicine's superiority.

Poor Scientific Productivity

Pharma's output has remained at a stable level for the past decade. Using the same discovering and developing processes, there is little reason to think its productivity will suddenly soar.

Cultural Sclerosis

A crisis of trust in pharma industry is a barrier to develop innovative patient-centered models for achieving culture change and facilitate scientific productivity. The prevailing management culture, mental models and strategies, on which the industry relies, are the same ones it's traditionally relied on, even though they have been eclipsed by new ways of doing business (PriceWaterhouseCoopers, 2015).

GLOBAL MARKET AND POLITICS

Uncertainty and Harmonization

Despite some more prohibitive market access trends in recent years, the first-call territory for global product launches in pharma happens absolutely in the developed nation. The accompanying country is a sigh of relief to share biopharma prices. Pharmaceutical and biotechnology industry is "getting away with murder" due to unpredictable sharp rise in prices. It is so-called "Big Pharma's Nightmare" by an expert. The national government must create favorable conditions including tax reform and rekindled investor enthusiasm; for a resurgence of biopharma mergers and acquisitions among life sciences industry trends in 2017. The considerable interest in the pharma industry such as uncertainty over regulation, mutual recognition, parallel imports, employee migration, R&D investment, and a number of other issues are popular to mandate.

Price-Gouging

Price-Gouging is a sharp criticism of both branded and generic products, as well as new and established medicines not particular to any country but globally extends to all pharma companies. This trend is also limited by recent action against companies accused of overcharging the National Health Service massively for generic drugs. Health care authorities from each country seek more transparency and cooperation in the way pharmaceutical companies negotiate pricing and reimbursement with purchasing authorities. Tougher price controls on medicine lead to greater volume-driven sales. The restraints on value-based pricing are influenced by the greater emphasis on 'enough is enough' and committing to voluntary price (Pharmas Almanac, 2015). In this challenging environment, major international markets need to show better price transparency while finding new ways to build, demonstrate and monetize drug value. It deals with more pay-for-performance deals, health plans and demanding criteria for pricing and reimbursement, with persistent variations from one country to the next, will continue to raise the bar for market entry.

The Convergence of Technology Sectors and Healthcare

Healthcare apps and other digital innovations have been converged to boosting connectivity and engagement between all players along the healthcare chain. The explosion in healthcare investment by technology giants, such as Apple, Google and IBM is also responsible for this trend in the pharmaceutical market. The emerging trend covers up the areas such as data-gathering, disease monitoring or drug compliance, goes in the same direction by placing medical or digital-health devices. The evolution of health wearables underlying these technology trends in the pharmaceutical industry is the rapid proliferation and paramount importance of data in healthcare. Yet, challenges around data integrity, collection, consolidation and reporting to be meet the pharmaceutical product launch checklist in addition. Increasing healthcare-technology convergence also reflects growing demand, in line with payer reliance on health economics, for real-time monitoring of patients and real-world evidence not only of drug efficacy but also of effectiveness and cost-effectiveness. Due to demand and complex operating environment, pharma cannot afford to be an island on offering wearables and other digital-health accessories.

Above all, it must learn technologies or innovations from digital technology, software, banking or fast-moving consumer goods for payers (Mulder, 2015).

Drug Access and Regulation

The viability of the health technology assessment is at risk. However, most of the pharma companies are encouraging the risk-benefit equation on their own strategies. For instance, the debate on Sarepta's-Duchenne's treatment Exondysin September 2016 put this still-evolving issue as a key component of the pharma industry outlook for 2017. For the approval of Exondys (www.fda.gov) through food and drug administration, came despite a negative advisory-committee verdict that found the evidence from clinical trials insufficiently compelling to support the product's claimed clinical benefits. To bring up the innovative drugs to market, several countries have already adopted regulatory mechanisms to speed up the progress. Many large-scale chronic diseases, such as diabetes and asthma, are now relatively well controlled. Now, there remain significant gaps in the therapeutic armamentarium, particularly for intractable conditions linked to population aging, such as Alzheimer's disease.

Public and Political Trust

Every year can be seen a number of pharma companies emerging and ruling the market such as Valeant, Turing, Mylan, Teva and Pfizer. These concerns centered mainly on drug pricing, exploitation of market monopolies, creative accounting and dubious promotional practices in developing and other markets. Pharma is being a genuine partner in healthcare industries that may reside in data- and technology-driven patient centricity. It helps to manage the entire disease spectrum. Patient involvement in decision making about research and development may be linked to information access/empowerment at ground level. This might be crucial to achieving these ends. Therefore, optimizing connectivity and plugging into the whole patient journey becomes one of the key challenges facing the pharmaceutical industry. Ethical stance on sales and marketing, along with its volume-driven business strategy seek to win back public and political trust is certainly one of the key pharma trends.

Multichannel

Marketing strategy has been struggling between the pharmaceutical sales teams and healthcare professionals due to the tight restrictions on face-to-face relationships. Therefore, pharma industry has been seeking to "non-personal promotions" such as email and mobile alerts, as well as direct mail and speaker programmes to outreach the medical professionals. While the trend towards more cost-effective multichannel marketing accelerates, there is also a risk of overload. Interactions via digital and other non-personal channels comes out with what customers really want and need so that they can deliver the right information and promotions through the right vehicle at the right time as part of a more tailored, smart multichannel strategy. That must also include educational initiatives to back up a growing trend in R&D and launches towards more complex, niche-oriented specialty and orphan drugs (Multichannel Marketing Report, 2014).

Trend to Specialty Drugs

The aforementioned trend towards specialty and rare-disease drugs looks set to continue during 2017. The volume of innovative medicines approved for entry to the market is declined last year about hitting a six-year low. In the EU, there were also signs of a slowdown. The European Medicines Agency's Committee for Medicinal Products for Human Use recommended a total of 81 medicines for approval – including innovative drugs, biosimilars and generics – in 2016, compared with 93 in the previous year. New options for conditions such as spinal muscular atrophy, Duchenne muscular dystrophy, hepatitis C virus, rare chronic liver disease, severe asthma and delusions experienced in Parkinson's disease must be figured strongly in the FDA's approval (http://www.regulations.gov/).

The launch pipeline for specialty drugs, 2017 remains well stocked with specialty therapies addressing anything from rheumatoid arthritis to osteoporosis, non-small cell lung cancer, melanoma, acute myeloid leukemia, asthma and tardive dyskinesia. The continuing emphasis on lower-volume, higher cost specialty assets will further raise market-access barriers at launch with escalating concerns about drug pricing and affordability.

Quality and cost efficiency are the twin intense factors at company level, which can promote by highly specialized teams across geographical and functional boundaries through optimal transparency, awareness, knowledge exchange and harmonization (Docteur, 2009). Smart digital tools that help pharmaceutical companies optimise launch readiness and market access. It is performed successfully by enhancing visibility and transparency, streamlining processes, utilizing business intelligence better, and driving communication and collaboration across brands, management layers, business functions and countries worldwide.

OPPORTUNITIES IN GLOBAL MARKET

Generic and Biosimilar Drugs

Pharmaceutical spending is increasingly affected by the generic drug market due to pro-generic policies in several regions, including Western Europe. The high-volume/low-margin generics market is generally fragmented-among the top leading players in pharma to thrive for double-digit market share. Analysts expect that increasing industry consolidation may partially offset the lower price advantage associated with generic drugs. Similar to generic impact on branded pharmaceuticals, biosimilars threaten to steal market share from more costly biotech drugs. For instance, since the first biosimilar approval in the European Union (EU) in 2006, there are now more than 700 biosimilars approved globally or in the pipeline (Ajay, 2016). The potential financial benefit of biosimilars is driving their uptake by regulators and payers of the major market. Experts expect the biosimilars market to reach $10 billion by 2020 with several challenges. The key differences between biosimilars and generic medications are illustrated in the table (see Table 1).

Medical Technology Trend

Global medical device and technology market growth were stagnant 2011-2015 due to the lasting impact of the 2009 recession, which resulted in lean financing from investors. However, the momentum of it is increased about 5.3 percent in 2016 (Medical Technology Report, 2016). It was leading to maintain or strengthen in the upcoming years by government support for the use of diagnostics to improve clinical outcomes and patient affordability, the rising preference for minimally invasive procedures, dramatic advances in digital health applications, and endorsements for branded devices such as diagnostic imaging and accessories.

Table 1. Difference between biosimilars and generics

S.No	Biosimilars	Generics
1.	Similar to, and not identical to the reference product	Bioequivalent and identical to the reference product
2.	20-30percent discount over reference product	80–90percent discount over reference product
3.	$100M – $200M in development costs	$1M–$5M in development costs
4.	8–10 year development timeline	3–5 year development timeline
5.	No interchangeability or automatic substitution	Interchangeable with the reference product

Source: (Pharmaceutical Processing, n.d.)

In vitro diagnostics (IVD) continues to be one of the fastest-growing areas, and is projected to gain momentum at a Compound Annual Growth Rate (CAGR) of 5.1percent from 2014 – 2020. It is a demand-driven technology for IVD testing by the prevalence of chronic diseases. Medicare Access and CHIP Reauthorization Act of 2015 (MACRA) has announced that a payment is a law intended to drive major health care payment and delivery system reform for clinicians, health systems, Medicare, and other government and commercial payers. Now a day, growth opportunities are welcoming the advancement in genomics, including gene editing and proteomics for the IVD market. Minimally invasive devices are the temptation such as MRI-compatible implantable cardioverter-defibrillators (ICDs), next-generation insertable cardiac monitors, and drug-coated balloons, as a result of increased minimally invasive cardiac procedures, should help drive the cardiology diagnostics market (Mauro, 2008).

Many industry players–both traditional organizations and new market entrants are capitalizing on recent and emerging technological advancements and providing digitally enabled healthcare solutions using mobile health applications, sensor technology, data analytics, and artificial intelligence (AI). In the next 10 years, the vast majority of devices are anticipated to have embedded sensors. New handheld diagnostics with built-in AI will revolutionize the way primary care is delivered outside the physician office. Diagnostics and AI will truly usher in the "personalized medicine" era. These new offerings will produce a huge new growth engine with the power to transform clinical care. Although, considerable attention and resources on IVD (Wilbert, 2014), minimally invasive devices, and digital health applications, the biggest challenges many faces are not at the product development level; rather, they are on the commercial side and along the supply chain. Questions arise about the strategies and tactics applied by the industry to more efficiently and cost-effectively manage a changing customer base, how best to the right size the organization, where to streamline distribution channels, or how to wrap services around products to differentiate themselves in the marketplace will be key to ongoing market success. If once it is answered, the pharma market cannot slide down.

Key Factors

Pharma stakeholders large and small, public and private are expected to pay close attention to five sector issues that have the potential to help and/or hinder their clinical, financial and operational plans:

- Managing cost and pricing,
- Driving clinical innovation,
- Connecting with customers & consumers,

- Transforming business & operating models,
- Meeting regulatory compliance.

The number of potential policy and regulatory changes is anticipated in 2017 for sector participants seeking to manage clinical and business risks and sustain growth in the pharmaceutical marketplace.

Digital Supply Networks

Forward-thinking pharma companies are transforming their traditional, linear supply chain into a dynamic, interconnected system that can more readily incorporate ecosystem partners and evolve to a more optimal state over time. This digital supply network (DSN) integrates information from many different sources and locations to drive the physical act of production and distribution. By implementing the new technologies, such as sensor-based data sets, DSNs enable integrated views of the supply network and rapid, use-case-appropriate latency responses to changing situations and current market positions. The "four Vs" (volatility, volume, velocity, and visibility) is must to reform according to the current demand & scenario of market situations by supply chain professionals. They must attempt to optimize results across a series of objectives that include total cost, service, quality, and support for innovation. Historically, supply chain making a decision depends on the traditional priorities, which are not likely to change but going forward in order to achieve higher levels of performance with capabilities developed using new digital technologies (Accenture, 2016).

Objectives of DSN

- Enabling end-to-end supply network visibility,
- Improve manufacturing operation efficiency and yield,
- Creating new options for enabling clinical trial supply.

Many life sciences organizations already on the path to creating DSNs are shifting their focus away from managing and optimizing discrete functions, such as procurement and manufacturing. Instead, they often use DSNs to focus more holistically on how the full supply chain can better achieve business objectives while informing corporate, business unit, and portfolio strategies. Indeed, DSNs increasingly enable supply chain professional to become an integral part of strategic planning and decision-making and to help create new sources of revenue by providing faster access to markets and supporting the production of smart products. To this end, organizations can develop and leverage multiple DSNs to complement different facets of their strategy and more effectively target specific needs.

TRENDS INFLUENCING PHARMACEUTICAL INDUSTRY

Until recently, any investments in R&D and innovation must result in patent-protected, high-margin revenue streams. The pharmaceutical business is lucrative. Today pharma industry is scrambling to deal with significant changes that include the below-mentioned issues.

The Patent Cliff

Billions in revenues will be lost due to patent expiry and the growing competition from low-cost generics. Pharma companies are trying different strategies and expanding their portfolios beyond prescription drugs.

Power Shift From Doctors Towards Payers and Patients

The patent cliff is an opportunity for payers and patients to accelerate generic penetration, stabilize costs, reduce price benchmarks and insist on value for money.

Cost-Containment to Curb Healthcare Deficits

Payers must find ways to contain healthcare costs. Exerting more control over the pharmaceutical industry is one tactic they will use.

Patients' Empowerment

Today's patients are aware more about their diseases, choices for medication and methods of treatment. They are taking more control of their treatment.

Implications for Pharma Companies

As pharma works to change strategies, many small and medium scale companies continue to struggle with implementation. To overcome, pharma companies must implement the below-described elements in the management.

Improve Market Access

Market Access is critical to sales and survival. It requires masterful orchestration of a complex web of activities with both internal and external stakeholders.

Growth in New Areas

Pharma still finds growth ahead in mature and fast-growing markets, value innovation, over-the-counter drug (OTC) (CSC, 2016) and health nutrition, generics, diagnostics, animal health, vaccines, orphan drugs and new drugs.

Be More Productive

Pharma companies must reduce costs while improving productivity. R&D, marketing and sales, and manufacturing and supply chains all present opportunities for greater efficiency and productivity.

Create Partnerships

Collaborating with neighbor industries, universities or smaller companies can increase Pharma's portfolio while reducing development costs and sharing risk. Partnering with payers could bring mutual benefits.

Be "Patient-Centric"

The patient is being placed at the center of strategy and operations, and focusing on health outcomes rather than medicines, distinguishes a pharma company from rivals and creates long-lasting value.

Patient-Centricity

Nowadays, patients are empowered as never before. They have access to free medical information on the internet. They search for the most effective, easy-to-use and best-priced treatments. Informed and networked patients are more active, organized, vocal and powerful. They involve themselves and exert their growing power in all aspects of healthcare and have become a central piece in most decision-making, individually or through their patient organizations and which regulates health technology assessment agencies. Healthcare professionals to deal with empowered patients with the importance of this new, growing reality to gain an advantage over your competitors.

Patient-centricity, the new source to compete in every step of the lifecycle of a pharmaceutical intervention: from product design to clinical demonstration and approval, from diagnosis to treatment initiation, monitoring and adherence. Patient-centric is the key functions of a biopharmaceutical organization for their top management and ruling "strategic" for the critical success of their company. Though, Patient-centricity "strategic" needs more recognition and declarations followed by implementation. Yet, implementing itself is a big challenge. (Kish, 2012/)

The difficulties are associated with:

- Mindset and cultural change,
- Lack of specific skills and experience,
- Lack of convergence between patient centricity and business.

Feasibility Analysis

Patient centricity is feasible, launched, reviewed by a large number of patient-centric initiatives with all critical functions. Several participating companies have proven the value of patient centricity at various development or commercial stages. However, despite the obvious, companies must overcome some of the challenges:

- A product-centric culture of the industry,
- Continued primary focus on relationships with the physicians,
- A too big distance between pharma managers and patients, making it easy to forget that the purpose of pharma companies is to help sick people get better,
- Fear (with some reason) that relationships built up over years with physicians would be damaged if they felt "bypassed" by going directly to patients,
- Assumptions (a few of them valid) about regulatory barriers to patient-centric practices,
- People in the organization do not perceive importance or urgency from their leaders,
- Insufficient priority given to patient-centricity topics and projects,
- Lack of long-term focus on a patient…,
- Lack of global strategies,
- Lack of supporting from internal decision makers and power brokers.

The organization must take necessary cross-functional alignment and collaboration to prevent systemic change (Feasibility Study, 2013). In order to apply it for work, top priority and support, a solution for major change and strategy implementation, alignment and concerted effort of the most powerful stakeholders is required through leadership.

Customer Value Proposition

At the center of the heart of competitive strategy lies the Customer Value Proposition to create a sustainable, differentiated competitive advantage. Identify:

- WHO are your target customers?
- WHAT market segment do you want to reach?
- WHAT is the Value Proposition you offer, in the eyes of the customer?
- WHERE are you positioned in relation to competitors, in the eyes of the customer?

Each Value Proposition (EVP)_leads to a different set of processes, metrics, systems and culture (http://www.AppliedProductMarketing.com). It answers for how someone manages the own organization very different, depending on Customer Value Proposition (CVP). Pharma industrialists must adopt CVP and implement internally to attain their goals, decisions and actions.

Cost and Pricing

Pharmaceutical companies facing the high pressure to reduce costs and prove value in life sciences is intense. Indeed, increasing demand for consumer out-of-pocket (OOP) (Baines, 2011) costs for popular treatments, uneven regional economic growth and reduced government health care are underpinning payer, provider, government, and patient demands for lower-cost drugs and devices; greater use of generic medicines; value- and outcome-based payment models; and more stringent regulatory processes. By improved targeting to the health group or diseases, life science companies are trying to justify the cost of their products. It is revealed by comparative effectiveness (CE) measures, and real-world evidence (RWE) in addition to hard clinical endpoints.

Adding to the pressure, the costs of bringing a new medicine to market have never been higher. Major pharma industries have drawn the cost figure from idea to R&D to commercialization. Significantly, researchers focus on challenging disease areas such as cancer to stabilize the healthcare market by providing a solution to the life-threatening disease. It will add up the other cost estimation range either higher or lower including expenses of complexities of drug development. Companies big and small are expending considerable time and effort to reduce the cost side of the equation by right-sizing their organizations, working more cross-functionally, and increasing operational efficiency through digital supply networks (DNS) and other technology advancements.

Virtually all countries of pharma industries are planning to institute drug price cost-containment measures or value-based pricing and reimbursement, models. The risk-based challenge is notably posing by research-based pharma companies.

For reference, in Japan, two new schemes were implemented in 2016 to strengthen pricing control–Health Technology Assessment (HTA) and "Huge Seller" Re-Pricing. If a drug meets certain criteria including sales forecast and level of premium requested by the manufacturer, certainly the submission of HTA data for Japan's National Health Insurance (NHI) price listing will be recommended (Hsu, 2015).

Interestingly, there is a new approach for cancer drugs gets appraised in the United Kingdom as the "new-look" Cancer Drug Fund (CDF). Such a financially sustainable funding system enables faster patient access to drugs even if the National Institute for Health and Care Excellence (NICE) reappraise the drug. The fund seems to be making a number of positive strides to being more sustainable. It also appears to be offsetting a lot more work to NICE; depending on how many new drugs are being pushed through the pipeline there may be more work for NICE (https://doi.org/10.1136/bmj.i5090) than the agency can handle, potentially resulting in a treatment backlog.

IMPORTANT ELEMENTS TO IMPLEMENT THE STRATEGY

Implementation of strategy is an interrelated system of tools and controls gets reinforced by all the control points. Sometimes changes may affect the strategy, day-to-day workflow, tasks and responsibilities. The Customer Value Proposition receive leadership support to deliver the internal implications of the strategy through the elements as described below.

- **Customer Proposition:** The Customer Value Proposition can only be realized if people know and understand what it is, and receive leadership support to deliver on it.
- **Strategy Commitment:** People need to understand the internal implications of the strategy, how their jobs contribute and how to act in support of it.
- **Performance Metrics:** Leaders focus on essential Key Performance Indicators (KPIs)(Health risk & assessment, 2014) that show whether the strategy is being implemented. Behaviours are considered as rewards that support the strategy contribute to better implementation.
- **Processes and Structure:** Leaders make sure the cross-functional processes, systems, structures and infrastructures in the company help people to implement strategy rather than work against them.

- **The Behaviour of Leaders:** It is leaders' responsibility to build and develop the team, deal with misaligned or low performers, clear the path for people to decide and act, and keep energy and motivation high.
- **Culture:** Culture is "the way we do things around here". It is the starting point for making changes in any company to implement current strategy. Each value proposition requires a different set of processes, metrics, practices and culture to be achieved successfully. (Baines, 2011).

Trends in Innovation and Sustainability

There is growing evidence that "sustainability" is no longer just optional. The most leading companies such as Unilever, SAP, Nestlé, P&G and Kraft have already announced that they are changing their business models to make the most of a changing business landscape. Using resources available for it efficiently and sustainably impact the consumer goods. Those companies analyze: What are the challenges involved in becoming more sustainable? What is the role of innovation? How does a company make it pay off for everyone? Whether is it needed to develop the link between sustainability and innovation or to plan, measure and manage sustainability?

These questions are asked to an organization to subject parties agree on a common strategy and work together to implement it to achieve business objectives. Hidden expectations about operational issues can lead to conflicts. Choosing the right partner, plan for success and outsourced activity actually builds up the network. Although businesses are beginning with sustainability that is not only about being environmentally friendly but ultimately means about money. If long-term plans are implemented well, sustainability can contribute positively to a company's financial results. Integration of sustainability into their strategy enables less risk towards economic, environmental and societal opportunities and turns them directly into actions. Sustainability Asset Management (SAM) is an approach, brings financial results in lifetime of the supply chain (Global life sciences outlook, 2017). Measuring "Sustainability Index" clearly indicates a positive relationship between sustainability and financial performance, as measured by stock returns. By extracting the right information from all operations on sustainability strategy, industrialists can make corrective adaptations on a continuous cycle.

According to the Office of Technology Assessment (OTA),

Innovation encompasses both the development and application of a new product, process, or service. Novelty must remain in the device, the application or both. Thus, innovation can include the use of an existing type of product in a new application or the development of a new device for an existing application. Innovation encompasses many activities, including scientific, technical, and market research; product, process, or service development; and manufacturing and marketing to the extent they support dissemination and application of the invention. (1995)

Innovation usually means the outcome itself — the actual creation or invention, and not just the process. Processes and resources that contribute to innovation are described as such. The 'Incremental Innovation' denotes innovations that are improvements, from modest to major, on existing innovations. As refer to pharmaceutical industry specifically, the modification of existing medicines — for example, by re-formulation — is often referred to as sequential innovation whereas a second- or third-generation product in a chemical class is often referred to as a follow-on innovation. Any drug that is not pioneering as a 'me-too', a tactic obviously intended to denigrate the practice of incremental innovation. Pioneering innovations, critics dispense with these formalities, which are also referred to as major, stand-alone, discontinuous or radical, usually describe the subset of innovations that represent something completely new and different. In pharmaceuticals, pioneering innovations are first-in-class drugs, although some critics also label first-in-class drugs that are similar to those in existing classes as 'me-too'.

Clinical Innovation

Driving and sustaining clinical innovation persists as a pharma sector priority in 2017, as tough competition and patent cliffs continue to jeopardize revenue. Growing market demand for generic pharmaceuticals and biosimilars, increasing pricing pressures and soaring R&D cost scrutinize the dampening effect on clinical innovation. Although regulations are stringent, health systems report substantial improvements in outcomes for infectious diseases, heart disease, and stroke as the result of the broad use of vaccines and antibiotics. Certain drugs are called "blockbuster" drugs as statins - the demand for new, innovative treatments is unrelenting, driven by the proliferation of age-related diseases such as cancer and dementia, and lifestyle-influenced or behavior-related chronic diseases, such as obesity and diabetes. Unfortunately, R&D is declined due to its competitiveness, funding, innovate deficiency and other elements of the value chain. The promising solution is to speed-up patient access to cost-effective and innovative medicines, devices, and diagnostics (Schneider et al., 2004).

Research and Development Market

Issues relating to the costs of pharmaceutical research, performance in developing drugs and decisions about investing drugs must be resolved. Other considerations are as follows

- Increasing the business performance to enhance competitiveness,
- Achieving customer loyalty,
- Managing supply chain risks and increasing commodity costs,
- Improving information for decision-making by focusing on data management and analytics,
- Managing regulatory change,
- Attracting, retaining and developing top talent,
- Realizing bottom-line value in mergers and acquisitions,
- Managing enterprise risk.

Importance of Incremental Innovation

In most pharmaceutical industries, innovation proceeds in evolutionary fashion perspectives with respect to obtain the source of R&D funds. Commercialization of emerging technologies reports that the flow of incremental innovations, policy changes dry up; the R&D well will inevitably run dry and, along with it, the resolve of this industry to pursue pioneering innovations. Motivations to innovate Pharmaceutical proponents generally suggest that the industry is primarily motivated to create two things: drugs that serve society and drugs that serve investors. If the industry is just motivated by profits alone, without concern for the welfare of society; an incentive for innovation becomes a question in general. Anyway, profits are directly related to R&D investment, appropriation of inventions (patents) and to innovative products themselves. On other hand, innovations improve sales, both in terms of volume and price by expanding the population being treated.

Innovation Metrics

Quality vs. Quantity

Quality and quantity are the deciding factors for the value of innovation in the pharmaceutical industry. Assessing the quantity of innovation is relatively easy compared to measuring quality. Many schemes are proposed for lumping together innovations into practical applications and labeling them a "highly innovative" and "moderately innovative". This is mainly assessed by the FDA's assessment of a drug's therapeutic potential at the time of New Drug Application filing. This approach provides a product reliable, subjective as well as selective. Combination of two drugs is more innovative? is decided by industrial critics. A reformulation of an existing drug in respect to a specific disease at a higher concentration over a longer duration, resulting in longer disease-free survival and reduced toxicity compared with the original formulation; or a novel. New Molecular Entity (NME) is designed to fast-track, supplants the original cytotoxic and demonstrates survival improvements and toxicities. Such molecular tags with identical indications for usage and indistinguishable safety have been demonstrated with a pair of drugs to improve survival (Healthcare Continuum, 2017). Therefore, unexpected benefit to treating a severe disease can be sorted out by comparable efficacy and safety in this way.

Pharma Tech

The pharmaceutical market is a growing economy not alone and, indeed, in combination with medical device companies – that are partnering and integrating with technology businesses. An increasing number of pharmaceutical firms must tackle the huge and rising blight of diabetes where millions of investment are done in a joint venture to combine devices, software and medicine. As of now, medical device companies are leading the cooperation with tech companies and R&D institutes. For example, in the diabetes space, one interesting partnership involves device giant Medtronic teaming up with tech firm Qualcomm, to develop a continuous "glucose monitoring system" that will also provide actionable insights to patients and providers. Software tools and access is becoming more and more important in our lives, and healthcare is no exception. Pharma tech alliance is trending until recently to develop cloud-based, electronic health records, data analytics and decision support software geared toward oncology patients. Such alliance positively explores the opportunities that will transform the global healthcare marketplace and address the advantage of the convergence. It is so far called "blurring the lines" (Little, 2006).

The New Pharmaceutical Playing Fields

It is apparent that some pharma companies could recognize the impact of two major shifts. One is downward pressure on pricing and moves towards prevention, diagnosis real cures. These changes negatively affect established order, opening door competition, forcing rethink where they play – who with, requiring a growing emphasis collaboration partnership. Second is disrupting factors that are genetics and immunotherapy.

Challenges for Sustainability Strategy

1. To shift the corporate view of sustainability away from focusing mainly on philanthropy and corporate social responsibility. Instead, companies need to see that there is a strong business case around sustainability, with a direct impact on their revenue and margins.

2. Sustainability needs to be an integral part of the goals and core processes of an organization and its supply chain. To make your sustainability strategy effective, data needs to reside in one place, where it can be analyzed for changes in a wide scope - and for potential opportunities.

Supply Chain Management and Manufacturing

Managing supply chains and manufacturing right away from the source to use and beyond in an increasingly globalized economy is more complex. However, when the supply chain is aligned to the organization's strategy, it can increase competitive advantage and be a driver of innovation and operational excellence. Methodology, processes and techniques must be drawn to align supply chain management with effect to corporate strategy for achieving operational excellence; focusing on time-to-market issues to improve financial aspects using IT as a key enabler; best practices in procurement and negotiations for contract life cycles in supply chains (Amegashie-Viglo, 2013).

Demand and Supply Scenario

Demand and supply are the primary factors governing pharma market globally. Hence, it becomes relevant to look into the demand-supply scenario for a particular product or industry by studying its past trends and forecasting outlook. Comparative analysis of other companies competing, in the same manner, is to find out the economic health of the company under consideration. Future demand and supply forecasting help investors understand the viability of future investments in terms of profits and losses.

Risk Management

Volatile fluctuations in the market prices of commodities, drugs and energy create havoc in pharma businesses everywhere. Indeed, they are unpredictable, certain practical ways are there to these kinds of risks; manage rational processes for hedging on pharmaceutical business.

- Strategy, tactics and methods for controlling the effect of volatile costs a business,
- Minimizing the impact of volatile costs and other risks on sales and marketing strategies,
- Project management–leading functions with specific skills and competencies to succeed,

- Estimating either go off-budget, off-specification or reach completion late,
- Quality, cost and time management in projects,
- Working cross-functionally to deliver client projects,
- Project management and risk accounting in projects,
- Fundamental project management techniques, tools and processes.

FUTURE RESEARCH DIRECTIONS

Long-term industrial competitiveness depends on national policies or abilities to build and upgrade production-related industrial capabilities and to address technological gaps in specific industries. The technological gaps can be found in value supply chains of consumer industries and factory suppliers. Recognition to the technological gaps in many countries links with manufacturing system elements includes production engineering; systems integration engineering; advanced materials processing; measurement and testing; standards and regulation; prototyping and testbed engineering; and scale-up processes and engineering. The quality of products related to the future viability of competitive national manufacturing systems. This is easily overcome by developing new business model possibilities that are a real differentiator from competitors for a better understanding of value generation based on collected information. It also draws guidelines for a quality standard for their customers.

CONCLUSION

The aim of this chapter is to elaborate on the current situation of the pharmaceutical industry and their policies. Industry analysis is the most important step to study the competitive scenario with industrial parameters including barriers to entry, supplier power and a threat of substitutes, buyer power and degree of rivalry. The macro-level factors influencing the industrial developments, innovations, sector valuations and global comparative valuations can be studied through industry dynamics. Lastly, give long-term and short-term valuations impacting the industry such as any foreseeable problems impacting the pharma industries in a negative fashion and potential corrective measures. The cutting-edge technologies and modern techniques are yet to be required for the massive change in the pharma industry.

ACKNOWLEDGMENT

The author of the chapter would like to thank Dr. Senthil Kumar Ponussamy for his assistance in gathering and conducting research for the chapter and in providing guidance toward the publication.

REFERENCES

A report from PWC entitled From Vision to Decision Pharma 2020. (n.d.). Retrieved from: www.pwc.in

Amegashie-Viglo, S. (2014). Supply Chain Management of the Pharmaceutical Industry for Quality Health Care Delivery: Consumer Perception of Ernest Chemists Limited as a Pharmaceutical Service Provider in Ghana. *Journal of Information Engineering and Applications*, *4*(8).

An interview with Jacques Mulder. (2015). *Cross-Sector Convergence in Health*, 1-8.

Applied Product Marketing. (n.d.). Retrieved from: http://www.AppliedProductMarketing.com

Aronow, W. S., & Wilbert, S. A. (2014). Indications for Implantable Cardioverter-Defibrillator Therapy and Recommendations for Implantable Cardioverter-Defibrillator Therapy in Patients not Included or not Well Represented in Clinical Trials. *Journal of Cardiovascular Diseases & Diagnosis*.

Baines, D. A. (2011). *Thesis on Problems Facing the Pharmaceutical Industry and Approaches to Ensure Long Term Viability*. University of Pennsylvania Scholarly Commons. Retrieved from: (http://repository.upenn.edu/od_theses_msod/33

Biffi, M., Ziacchi, M., Bertini, M., Sangiorgi, D., Corsini, D., Martignani, C., ... Giuseppe, B. (2008). Longevity of implantable cardioverter-defibrillators: Implications for clinical practice and health care systems. *Europace*, *10*(11), 1288–1295. doi:10.1093/europace/eun240 PMID:18772164

Business health care group, Towers Watson/National Business Group on Health. (2014). *Trends in Benefit Design Evolution & National Employer Initiative on Specialty Pharmacy*. Business health care group, Towers Watson/National Business Group on Health, 2014. The New Health Care Imperative.

Cancer Drugs Fund: The bigger picture. (n.d.). . doi:10.1136/bmj.i5090

Delivering at the Speed of Business: Digital Supply Networks in Life Sciences. (2016). Accenture. *Life Sciences*, 1–12.

Docteur, E. (2009). *Ensuring Efficiency in Pharmaceutical Expenditure*. Achieving Better Value for Money in Health Care.

Embracing Innovation. (2017). Driving Growth Across Healthcare Continuum.

Embracing the change: An Introduction to Multichannel Marketing. (2014). *Eye for Pharma*, 1-3. Retrieved from: www.eyeforpharma.com/multichannelreport

Feasibility Study Measuring the Economic Footprint of the Pharmaceutical Industry. (2013). Retrieved from: https://www.ifpma.org/wp-content/uploads/2016/02/wifor_feasibility_study_2013.pdf

Gassmann, O., & Oliver, G. (2002). Global Corporate R&D to and from Emerging Economies. In *Global Corporate R&D to and from Emerging Economies*. Retrieved from: http://www.glorad.org

Gautam, A., Pan, X., & Ajay, G. (2016). The changing model of big pharma: Impact of key trends. *Drug Discovery Today*, *21*(3), 379–384. doi:10.1016/j.drudis.2015.10.002 PMID:26477304

Global Life Sciences Outlook Thriving in today's uncertain market. (2017). Retrieved from: https://www2.deloitte.com/global/en/pages/life-sciences-and-healthcare/articles/global-life-sciences-sector-outlook.html

Guidance for Industry Best Practices in Developing Proprietary Names for Drugs. (2014). Food and Drug Administration, Drug Safety. Retrieved from: http://www.regulations.gov/

Hsu, J. C., & Lu, C. Y. (2015). The evolution of Taiwan's National Health Insurance drug reimbursement scheme. *DARU Journal of Pharmaceutical Sciences, 23*(15).

Kish, L. (2012). *The Blockbuster Drug of the Century: An Engaged Patient*. Retrieved from http://www.hl7standards.com/blog/2012/08/28/drug-of-the-century/

KMPG. (n.d.). *Pharma 2030: From evolution to revolution*. Retrieved from: https://assets.kpmg.com/content/dam/kpmg/xx/pdf/2017/02/pharma-outlook-2030-from-evolution-to-revolution.pdf

Light, D. L., Donald, W. L., Warburton, R., & Rebecca, W. (2011). Demythologizing the high costs of pharmaceutical research. *Biosocieties*, 1–17. Retrieved from www.palgrave-journals.com/bioso/

Little, A. D. (2016). *Presentation on Trends in the pharmaceutical industry*. Retrieved from: http://i3health.eu/wp-content/uploads/2016/01/Presentation-E.Croufer-.pdf

Management Centre Europe. (2017). Retrieved from: www.mce.eu

Measuring Pharmaceutical Quality through Manufacturing Metrics and Risk-Based Assessment. (2014). Engelberg Centre for Healthcare Reform at Brookings.

Novel Drugs Summary. (2016). U.S. Food and Drug Administration. Retrieved from: www.fda.gov

Pharma Processing. (n.d.). Retrieved from http://www.pharmpro.com

Report, M. T. (2016). *Pulse of the industry*, 1-62.

Schneider, J., & Jennifer, S. (2004). *Thesis on Integrated sustainability in the pharmaceutical industry*. Rochester Institute of Technology RIT Scholar Works. Retrieved from: http://scholarworks.rit.edu/article

U.S. Congress, Office of Technology Assessment (OTA), Innovation and Commercialization of Emerging Technology, OTA-BP-ITC-165. (1995). Washington, DC: U.S. Government Printing Office.

5. ways the digital supply chain drives success for life sciences. (2016). Retrieved from: https://assets1.dxc.technology/life_sciences/downloads/DXC_Digital_Supply_Chain_Drives_Success_for_Life_Sciences.pdf

ADDITIONAL READING

Chatawaya, J., Hanlin, R., Mugwagwa, J., & Muraguri, L. (2010). Global health social technologies: Reflections on evolving theories and landscapes. *Research Policy*, *39*(10), 1277–1288. doi:10.1016/j.respol.2010.07.006

Chittoor, R., Preet, S. R., Aulakh, S., & Sarkar, M. B. (2008). Strategic responses to institutional changes: 'Indigenous growth' model of the Indian pharmaceutical industry. *Journal of International Management*, *14*(3), 252–269. doi:10.1016/j.intman.2008.05.001

Gauld, N. J., Kelly, F. S., Emmerton, L. M., Kurosawa, N., Bryant, L. M., & Buetow, S. S. (2018). Medicines reclassification from a pharmaceutical industry perspective: An international qualitative study. *Research in Social & Administrative Pharmacy*. doi:10.1016/j.sapharm.2018.06.004

Gupta, A., Pawar, K. S., & Smart, P. (2007). New product development in the pharmaceutical and telecommunication industries: A comparative study. *International Journal of Production Economics*, *106*(1), 41–60. doi:10.1016/j.ijpe.2006.04.008

Papaioannou, T., Watkins, A., Mugwagwa, J., & Kale, D. (2016). To Lobby or to Partner? Investigating the Shifting Political Strategies of Biopharmaceutical Industry Associations in Innovation Systems of South Africa and India. *World Development*, *78*, 66–79. doi:10.1016/j.worlddev.2015.10.017

Traulsen, J. M., & Druedahl, L. C. (2018). Shifting perspectives – Planning for the future of the pharmacy profession taking current labor market trends into consideration. *Research in Social & Administrative Pharmacy*. doi:10.1016/j.sapharm.2018.02.006 PMID:29478833

KEY TERMS AND DEFINITIONS

Biologic Drug: Biologic drugs are made by a living cell, typically an engineered bacterium or a yeast. That gives them the capacity to be chemically much more complicated.

Biosimilar Drug: When the patent surrounding a biologic's formula is no longer protected, multiple companies can release a drug with the same chemical recipe, driving the cost down. That new biologic drug is a biosimilar.

Cultural Sclerosis: The prevailing management culture, mental models and strategies on which the industry relies are the same ones it's traditionally relied on, even though they've been eclipsed by new ways of doing business.

Generic Drug: A term referring to the chemical makeup of a drug rather than to the advertised brand name under which the drug is sold. A term referring to any drug marketed under its chemical name without advertising.

Harmonization: Lack of clarity of pharmaceutical product exists, even around such deceptively obvious concepts as regulatory cooperation is a stumbling block to harmonization.

Price-Gouging: Price-gouging is a sharp criticism of both branded and generic products, as well as new and established medicines not particular to any country but globally extends to all pharma companies.

Section 3
Primary and Support Processes in the Pharmaceutical Industry

This section presents the details of the production process (the primary process) in the pharmaceutical industry and the chosen functions of the support (logistics) process in this sector (product development, sales, and distribution).

Chapter 5
Product Lifecycle in the Pharmaceutical Industry

Senthil Kumar Ponnusamy
SSN College of Engineering, India

Yaashikaa Ponnambalam Ragini
SSN College of Engineering, India

ABSTRACT

The composite of the present pharmaceutical industry requires more effective medication improvement and generation. A product lifecycle (PLC) is the progression of stages from the product's production to the world until its last withdrawal from the market. Product lifecycle comprises various stages that a product must possess in its lifespan, for example, launching, growth, maturity, and decline stage. While each stage brings huge changes, a progression of procedures for the administration of product lifecycle is required. Product lifecycle management (PLM) is a precise, controlled idea for overseeing and creating products and product-related data. Enhanced patient consistency, income development, extended clinical advantages, and faster market dispatch are among the primary utilization of product lifecycle management. To create a viable and productive product lifecycle management program many qualities are viewed like promising start, vital arranging clear authority, supporting information and abilities, readiness for changing tenets of government and associations.

DOI: 10.4018/978-1-5225-5921-4.ch005

INTRODUCTION

Product advancement basically defines the pharmaceutical industry. Research on the front line of science, the production of new learning bases, the innovation in the form of the new solutions and the change of existing medications constitute the fuel that drives the firms in this industry. The incidental success of making a novel treatment in a range with no earlier medications considers as a part of the pharmaceutical sectors' most defining trademarks. This is the main industry whose yield can have any kind of effect by influencing the particles we are made of. Current time drugs can impact the quality and the term of human life in ways that were never conceivable. Effective and constant new medication presentations constitute the wellspring of practical upper hand for the organizations in this industry (Phelps, 2011). A portion of the difficulties the pharmaceutical industry faces incorporate R&D (innovative work) disappointments, changes in administrative viewpoints, patent expiries, and remote cash developments. The legislatures over the world are endeavouring to check these medicinal services costs either by sedate value modifications, requesting higher rebates and refunds to the makers or by advancing nonspecific medications. In any case, with the dispatch of inventive medications, pharmaceutical organizations can get deals with development. The sector development is driven by particular functions, for example, invulnerable oncology. With expanding occurrence of disease, oncology drugs are relied upon to witness solid request. The life-sparing capacities of these medications get higher costs and more extensive edges (Zannou et al., 2009).

Even though creation and advancement is the backbone of any industry, the revelation and improvement of new drugs are joined by a large group of difficulties, ethical issues, moral suggestions, and social duties. One will be unable to think about another industry where fastidious research, thorough testing, and stringent product principles can have such a significant effect on human prosperity. The central part of the pharmaceutical industry in keeping up and upgrading human life is additionally reflected in the greatness of its R&D action. The production of new medications is not really a deliberate, unsurprising procedure. There are tremendous troubles related to the making of a protected and effective medication. Regardless of phenomenal late advances in science and innovation, good fortune and chance still assume a part in the revelation and combination of compelling mixes. There is essentially no chance to get of guaranteeing the extreme R&D endeavours and immense expenses will pay off liberally, at last, as the rates of achievement in sedate revelation remain consistently low. Imperatively, the execution vulnerability is intensified by the nearness of stringent directions and extraordinary examination over the whole improvement process. The basic choice to go to advertise is basically outside the control of the firm. The market endorsement for another drug at last rests with the American Food and Drug Administration (FDA), the administration office depended to practice administrative furthermore, and control works over the pharmaceutical business. These characteristics consolidate to influence the advancement and the life to cycle of medications not the same as the development procedure in some other innovation serious industry (Bruce, 2003).

TYPES OF PHARMACEUTICAL PRODUCTS

Pharmaceutical products more regularly known as drugs or medications are a central part of both present day and ancient drug. It is basic that such items are protected, viable, and of good quality. The following are a few types of pharmaceutical products.

Drugs

A drug or medication is a chemical substance taken to cure or improve any side effects of a disease or medical condition. Its utilization may likewise be as a preventive prescription that has future advantages, however, does not treat any current or prior infections or side effects. Generally, drugs were obtained by extraction from therapeutic plants. Drugs are the most important product of the pharmaceutical industry with high revenue range. These drugs reduce the effect caused by disease/ infection by reacting against it. There are various routes of drug inhalation such as oral, bolus, injection, inhalation, rectal, sublingual, etc. (Norman et al., 2017).

Generic Drugs

Generic or non-specific drugs are copies of brand-name medications that have a similar estimation, utilization, impacts, manifestations, the course of association, threats, prosperity, and quality as the primary, basic pharmaceuticals. Their pharmacological effects are exactly the same as those of their picture name accomplices. Generic medications are used proportionally with checked meds in the market. Fundamentally, a generic drug is immediately endorsed in the market. Controllers of medications would not really require point by point testing and clinical trials for these medications. The FDA requires that generic medications be as sheltered and powerful as brand-name drugs. Generic medications are less expensive because the makers have not had the costs of creating and showcasing another medication. At the point when an organization brings another medication onto the market, the firm has effectively spent significant cash on explore, improvement, advertising, and advancement of the medication. A patent is conceded that gives the organization that built up the medication all rights to offer the medication as long as the patent is in actuality.

Biologics

Biologics include a variety of products like antibiotics, blood products, vaccines, therapeutic proteins, etc. These products are used for medicinal purposes. A biologic is made in a living framework, for example, a microorganism, plant or animal cells. Most biologics are huge, complex particles or blends of atoms. Numerous biologics are delivered utilizing recombinant DNA technology. It is quite complex and not possible to distinguish a complex biologic by characterization techniques accessible in the research facility, and a portion of the segments of a completed biologic might be unknown. Because the completed biologic product cannot be completely tested in the lab, producers must guarantee product consistency, quality, and sterility by protecting that the assembling procedure remains considerably the same after a certain period. The living frameworks used to create biologics can be delicate to small changes in the assembling procedure. Slight changes in process can essentially influence the completed biologic and also the way it works in the human body (Ratajczak et al., 2015).

Orphan Drugs

Orphan drugs are those drugs approved only when a specific disease affects small population of people. Sometimes this condition is termed as an orphan designation. An orphan drug is a pharmaceutical operator that has been created to manage an uncommon restorative condition, the condition itself being alluded to as an uncommon disease. An uncommon disease additionally alluded to as an "orphan illness", is any sickness, which influences a little level of the human community. Most uncommon diseases are hereditary, and are available all through the individual's whole life, regardless of the possibility that manifestations do not quickly show up. The task of an orphan status to a disease and to any medications created to treat it involves open arrangement in numerous nations and has brought about medicinal leaps forward that might not have generally been accomplished because of the financial aspects of medication innovative work.

Over-the-Counter (OTC) Drugs

OTC drugs are those medications that patients can buy from pharmacies without the prescription of a doctor. There are many sorts of over the counter medications in the market. It may be utilized as a part of curing sicknesses and diseases like foot and tooth disease. Headaches and other repeating issues may likewise be dealt with utilizing OTC medications. A medication should be appropriately considered as OTC, must be studied by an administrative body that it is without a doubt all right for open utilize and be sold over the counter. Care should be taken in overseeing OTC medications particularly to individuals with exceptional and particular restorative conditions. Over a period, if the drug turns out to be secure and viable as a recommended pharmaceutical, it might be considered as an OTC medication (Gaisford, 2017).

PRODUCT LIFECYCLE

Product lifecycle can be characterized as "the adjustment in deals volume of a particular product offered by an association, over the normal existence of the product". Product lifecycle is a normative and spellbinding model for the life of products. Singular products will encounter their own variety. A few products may have a higher deals curve - advance to a bigger number of fragments than typical. A few products may have lower deals curve - offer to a little fragment than typical. A few products may have a more drawn out section in the curve or a more extended curve. The PLC's significance to promoting chiefs is to help distinguish suitable techniques also, strategies for introducing a product. Each stage speaks to an alternate arrangement of wild factors to consider in the improvement of product and market procedures. The lifespan of a product's lifecycle and the length of each stage fluctuate from product to product. The lifecycle of one product can be over in a couple of months, and of another product may keep going for a long time. One product reaches to development in years, and another can achieve it in a couple of months. One product remains at the development for a considerable length of time and another only for a couple of months. Subsequently, it is consistent with saying that length of each stage changes from product to product. Product lifecycle is related to variations in the commercializing circumstance, level of demand, product request, customer understanding, etc. in this way advertising supervisors need to change the promoting methodology (Twiss, 1984). The steps involved in the product lifecycle are shown in Figure 1.

The product lifecycle portrays the timeframe over which a thing is produced, conveyed to advertise and in the long run expelled from the market. The possibility of the product lifecycle is utilized as a part of promoting to choose when it is fitting to publicize, decrease costs, investigate new markets or make new bundling. Initially, a product manufacturing idea is executed at the presentation stage, and the thought experiences innovative work. In case the innovation is resolved to be possible and conceivably beneficial, the product is created, advertised and taken off in the development stage. Expecting the product ends up in success, its generation will develop to the point that the product turns out to be generally accessible and develops in the third stage. Inevitably, interest in the product decays, and it ends

Figure 1. Product lifecycle
Source: (Twiss, 1984)

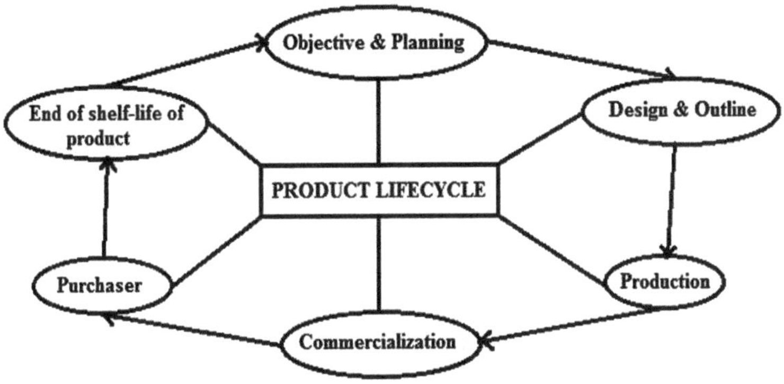

up noticeably out of date, bringing about the decline phase. Toward the start of a product's life, it might have a next to zero rivalries in the commercial centre, until the point that contenders begin to imitate its prosperity. As the product turns out to be more successful, it faces expanding quantities of contenders and may lose its share in the market, inevitably declining. The phase of a product's lifecycle impacts the route in which it is promoted to customers. The course of occasions brings another product into reality and takes after its development into a perfect product and into inevitable minimum amount and decay (William & McCarthy, 1997).

STAGES OF PRODUCT LIFECYCLE

A new product undergoes through an arrangement of stages known as product lifecycle. It applies to both brand and classification of products. Its generation change from one product to another. The condition of product in the market differs at each stage in the market as shown in Table 1. Present day product lifecycles are getting to be noticeably shorter and shorter as products in developing stages are being recharged by division and product separation. Organizations dependably endeavour to augment the benefit and incomes over the whole lifecycle of a product. With an end goal to accomplish the expected level of benefit, the presentation of the new product at the correct time is critical. In the event that new product is engaging the purchaser and no hardened rivalry is out there, an organization can charge high costs and acquire high benefits (Qureshi et al., 2014). The curve in Figure 2 shows the stages of the product lifecycle.

Table 1. Comparison of Product Condition at Different Stages of Product Lifecycle

S. No	Stage	Product Condition	Cost	Position	Development
1.	Launch	Unspecified	High	Particular	Customized and Instructive
2.	Growth	Identified	Decrease with volume	Well-known (Universal)	Satisfies the demand
3.	Maturity	Competitive	Low	Extreme	Competition and Marketing
4.	Decline	Reduced conflict	Increase with decreased volume	Discriminatory	Focuses on leftover products

Source: (own elaboration)

Figure 2. Stages of the product lifecycle
Source: (Qureshi et al., 2014)

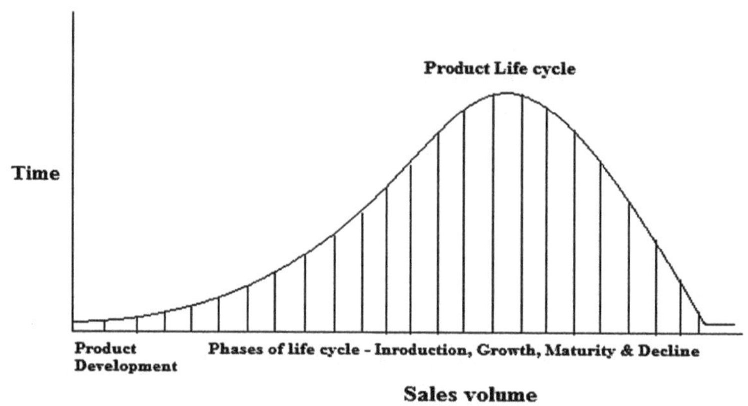

Launch Stage

The first stage of the four product lifecycle stages is the launch stage. Any business that is propelling another item needs to welcome that this underlying stage could require noteworthy capital. It is not necessarily the case that spending a great deal of cash at this stage will ensure the fortune of the product. Any interest in research and new product development must be weighed up against the conceivable come back from the new product, and a powerful promoting arrangement should be created, with a specific end goal to give the new product the most obvious opportunity with regards to accomplishing this arrival. This phase of the cycle could be the most costly for an organization propelling the product. The measure of the market for the product is little, which implies deals are low, in spite of the fact that they will raise. Then again, the cost of things like innovative work, purchaser testing, and the promoting expected to dispatch the product can be high, particularly if it is an aggressive area.

A product is presented in the market with the aim to manufacture a reasonable personality and overwhelming advancement. Before genuine offering of the product to clients, the product goes through improvement, includes model and market tests. Organizations notice at this stage more expenses and furthermore bear extra cost for circulation. Then again, there are a couple of clients at this stage, implies low deals volume. During this introductory stage, the organization's benefits demonstrate negative amounts due to enormous cost yet low deals volume. The organization concentrates on building up a market and emerging an interest for the product. Development is made with an aim to create the brand awareness Tests/trials are given that is productive in pulling in early adopters and potential clients. Special projects are basic at this stage. It is as much vital as to create the product since it places the product at a standard level in the market. Since there is no need or interest for the product, retailing and marking are vital for attracting people. The essential goal of this stage is to dispatch the product and assemble product request.

Advantages of the Launch Stage

1. **Constrained Competition:** If the product is unique and a trade is the first to produce and market it, the absence of direct competition would be an unmistakable profit. Being first could enable an association to catch a substantial market share before other organizations begin propelling products, and in a few cases can empower a business brand name to wind up noticeably with the entire scope of products.
2. **Price:** Manufacturers that are propelling unique product are frequently ready to charge costs that are essentially above what will turn into the normal market cost. This is on the grounds that early adopters are set up to pay this higher cost to get their most recent products, and it enables the organization to recover a portion of the expenses of creating and propelling the product. In a few circumstances, producers may do the correct inverse and offer moderately low costs, with a specific end goal to invigorate the request.

Obstacles in the Launch Stage

1. **Little or No Market:** When another product is in market, suppose if there is no market for it, or if a market exists, it is probably going to be little. Basically,

this implies deals to be low to start. There will be events where an awesome new product or fabulous promoting effort will make, to the point that business faces loss, yet these are for the most part unique cases, and it frequently requires some investment and exertion before most products accomplish this sort of force.

2. **High Price:** A couple of products are made without some innovative work, and once they are made, numerous producers should put resources into advertising and advancement keeping in mind the end goal to accomplish the sort of interest that will make their new product a successful outcome. Both of these can cost a huge amount of money, and by virtue of a couple of business sectors, these costs could continue running into an increasing amount.
3. **Misfortunes, No Profits:** When everyone expenses of getting another product to advertise, most organizations will see negative benefits for part of the Initial Stage of the product lifecycle, in spite of the fact that the sum and length of these negative benefits vary starting with one market then onto the next. A few producers could begin demonstrating benefit rapidly; while for organizations in different parts it could take few years.

Growth Stage

The growth stage is the second stage of the product lifecycle, and for some producers this is the key stage for setting up a product's position in a market, expanding deals, and enhancing net revenues. This is accomplished by the proceeded with an improvement of shopper request using showcasing and limited time movement, joined with the decrease in assembling costs. The rapid development of products from an introductory (launching) stage through the growth stage and its expansion varies in selling rate starting with one market then onto the next. The advancement sort out is conventionally depicted by a strong improvement in arrangements and benefits, and the way that the association can start to benefit by economies of scale in progress, the net incomes, and furthermore the general measure of advantage, will increase. This makes it workable for organizations to put more cash in the limited time movement to boost the capability of this stage. In this phase, organization's deals and benefits begin expanding and rivalry likewise start to increment. The product turns out to be perceives as attractive and a numberof the purchasers start to buy it. It is advertised acknowledgment stage. In any case, because of rivalry on the market, an organization invest in a promotion to persuade clients so benefits may decay close to the finish of development or growth stage.

Advantages of the Growth Stage

1. **Minimized Expenses:** With new product advancement and promoting, the first, launching stage is generally the most exorbitant period of a product lifecycle. Interestingly, the growth stage can be the most productive phase of the entire cycle for a producer. As creation increases to take care of demand, producers can decrease their expenses through economies of scale, and built up courses to market will likewise turn into significantly more proficient.
2. **Consumer Awareness:** During the growth stage an ever-increasing number of buyers will wind up noticeably aware of the new product. This implies the extent of the market will begin to increment and there will be a more significant interest in the product; all of which prompts the moderately sharp increment in deals that is normal for the growth stage.
3. **An Increment in Profits:** With bring down expenses and a critical increment in deals, most producers will see an expansion in benefits during the growth stage, both as far as the general measure of benefit they make and the net revenue on every product they offer.

Obstacles in the Growth Stage

1. **Expanding Competition:** When an organization is the first to bring a product to the market, they have the advantage of practically no competition. In any case, when the interest for their product begins to rise, and the organization moves into the growth period of the item lifecycle, they are probably going to confront expanded rivalry as new producers hope to profit by another, creating a market.
2. **Reduced Cost:** During the launch stage, organizations can frequently charge early starters a top-notch cost for another product. Nonetheless, in light of the developing number of contenders that are probably going to enter the market during the growth stage, producers may need to bring down their costs with a specific end goal to accomplish the expected increment in deals.
3. **Diverse Marketing Strategies:** Marketing efforts during the launch stage arrange tend to profit by all the buzz and buildup that encompasses the dispatch of the new product. In any case, once the item winds up noticeably settled and is never again 'new', a more advanced showcasing approach is probably going to be required keeping in mind the end goal to benefit as much as possible from the development capability of this stage.

Maturity Stage

After the launch and growth stage, the product goes into the maturity stage. The third of the product lifecycle stages can be a significant testing time for producers. In the initial two phases, organizations attempt to build up a market and afterward develop offers of their product to accomplish as substantial an offer of that market as could reasonably be expected. In any case, at the maturity stage, the essential concentration for most organizations will keep up their share despite various distinctive difficulties. At the development stage, the product is set up and the go for the producer is present to keep up the piece of the overall industry they have developed. This is presumably the toughest time for most products and organizations need to put carefully in any promoting they embrace. They additionally need to consider any product alterations or enhancements to the creation procedure, which may give them an upper hand. At the development stage, product name awareness is solid so deal keeps on developing yet at a declining rate when contrasted with past. At this stage, there are more contenders with similar items. In this way, organizations safeguard the piece of the overall industry and expanding product lifecycle, as opposed to making the benefits, by offering deals advancements to urge the retailer to give more retire space to the product than that of contenders.

Advantages of the Maturity Stage

1. **Proceeding With Price Reduction:** The cost can be minimized with the help of the economies of scale in the growth stage of the product lifecycle. Advancements underway can prompt more effective approaches to fabricate high volumes of a specific product, bringing down expenses considerably further.
2. **Expanded Market Share via Differentiation:** While the market may achieve immersion at the maturity stage, producers may have the capacity to develop their share in the market and increment benefits in different ways. Using inventive advertising efforts and by offering more various products includes, organizations can really enhance their piece of the overall industry through separation and there are many product lifecycle cases of organizations having the capacity to accomplish this.

Obstacles in the Maturity Stage

1. **Deals Volumes Peak:** After the consistent increment in deals at the growth stage, the market begins to wind up plainly immersed, as there are less new

clients. Most of the shoppers who are consistently going to buy the product have officially done as such.

2. **Diminishing Market Share:** Another feature for the maturity stage is the huge volume of producers who are generally seeking an offer of the market. With this phase of the product lifecycle frequently observing the most abnormal rivalry, it turns out to be progressively trying for organizations to keep up their share.
3. **Benefits Start to Decline:** While this stage might be the point at which the market makes the most benefit, it is regularly the segment of the product lifecycle where a considerable measure of producers can begin to see their benefits diminish. Benefits should be shared among the majority of the rivals in the market, and with deals liable to be high at this stage, any producer that loses market share, and encounters a fall in deals, is probably going to see a consequent fall in benefits. This decline in benefits could be aggravated by the falling costs that are regularly observed when the sheer number of contenders constraints to have a go at pulling in more clients by contending on cost.

Decline Stage

The remainder of the product lifecycle stages is the decline stage, which is considered as the start of the end for a product. In the product lifecycle curve, this last decline stage is plainly exhibited by the fall in the two deals and benefits. Despite the undesirable difficulties of this decrease, there may even now be open doors for producers to keep making a benefit from their product. A decrease in deals, changes in patterns and troublesome monetary conditions clarify the decline stage. At this stage, the market ends up noticeably soaked, so deals decrease. It might be because of specialized out of date quality or client taste has been changed. The offers of most products will decrease at some stage. This can be because of variables, for example, mechanical advances, patterns, development or changing customer tastes. At the declining stage, promoting blend choices rely upon the organization's system. In the end, the market for a product will begin to diminish, and this is what is known as the decline stage. This reduction could be because of the market getting to be plainly immersed, or the fact that the buyers are changing to an alternate kind of product. While this decrease might be unavoidable, it might be feasible for organizations to make some benefit by changing to more affordable creation strategies and less expensive markets. At the declining stage organization has following alternatives:

- Keep up the product; reduce cost and finding new applications of the product.
- Collect the product by decreasing advertising expense and keep offering the product to faithful specialty until the point reaches zero benefits.

Advantages of the Decline Stage

1. **Less Expensive Production:** Even at the decline stage, there might be open doors for a few organizations to keep offering their products at a benefit in the event that they can decrease their expenses. With a view on the different producing strategies, utilizing distinctive procedures, or moving the generation to another area, a sector might have the capacity to broaden the beneficial existence of a product.
2. **Less Expensive Markets:** For a few producers, another approach to keep influencing a benefit from a product at the decline stage might be to look to new, less expensive markets for deals. Previously, the benefit potential from these sectors might not have legitimized the speculation need to enter them, yet organizations regularly observe things distinctively.

Obstacles in the Decline Stage

1. **A Market in Decline:** During this last period of the product lifecycle, the market for a product will begin to decrease. Buyers will regularly quit purchasing this product for something more up to date and better, and there is very little producer will have the capacity to do to keep this.
2. **Fall in Sales and Profits:** Because of the declining market, deals will begin to fall, and the general benefit that is accessible to the producers in the market will begin to diminish. One route for organizations to moderate this fall in deals and benefits is to attempt and increment their share, which, while testing enough at the maturity phase of the cycle, can be much harder when a market is decreasing.
3. **Product Withdrawal:** For a considerable measure of producers it could get to a point where they are never again making a benefit from their product. As there might be no real way to turn around this decrease, the main choice numerous organizations will have is to pull back their product before it begins to lose the cash.

PHASES OF LIFECYCLE IN PHARMACEUTICAL INDUSTRY

One significant and comprehensive way to deal with the present current difficulties inside the pharmaceutical sector is to concentrate on Product Lifecycle Management (PLM), which is a business change way to deal with overseeing items and related data over the endeavour. As of late PLM has given numerous pharmaceutical associations the capacity to expand their capacity to motivate products to advertise faster, guarantee more remarkable administrative consistency and efficiencies while decreasing advancement costs (Itkar, 2007). The following are four phases of product lifecycle in a pharmaceutical industry.

Phase 1: Originate - Planning, Creating, Identifying, Conceive

The primary stage is the meaning of the product necessities in light of consumer, organization, advertise and administrative bodies' perspectives. From this determination, the product's significant specialized features can be characterized. Along with this, the underlying idea configuration work is performed characterizing the style of the product together with its principle utilitarian perspectives. A wide range of networks is utilized for these procedures, from pencil and paper to dirt models to PC supported mechanical plan programming. The venture of assets into research or examination of choices might be incorporated into the origination stage – for e.g. conveying the innovation to a level of development adequate to move to the following stage. The life-cycle building is frequentative. It is constantly conceivable that something doesn't function admirably in any stage enough to go down into an earlier stage – may be the distance back to origination or research.

Phase 2: Pattern - Details, Significance, Advance, Analyze and Verify

This is the place the full plan and improvement of the product frame begins, advancing to model testing, through pilot discharge to full product dispatch. It can likewise include an update and incline for development to existing items and in addition arranged out of date quality. Computer Aided Design (CAD) is the principle apparatus utilized for outline and improvement. This can be basic 2D drawing/drafting or 3D parametric element based strong/surface demonstrating. Such programming incorporates innovation, for example, hybrid modelling, reverse engineering, learning-based designing, NDT (Non-destructive testing), and assembly development. This progression covers many building disciplines including mechanical, electrical, electronic, installed programming and space. Alongside the real making of geometry, there is the investigation of the segments and product congregations. Reproduction, approval, and advancement assignments are done utilizing Computer Aided Engineered programming either incorporated into the CAD bundle or remain solitary. Another errand performed at this stage is the sourcing of purchased out segments, perhaps with the guide of acquirement frameworks.

Phase 3: Discover - Production, Develop, Market, Commercialize

Once the outline of the product's parts is finished, the strategy for assembling is characterized. This incorporates Computer Aided Design undertakings, for example, apparatus outline; formation of CNC Machining directions for the product's parts and also instruments to fabricate those parts, utilizing coordinated or isolate CAM PC supported assembling programming. This will likewise include investigation instruments for process simulations. Once the assembling strategy has been recognized CPM becomes possibly the most important factor. This includes CAPE (PC supported creation designing) or CAP/CAPP – (generation arranging) devices for doing manufacturing plant, plant and office format and creation reproduction. Similar to the designing undertakings deals with product setup, and advertising documentation work occur. This could incorporate exchanging building information to an electronic deals design.

Phase 4: Solution - Utilization, Maintenance, Recycle, Reuse and Management

The last period of the lifecycle includes overseeing of in-benefit data by providing clients and administration engineers with supporting data for repair and support, and additionally, squander administration/reusing data. This includes utilizing instruments, for example, maintenance, repair and operations management programming. There is a lifespan to each product regardless of whether it be transfer or obliteration of material items or data, this should be considered since it may not be free from consequences.

PRODUCT LIFECYCLE MANAGEMENT

Product Lifecycle Management (PLM) is a deliberate, controlled idea for overseeing and creating products and product-related data. PLM offers administration and control of the process and the request conveyance process, the control of product-related data all through the product lifecycle, from the underlying basic plan to the final stage. Product Lifecycle Management (PLM) has existed for a long time beginning in hardware and car parts. It enables an organization to effectively deal with the route in which a product is being sourced, produced and arranged all through its lifecycle. PLM is a vital approach for making and dealing with an organization's product-related scholarly capital beginning from its underlying origination to retirement (Prajapati & Dureja, 2012). PLM enhances an organization's product advancement procedures and its capacity to utilize the product-related data to settle on better business choices and convey more noteworthy incentive to clients. Numerous producers seek lifecycle management strategies in a receptive way. Exchanging a professionally prescribed medication to an over-the-counter medication is likewise another strategy to have an edge over generics. These strategies, in spite of awesome endeavours, sooner or later offer the approach to generics even though they improve the arrival on speculation. The PLM program ought to be founded on the advancement and usage of Intellectual Property. Fast changes in business sectors, advancements, and controls also, laws and new contender products and offerings make lifecycle management programs profoundly unique. Therefore, PLM procedures ought to be further continued for new programs. The PLM program has turned into an undeniably difficult due to current advancements in the U.S. courts and potential administrative changes. Hence, organizations ought to continue their techniques as well as approaches towards PLM (Dennis, 2008). For a successful PLM, the few characteristics important are shown in Figure 3.

PLM AND PHARMACEUTICAL INDUSTRY

Pharmaceutical industries are presently resolved to expand the life of their medication above patent termination, contriving methodologies to deal with the lifecycle of their most imperative drugs that start in the clinical stages. PLM has turned into a need to the proceeded with an accomplishment of pharmaceutical industries. Organizations that have initiated a complete lifecycle management procedure and a specific arrangement to control their advance toward their objective are receiving

Figure 3. Factors for successful PLM
Source: (Prajapati & Dureja, 2012)

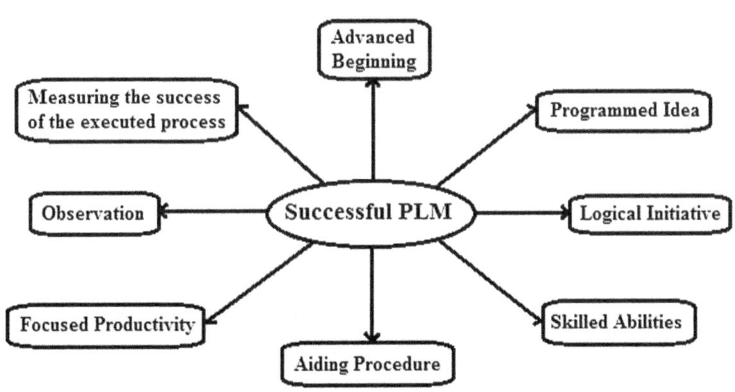

monetary and clinical benefits. Effective PLM includes the advancement of logical, specialized, administrative and promoting systems that improve the esteem and broaden the life of pharmaceuticals (Kvesic, 2008).

The centre of product lifecycle management is the creation, protection, and capacity of data identifying the organization's product and exercises, keeping in mind the end goal to guarantee the quick, simple and convenient discovering, refining, dissemination, and use of the information required for day-to-day operations. As such, work that has once been done ought to stay exploitable. In the meantime, the thought is to change over information controlled by the organization's representatives, talented people, and authorities into organization capital in an effortlessly reasonable and shareable frame.

NEED FOR PHARMACEUTICAL PRODUCT LIFECYCLE MANAGEMENT

Pharmaceutical and biopharmaceutical sectors are under extreme strain to enhance product pipelines, quicken time to commercialize, and enhance edges on available products—while additionally keeping up strict adherence to quality standards and administrative necessities. Product lifecycle management concentrates on helping associations use their research and innovative work (R&D) endeavours to grow new infection treatments and move them through all elements of an association to inspire them to advertise rapidly, gainfully, and inconsistency. A PLM approach additionally furnishes a medication organization with the stage to oversee change as the product travels through its valuable financial life. Picking special arrangements that exclusively address one part of the drug lifecycle may really cause more issues that the arrangements do not consider different parts of dealing with the drug through its whole lifecycle. Currently, the pharmaceutical business is confronting more rivalry from generics, Patent terminations that will lessen incomes. Small product portfolios that depend too intensely on drugs, unrealized advantages from solidification, etc. The pharmaceutical sector is confronting numerous business challenges today. To increase the benefit, pharmaceutical organizations must quicken new medication improvement, allocate R&D assets successfully by enhancing the capacity to dispense with poor applicant mixes, manage adequately the change to products, bundling parts, and procedures, and etc. Embracing product lifecycle management is an exploration-based organization's most important resource. Basic mechanization regularly gives them more information that does not promptly convert into more-educated choices in the lifecycle of a particular medication. This is particularly critical to pharmaceutical organizations on the grounds that expelling even a solitary day from the advancement and administrative acceptance process can pay an enormous profit. Product lifecycle management makes a key structure for settling on educated choices through the disclosure, preclinical, clinical, administrative acceptance, and commercialization forms. This structure empowers organizations to have an abnormal state of clarity and cooperation over the operations and choices important to deal with a medication for ideal gainfulness all through its lifecycle (Daly & Kolassa,2004).

ISSUES OF PRODUCT LIFECYCLE MANAGEMENT

These days, product lifecycle management did nearly no matter what with the assistance of various data handling frameworks. In many organizations, basic operations can be made to create data administration without an uncommon and committed data-preparing framework. The creation and following of normal methods of activity is the way to enhancements in the creation and examination of data. It is conceivable to take care of huge numbers of the issues and circumstances portrayed above utilizing data handling frameworks that help product lifecycle management (Saaksvuori,&,Immonen, 2004). Data handling frameworks have advanced rapidly in the most recent couple of years, yet it has not been conceivable to expel all issues. The most exceedingly terrible issues result ordinarily from various methods of operation, the wide range of various programming used to deliver the data, utilitarian contrasts in programming, and the various interfaces between various data handling frameworks. The following are a few issues related to product lifecycle management.

1. The ideas, terms, and acronyms inside the zone of product lifecycle management are not clear and not characterized inside organizations. This implies the data content associated with specific terms is not clear and the ideas how to use the product related data are considerably not clear.
2. The utilization of the data and the configurations in which it is spared and recorded might differ. Data has more often than not been created for various purposes or in some other association however it should be conceivable to use it in settings other than the assignment for which it was delivered: in an alternate way or even in a different organization.
3. The fulfilment and consistency of data delivered in various units, offices or organizations can't be ensured. This issue emerges when the product information is created and put away on various information media or even as records in papers, and when the gatherings concerned have distinctive ways to deal with the security and treatment of data.

CONCLUSION

Progressively, pharmaceutical organizations try to have a bound together perspective of their whole product development lifecycle with the capacity to view and follow each product detail all through the whole procedure. Product Lifecycle Management gives the ability to both oversee and concentrate product data, helping pharmaceutical organizations understand their investments by tending to some of a fundamental needs including speeding time to advertise, bringing down general working and generation costs and acknowledging quality norms. PLM benefits both substantial and small-scale businesses and can be connected to enhance understanding consistency, giving income development, increasing clinical advantages getting cost focal points and quick dispatch. For an effective PLM, an early begins, a key arranging, perfect initiative and supporting information and abilities are required. Most systems expand the lifecycle include interdisciplinary information on showcasing, R&D, and controls. This makes it trying to explore different lifecycle augmentation procedures top to bottom. The utilization of PLM frameworks as indicated by the lifecycle model will help in the different business works in most authoritative forms in the entire lifecycle of the product.

REFERENCES

Bruce, L. (2003). Defending value and maximizing profitability of innovative pharmaceuticals over their entire life cycles. *International Journal of Medical Marketing*, *3*(3), 195–197. doi:10.1057/palgrave.jmm.5040119

Daly, R., & Kolassa, M. (2004). Start early, sell more, sell longer. *Pharmaceutical Executive*, *1*, 8–20.

Dennis, Z. K. (2008). Product lifecycle management: Marketing strategies for the pharmaceutical industry. *Journal of Medical Marketing: Device Diagnostics Pharmaceutical Market*, *8*(4), 293–301. doi:10.1057/jmm.2008.23

Gaisford, S. (2017). 8 – 3D printed pharmaceutical products. In 3D Printing in Medicine (pp. 155-166). Woodhead Publishers.

Itkar, S. (2007). Pharmaceutical management. Pune. *Nirali Prakashan*, *3*, 12–17.

Kvesic, D. Z. (2008). Market Strategy Product Lifecycle Management: Marketing stratergies for the pharmaceutical industry. *Journal of Medical Marketing*, *8*(4), 293–301. doi:10.1057/jmm.2008.23

Norman, J., Madurawe, R. D., Moore, C. M. V., Khan, M. A., & Khairizzaman, A. (2017). A new chapter in pharmaceutical manufacturing: 3D-printed drug products. *Advanced Drug Delivery Reviews*, *108*, 39–50. doi:10.1016/j.addr.2016.03.001 PMID:27001902

Phelps, K. (2011). Repositioning to enhance a product's lifecycle. *Drug Discovery Today. Therapeutic Strategies*, *8*(3-4), 97–101. doi:10.1016/j.ddstr.2011.09.006

Prajapati, V., & Dureja, H. (2012). Product Lifecycle management in pharmaceuticals. *Journal of Medical Marketing*, *12*(3), 150–158. doi:10.1177/1745790412445292

Qureshi, A. J., Gericke, K., & Blessing, L. (2014). Stages in Product Lifecycle: Trans-disciplinary Design Context. *Procedia CIRP*, *21*, 224–229. doi:10.1016/j.procir.2014.03.131

Ratajczak, M., Kubicka, M. M., Kaminska, D., Sawicka, P., & Długaszewska, J. (2015). Microbiological quality of non-sterile pharmaceutical products. *Saudi Pharmaceutical Journal*, *23*(3), 303–307. doi:10.1016/j.jsps.2014.11.015 PMID:26106278

Saaksvuori, A., & Immonen, A. (2004). Product lifecycle management systems. In *Product Lifecycle Management*. Berlin: Springer. doi:10.1007/978-3-540-24799-9_3

Twiss, B. C. (1984). Forecasting Market Size and Market Growth Rates for New Products. *Journal of Product Innovation Management*, *1*(1), 19–29. doi:10.1016/S0737-6782(84)80039-9

William, D., & McCarthy, J. E. (1997). *Product Life Cycle: "Essentials of Marketing"*. Richard D Irwin Company.

Zannou, E. A., Li, P., & Tong, W. Q. (2009). Chapter 40 – Product Lifecycle Management (LCM). In Developing Solid Oral Dosage Forms, Pharmaceutical Theory and Practice (pp. 911-921). Academic Press.

ADDITIONAL READING

Ding, B. (2018). Pharma Industry 4.0: Literature review and research opportunities in sustainable pharmaceutical supply chains. *Process Safety and Environmental Protection*. doi:10.1016/j.psep.2018.06.031

Haleem, R. M., Salem, M. Y., Fatahallah, F. A., & Abdelfattah, L. E. (2015). Quality in the pharmaceutical industry - A literature review. *Saudi Pharmaceutical Journal*, *23*(5), 463–469. doi:10.1016/j.jsps.2013.11.004 PMID:26594110

Klatte, S., Scharfer, H. C., & Hempel, M. (2017). Pharmaceuticals in the environment - A short review on options to minimize the exposure of humans, animals and ecosystems. *Sustainable Chemistry and Pharmacy*, *5*, 61–66. doi:10.1016/j.scp.2016.07.001

Low, Y. S., Halim, I., Adhitya, A., Chew, W., & Sharratt, P. (2016). Systematic Framework for Design of Environmentally Sustainable Pharmaceutical Supply Chain Network. *Journal of Pharmaceutical Innovation*, *11*(3), 250–263. doi:10.100712247-016-9255-8

Norman, J., Madurawe, R. D., Moore, C. M., Khan, M. A., & Khairuzzaman, A. (2017). A new chapter in pharmaceutical manufacturing: 3D-printed drug products. *Advanced Drug Delivery Reviews*, *108*, 39–50. doi:10.1016/j.addr.2016.03.001 PMID:27001902

Seuring, S., & Muller, M. (2008). From a literature review to a conceptual framework for sustainable supply chain management. *Journal of Cleaner Production*, *16*(5), 1699–1710. doi:10.1016/j.jclepro.2008.04.020

Singh, H., Khurana, L. K., & Singh, R. (2018), Chapter 3 - Pharmaceutical Development. Pharmaceutical Medicine and Translational Clinical Research, 33-46.

Zannou, E. A., Li, P., & Tong, W.-Q. (2009) Chapter 40 - Product Lifecycle Management (LCM). Developing Solid Oral Dosage Forms, 911-921.

KEY TERMS AND DEFINITIONS

Biologics: Is defined as the type of drugs produced from living creatures such as microbes, plant, or animal cells.

Generics: Are defined as drugs that are equal to brand-name drug in its dosage level, method of administration, efficiency, its applications, etc.

Orphan Drugs: Are defined as engineered pharmaceutical medications for treatment of rare uncommon diseases.

Over-the-Counter Drugs: Are defined as the medications that are given directly to the consumers without any prescriptions or concern from professionals.

Product Lifecycle (PLC): Is defined as the cycle the entire product undergoes through four stages such as introduction, growth, maturation, and decline stage.

Product Lifecycle Management (PLM): Is defined as the way toward dealing with the whole lifecycle of a product from the origin, through building plan and fabricate, to administration and commercialization of produced products.

Chapter 6
Pharmaceutical Development Process

Yaashikaa Ponnambalam Ragini
SSN College of Engineering, India

ABSTRACT

The most significant attribute of the pharmaceutical industry is its creations and advancements. The innovation of new drugs is necessary for improving the quality of human life and duration. Pharmaceutical drug development is a time-consuming, costly, and crucial process. The essential goal of drug development is to discover a dosage or dosage scale of a drug application that is both efficient in curing the desired disease and safe. Clinical trials including newly developed drugs that are directed in a progression of successive steps called stages to decide the security and efficacy of the new drug moreover the viability against the targeted diseases. There are four phases through which clinical trials are conducted. An investigational item can be assessed in more than one stage all the while in various clinical trials, and some clinical trials may cover two unique stages.

INTRODUCTION

The pharmaceutical sector is basically characterized by its development. Persistent advancement is one of the pharmaceutical industry's most characterizing attributes. New solutions can be urgent for keeping up the nature of human life, and may even influence its duration. Research on the front line of science, the formation of new information bases, the development of new pharmaceuticals, and the change of existing medications constitute the fuel that impels the organizations in this industry. The periodic triumph of making a novel treatment in a region with no earlier medicines

DOI: 10.4018/978-1-5225-5921-4.ch006

considers as a real part of the pharmaceutical sector's most characterizing trademarks. This is the main business whose yield can have any kind of effect by influencing the small molecules. The mission of innovative medication work (R&D) is to convey new protected and strong prescriptions to patients. Many have revealed that the way toward building up another pharmaceutical is long and expensive. Pharmaceutical development is not really a methodical, unsurprising procedure. It takes after an innovation push demonstrates reliant on a winding way of logical leaps forward with uneven planning and difficult to anticipate results. Mechanical competency, many years of thorough research, and significant comprehension of neglected client needs, while vital, may demonstrate insufficient for global accomplishment as the basic choice for commercialization stays outside the firm (Haleem et al., 2015).

Drug development as a business procedure requires vital, hierarchical, and administrative choices. It is as of now getting a charge out of serious research scope, offering to ascend to rich yet generally scattered information of the components driving medication disclosure and advancement. Medication development raises at the juncture of best in class disclosures in the life sciences, helped by forefront progressions in different fields, for example, building, informatics, and streamlining. Flourishing in the wake of the most recent accomplishments in these controls, it frequently unites them to cross and connect in a path adapted to enhance human well-being and broaden human life. During the time spent in finding the best structures and the most productive methodologies, novel choice openings and difficulties emerge, and new authoritative structures and game plans rise to address them. Discovering novel medications is eventually a business procedure needing strict financial train and compelling key, hierarchical, and administrative choices. Different parts of pharmaceutical development have been the protest of extreme investigation in various fields, for example, financial aspects, business methodology, etc. In any case, the acquired discoveries and derivations have remained to some degree isolated, restricted to the beginning order regardless of their more extensive relevance and criticalness. There are numerous ranges that warrant advance investigation and improvement. This is the reason a complete review of the business procedures, methodologies, and practices identified with pharmaceutical advancement appears to be fundamental and convenient (Hughes et al., 2010).

OVERVIEW OF THE PHARMACEUTICAL INDUSTRY

The pharmaceutical industry finds, creates, delivers, and commercialise medications or pharmaceutical medications for use as drugs (see Figure 1). Pharmaceutical organizations may bargain in non-exclusive or mark solutions and medicinal instruments. They are liable to an assortment of laws and directions that administer the licensing, testing, well-being, adequacy and promoting of medications. The pharmaceutical sector is the piece of the human services area that assigns with solutions. The industry contains distinctive subfields relating to the advancement, creation, and advertising of prescriptions. These pretty much-related subfields comprise of medication producers, drug advertisers, and biotechnology organizations. The principal objective of the pharmaceutical industry is to give sedates that avoid contaminations, maintains human health, and cure sicknesses. This industry influences explicitly the worldwide community, so various universal administrative bodies screen things like medication safety, licenses, quality, and estimation (Rousseaux & Bracken, 2013). The pharmaceutical sector has gained a lot of ground in the course of the most recent decade because of an exploration-based approach that has enhanced advances, created foundations, and expanded research in the field of bioscience.

Figure 1. Basic procedure of drug development and commercialization by pharmaceutical industry
Source: (Sinha & Vohora, 2018)

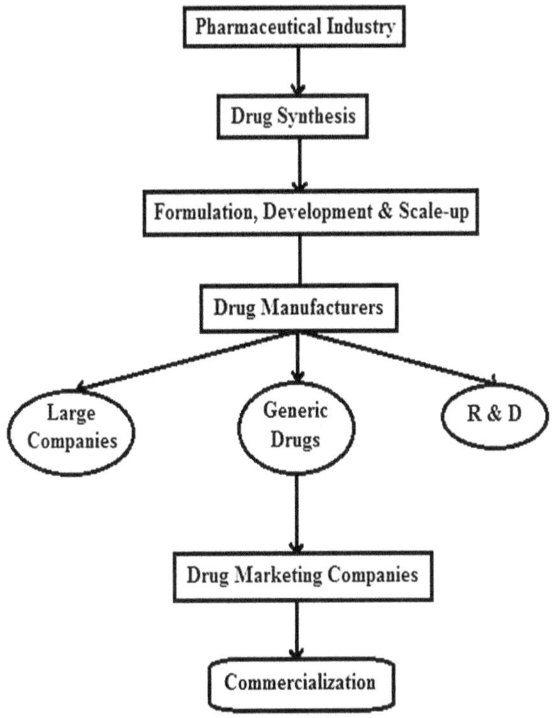

GLOBAL NEED FOR PHARMACEUTICAL INDUSTRY

The pharmaceutical industrial sector works simply like any other industry. It has crude materials producers, completed merchandise makers, R&D (innovative work) organizations, commercialising organizations, and most importantly consumers. However, it is much more managed and capital-concentrated than any other sectors. Around the world, the average human life expectancy has grown considerably since last few decades. In addition, more contamination and illnesses have joined this lifespan development. This has prompted expanded research on maturing community. The objectives are to avoid diseases and keep up well-being so these people are healthier. Rushed everyday plans have prompted unfortunate dietary patterns, absence of activity, less rest, and another tricky way of life decisions. This has brought about high weight rates, poor absorption, breathing troubles, and other physical issues. Well-being supplements have been acquainted with the aim of curing these issues, decreasing the possibility of becoming ill, and meet day by day nourishing requirements through vitamins and minerals. The working class has been developing in both the rising and created markets. Individuals in these business sectors have more extra cash and expect better medical services arrangements (Kontoravdi et al., 2013). Chronic ailment cases have ascended in number. This has made individuals turn out to be more subject to prescriptions and wellbeing supplements. Globalization and urbanization have prompted expanded ecological unsettling influences. These are real main thrusts in the developing interest for enhanced prescription and wellbeing supplements for different age people and geographic area. The figure shows the reasons for the need for pharmaceutical industry as a whole (see Figure 2).

INNOVATION IN PHARMACEUTICAL INDUSTRY

Presently the pharmaceutical sector is underweight to convey its finished results less expensive, quicker and that's only the tip of the efficient productivity. Conflict from non-specific medication producers is without a doubt one of the primary drivers and has just activated emotional changes. With no doubt, a number of the customary research-based pharmaceutical organizations have begun the creation of non-exclusive medications amid the previous few years, and are in this manner in coordinate rivalry with non-specific medication makers. Such conflict requests specific concentrate on the generation cost. The last request starts from a developing mindfulness that medication-producing forms have a huge natural effect. Customarily, the pharmaceutical sector has been somewhat hesitant to present imaginative strategies in its creation forms, regardless of the way that the cost for the advancement of another medication constantly increments, while the patent lifetime is stable.

Figure 2. Need for drug development
Source: (Kontoravdi et al., 2013)

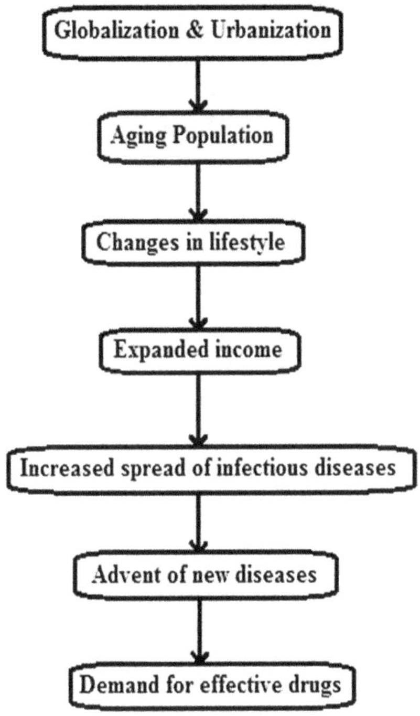

Considering the drug development cycle, two evident methods for expanding benefits are: (1) more fast process advancement, and along these lines expansion of the time between item discharge and patent termination; and (2) optimizing the full-scale generation framework to lessen creation costs, with the end goal that conventional research-based medication producers can likewise contend with generic medication producers when the patent of a medication has lapsed. In the two cases, expanded and precise utilization of Process Systems Engineering (PSE) techniques can be invaluable (Gernaey et al., 2011).

DRUG DEVELOPMENT

Drug development is the way toward conveying another pharmaceutical medication to the market once a lead compound has been recognized through the procedure of medication disclosure. It incorporates pre-clinical research on microbes and creatures, petitioning for administrative status, for example, by means of the United States' Food and Drug Administration (FDA) for an investigational new medication to start clinical trials on people, and may incorporate the progression of getting administrative endorsement with another medication application to advertise the drug in the market. The figure depicts the stages involved in the drug development process and its final approval (see Figure 3). The major target of pharmaceuticals improvement is to discover a dosage or dosage limit of a medication applicant that is both viable (for enhancing or curing the proposed ailment condition) and safe (with a worthy danger of dangerous impacts) (Das & Chakra borty, 2015). Failing to discover the right dosage range will not result in disease recovery or then again industrially suitable pharmaceutical item, nor should it be affirmed by administrative organizations. Each pharmacological firm will generally have many impacts, both sought, (for example, circulatory strain decrease) and undesired (unfavourable impacts, for example, nausea or sickness). The extent of a pharmacological impact expands monotonically with expanded dosage.

CLASSIFICATION OF DRUG DEVELOPMENT PROCESS

The drug development process can be extensively divided into two stages, namely:

- Non-clinical development,
- Clinical development.

Figure 3. Steps involved in the drug development process
Source: (Das & Chakra Borty, 2015)

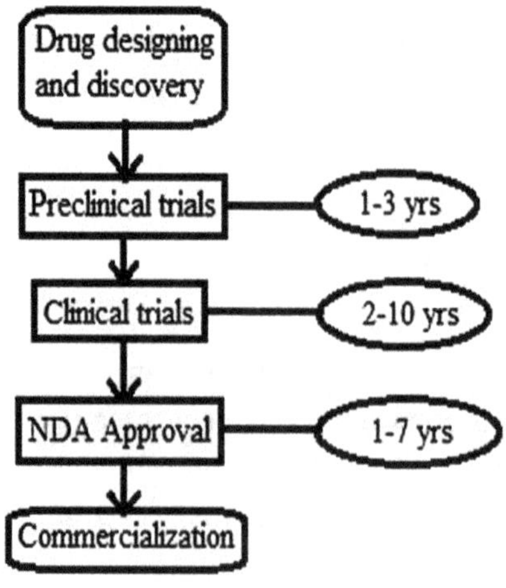

Non-clinical advancement incorporates all medication testing carried outside of the human body. Non-clinical improvement can additionally be extensively separated into pharmacology, toxicology, and detailing. In the case of those procedures, tests are performed in research centres or pilot plants. Perceptions from cells, tissues, creature bodies, or medication parts are gathered to determine inductions for potential new medications. Synthetic procedures are included in detailing the new compound into medications to be conveyed into the human body. Non-clinical improvement may likewise be termed to as preclinical development since these tests are performed before human trials.

The clinical improvement depends on tests led in the human body. Clinical improvement can be additionally isolated into phases I, II, III, and IV. Clinical investigations are intended to gather information from typical volunteers and subjects with the objective infection, to help see how the human body follows up on the medication applicant, and how the medication hopeful helps patients with the malady. Another chemical or biological compound can be assigned as a medication hopeful since it exhibits some attractive pharmacological exercises in the research facility. At the beginning period of medication improvement, the attention is mostly on cells, tissues, organs, or creature bodies. Examinations on people are performed after the volunteer overcomes the early stages of tests without any negative impacts of the medication.

STAGES OF DRUG DEVELOPMENT

Drug development involves the following stages (phases) to commercialise as a successful medication:

- Drug discovery,
- Target and lead identification,
- Nonclinical development,
- Clinical development.

Drug Discovery

A drug discovery program starts in light of the fact that there is an ailment or clinical condition without appropriate medicinal solutions accessible and it is this neglected clinical requirement, which is the fundamental driving inspiration for the venture. The underlying investigation, frequently happening in the research world, produces information to build up a theory that the restraint or initiation of a protein or pathway will bring about a helpful impact in an infectious state. The result of this action is the choice of an objective, which may require assist approval preceding movement into the lead revelation stage with a specific end goal to legitimize a medication disclosure. At the time of lead discovery, a serious hunt results to a discovery of a new pharmaceutical like a little atom or therapeutic, regularly named an advancement applicant, that will advance into preclinical, and if effective, into clinical advancement and eventually be a commercialized pharmaceutical product.

Drug Target Identification

Failure of drugs in the health centre for two primary reasons; the first is that they do not work and the second is that they are not secure. A standout amongst the most important strides in building up another medication is target identification and approval. A target is, for the most part, a solitary particle, for example, a gene or protein that is engaged with ailment pathway and upon intercession prompts changes in ailment movement. Regular techniques for target distinguishing proof incorporate hereditary affiliation, genomic affiliation and phenotypic screening. The best target should be reliable, secure, meet clinical and commercial needs and, most importantly, be 'druggable'. A "druggable" target is available to the reputed medication atom, be that a little particle or bigger biological and after official, inspire a natural reaction which might be measured both in vitro and in vivo. Great target identification and approval empowers expanded trust in the connection amongst target and ailment and enables us to investigate whether target regulation will prompt instrument-based symptoms.

Target Validation

When potential targets are distinguished, they should be completely validated. Approval strategies run from in vitro devices using entire animal models, to balance an essential focus in ailment patients. While each approach is substantial in its own particular right, trust in the result is essentially expanded by a multi-approval approach. Antisense technology is a conceivably effective procedure that uses RNA-like artificially changed oligonucleotide, which is intended to be complementary to an area of an objective mRNA atom. Transgenic creatures are an important approval method as they include the entire animal's phenotypic endpoints to clarify the utilitarian outcome of quality control. Monoclonal antibodies are an incredible target validation device as they interface with a bigger area of the objective atom surface, taking into consideration better separation between even firmly related targets and frequently giving higher partiality. All the more as of late, synthetic genomics, a foundational utilization of hardware particles to target identification and approval has developed. Chemical genomics can be characterized as the investigation of genomic reactions to substance mixes. The objective is the quick identification of novel medications and medication targets grasping different early stage sedate disclosure advancements going from target identification and validation, over the compound plan and substance blend to natural testing. The yield of a compound screen is commonly named as a hit particle, which has been exhibited to have particular movement at the objective protein. Screening hits shape the premise of a lead improvement science program to build the power of the synthetic arrangement at the essential medication target protein.

Properties of an Ideal Drug Target

A target molecule, biologically, may be a protein or genetic material, which function can be altered by the application of any external agency. An ideal target must possess the following features:

- Selectivity,
- Essentiality,
- Functionality.

Optimization of the Lead Compound

The subsequent stage is to discover a drug aspirant that corresponds with the desired target. This process incorporates screening, lead identification and lead validation. A lead compound in drug development is a substance that has pharmacological or natural action prone to be therapeutically or biologically valuable. Its substance structure is utilized as a beginning stage for chemical alterations with a specific end goal to enhance power, selectivity, or pharmacokinetic factors. In screening, the technique is to look through a library of substances to distinguish a shorter rundown with solid connections with the objective of attaching or cell-based tests. One such approach is high-throughput screening and the subsequent rundown is called hits. During identification of lead process, a hit is viewed as a lead in the event that it has many "medication like" chemical and organic properties in ingestion, dispersion, digestion, discharge and danger and pharmacokinetics. During the lead optimization phase, structure alterations are made to make them more powerful and more secure, e.g., to build the selectivity, the capacity to tie to the objective rather than different proteins. The ideal leads progress toward becoming medication and move to the following advancement stage. The procedure of hit phase period to preclinical competitor choice regularly takes much time.

Non-Clinical Development

A drug volunteer is investigated broadly for pharmacological and toxicological properties through in vitro and in vivo analysis. Non-clinical protection evaluation involves pharmacology analysis, lethal research, toxicokinetic and nonclinical pharmacokinetics contemplates, proliferation harmfulness examines, genotoxicity studies and for some situation, cancer-causing contemplates. Other nonclinical concentrates to evaluate phototoxicity, immunotoxicity, adolescent animal poisonous quality and mishandle risk ought to be led on a case-by-case premise. During this process, studies on manufacturing drug and its formulation methods should be conducted. After satisfactory data of the wellbeing profile is picked up from animal examines, the organization will document an investigational new drug (IND) application to administrative organizations, for example, FDA for starting clinical trials. All examinations before IND constitute a preclinical improvement. Few animal research studies, considering cancer-causing nature thinks about and long-time poisonous quality examinations will be led amid the clinical improvement phase. Hence, these animal studies are termed as nonclinical developments.

Pharmacological Activity

Pharmacology is defined as the investigation of the particular organic movement of compound substances on living issue. A substance has natural activity when, in suitable measurements, it causes a cell reaction. It is particular when the reaction happens in a few cells and not in others. Accordingly, a synthetic compound or a biologic has to show these activities before it can be additionally created. In the early phase of medication testing, it is critical to separate a "dynamic" hopeful from an "idle" competitor. There are screening techniques to choose these applicants. Two properties specifically noticeable are affectability and specificity. Given that a compound is dynamic, affectability is the contingent likelihood that the screen will order it as positive. Specificity is the restrictive likelihood that the screen will call a compound negative given that it is inert. Normally, affectability and specificity can be an exchange off; notwithstanding, in the perfect case, one can trust both of these qualities to be high and near one. Amount of these pharmacological actions might be seen as the medication power or quality. The estimation of medication strength by the responses of living beings or their segments is known as bioassay. Relationship between given dose and response is the most important research for determining pharmacological action. In these tests, a few dosages of the medication are chosen, and the reactions are measured for each relating measurement. After reaction information is gathered, relapse or non-parametric strategies might be connected to examine the outputs. By expanding the measurement or grouping of the medication hopeful, the pharmacological reaction does not change and remains at the low level of action, at that point, it can be inferred that this candidate does not have the movement under examination and there is no compelling reason to build up this applicant. Suppose the medication candidate is dynamic, at that point the data about how much reaction can be normal for a given dose can be utilized to help control the outline of measurement choice clinical trials in human examinations (Dingemanse & Krause, 2017).

Toxicity and Drug Safety

Medication security is a standout amongst the most essential step through all phases of drug improvement. In the preclinical stage, the safety of drugs should be examined for diverse types of creatures (e.g. mice, rabbits, rodents). Studies are outlined to watch antagonistic medication impacts or dangerous occasions experienced by creatures treated with various measurements of the medication. Creatures are likewise presented to the medication for different time spans to check whether there are unfavourable impacts caused by aggregate dosing after a certain period. These outcomes are compressed and dissected by utilizing measurable strategies. At the point when the after-effects of animal studies demonstrate possibly adverse symptoms, drug development is either ended or stopped from further examinations of the issue. Based upon the length of introduction to the medication applicant, toxicity studies on animals are named intense investigations, subchronic considers, chronic examinations, and regenerative investigations. Typically, the primary few studies are intense investigations; i.e. the creature is given one or a couple of measurements of the medication applicant. If just a single dosage is given, it can likewise be known as solitary measurements contemplate. Just those medication applicants exhibited to be protected in the single-dosage studies can be advanced into numerous measurements examines. Single-measurements intense examinations in creatures are essentially used to set the dosage to be tried in perpetual investigations. Intense investigations are ordinarily around 2 weeks in the term. Continuous dosage investigations of 30 to 90 days span are called subchronic contemplates. Chronic investigations are typically composed with over 90 days of length. These examinations are led in creatures like rodents and in no less than one non-rat animal types. Some interminable investigations may likewise be seen as cancer-causing nature. Regenerative investigations are completed to evaluate the medication's impact on fruitfulness and origination; they can likewise be utilized to think about medication impact on the baby and creating posterity. Once more, outcomes from creature toxicological investigations are extremely valuable in helping configuration measurements choice clinical trials in people.

Drug Formulation and Development

An effective new drug can be either a synthetic compound or a biologic one. In the event that the medication competitor is a biologic, at that point, the plan is normally a solution, which contains a high grouping of such a biologic, and the arrangement is infused into the subject. Then again, if the potential medication is chemical in nature, at that point the detailing can be tablets (pills), containers, arrangement, patches, suspension, or different structures. There are numerous detailing issues that require measurable examinations. Formulation issues that arise due to these chemical substances can be validated using statistical methods. A medication is the blend of the integrated synthetic compound and other latent fixings intended to enhance the retention of the dynamic substances. How the blend is made relies upon after effects of a progression of examinations. Generally, these tests are performed under some physical imperatives, e.g. the measure of the supply of crude materials, limit of the compartment, size and state of the tablets. In the beginning time of medication advancement, the formulation should be adaptable with the goal that different dosage qualities can be tried in creatures and in people. Frequently in the nonclinical advancement phase or in the early period of clinical trials, the medication competitor is provided in powder pattern. When the medication hopeful advances into late Phase I or early Phase II, fixed measurements shape, for example, tablets, capsules, or different details are more attractive. The measurement quality relies upon both nonclinical and clinical data. The medication plan assembles works intimately with research centre researchers, toxicologists and clinical pharmacologists to decide the conceivable dosage qualities for each medication. As a rule, the initially proposed measurements qualities should be changed relying upon outputs acquired from Phase II analysis. These definitions are produced for clinical trial use and are regularly not quite the same as the formulation. After the new medication is endorsed for commercialization, formulation ought to be promptly accessible for circulation in the market.

Clinical Development

In the event that a synthetic compound or a biologic overcomes the determination procedure from animal testing and it appeared to be secured and suitable to be tried in human, it advances into clinical improvement. In drug development for human utilize, the major refinement between "clinical trials" and "nonclinical testing" is the investigational unit. In clinical trials, the trial units are individuals, and the trial units in "nonclinical testing" are nonhuman subjects. As specified before, the consequences of these nonclinical studies will be utilized as a part of the IND accommodation preceding the primary clinical trial. In the event that there is no concern from the FDA following 30 days of the IND accommodation, the support would then be able to begin clinical testing for this medication applicant. At this stage, the synthetic compound or the biologic might be termed to as the "test medicate" or the "study drug". An IND is a report that contains all the data thought about the new tranquilize up to the time the IND is developed. A classic IND incorporates the name and depiction of the medication, how the medication is handled; data about any preclinical encounters identifying with the security of the medication; promoting data. Such a portrayal ought to contain the greater part of the instructive materials to be provided to clinical examiners, consented to arrangements from specialists, and the starting conventions for clinical examination (Pandey et al., 2017).

Stages in Clinical Development Process

The clinical trials in drug development process can be classified into two periods namely the preclinical and clinical trials. The initial step, a preclinical stage, is to locate a promising compound, which includes exploiting the advances made in understanding a disease, pharmacology, software engineering, and science. On separating a disease development process into its parts can give, pieces of information to focusing on medicate advancement. After the preclinical trials, animal models are used for testing the new drug. Food and Drug Administration (FDA) has demands positive results on animal experiments before being tested on humans. After FDA approval, clinical trials are conducted by dividing into four phases as shown in the table (see Table 1).

Clinical Trial: Phase 1

Phase I investigations are experimental first-into-human or early-stage trials, intended to make an evaluation of the safety and withstanding effect of new medication or antibody in a little group of individuals (ordinarily nutritious volunteers, however

Table 1. Phases involved in Clinical Development Process

Clinical Phase	Purpose	Duration
Phase 1	Safety and pharmacology	Several months (20-100 volunteers)
Phase 2	Effectiveness and Side effects	2 years (300 volunteers)
Phase 3	Efficacy and monitoring of reactions	4-10 years (3000 volunteers)
Phase 4	FDA approval	1-3years (several thousand patients with the same infection/disease)

Source: (Pandey et al., 2017)

in the case of diseases like cancers, the members are patients) and additionally to decide the most extreme tolerated dosage (MTD). The new investigation medication is directed in little measurements at first and afterwards rose to bigger dosages to assemble preparatory information on the pharmacokinetic (the grouping of the new medication and its metabolites and where it is consumed) and pharmacodynamic (effect of the drug in the human body) impacts. Phase I trials help to decide the right dosage and recurrence that are secured and important to have an impact. In this stage, it is basic to screen, recognize, and report every single reaction. An endeavour is made to set up the measurements run endured by volunteers for single and for various dosages. Phase I trials are now and then directed in seriously sick patients mainly in case of cancer or in less sick patients when pharmacokinetic issues are directed. Pharmacokinetic trials are typically viewed as Phase I trials during drug development.

Clinical Trial: Phase II

Without any security concerns, the trial can move into Phase II. The new medication is presently tried on a bigger number of members and the procedure is intended to evaluate the adequacy of the medication. The point is to survey the movement, practical, and poisonous quality of a given dosage. Remedial medications are tried on patients and antibodies in healthy members to evaluate immunogenicity. Security assessments are preceded and duration between dosages may keep on being resolved. The new examination medication might be tried in various Phase II trials, assessing its execution under various conditions, for instance, at first tried in grown-ups, then tried in more adults until tried in the last target population of newborn children. Once a dosage or scope of measurements is resolved, the following objective is to assess whether the medication has any organic action or impact. Phase II trials are performed on a bigger group (100-300) and are intended to evaluate how well the medication functions, and in addition to proceed with Phase I safety evaluation in a bigger gathering of volunteers and patients. Hereditary testing is reasonable, especially when there is confirmation of difference in metabolic rate. At the point when the improvement procedure for another medication comes up short, this generally happens during Phase II trials when the medication is found not to fill in as arranged or to have poisonous impacts.

Phase IIa

The efficiency of the medication competitor is investigated in trials with up to a few hundred target patients treated for normally a little while or a couple of months. All safety evaluations incorporated in Phase I would now be able to be periodic on a considerably bigger member gathering. Stage IIa trials are pilot clinical trials that assess viability in chosen populaces of patients with the illness or condition to be dealt with, analyzed, or avoided. Targets concentrate on measurements necessities, what is the maximum tolerable dosage that is suitable for members to take, dosage reaction, sort of patients, recurrence of dosing, or various different attributes of security and viability.

Phase IIb

If the medication exhibits certain level of impact, more dosage level examination including 3–5 dosage levels are led to building up the medication applicant's dosage reaction including viability and security, with the goal that an ideal measurement might be chosen for the following stage III testing. Stage IIb trials concentrate on how effectively the medication functions at the endorsed dosage. Stage IIb trials are in some cases alluded to as urgent trials. A critical trial is expected to give proof to a medication marketing acceptance. Stage III trials are thought to be crucial, so the expression is regularly utilized for the uncommon essential stage II trials.

Clinical Trial: Phase III

Phase III trials plan to give an authoritative evaluation of the viability of the medication against the essential consequence and also giving security information in a huge gathering of members. The medication is given to much bigger gatherings of individuals mostly 1000-3000 or more) to affirm its adequacy, screen symptoms, look at it to ordinarily utilized drugs, and gather data that will enable the medication or treatment to be utilized securely. The example and profile of often-severe system are examined and unique elements of the medication are researched. These trials ought to be of a randomized twofold visually impaired outline, however, different plans are worthy. They are regularly alluded to as "critical trials" as they are directed to create the proof of adequacy and security required to present another medication to a permitting specialist. This period of trials is additionally called corroborative trials, which frequently include a large number of patients, satisfactorily long development, and legitimate measurable plan. The after-effects of this phase III trials shape the establishment of another medication application (NDA) for administrative endorsement of promoting approval. Because of their size and similarly long-term, Phase III trials are the most costly, tedious and troublesome trials to outline and run, particularly in treatments for endless therapeutic conditions. Phase III trials of ceaseless conditions or sicknesses frequently have a short follow-up period for assessment, with respect to the time the mediation may be utilized as a part of practice. This is at times called the "pre-promoting stage" since it really measures consumer reaction to the medication.

Phase IIIa

These trials are directed after adequacy of the examination drug is exhibited yet before the accommodation of a New Drug Application. They are directed in victims for whom the drug is required. Extra information is created on wellbeing and adequacy in vast quantities of patients. They regularly give a great part of the data required for the collection and naming of the pharmaceutical.

Phase IIIb

Phase IIIb trials are led after the administrative accommodation of a New Drug Application, yet before the pharmaceutical's acceptance and promoting. This stage gathers extra discoveries and data which might be required by the administrative specialist before acceptance. These trials supplement prior trials, finish prior trials, or might be coordinated toward new sorts of trials or Phase IV trials.

Clinical Trial: Phase IV

Phase IV trials are done after the medication or treatment has been promoted to assemble data on the medication's impact in different populaces and any side impacts related with usage over longer time period. They are generally post-registration or post-license trials and give extra insights about the prescription's long-term viability or security profiles. These trials are directed to evaluate the viability of another medication when it is utilized as a part of an open domain when contrasted with the adequacy evaluated in a deliberately controlled Phase III trial. New age gatherings, populaces, and other solution correlations can be assessed. Imperative safe issues that exclusively emerge in a moderately little extent of individuals may just be accounted for this stage because of the far-reaching utilization of the new medication. These trials should utilize indistinguishable logical and moral principles as in premarketing investigations. One of the real targets in post-marketing improvement is to build up a superior security profile for the new medication. Vast scale Well-being observations are extremely regular in Phase IV. Patients selected in Phases I, II, and III are frequently to some degree confined (patients would need to be inside a particular age extend, sexual orientation, sickness seriousness or different confinements). After the new medication is endorsed and is accessible to the general patient populace, each patient with the fundamental infection can be presented to this medication. Issues identified with medicate wellbeing that have not been recognized from the pre-marketing considers (Phases I, II, and III) may now be seen in this substantial, all-inclusive community.

ROLE OF FDA IN DRUG DEVELOPMENT

The FDA is the most established purchasers assurance organization in the United States, starting in the U.S. Patent Office in 1848, and later acquired by the Department of Agriculture in 1862. The Federal Food, Drug, and Cosmetics Act of 1938 required all medications to be endorsed for security by the FDA (Williams, 2015). This mission was extended in 1962 by adding the prerequisite that medications be demonstrated "compelling" and additionally sheltered and set strict controls on the utilization of investigational drugs. Controls with respect to drug well-being oversight were extended in 1976 to incorporate medicinal instruments. The direction of the advancement, generation, advertising, and offers of restorative pharmaceuticals and gadgets involves incomprehensible objectives. It must guarantee that new and viable restorative medicines achieve general society quickly while at the same time giving security from insufficient or even risky treatments. In the United States, these administrative capacities tumble to the U.S. Food and Drug Administration (FDA) (Ning & Maher, 2015). At the point when a substance is prepared for clinical examination, however, before any testing in human subjects, the medication designer must include the FDA. This procedure starts when the medication's support (for the most part the medication producer or merchant) documents an investigational new drug (IND) application with the office. Government law requires that a medication be the subject of an endorsed promoting application for it to be lawfully transported crosswise over state lines. An affirmed IND application furnishes the engineer with a specialized exception to this government control, so clinical examiners can issue a drug to various examination focuses over the country (Berkman & Eugster, 2017,).

Basic Steps for Approval

There are three basic steps of IND applications as follows (Yao et al., 2017):

- Investigator IND
- Emergency IND
- Treatment IND

Investigator IND

An Investigator IND is put together by a medical practitioner who starts and leads an examination, and under whose quick course the investigational medicate is controlled or distributed. A physician may present an exploration IND to propose considering an unapproved medication, or an endorsed item for another sign or in another patient. The investigator will initiate and assist the examination by distributing and organising the drug. The specialist must hold up not less than 30 days subsequent to presenting an IND application to start any clinical trials. In the event that the FDA does not question, clinical Phase I testing can start. The FDA may react to the application with proposals for the examination or with obligatory change prerequisites. In spite of the fact that proposals are changes that are not required for the IND analysis to continue, they should be considered important. The FDA audit board comprises of clinicians and specialists who may have extensive involvement with related medications or medications in a comparable class, and such proposals are not made delicately. Moreover, it is a key for the endorsement procedure that the agent keeps up an integrated association with the FDA commentators. Although the FDA must react within 30 days to difficulties of a clinical hold by the examiner, in fact, there is no due date for the determination of issues causing clinical holds. The clinical hold may end up in delay of development of a year or more.

Emergency IND

An emergency IND solicits the FDA to support use from an exploratory medication in a crisis circumstance that does not permit time for a standard IND process or institutional review board (IRB) endorsement. It is likewise utilized for patients who do not meet the criteria of a current investigation convention, or if an endorsed think about convention does not exist. This sort of utilization may likewise be submitted to approve use in a patient or patients who do not meet investigation criteria or if no endorsed examination, convention exists. Emergency INDs are started by coordinate contact with the suitable division of the FDA. In emergency condition, the FDA will regularly approve utilization of the operator ahead of time of a full IND, which should then be finished in an auspicious manner.

Treatment IND

Treatment IND is submitted for exploratory medications demonstrating guarantee in clinical testing for genuine or quickly hazardous conditions while the last clinical work is directed and the FDA audit happens. Treatment IND applications request endorsement to utilize a test drug that is demonstrating guarantee in clinical investigations previously fulfillment of the investigations, FDA audit, and last endorsement. These are likewise called extended utilize INDs. Four necessities must be considered before issuance of a treatment IND: 1) the medication is expected for treatment of a hazardous disease; 2) there is no acceptable elective treatment; 3) the medication is as of now under scrutiny or trials are finished; and 4) the medication support is effectively seeking after endorsement. Possible IRB audit and educated assent are compulsory. The procedure and courses of events for treatment IND applications take after a comparable pathway to those of customary INDs, yet prerequisites for clinical confirmation varies.

STRATEGIES FOR DRUG DEVELOPMENT

Throughout the period of drug development, various methodologies have been taken up which could be further subcategorized as in vivo, in vitro, and in silico in their actual structures. The advantages of in vitro tests lie in the certainty that they render fast outcomes, generally practical, and their exact methods of action can be tried. The disadvantage of these tests is that the homeostatic systems and pathways found in creatures are not present. In vitro thinks about plainly imply conspicuous impacts of an operator in a controlled domain outside of a living being and henceforth affirm the validity of a medication. In any case, the affirmation through in vivo considers is more qualified for its impacts of an investigation on a living subject including the instruments of activity (Fielden & Kolaja, 2008). On the other hand, in silico investigations imply a moderately novel part of examining and analysing. Significant conclusions attracted by executing in silico approaches happen to be in the radar of forecast, displaying, and reproduction in regards to medicating collaboration inside the victim. While in silico and in vitro models will consistently be produced and refined, in vivo preclinical security models remain the highest quality level for surveying human hazard.

In vitro Studies

For setting up a relationship between medication and dosage, the minimum inhibitory concentration (MIC) for a microbe, and result of the medication on the victim, both in vitro and in vivo models have turned out to be effective. Through the span of antimicrobial movement, their examples have been portrayed by testing the connection between drug focus and antimicrobial impact. At the point when expanding drug levels upgrade antimicrobial killing, the example of movement is termed as "focus subordinate". Some different medications are termed to as "time subordinate" where their belongings are not adjusted by upgrading the concentrations but rather by expanding the term of presentation. Analysts consider that in vitro poisonous quality investigation examines and methods are generally huge as for time and cost compels when contrasted with in vivo toxicology tests in creature models. Cytotoxicity test of medications is done to dissect its relative harmfulness to growths, however, not to different human cell lines. For contemplating drug weakness tests fundamentally MIC and minimum fungicidal concentration (MFCs) are resolved, and pathogens' development is checked outwardly. The MIC was characterized as the most reduced centralization of medication demonstrating no noticeable development. The MFC was characterized as the least convergence of drug which lessened the colony forming unit by a distinct esteem (Samaranayake et al., 2005).

In vivo Studies

The period of in vivo analysis ranges from administering drug from short-term to lifetime exposure. Short-term examinations are typically directed in at least one-rat animal categories with the sole plan to choose the test medication's lethality. In addition, measurement run and the state of the dosage, reaction bend are additionally contemplated with in vivo models. Deciding the bioavailability of drug is done through a pharmacokinetic analysis in clinical trials decisively in Phase 1 and Phase 2 trials. Bioavailability refers to the degree and rate of assimilation of the medication. Medications are directed to human and examination of how and place of administration the drug gets absorbed by the body are observed. To decide the right dose for non-intravenous administrations of a medication like oral, rectal, transdermal, subcutaneous, and sublingual, this parameter is fundamental. Administration direction, medicate digestion, furthermore, the plan of medication impact the retention rate. Understanding the poisonous quality of medications is vital in light of the fact that the greater part of medications breaks because of its danger and security issues. Danger examines give an intensive examination of the measurement impact of a medication on different purposes of the victim (Andes et al., 2008).

In silico Studies

Computer-aided drug discovery utilizes computational ways to deal with finding, creating and investigating drugs. The ligand-based computer-aided drug discovery approach includes the examination of ligands known to cooperate with an object of desire. These techniques utilize an arrangement of reference structures gathered from substances known to communicate with the desired object and break down their 2D or 3D structures. The essential target of these techniques is to focus on the type and binding strength of the target. Docking is a pharmacologically essential apparatus in the field of drug discovery and computational science. It likewise gives other imperative data like the degree and specificity of association, official and change energies. An in silico approach with significant capacity in the field of medication outline and medication disclosure, molecular modelling is a strategy for contrasting and investigating sub-atomic structures and 3D structure-based properties. Over the span of the drug discovery process, computational screening of new lead compounds is named as virtual screening. It is the key approach connected in medicate revelation examines for the recognizable proof of new hits. Receptor and non-receptor based techniques could be utilized to outline ligand (Sliwoski et al., 2014).

RISK MANAGEMENT IN DRUG DEVELOPMENT PROCESS

The beginning stage of risk management through advancement i.e. once the essential plan and the related assembling process have been chosen is the lead of an underlying danger evaluation. Regardless of the particular risk evaluation mechanism that is used to survey the information factors and their potential effect on item quality, and free of the point in the item improvement lifecycle at which the device is connected, the general results can be classified as described in the table (see Table 2).

The quality desires for a specific drug item are characterized by its basic quality traits, which are in view of the necessities for quiet well-being and viability. The production and utilization of a pharmaceutical item fundamentally involve some level of hazard. The key, in this way, is minimizing the danger to a worthy level by building up a strong procedure understanding and executing suitable control measures to give an abnormal state of affirmation that the item will reliably meet the basic quality ascribes important to guarantee item security and adequacy for the patient. Risk administration is a continuous procedure all through the medication's whole lifecycle, and at entering focuses in the lifecycle, reassessments of hazard

Table 2. Different types of risks faced during drug development process

S.No	Type of Risks	Description
1.	Adequate risk	No advance examination is justified
2.	Potential risk	An advance examination is justified
3.	Critical risk	A characterized risk management methodology is required
4.	Improper risk	Analysis, re-designing or quitting of procedure or outcome

Source: (Hulbert et al., 2008)

are required. From one evaluation to another, the base of logical information and experience will vary and, along these lines, the methodologies and the instruments connected in the evaluations will usually contrast (Hulbert et al., 2008).

CONCLUSION

Drug disclosure and advancement are a time consuming and expensive process. The disappointment rate of medication entries has been expanding. To enhance the rate of progress, advancement has been started in clinical improvement through FDA's basic way of activity. Clearly choosing the correct measurement for another drug is a vital process. Without dosage data, it is impractical for a doctor to endorse the medication to patients. Stage I clinical trials are intended to gather data that will reinforce the investigation of dose– reaction relationship for Phase II. Dosing data is a standout amongst the most critical contemplations in Phases II and III clinical examinations. Finally, recently, amid and after the NDA procedure, measurements determination is being considered by the support, the administrative organizations, and the overall population. Indeed, even after the medication is affirmed and accessible available, new medication dosages are yet examined precisely and the level of the examination relies upon reactions noticed from the general patient population.

ACKNOWLEDGMENT

The author of the chapter would like to thank Dr. Senthil Kumar Ponussamy for his assistance in gathering and conducting research for the chapter and in providing guidance toward the publication.

REFERENCES

Andes, D., Diekema, D. J., Pfaller, M. A., Prince, R. A., ... Jou, J. (2008). In vivo pharmacodynamic characterization of anidulafungin in a neutropenic murine canddiasis model. *Antimicrobial Agents and Chemotherapy*, *52*(2), 539–550. doi:10.1128/AAC.01061-07 PMID:18070979

Berkman, H., & Eugster, M. (2017). Short on drugs: Short Selling during the Drug Development Process. *Journal of Financial Markets*, *33*, 102–123. doi:10.1016/j.finmar.2017.02.001

Das, M. K., & Chakraborty, T. (2016). ANN in Pharmaceutical Product and Process Development. Artificial Neural Network for Drug Design, Delivery and Disposition, 277-293.

Dingemanse, J., & Krause, A. (2017). Impact of pharmacokinetic-pharmacodynamic modelling in early clinical drug development. *European Journal of Pharmaceutical Sciences*, *109*, S53–S58. doi:10.1016/j.ejps.2017.05.042 PMID:28535992

Fielden, M. R., & Kolaja, K. L. (2008). The role of early in vivo toxicity testing in drug discovery toxicology. *Expert Opinion on Drug Safety*, *2*(2), 107–110. doi:10.1517/14740338.7.2.107 PMID:18324874

Gernaey, K. V., Cervera, A. E., & Woodley, J. M. (2011). PSE in Pharmaceutical Process Development. *Computer-Aided Chemical Engineering*, *29*, 1628–1632. doi:10.1016/B978-0-444-54298-4.50104-5

Haleem, R. M., Salem, M. Y., Fatahallah, F. A., & Abdelfattah, L. E. (2015). Quality in the pharmaceutical industry – A literature review. *Saudi Pharmaceutical Journal*, *23*(5), 463–469. doi:10.1016/j.jsps.2013.11.004 PMID:26594110

Hughes, J. P., Rees, S., Kalindjian, S. B., & Philpott, K. L. (2010). Principles of early drug discovery. *British Journal of Pharmacology*, *162*(6), 1239–1249. doi:10.1111/j.1476-5381.2010.01127.x PMID:21091654

Hulbert, M. H., Feely, L. C., Inman, E. L., Jophnson, A. D., ... Zour, E. (2008). Risk Management in Pharmaceutical Development Process. *Journal of Pharmaceutical Innovation*, *3*(4), 227–248. doi:10.100712247-008-9049-8

Kontoravdi, C., Samsatli, N. J., & Shah, N. (2013). Development and design of bio-pharmaceutical processes. *Current Opinion in Chemical Engineering*, *2*(4), 435–441. doi:10.1016/j.coche.2013.09.007

Ning, Y. M., & Maher, V. E. (2015). Food and Drug Administration Process for development and approval of drugs radiopharmaceuticals: Treatment in urologic oncology. *Urologic Oncology: Seminars and Original Investigations*, *33*(3), 137–142. doi:10.1016/j.urolonc.2014.12.008 PMID:25613202

Pandey, P., Bharadwaj, R., & Chen, X. (2017). Modeling of drug product manufacturing processes in the pharmaceutical industry. *Predictive Modeling of Pharmaceutical Unit Operations*, 1-13.

Rousseaux, C. G., & Bracken, W. M. (2013). Overview of Drug Development. Haschek and Rousseaux's Handbook of Toxicologic pathology, 647-685.

Samaranayake, Y. H., Ye, J., Yau, J. Y. Y., Cheung, B. P. K., & Smaranayake, L. P. (2005). In vitro method to study antifungal perfusion in Candida biofilms. *Journal of Clinical Microbiology*, *43*(2), 818–825. doi:10.1128/JCM.43.2.818-825.2005 PMID:15695686

Sinha, S., & Vohora, D. (2018). Drug Discovery and Development: An Overview. Pharmaceutical Medicine and Translational Clinical Research, 19-32.

Sliwoski, G., Kothiwale, S., Meiler, J., & Lowe, E. W. Jr. (2014). Computational methods in drug discovery. *Pharmacological Reviews*, *66*(1), 334–395. doi:10.1124/pr.112.007336 PMID:24381236

Williams, C. T. (2015). Food and Drug Administration Drug Approval Process: A History and Overview. *The Nursing Clinics of North America*, *51*(1), 1–11. doi:10.1016/j.cnur.2015.10.007 PMID:26897420

Yao, X., Ding, J., Liu, Y., & Li, P. (2017). The New Drug Conditional Approval Process in China: Challenges and Opportunities. *Clinical Therapeutics*, *39*(5), 1040–1051. doi:10.1016/j.clinthera.2017.03.016 PMID:28431767

ADDITIONAL READING

Adam, C. P., & Brantner, V. V. (2010). Spending on new drug development. *Health Economics*, *19*(2), 130–141. doi:10.1002/hec.1454 PMID:19247981

Aranyi, P. (2018). Ethical aspects of drug development. *Microchemical Journal*, *136*, 244–246. doi:10.1016/j.microc.2016.11.015

Dimitri, N. (2008). On the stage division mechanism in pharmaceuticals development processes. *Drug Discovery Today*, *13*(19-20), 902–906. doi:10.1016/j.drudis.2008.07.001 PMID:18678274

Hughes, J. P., Rees, S., Kalindjian, S. B., & Philpott, K. L. (2011). Principles of early drug discovery. *British Journal of Pharmacology*, *162*(6), 1239–1249. doi:10.1111/j.1476-5381.2010.01127.x PMID:21091654

Pandeya, S. N., & Thakkar, D. (2005). Combinatorial chemistry: A novel method in drug discovery and its application. *Indian Journal of Chemistry*, *44B*, 335–348.

Paul, M. S., Mytelka, D. S., Dunwiddie, C. T., Persinger, C. C., Munos, B. H., Lindborg, S. R., & Schacht, A. L. (2010). How to improve R&D productivity: The pharmaceutical industry's grand challenge. *Nature Reviews. Drug Discovery*, *9*(3), 203–214. doi:10.1038/nrd3078 PMID:20168317

Salazar, D. E., & Gormley, G. (2017). *Modern Drug Discovery and Development* (2nd ed., pp. 719–743). Clinical and Translational Science.

Singh, A., & Aggarwal, G. (2010). Technology transfer in pharmaceutical industry a discussion. *International Journal of Pharma and Bio Sciences*, *13*, 1–5.

KEY TERMS AND DEFINITIONS

Clinical Development: Is defined as trials in which individuals are involved.

Drug Development: Is defined as the process of developing new medications according to the demand and need in the market for curing of diseases and protecting from further infections.

Food and Drug Administration (FDA): Monitors the drug and its safety issues once the drug is commercially available in the market.

Investigational New Drug (IND): Application is the successful outcome of preclinical development process and is the step for the drug for entering into clinical development stage.

Nonclinical Development: Is defined as the process in which a drug volunteer is investigated broadly for pharmacological and toxicological properties through in vitro and in vivo analysis.

Chapter 7
Production Process in the Pharmaceutical Industry

Senthil Kumar Ponnusamy
SSN College of Engineering, India

Femina Carolin Christopher
SSN College of Engineering, India

ABSTRACT

The most important stress related to the industrialized societies are diseases and health issues caused by taking medicines that are in unfavorable condition. The health issues caused due to the medications mainly depend on the quality of drugs. This is the main test confronted by any pharmaceutical organization wishing to guarantee its survival. The benefit in the pharmaceutical industries is higher. But now, the cost of the medicines is reduced as per the estimation is given by the government. Hence, pharmaceutical organizations now confront a moment of challenge to diminish costs through upgrading and enhancing their production methods. Based on the production process following in the pharmaceutical industries, the product quality can be varied and improved. This chapter prescribes the detailed information regarding the production practices that are followed in the pharmaceutical industries for the production of high-quality products.

DOI: 10.4018/978-1-5225-5921-4.ch007

INTRODUCTION

Pharmaceutical industries bring out the major changes in the developed countries as well as in developing countries. Pharmaceutical industries use chemical materials for the production of antibiotics through research and development investment, which was useful to both the animals and humans. They tend to produce a profit source for the next generation and less expensive drugs that increase the enterprise value (Lee & Choi, 2015). Pharmaceutical industries get involved in the production of pharmaceuticals that represses the contaminants and infections of the living creatures. The pharmaceutical enterprises grew new methodologies in advances, explore fields and framework. The drug produced by the pharmaceutical industries contains various toxicological properties and therapeutic activity. Advancement in the research and technology innovation prompts the discovery of new pharmaceuticals that aid in the diminishment of symptoms. The manufacturing techniques of pharmaceuticalsinclude two major processing techniques namely primary processing and secondary processing. In the primary processing, active drug production takes place and in the secondary processing, the alteration of the drug takes place and converts them into a good product for administration. These drugs inhibit the infections and diseases of the living beings. The manufactured pharmaceutical groups include patented products like Proprietary ethical products or prescription only medicines (POM), general ethical products and over-the counter (OTC), or non-prescription products.

The entire pharmaceutical part is in need of creative technological solutions and basic scientific work which empowers in the generation of highly engineered drug materials. The product development process in the pharmaceutical industries includes logical and systematic process. The dosage form is created based on the successful outcome. Due to a deficiency in the control steps of product production, the above-mentioned developmental process becomes difficult. Based on the risk, regulatory demands are increasing rapidly in which the pharmaceutical industries are trying to change and match with the regulatory measures. The achievement of the pharmaceutical industry is due to the increase in population, high sale of drugs in the pharmaceutical industries and product innovation to treat various diseases. Research and development labs play out the work of medication discovery and improvement while fabricating plants create the final medications for purchasers. Most R&D research facilities are found independently from assembling plants, yet a few labs and generation plants are incorporated. In order to safeguard the characteristics of quality of the product regulatory conditions were developed which regulates the manufacturing process of products in the pharmaceutical and similar industries (Rantanen & Khinast, 2015). This chapter gives a short description of the production methods along with significance and limitations

PRODUCTION PROCESS IN PHARMACEUTICAL INDUSTRIES

The production process acts as a platform for the research and consumers. It is an industrial scale level of producing pharmaceutical drugs and several unit operations involved in the production of drugs are milling, drying, compression, and coating etc. A progression of creation procedures is following in the pharmaceutical enterprises for the production of pharmaceutical medications. It includes drug design, manufacturing, extraction, supply, packaging, release, and storage. The pharmaceutical industry undergo these steps to produce the essential drugs.

Design Conception

A drug is a molecule, which represses the activity of the target particle that prompts therapeutic aid to the people. The drugs can be a single compound or mixture of compounds. The design of the drugs also depends on the shape and size of the target molecule. Through drug designing process, a new drug compound can be discovered and utilized in clinical studies. Than the pharmacologically active compound, the drug configuration is more troublesome. The drug has the features like bioavailable, safe effective, absorbed orally, high stability, non-toxic, fewer side effects, and selective distribution to the target molecules. The more efficient drug configuration mainly depends on the improvement of computer programs to adapt with the flexibility of the target molecule and exact method for scoring interactions. Computer-aided drug design and structure-based design are the strategies widely used to refine the drugs. After knowing the details regarding the target molecule, the drug is composed with the assistance of computer devices. The alterations carried out in the drug design is dissolution, absorption, metabolic stability, distribution, elimination, toxicological profile, the cost of synthesis, and pharmaceutical properties.

Computer-Aided Drug Design

Computational instruments have turned out to be progressively essential in drug configuration forms. In order to study the atomic information regarding drug receptor and to forecast the properties of small molecule of drugs, computational chemistry is used frequently. The computational methods increase the affinity, selectivity, and stability of the protein-based therapeutics (Shirai, 2014). The major need to arrange and deal with large chemical and natural activity databases that all the pharmaceutical organization presently have are devices from data sciences and statistics. Furthermore, the demonstration of producing chemical substances is exceptionally amiable to mechanized computerization. The important aspects of the computer-aided design are storing and recovering data, provide information about the harmfulness and their relation to structure and target molecules visualization. Sub-atomic mechanics or sub-atomic progression is regularly used to assess the quality of the intermolecular communication between the little particle and its organic target. These techniques are used to anticipate the adaptation of the small molecule and to display conformational changes in the target that may happen when the small molecule binds to it. Some of the useful hypothesis is regularly used to give optimized parameters to the subatomic mechanics and furthermore give an estimate regarding electronic properties of the drug that will influence restricting affinity.

Structure-Based Drug Design

Distinguishing a reasonable target is the primary thought when beginning any structure-based drug configuration program. In the structure-based drug design, the drug is integral to the target molecule (Zeng et al., 2017). It is most effective when coordinated with data from diverse sources. It is widely used for the development of a new type of drugs. This method is exactly termed as rational drug design. The main objective is to optimize the intensity of ligand in a basic in-vitro assay. The modifications occurring in the existing compounds can be determined using this method. Additionally, it also enhances the binding between the compounds. In 1980s, various pharmaceutical industries invested heavily in the structure-based design for drug designing process. For good integrity, the complementarity between the target molecule and the drug is more essential. It is a powerful and inventive methodology applied in drug designing. Some of the methods like virtual screening and ligand synthesis used to produce high-affinity inhibitors or drugs. Examples of structure based design techniques are explained in the below-mentioned table (see Table 1). Though the mentioned technologies in the table have several advantages, their applications have certain limitations. Designed compounds are then tried in proper tests, and the data is additionally used to manage this method. The new modern technique in this method is high throughput screening which creates a great hope in the design conception. Because of its advancements, it can able to configure the drugs with various homologous targets at the same time (Baldi, 2010). However, the opportunities in the structure-based design have never been greater in the drug designing and discovery. The structure-based configuration will turn into anoticeable tool for antibacterial drug discovery. In fragment-based drug design, the drug will target different types of target molecules (Baker, 2013). The fragment-based drug design mainly focus on the proteins even though there are an expanding number of illustrations where this drug design has been utilized for non-protein targets, for example, RNA.

Manufacturing Process

Depending upon the physical and chemical properties, the proper unit operations are chosen for the manufacturing process. In the pharmaceutical industries, the drugs are produced through a various combination of operations includes formulation, pre-formulation development, powder mixing, processing, granulation, compression, hot melt extrusion, and so on. The assembling procedure in the pharmaceutical industries, biochemical industries, and chemical industries are the same but their applications are distinctive. The manufacturing process relies on specific variables like design and format of the manufacturing process, crude materials utilized as a part of the manufacturing process, people required in the manufacturing process and the accessibility of control system. Below are some of the brief explanation of the manufacturing process used for the synthesis of drugs.

Formulation of Drugs

The chemical substances incorporated together to form a medical compound like drug are called pharmaceutical formulation. Around 40percent of the small molecules that are developing as a new medication has worse water solubility. Poor solubility is a major problem in the drug formulation process. Different methodologies have been created with an attention on the upgrade of the dissolvability, disintegration rate, and oral bioavailability of poor water-soluble pharmaceutical products. The foundation of an appropriate definition methodology ought to be a key thought for the pharmaceutical advancement of drug (Kawabata et al., 2011). Drug formulation gives a way to abuse completely the remedial capability of inadequately soluble agents. The major types of pharmaceutical formulation are oral formulation and topical medication forms (Hassan, 2012). The most commonly used approach in the pharmaceutical industries for ionizable medication to expand dissolvability and

Table 1. Some of the structure-based design methods

S.No	Structure Based Design Techniques	Purpose
1	Ligand docking	Predict the orientation of the ligand
2	De novo design	Design the target modifications using molecular tools
3	Virtual screening	Structural determination of target molecules
4	High throughput screening	Evaluate the activity of drug molecules
5	Quantitative structure–activity relationship (QSAR)	It creates the relationship between activity and properties of complex molecules

Source: (Anderson, 2003)

disintegration rate is salt formation approach. From acid to base, the salt formation takes place through proton transfer. In formulation design, particle size reduction, amorphization, emulsification, cyclodextrin complexation, and pH adjustment would be reasonable choices to enhance the disintegration conduct of ineffectively water-dissolvable pharmaceuticals. A better understanding of the physical and chemical properties of drug substances enhances the formulation method for poorly soluble medications.

Powder Mixing

Next, to the formulation process, the powder mixing process decides the delivery of the accurate dosage of pharmaceuticals. It is a basic manufacturing step in the pharmaceutical industries. It widely takes place during the batch process. Nevertheless, nowadays industries are focusing on the continuous process of powder mixing in order to increase the quality of finished products (Osorio & Muzzio, 2016). Obtaining the uniform mixtures of powders is critical in pharmaceuticals. Various studies have been used in several types of mixing equipment to recognize the mixing mechanism through convection, diffusion, and shearing. The mixing process followed in the pharmaceutical industries are dry blending, high shear mixing and emulsification, high shear mixing and powder dispersion into liquid, inline ultra-high shear mixing, in-line static mixing, dual-shaft and triple shaft mixers, double planetary mixing, high-speed planetary mixing. Some of the parameters like operation temperature, pressure, raw materials, and additives will affect the powder mixing process. It is basic for R&D researchers and process designers to be persistently refreshed on new blender frameworks and enhanced plans. In today's situations, combined usage of two or more mixing technologies only will give a successful application. Hence, while designing such type of blenders cost investment and efficiencies need to be considered.

Granulation

In the granulation process, the number of powder particle combine together to form larger particles and that larger particle or multi-particleis called granules. In this way, the particles gather together to make a bond between. Bonds are shaped by pressure or by utilizing a coupling operator. Granulation is broadly utilized as a part of the assembling of tablets and pellets (or spheroids). Granulation changes fine powders into free-streaming and tidy free granules. Additionally, the granulation process increases the substance consistency and physicochemical properties of mass thickness, porosity, hardness, compressibility and stability of the drug (Shanmugam, 2015). There are two types of granulation process. They are wet and dry granulation process. Using a granulating fluid, the powders are mix together to form a mass of mix are called wet granulation. Wet granulation is utilized to enhance the stream, compressibility, bioavailability, also, homogeneity of low-dosage mixes, electrostatic properties of powders and the stability of dosage forms. Dry granulation is a simple and less expensive method. Dry granulation expands the size of the granules, which helps to form tablets or capsules.

Compression

Compression is an effective way to produce tablets. The major benefit of the compression process is no additional processing steps are needed. The compression stage consists of upper and lower punch, which forms shape to the tablet. These punches are present in the pressure rolls and form the tablets. The separation between the upper and lower punches decides the thickness and the hardness of the tablet. When the punches are near with one another, a thin and hard tablet is made. When the punches are more separated, the tablet made is gentler and thicker. Tablets are prepared by compressing a drug or a mixture of drugs to form solid flat or biconvex dishes (Harbir, 2012). Depending upon the substance, the shape, size, and weight of the tablets vary. Granulation techniques like wet and dry granulation are also used to produce the tablets. Due to certain disadvantages in the granulation process, the compression process is widely preferred for the preparation of tablets.

Hot Melt Extrusion

It is an increasing technology in the pharmaceutical industry because using this method a novel compound can be generated. By the hot melt extrusion technology, the novel drugs with low solubility can be changed through hot melt extrusion method. To achieve a molecular level mix of some compounds like binders and polymers, they are pumped into the system using a rotating screw at a temperature greater than the melting temperature or transition temperature (Patil et al., 2016). Using heat and pressure, the channels in the hot melt extrusion method mix to materials together to increase the solubility (Wilson et al., 2012). In pharmaceutical industries, the supply of chemicals and equipment related to the hot melt extrusion method are increasing rapidly due to their application in solubility and soli-dispersion production.

Pharmaceutical Extraction and Separation

When the pharmacological activity is present in the plants or some other sources, it is important to build up an extraction method using the appropriate solvents. The determination of solvents relies on the dissolvability and stability of the active substance. The most generally utilized solvents for the extraction procedure are water, acetone, alcohols, ether, ethyl acetate etc. The partition strategies are practiced acquiring the active drug and eliminate the inert material by treatment with the suitable solvent which is known as the menstruum. The extracts which were obtained from the sources are further processed to form tablets and capsules. The solvent is selected based on the following factors like high capacity, highly selective, completely volatile, non-toxic to human beings etc. The different strategies for the extraction process incorporate maceration, percolation, infusion, decoction, digestion, supercritical fluid extraction and so on. These sorts of extraction play a noteworthy part in the composition of qualitative and quantitative extracts. The choice of extraction process depends upon factors like nature and stability of the crude drug, the cost of the drug, and concentration of the product and recovery of solvent.

Maceration

The maceration process is less complex for the extraction of active material from the plant source and is more suitable for the temperature stability compounds and non-volatile compounds which are widely used in the pharmaceutical products (Jovanovic et al., 2017; Siqueira et al., 2011). Because of its suitability and simplicity, it is applied from laboratory scale to industrial level. In as toppered container, solvents and solid ingredients are added and mixed and allowed to remain standing for about few days with adequate agitation process. The agitation process in the maceration increases the contact between the solvent and ingredients. After some time, the mixture is strained by using sieving and then filtered by decantation process. This process is widely used for the organized drugs like roots, stems and unorganized drugs like oleoresins and gum resins. Various active substances were extracted using the maceration process are explained in the table (see Table 2). The certain downside of the maceration process is the utilization of large volumes of solvents and extended concentration steps, which limit their usage.

Table 2. Maceration method applied for the separation of the active substance

S.No	Source	Extracts
1	*Thymus serpyllum L.*herb	Polyphenols
2	Peel of kinnow (*Citrus reticulate* L.)	Polyphenols
3	*Olea europaea* L.	Olive oil
4	*Chrysanthemum cinerariifolium*	Pyrethrins
5	*Arbutus unedo* L.	Catechin-based extract

Source: (Jovanovic et al., 2017; Safdar et al., 2016; Deng et al., 2017; Gallo et al., 2017; Albuquerque et al., 2017)

Percolation

Percolation is generally used for the establishment of tinctures and fluid extract. The solvent is allowed to flow continuously downward in the bed which consists of crude material. The substance gets moistened by the solvent and stands for few hours in a closed container. After some time, the mass is removed from the equipment. The extra solvent is added to the mass to form a layer and menstruum is added continuously to obtain the required volume. Then the liquid is removed and filtered over decantation process. The major advantage of the percolation process is less time and complete extraction occurs than the maceration.

Infusion

In this method, warm or cold water is used to remove the active substances or soluble compounds present in the plant material within a short period of time. The infusion technique is different from percolation and decoction process. The most widely used source in the infusion method is herbs, flowers, and berries of the plant material. The boiling liquid is poured over the plant material and dissolve readily. The active ingredients from the source are released within a short time period. Infusions are divided into two types. They are fresh infusions and concentrated infusions. The fresh infusion is prepared by infusion process that contains active constituents of vegetable drugs. Maceration or percolation process and alcohol prepare concentrated infusions are used as a preservative in this method. The hot infusion is the perfect medium for enhancing the therapeutic sweet. The cold infusion is prepared overnight though steeping method. Based on the quantities of solvent and plant material, the efficiency of the infusion will vary.

Decoction

In this procedure, the hot liquid (water) is used to boil the crude drug for a defined time and then cooled and filtered. It is most reasonable for separating water soluble and heat stable constituents. It is commonly utilized in the preparation of ayurvedic extracts. This method is different from infusion in which the boiling liquid is poured over the crude drug. This is most reliable to the materials like roots, seeds, berries, and barks. Decoctions can be taken either in hot or cold form. This process is used to produce herbal teas, leaf teas, tinctures and similar solutions. Despite the fact that this strategy for extraction distinct from infusion and percolation, the resultant fluids can sometimes the same in their effects, or general appearance and taste.

Digestion

It is the modified form of maceration and percolation method. At a specific pressure, the drug is separated from the plant material by heating in which the temperature is higher than the room temperature. The generally used temperature for this process is 35° and 40°C but not more than 50°C. This will raise the diffusion power of the solvent into the crude drug. Protection should be taken to avoid the harm to the active substance of the drug. It is widely used for the separation of wood and bark of the plant material which has poor solubility. The apparatus used in the digestion process is the digester. This digester is made up of metal in which the drug and menstruum are treated for a specified of time under particular temperature and pressure.

Supercritical Fluid Extraction

The supercritical fluid extraction method has several benefits than the other traditional extraction methods because it used solvents with different physical and chemical properties like density, diffusivity, viscosity and dielectric constant (Silva et al., 2016). It is recently entered into the pharmaceutical applications. In this method, supercritical fluids are used at temperature and pressure greater than the critical point. At higher temperature, the liquids get changed into gases through higher pressure and at higher pressure gases gets changed into a liquid through higher temperature (Deshpande et al., 2011). Hence, the fluid properties were changed and they behave like liquid and gas like properties. Liquid-like properties provides extraction of active substances from the materials and gas like properties provide mass transfer process. It has turned into a more flexible and environmentally friendly technology that can deal with an assortment of complicated issues in the pharmaceuticals. Unique solvating properties are obtained in the fluid due to the changes in properties like surface tension and strength of the solvent. High degree of selectivity is increased in the supercritical fluid over the modification of properties of the fluid. Due to the easy diffusion of solvents into the solid materials, faster transportation rate takes place than the other methods. One of the fundamental qualities of a supercritical liquid is adjusting the thickness of the liquid by changing its weight as well as temperature. Since thickness is identified with dissolvability, adjusting the extraction pressure, the strength of the solvent can be altered. It has some advantages like higher efficiency, time requirement is low, safe and gives a higher yield. The most widely used supercritical solvents are ethane, water, methanol, carbon dioxide, nitrous oxide, sulfur hexafluoride, ethane, xenon, ethylene, propane, methane, etc. The different types of supercritical fluids applied in the extraction of active substances are explained in the table with their critical temperature and pressure. The molecules present in the supercritical solvent are transferred from the bulk solvent and reaches the surface of the particles through the boundary layer. Solvent molecules permeate to the solid particle and solute molecules that adhere to the solid matrix by Van der Waals forces and/or chemical forces. At that point, solute molecules diffuse and moves over the film into the bulk fluid phase (Rai et al., 2016). Based on the environmental point of view, the super-critical fluid extraction process is an advantageous technology but in the case of economic considerations, the focus needs to be increased to enhance the application of supercritical technology. This technology is not widely applied in the pharmaceutical industry but it employed in the formulation of drugs in the pharmaceutical industries (see Table 3).

Supply Chains in the Pharmaceutical Industry

In the health sectors, the pharmaceutical industry plays a major role and pharmaceutical supply chain is more important in the health sectors (Nematollahi et al., 2017; Naryana et al., 2014). The supply chain is a more complex framework and very fragmented. The supply chain of pharmaceutical enterprises is undifferentiated from alternative enterprises simultaneously. At each level of the supply chain, industries are very cautious regarding the quality of the drug and the safety of the people. The supply chain is more unpredictable than other numerous supply chains as it can influence social and political viewpoints. Dealing with the pharmaceutical supply chain is troublesome as a result of its complexity and government regulations in this field. The pharmaceutical supply chain is mainly incorporated with five supply chain namely primary manufacturers, secondary manufacturers, main and local distribution centers (DCs), and destination zones/demand points (Zahiri et al., 2017).The policy created in the pharmaceutical industry allows the usage of a wide variety of materials in high quantities. The primary manufacturers produce the active substances and the production process involves the synthesis of chemicals, extraction stages, purification and product recovery. Secondary producers are in charge of further creation forms with various innovation levels packaging and finishing the items. The secondary manufacturers play a major role in the storage of a large number of products in the available facility. The main and local distribution centers are a charge of stocking products to fulfill the market request.

The pharmaceutical industry uses fixed suppliers of raw materials and saves the raw materials in different warehouses. Then further the stored raw materials are passed into the manufacturing section to produce the drug. The company with a single manufacturing section will use asingle warehouse and the company with more manufacturing section use different warehouses. In spite of combining with refined advancements and enhancements in amount and nature of related items in the pharmaceutical supply chain, many organizations are a long way from adequately fulfilling market requests as for emerged concerns (Masoumi et al., 2012). Decisions

Table 3. Types of supercritical fluids and their critical temperature and pressure

S.No	Supercritical Fluid	Critical Temperature (TC) °C	Critical Pressure (PC) MP
1.	Water	374	22
2.	Xenon	16.6	5.9
3.	Nitrous oxide	36.5	4.1
4.	Ethylene	9.1	5.1
5.	Propene	36.5	4.6

Source: (Deshpande et al., 2011)

based on cost, quantity taken by the members in the supply chain can affect the other supply chain actors also. In that case, individual decisions lead to the worse supply chain. The transportation of pharmaceutical items is carried out through pharma-providers who visit retailers and convey the orders. In this circumstance, pharma-providers who are frequently more capable position than the retailers make decisions based on their meeting consistency. Supply chain service level is decided by the retailers which affect the number of stocks in the system and profit of the suppliers (Heydari, 2014). The demand percentage of stocks within a time period are called service level. Low service level leads to a reduction in the market share, hence pharmaceutical retailers are trying to increase the service level to reduce the probability of stock-outs.

The requirement of the stock level is high because this will buffer the slow supply chain in the pharmaceutical industry. The major advantage of the pharma supply chain is improved the business efficiency, reduces the waste, increases the security of supplies and market share. The most priority considered in the designing of the pharmaceutical drugs are the safety and efficiency of drugs. Manufacturers, providers, and distributors play a vital role in supply chain strategy. Manufacturers organize a partnership with the distributors and guarantee that particular drug is accessible and open to suppliers. Providers have numerous options from whom they will secure item, and distributors provide safety services that support suppliers to safeguard the patient. Pharmaceutical supply chain strategies are used to supply the product to the market in an effective way. Nowadays, pharmaceutical companies are trying to extract benefits from the components of theirsupply chain due to the recent changes in the working conditions. There are a lot of falls regarding pharmaceutical supply chain are facing the pharmaceutical industry. Hence, every pharmaceutical industry should aware about that and methodologies are required to manage them. Obtaining the raw materials, change of raw materials into completed products and transportation of those products are incorporated into the effective supply chain management all the pharmaceutical industries. Previously, industries are focused more on the research and development, sales and marketing than the supply chain management. Hence, the pharmaceutical organizationis lagging in developing bets methodologies for supply chain management. Supply chain management in the pharmaceutical industry is important because it plays a vital role in the cost reduction and maintain the product quality standards and additionally increases the competitive advantages over the companies.

Packaging

The packaging of pharmaceuticals or drugs is necessary to reduce the contamination and decrease the growth and activity of microbes. In the pharmaceutical industry, packing is a tool preserving which preserves the integrity of the product. Packaging is the process in which the pharmaceuticals are appropriately held their therapeutic efficiency and allows to store the drugs till it used for other purposes. Based on the physical and chemical characteristics, the packaging of the pharmaceutical is selected. It plays a vital role in saving the drugs, blood, blood products, liquid and solid dosage forms etc (Pareek & Khunteta, 2014). The most continuous challenges faced by the pharmaceutical industries are packaging. It is continuously evolving and noteworthy achievement in the pharmaceutical industries. The main objective of pharmaceutical packaging is to provide information, convenience, and stability to the final product. Packaging greatly helps in the identification of products and additionally protects the drug or pharmaceutical from breakage, leakage, spoilage etc. It also allows convenience to open and handle the substance. It increases the attraction of people while purchasing. A few regular variables include patient safety, affirmation related to the efficiency of medication through the planned time span of usability, consistency of the medication through various creation, careful documentation of all materials and procedures, regulation of transport of packaging materials into drug, control of degradation of final product by oxygen, temperature, warm and so on. Packaging is regularly required in administering, dosing, and utilization of the pharmaceutical item. Secure packaging is essential in identifying the fake items. This prompted to develop the legislations to guarantee secure packing of pharmaceuticals. By utilizing new anti-counterfeiting technology manufacturers undoubtedly deliver secure packaging and satisfy the government strategies. The World Health Organization (WHO) finds that the exchange of fake medicines around the world is increasing continuously (Cozella et al., 2012). Packaging is the combined system forgenerating final products for transport. Logistics, warehousing, sale and final use.

Pharmaceutical packaging is classified into three types. They are primary packaging, secondary packaging and tertiary packaging (Zadbuke et al., 2013). The primary packing component has a direct contact with the product but there is no interaction with the drug. It prevents the external actions from biological, physical and chemical hazards. It is a part of the container closure system. E.g. Blister packages, strip packages, aseptic filling, and sealing equipment, bottle filling and capping equipment, soft tube filling and sealing equipment, sachet packaging equipment etc. Secondary packaging is back to back covering or bundle which stores pharmaceuticals bundles in it for their gathering. Additionally, the secondary packing component does not have a direct contact with the final product. E.g. Cartons, boxes, case packaging equipment, wrapping equipment etc. Tertiary pharmaceutical deals with the bundle of pharmaceuticals and transfers the drugs from one area to another. E.g. Containers, barrels, etc. The package must have the following characteristics like it should protect the preparation form the environmental conditions, must be inert, must non-toxic, must not transmit the odor/ taste with the product. Must meet tamper-resistant requirements. The primary and secondary packaging of the pharmaceutical items is firmly connected to their creation and constitutes.

Types of Materials Used in Packaging

Packaging materials including their distinguishing proof, examining, testing, elimination of medication item compartments and closures are in charge of the quality of control unit. They are more responsible for the above-mentioned functions in the pharmaceutical companies. The most widely used materials for packaging are glass containers, plastic containers, rubber, metal, paper/cardboards. The selection of packaging material depends on the conservation of the product, the satisfaction of the peoples or customer, stuffing method, and sterilization technique. Frequently used packaging materials is glass. It has higher qualities, transparent, best preservation power, economical and their availability is high in different shapes and sizes. They should be chemically inert, strong, impermeable and should protect the product from the light. The glass is made up of sand, soda ash, silica etc. The decrease of sodium ion in the glass material rises the chemical resistance of the glass. Amber glass and red glass are able to save or protect the product in the glass containers from sunlight. The downside of the glass material is weak, weight and release alkali to the aqueous preparation. Plastic materials are easy to design and have high quality. They are highly breakage resistant, lower weight than the glass materials and thus provide more safety in handling. The drawback in the plastic materials is the entry of humidity into the product is easy than the glass containers. Plastic materials are composed of polymers like polyethylene, polypropylene, polyvinylchloride, polystyrene, polycarbonate etc. The additive added to the plastic materials are plasticizers, fillers, and antioxidants. Drug plastic consideration is divided into five types like leaching, permeation, sorption, chemical reaction, and changes in the physical properties of the plastics. Metals are commonly used for the development of containers. Aluminium, stainless steel, iron, and lead are widely utilized metals for the construction of containers. The benefits of metals in packing are impermeable to light, moisture and gases, less weight, easy labeling and provide strong rigid containers for packing. Metals give adequate safety to the final product. Although metals have some advantages, it has some disadvantages like high cost and reacts with some chemicals. The rubber material is commonly applied in closure meant for vials, dropping bottles etc. They are cheaper than the other packaging materials and additionally, the absorption of water is also low. Types of rubbers used as a packaging substance are butyl rubber, nitrile rubber, chloroprene rubbers and silicone rubbers. The packaging materials must be approved by the Food and Drug Administration (FDA). The manufacturer is more responsible for the security of packaging material. The obligation regarding the tests lies now more with the producers of packaging materials. Notwithstanding, as a precondition for this, extra QA measures, similar to merchant capability, provider review, and technical contracts must be taken. Packaging system will keep on becoming more vital, particularly in therapeutic areas and for taking care of industrial issues, for example, drug-product counterfeiting. The pharmaceutical packaging market is continuously increasing and has encountered yearly development of at least 5percent per annum.

Storage

The important authority to the person in the pharmaceutical industries is storing the pharmaceuticals at a particular place. Storage facilities are an important segment of the pharmaceutical industry. Facilities need to consent to Good Manufacturing Practices (GMP) for safekeeping of stock in the pharmaceutical industries. Prior to any storage facility, it is fundamental to recognize and measure the products to be kept in the facility and build up the safety conditions in which products must be kept. It is an essential activity in the supply chain management of the drug products. Pharmaceutical organization and institutions follow different techniques for storing pharmaceutical products. When the pharmaceutical items are stored in a proper condition, the power of item stays as it generally loses its strength before the expiry date. It is an important pharmacy practice followed in pharmaceutical industries. Storage is required for the materials like drugs, excipients and finished products etc. Storage of such materials maintains physical, chemical and biological properties. The manufacture and storage of pharmaceutical items at a particular condition create a great effect on the quality of the item. Storage conditions like cool storage are required for some of the products and hence refrigeration plant is widely used but needs to be monitored regularly to ensure the correct temperature are maintained. The loss of power amid capacity may impact the viability and security of pharmaceuticals. There is no guarantee when the drugs are kept away from the no-pharmaceuticals. Until it reaches the consumer, the pharmaceuticals should be stored in order to maintain the quality and safety of the product (Kassie & Mammo, 2014). Pharmaceutical items require controlled storage also, travel conditions to guarantee that their quality is most certainly not compromised. It is a vital part of the drug control system. Proper storage is required to prevent the spoilage or degradation. Generally, the natural risk involved are mix-ups, contamination and cross-contamination and these risks arise due to the improper storage of the products. Certain conditions like appropriate temperature, light, moisture, states of sanitation, ventilation, and isolation must be maintained properly wherever medications and supplies are stored (Shafaat et al., 2013). Based on the stability and nature of the product, the storage facility is chosen. Labeling of the pharmaceutical product depends on the stability test carried out on the product. Relevant storage practices are available for the pharmaceutical products in all the conditions. The pharmaceutical products enclosed in a closed container should be free from solids, liquids, and gases. Pharmaceutical companies and government regulations should focus on the significance of storage conditions of pharmaceutical products. Based on the necessity, the storage conditions vary for pharmaceutical products. At the temperature range from 20 to 25^{0}C, pharmaceuticals procedures are carried out and it is decided as a room temperature for most of the pharmaceuticals. The drug materials stored in warehouses which get degraded at the room temperature will store at the temperature range from 8 to 15^{0}C. Monitoring of storage conditions is required to main the quality of the product. Equipment utilized in the monitoring process should be calibrated regularly at different time intervals. Handling of intravenous medicines is required because it becomes fragile when it is frozen and these medicines should be stored until they are transported to the specific wards.

FUTURE TRENDS

The huge challenge for the pharmaceutical industry is that the product quality should match the international standards or regulations prescribed by the government. Hence, it is necessary that pharmaceutical industries should upgrade the research in the manufacturing process based on the security, cost, safety of the people. Based on the cost factor, industries need to implement new advancements in the manufacturing process. Additionally, it is needed to understand the scientific methods involved in the production practices. Though basic learning and specialized instruments are available today in the innovative manufacturing process, huge work is required in order to create most inventive pharmaceutical quality. Research and development are now focusing more on the production of new drugs that could achieve good financial performance. Hence, R& D will play a significant role in the future to secure the medicinal field.

CONCLUSION

In this chapter, the methods involved in the production of pharmaceuticals in the pharmaceutical industry were demonstrated. In the medical improvement and research, the pharmaceutical industry gives a tremendous contribution towards the medicinal services. Depending upon the generation system, the nature of the pharmaceutical item is resolved. These procedures build up pharmaceutical quality in order to ensure guaranteed to the people. The creative medications are delivered from the pharmaceutical ventures by following these generation methodologies. These procedures play a vital role in industries which impacts the manufacturing procedure of pharmaceuticals to the best quality level. Specialized and technological developments that progress furthermore and the available process may afford to improve quality ofthe product and creates a generous effect on the product improvement. The pharmaceutical production patterns are on the verge of creative fast development which gives the requirements for the item based on cost, preservation and human satisfaction is taken into consideration to increase the quality. In the pharmaceutical industries, the effective and cost-efficient manufacturing process is developing away from the interdisciplinary scientists of industries. Finally, the process explained in this chapter could provide the best platform for further innovation in the quality of the pharmaceutical product and the discovery of a new product.

REFERENCES

Albuquerque, B. R., Prieto, M. A., Barreiro, M. F., Rodrigues, A., Curran, T. P., Barros, L., & Ferreira, I. C. F. R. (2017). Catechin-based extract optimization obtained from *Arbutus unedo* L. fruits using maceration/microwave/ultrasound extraction techniques. *Industrial Crops and Products*, *95*, 404–415. doi:10.1016/j.indcrop.2016.10.050

Anderson, A. C. (2003). The Process of Structure-Based Drug Design. *Chemistry & Biology*, *10*(9), 787–797. doi:10.1016/j.chembiol.2003.09.002 PMID:14522049

Baker, M. (2013). Fragment-based lead discovery grows up. *Nature Reviews. Drug Discovery*, *12*(1), 5–7. doi:10.1038/nrd3926 PMID:23274457

Baldi, A. (2010). Computational Approaches for Drug Design and Discovery: An Overview. *Systematic Reviews in Pharmacy*, *1*(1), 99–105. doi:10.4103/0975-8453.59519

Cozzella, L., Simonetti, C., & Spagnolo, G. S. (2012). Drug packaging security by means of white-light speckle. *Optics and Lasers in Engineering*, *50*(10), 1359–1371. doi:10.1016/j.optlaseng.2012.05.016

Deng, J., Xu, Z., Xiang, C., Liu, J., Zhou, L., Li, T., ... Ding, C. (2017). Comparative evaluation of maceration and ultrasonic-assisted extraction of phenolic compounds from fresh olives. *Ultrasonics Sonochemistry*, *37*, 328–334. doi:10.1016/j.ultsonch.2017.01.023 PMID:28427640

Deshpande, P. B., Kumar, G. A., Kumar, A. R., Shavi, G. V., Karthik, A., Reddy, M. S., & Udupa, N. (2011). Supercritical fluid technology: Concepts and pharmaceutical applications. *PDA Journal of Pharmaceutical Science and Technology*, *65*(3), 333–344. doi:10.5731/pdajpst.2011.00717 PMID:22293238

Gallo, M., Formato, A., Ianniello, D., Andolfi, A., Conte, E., Ciaravolo, M., ... Naviglio, D. (2017). Supercritical fluid extraction of pyrethrins from pyrethrum flowers (*Chrysanthemum cinerariifolium*) compared to traditional maceration and cyclic pressurization extraction. *The Journal of Supercritical Fluids*, *119*, 104–112. doi:10.1016/j.supflu.2016.09.012

Harbir, K. (2012). Processing technologies for pharmaceutical tablets: A Review. *International Research Journal of Pharmacy*, *3*(7), 20–23.

Hassan, B. A. R. (2012). Overview on Pharmaceutical Formulation and Drug Design. *Pharmaceutica Analytica Acta*, *3*(10).

Heydari, J. (2014). Lead time variation control using reliable shipment equipment: An incentive scheme for supply chain coordination. *Transportation Research Part E, Logistics and Transportation Review*, *63*, 44–58. doi:10.1016/j.tre.2014.01.004

Jovanovic, A. A., Dordevic, V. B., Zdunic, G. M., Pljevljakusic, D. S., Savikin, K. P., Godevac, D. M., & Bugarski, B. M. (2017). Optimization of the extraction process of polyphenols from *Thymus serpyllum L.* herb using maceration, heat- and ultrasound-assisted techniques. *Separation and Purification Technology*, *179*(31), 369–380. doi:10.1016/j.seppur.2017.01.055

Kassie, G.M., & Mammo, S. (2014). Assessment of pharmaceutical store management in woreda health offices of westhararghe zone, Ethiopia. *International Research Journal of Pharmacy, 5*(8), 642-645.

Kawabata, Y., Wada, K., Nakatani, M., Yamada, S., & Onoue, S. (2011). Formulation design for poorly water-soluble drugs based on biopharmaceutics classification system: Basic approaches and practical applications. *International Journal of Pharmaceutics*, *420*(1), 1–10. doi:10.1016/j.ijpharm.2011.08.032 PMID:21884771

Lee, M., & Choi, M. (2015). Analysis on Time-Lag Effect of Research and Development Investment in the Pharmaceutical Industry in Korea. *Osong Public Health and Research Perspectives*, *6*(4), 241–248. doi:10.1016/j.phrp.2015.07.001 PMID:26473091

Masoumi, A. H., Yu, M., & Nagurney, A. (2012). A supply chain generalized network oligopoly model for pharmaceuticals under brand differentiation and perishability. *Transportation Research Part E, Logistics and Transportation Review*, *48*(4), 762–780. doi:10.1016/j.tre.2012.01.001

Narayana, S. A., Pati, R. K., & Vrat, P. (2014). Managerial research on the pharmaceutical supply chain – A critical review and some insights for future directions. *Journal of Purchasing and Supply Management*, *20*(1), 18–40. doi:10.1016/j.pursup.2013.09.001

Nematollahi, M., Hosseini-Motlagha, S. M., & Heydari, J. (2017). Economic and social collaborative decision-making on visit interval and service level in a two-echelon pharmaceutical supply chain. *Journal of Cleaner Production*, *142*, 3956–3969. doi:10.1016/j.jclepro.2016.10.062

Osorio, J. G., & Muzzio, F. J. (2016). Effects of processing parameters and blade patterns on continuous pharmaceutical powder mixing. *Chemical Engineering and Processing*, *109*, 59–67. doi:10.1016/j.cep.2016.07.012

Pareek, V., & Khunteta, A. (2014). Pharmaceutical packaging: Current trends and future. *International Journal of Pharmacy and Pharmaceutical Sciences*, *6*(6), 480–485.

Patil, H., Tiwari, R. V., & Repka, M. A. (2016). Hot-Melt Extrusion: From Theory to Application in Pharmaceutical Formulation. *AAPS PharmSciTech*, *17*(1), 20–42. doi:10.120812249-015-0360-7 PMID:26159653

Rai, A., Bhargava, R., & Mohanty, B. (2016). Simulation of supercritical fluid extraction of essential oil from natural products. *Journal of Applied Research on Medicinal and Aromatic Plants*, *5*, 1–9. doi:10.1016/j.jarmap.2016.09.005

Rantanen, J., & Khinast, J. (2015). The Future of Pharmaceutical Manufacturing Sciences. *Journal of Pharmaceutical Sciences*, *104*(11), 3612–3638. doi:10.1002/jps.24594 PMID:26280993

Safdar, M. N., Kausar, T., Jabbar, S., Mumtaz, A., Ahad, K., & Saddozai, A. A. (in press). Extraction and quantification of polyphenols from kinnow (*Citrus reticulate* L.) peel using ultrasound and maceration techniques. *Journal of Food and Drug Analysis*. PMID:28911634

Shafaat, K., Hussain, A., Kumar, B., Hasan, R. U., Prabhat, P., & Yadav, V. K. (2013). *World Journal of Pharmacy and Pharmaceutical Sciences*, *2*(5), 2499–2515.

Shanmugam, S. (2015). Granulation techniques and technologies: Recent progresses. *BioImpacts*, *5*(1), 55–63. doi:10.15171/bi.2015.04 PMID:25901297

Shirai, H., Prades, C., Vita, R., Marcatili, P., Popovic, B., Xu, J., ... Ikeda, K. (2014). Antibody informatics for drug discovery. *Biochimica et Biophysica Acta (BBA) -. Proteins and Proteomics*, *1844*(11), 2002–2015. doi:10.1016/j.bbapap.2014.07.006

Silva, R. P. F. F., Rocha-Santosa, T. A. P., & Duarte, A. C. (2016). Supercritical fluid extraction of bioactive compounds. *TrAC Trends in Analytical Chemistry*, *76*, 40–51. doi:10.1016/j.trac.2015.11.013

Siqueira, S., Falcao-Silva, V. D. S., Agra, M. D. F., Dariva, C., Siqueira-Junior, S. P. D., & Fonseca, M. J. V. (2011). Biological activities of Solanum paludosum Moric. extracts obtained by maceration and supercritical fluid extraction. *The Journal of Supercritical Fluids*, *58*(3), 391–397. doi:10.1016/j.supflu.2011.06.011

Wilson, M., Williams, M. A., Jones, D. S., & Andrews, G. P. (2012). Hot-melt extrusion technology and pharmaceutical application. *Therapeutic Delivery*, *3*(6), 787–797. doi:10.4155/tde.12.26 PMID:22838073

Zadbuke, N., Shahi, S., Gulecha, B., Padalkar, A., & Thube, M. (2013). Recent trends and future of pharmaceutical packaging technology. *Journal of Pharmacy & Bioallied Sciences*, *5*(2), 98–110. doi:10.4103/0975-7406.111820 PMID:23833515

Zahiri, B., Zhuang, J., & Mohammadi, M. (2017). Toward an integrated sustainable-resilient supply chain: A pharmaceutical case study. *Transportation Research Part E, Logistics and Transportation Review*, *103*, 109–142. doi:10.1016/j.tre.2017.04.009

Zheng, Y., Tice, C. M., & Singh, S. B. (2017). Conformational control in structure-based drug design. *Bioorganic & Medicinal Chemistry Letters*, *27*(13), 2825–2837. doi:10.1016/j.bmcl.2017.04.079 PMID:28479196

ADDITIONAL READING

Breen, L., & Crawford, H. (2005). Improving the pharmaceutical supply chain: Assessing the reality of e-quality through e-commerce application in hospital pharmacy. *International Journal of Quality & Reliability Management, 22*(6), 572–590. doi:10.1108/02656710510604890

Cook, J., Addicks, W., & Wu, Y. H. (2008). Application of the Biopharmaceutical Classification System in Clinical Drug Development—An Industrial View. *The AAPS Journal, 10*(2), 306–310. doi:10.120812248-008-9036-5 PMID:18500563

Davies, O. R., Lewis, A. L., Whitaker, M. J., Tai, H., Shakesheff, K. M., & Howdle, S. M. (2008). Applications of supercritical CO_2 in the fabrication of polymer systems for drug delivery and tissue engineering. *Advanced Drug Delivery Reviews, 60*(3), 373–387. doi:10.1016/j.addr.2006.12.001 PMID:18069079

Guzman, H. R., Tawa, M., Zhang, Z., Ratanabanangkoon, P., Shaw, P., Gardner, C. R., & Remenar, J. F. (2007). Combined use of crystalline salt forms and precipitation inhibitors to improve oral absorption of celecoxib from solid oral formulations. *Journal of Pharmaceutical Sciences, 96*(10), 2686–2702. doi:10.1002/jps.20906 PMID:17518357

Ku, M. S. (2008). Use of the Biopharmaceutical Classification System in Early Drug Development. *The AAPS Journal, 10*(1), 208–212. doi:10.120812248-008-9020-0 PMID:18446521

Pasquali, I., Bettini, R., & Giordano, F. (2008). Supercritical fluid technologies: An innovative approach for manipulating the solid-state of pharmaceuticals. *Advanced Drug Delivery Reviews, 60*(3), 399–410. doi:10.1016/j.addr.2007.08.030 PMID:17964684

Rodriguez-Spong, B., Price, C. P., Jayasankar, A., Matzger, A. J., & Rodriguez-Hornedo, N. (2004). General principles of pharmaceutical solid polymorphism: A supramolecular perspective. *Advanced Drug Delivery Reviews, 56*(3), 241–274. doi:10.1016/j.addr.2003.10.005 PMID:14962581

Schultheiss, N., & Newman, A. (2009). Pharmaceutical Cocrystals and Their Physicochemical Properties. *Crystal Growth & Design, 9*(6), 2950–2967. doi:10.1021/cg900129f PMID:19503732

KEY TERMS AND DEFINITIONS

Drug Design: It is the process of inventing a new product based on the biological target.

Extraction: It is a separation process in which the components gets separated from the matrix.

Formulation: The chemical compounds are joined together to form a medicinal drug.

Granulation: Granulation is the process of collecting particles together and creating a bond between them and these bonds are formed by compression or binding agent.

Maceration: Maceration involves soaking of coarse material in a container with the solvent and allowed to remain at room temperature for about 3 days with adequate agitation.

Packaging Material: The material which is used for packing the final product (e.g., glass, rubber, metals, etc.).

Pharmaceuticals: A compound that is manufactured from the active material for use as a medicinal drug.

Storage Conditions: The conditions specified for storing the product e.g. temperature, humidity, etc.

Section 4
Supply Chain Management in the Pharmaceutical Industry

This section provides enhanced knowledge about supply chain management in the global pharmaceutical industry. It gives a detailed analysis of all functional areas related to the pharmaceutical supply chains including the newest solutions and current problems.

Chapter 8
Characteristics of Pharmaceutical Supply Chains

Senthil Kumar Ponnusamy
SSN College of Engineering, India

Anbalagan Saravanan
Rajalakshmi Engineering College, India

ABSTRACT

The pharmaceutical supply chain is presently a noteworthy research topic in process operations and administration. A lot of research has been embraced on office area and configuration, stock and circulation arranging, limit and generation arranging, and point-by-point planning. Just a little extent of this work straightforwardly addresses the issues confronted in the pharmaceutical division. The pharmaceutical industry is facing extraordinary difficulties caused by a maturing population, the expanding expense of medicinal services, the priority given by the governments to bring down the cost of medications, boundaries to a passage in developing markets, and the more extensive reception of non-specific medications. These are quite recently a portion of the many difficulties making weight on the overall revenue of pharmaceutical firms. Expanded expenses of R&D and a diminished number of affirmed sedates additionally demonstrates that the lion's share of prescription, which is anything but difficult to find, has just been found.

DOI: 10.4018/978-1-5225-5921-4.ch008

INTRODUCTION

The pharmaceutical business can be characterized as a complex of procedures, operations and associations engaged with the revelation, improvement and produce of medications and meds (Jarrett, 1998). The World Health Organization (WHO) characterizes a medication or pharmaceutical readiness as: any substance or blend of substances made, sold, offered available to be purchased or spoken to for use in the conclusion, treatment, moderation or avoidance of malady, strange physical state or the manifestations thereof in man or creature; reestablishing, redressing or adjusting natural capacities in man or creature (Burns, 2002).

Pharmaceuticals merit unprecedented thought in controlling stock, including the essential contrasts amongst medications and other customer items: they are produced, made, and distributed by meeting the strict administrative prerequisites; medications are regularly chosen by a physician for a particular patient and can be repaid in entire or to some degree by an outsider guarantor or the state. These particular attributes make the pharmaceutical business an intense power in its own right, representing 15.4% of aggregate well-being consumption.

Generally, pharma organizations have complex supply chains that are under-used and wasteful. More terrible still, they are badly prepared to adapt to the kind of items that are coming down the pipeline. By 2020, huge numbers of the meds the business makes will be master treatments that require entirely distinctive assembling and conveyance systems from those used to deliver little particles. The pharmaceutical supply chain needs a radical upgrade, and it will experience three key changes over the following decade:

1. It will piece, with various models for various item sorts and patient fragments,
2. It will end up being a method for advertising separation and wellspring of monetary esteem; and
3. It will end up being a two-route road, with data streaming upstream to drive the downstream stream of items and administrations (Booth, 1999).

This is a wide definition, and correspondingly, there is a number of key players in the pharmaceutical business, counting:

1. The huge, innovative work-based multinationals with a worldwide nearness in marked items, both moral/remedy and over-the-counter. They tend to have production destinations in numerous areas,
2. The extensive non-specific makers, who create out-of-patent items and over-the-counter items,

3. Local assembling organizations that work in their home nation, delivering both non-branded items and brand items under permit or contract,
4. Contract makers, who do not have their own item portfolio, yet deliver either key intermediates, dynamic fixings (AI) or even last items by giving outsourcing administrations to different organizations,
5. Drug disclosure and biotechnology organizations, frequently moderately new businesses with no critical assembling limit.

A supply chain is the strategies by which an association trades its things from change to the business focus all together to offer them and deliverthe added value. It incorporates all the hierarchical, operational furthermore, esteem adding exercises expected to fabricate those items and get them to the final customer. In this way, for a pharma organization, it covers everything from new item improvement through to conveyance to the hospital, retail drug store or patient (Butler, 2002).

PHARMACEUTICAL SUPPLY CHAIN:BACKGROUND

The Pharmacy Supply and the Significant Choices of the Case Healing Center Drug Store

The hospital applies propelled innovation in controlling prescription all through itself. It is imperative to perceive that pharmaceutical stock administration is as yet an extremely work escalated process because of the quantity of nearby stops in the clinic that should be recharged, the vast volume of medications in every warehouse, and the drug store staff workload required amid the restocking procedure. The staff must be administered by much-aught drug specialists, a profitable and at times rare asset for the healing center. The interest for each medication is questionable and visit occasional changes happen. In the medication supply, a high administration level is basic (Pitta & Laric, 2004). If there should be an occurrence of a lack at a neighborhood, distribution center an emergency transport is fundamental and this crisis refill is exorbitant and can be hazardous for the patient's recuperating procedure, so for these medications a high administration level is significant. The figure shows this part of the pharmaceutical supply chain (see Figure 1).

One noteworthy objective of the healing center drug store is to limit the number of refills every day. In the event that the quantity of refills every day is very high, it is impossible in two movements. To have additional time or an additional move is troublesome and exorbitant. This shortsighted arrangement brings about incessant deficiencies and crisis refills for a few medications and furthermore countless refills putting an over-burden on the drug store staff. In view of encounters, the drug

Figure 1. Pharmaceutical supply chain
Source: (Pitta & Laric, 2004)

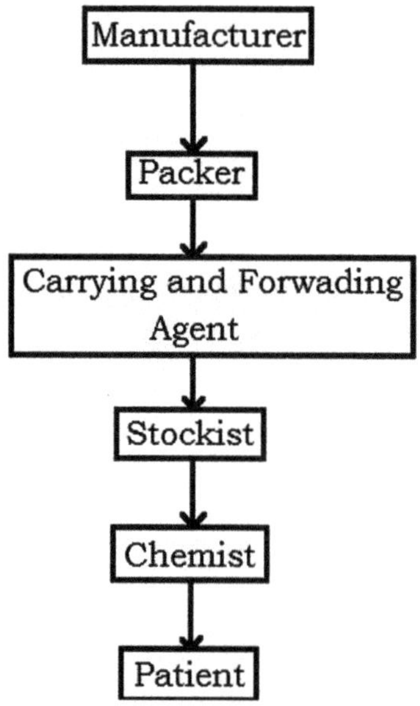

Table 1. Chosen characteristics of the pharmaceutical supply chain

S.No	Industry Characteristics	Implications
1	Low likelihood of progress amid item improvement	Contribute vast capital at high hazard
2	Control binds showcase access to process approval	production network configuration finished a long time before dispatch
3	Until endorsement, you don't realize what you have	Need adaptable advantage for overseeing the portfolio
4	An excessive number of leaders included recommending a medication	Interest for a medication or treatment depends on specialist's inclination, wellbeing design, and accessibility in addition to other things
5	Enrollment binds sourcing choice to showcase get to	Restricted, moderate, and expensive sourcing changes
6	Cost of stock versus estimation of a deal	Client benefit - need, Stock control – optional

Source: (Pitta & Laric, 2004)

specialists are as often as possible changing the settled day supply strategy. The essential, some of the time clashing, operational objectives of the doctor's facility are to (a) decrease workloads (crisis furthermore, every day refills) and refilling costs at the nearby stockpiling stations, (b) lessen holding expenses, and (c) help in a drug store choice emotionally supportive network to investigate the impact of upper-level choices on the operational expenses. Table 1 shows diverse characteristics of the pharmaceutical supply chain.

Segments of the Pharmaceutical Business Assembling and Dispersion Chain

A run of the mill pharmaceutical production network will comprise of the at least one of the accompanying hubs:

- Essential assembling (perhaps including contractual worker locales),
- Auxiliary assembling (potentially including contractual worker locales),
- Showcase stockrooms/circulation focuses,
- Wholesalers,
- Retailers/hospitals.

Essential Assembling

The essential assembling site is in charge of the generation of the dynamic fixing. This regularly includes either a few compound amalgamation and partition stages to develop the unpredictable atoms included, or maturation and item recuperation and cleansing for the situation of biochemical procedures. The assembling procedure is described by long assignment handling times, frequently adjusted to products of movements. Where multistage forms are worked, extensive inventories are regularly held between stages. Besides, material from a moderate stage should regularly pass some type of value control check before being endorsed for utilizing downstream in the process. This can bring extra deferrals into the framework (Moser et al., 2000).

The customary procedure innovation includes group hardware and adaptable pipework. The generally low creation volumes result in multipurpose plants to spread the capital cost between items. The need to maintain a strategic distance from cross-defilement of items and necessities for approved cleaning and changeovers brings about long downtimes between products. Since most complex pharmaceuticals are delivered through multistage forms, the same frequently remains constant for the steady intermediates. Naturally, this method of operation does not loan itself well to responsiveness, and contributes altogether to a few of the poor store network measurements showed by this industry.

Secondary Industrialized

This is worried about taking the dynamic fixing delivered at the essential site and including "excipient" idle materials alongside additionally preparing and bundling to deliver the last items. The auxiliary assembling areas are frequently geologically isolated from the essential assembling areas. This is as often as possible the result of assessment and exchange value enhancement inside the undertaking. There are regularly numerous more auxiliary assembling destinations than essential ones, serving nearby or provincial markets.

The Outfitted Concern in the Pharmaceutical Supply Chain

All real pharmaceutical organizations take after a business procedure along the accompanying lines:

- **Request Administration:** In each geological area, forward figures are produced, based on authentic information, showcase knowledge, and so forth. Tenders for fabricating may likewise be assessed and perhaps acknowledged at this stage,
- **Inventory Administration and Conveyance Prerequisites Arranging:** The requests decided are accumulated and forced on the suitable stockroom/ dispersion focus. The effect on completed merchandise stock is evaluated, and if vital, orders are put on upstream optional fabricating locales.
- **Secondary Generation Arranging and Booking:** The requests put on the auxiliary destinations are arranged and after that booked in detail. The effect of creation designs on dynamic fixing crude material stocks is assessed and on the off chance that fundamental, orders for AI are set on the upstream.
- **Primary Assembling Effort:** Is arranging as is the AI stock administration. Here, the requests put by auxiliary fabricating are fulfilled via cautious administration of stock also, creation arranging.

Another element of this procedure is a result of its vast scale and topographical traverse. This is the dispersed idea of basic leadership, which can prompt strains and imperfect choices. Diverse hubs are not by any means mindful of upstream hubs' asset imperatives, and requests might be dispatched all together of receipt, as opposed to on a financial premise. Obviously, brought together arranging would not be without its troubles in this unique situation.

For the most part, the accompanying supply chain execution measures are average of the business

- The stock levels in the entire chain regularly sum to 30– 90% of the yearly requests in amount; also, there are normally 4–24 weeks of completed products.
- Stock turns (characterized as yearly deals/normal stock) are normally near one and eight.
- Supply chain process durations (characterized as slipped by the time between material entering as crude material and leaving as an item- finished product) are frequently approximately 1000 and 8000 hours.
- The esteem included (the time when something happens to a material as a level of chain process duration) is of request 0.3– 5%.
- Material usage efficiency (the measures for an item created per unit measure of aggregate materials utilized) is 1– 10%.

Vital and Configuration Issues in the Pharmaceutical Supply Chain

The choices to be taken at this level incorporate:

- **Pipeline and Improvement Administration:** This includes the determination of potential medications to grow further, and the arranging of the improvement action,
- **Process Improvement:** The examination of assembling courses and the era of assembling forms,
- Capacity arranging and plant and organizing the store network plan,
- **Plant Outline:** The choosing and estimating of the real hardware and stockpiling units,
- Vulnerability in the requests for existing medications,
- **Uncertainty in the Pipeline of New Medications:** Specifically, which ones will be effective in trials, what kind of dose furthermore, treatment administration will be ideal,
- **Process Improvement:** This is an overwhelming issue, driven by science and yield improvement. It frequently brings about wasteful procedures that are worked significantly more gradually than the inborn rates, offering ascend to bunch forms and long process durations in charge of a portion of the issues seen at the essential generation arranging stage,
- **Capacity Arranging:** The long lead times to make limit powerful imply that choices frequently should be taken at times of high vulnerability. Sitting tight for the vulnerabilities to be settled may defer an opportunity to advertise by an unsuitable sum,

- **Network Configuration:** Regularly charge suggestions outweigh everything else over co ordinations issues, these outcomes in financial however possibly confused supply chains,
- **Plant Outline:** This tends to be exceptionally conventional, with no genuine change in assembling innovation for a long time (the workhorse of the essential assembling site is the glass-lined stainless steel group reactor). There are noteworthy open doors for escalated, constant handling. The figure shows composites of the pharmaceutical supply chain (see Figure 2).

SUPPLY CHAIN CHALLENGES

There are a number of difficulties influencing the general execution of supply chains. In view of their reactions, four issues occur.

Quality and Administrative Issues

Quality keeps on being a hotly debated issue in the pharmaceutical industry, with more noteworthy examination originating from global administrative agencies.

Figure 2. Composites of the pharma supply chain
Source: (own elaboration)

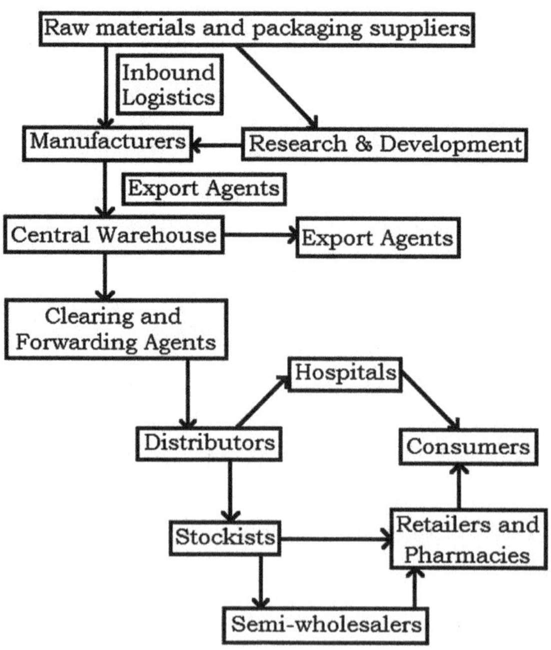

Plant shutdowns, import bans on particular items, and basic perceptions over the esteem chain have put a focus on trades, which is influencing organizations' income and credibility (Breiger et al., 2004). Quality issues have extended and broadened after some time and are not confined to the creation floor. Indeed, more issues are happening over the esteem chain:

- **Acquisition:** Issues with the nature of crude materials have spiraled in the course of recent years, prompting group disappointments, creation postponements, and absence of accessibility of assets over the plant.
- **Assembling:** Plant shutdowns and powerlessness to be ensured by worldwide administrative organizations have made noteworthy unused limit over the system.
- **Coordination:** Post-advertise issues, for example, protests, rejects, and item disappointments are directly affecting capacity, dealing with, and cost to dispose of rejected items.
- **Research and Development:** Particularly for trade items, the absence of value control in R&D has prompted more disappointments of trial clusters, causing delays in item dispatches.

Product Multiplication

New item improvement, new measurements frames, upgraded plans, and changes in bundling and naming to take into account new markets are growing the item portfolio. This has a few ramifications for the store network, including higher assembling and conveyance costs, stock, and a more significant provider base. A few fundamental elements add to this

1. Changing shoppers' socioeconomics. Non-transferable illnesses, for example, diabetes, cardiovascular malady, growth, and endless agony are on the ascent in India and are quickly pushing toward the early-age beginning. Studies show the pinnacle event could be 10 years sooner than in Western nations. Top pharma players are incorporating new atoms in their portfolios to oblige these rising remedial fragments. This could call for more plants, additionally fabricating lines, and innovations to help creation, along these lines adding critical multifaceted nature to the current production network organizing.
2. Expanded rivalry. Different items are available with fundamentally the same as determinations, bio equality, and value focuses, advertised by both Indian and multinational firms. This fills the need to ceaselessly improve and decrease the expenses of existing medications to stay aggressive. Process upgrades are a substantial piece of a pharma organization's pipeline. Truth be told, our

investigation shows 10 to 12 percent of limit is utilized as a part of unsuccessful trial groups, influencing the creation office's general utilize and assembling adaptability.

3. Fluctuating administrative necessities crosswise over fare markets. As organizations venture into new markets, directions shift crosswise over districts. The correlated wellbeing experts represent particular prerequisites and rules for naming and bundling. Item particulars should be altered, and names should be printed by rules, which expands the quantity of generation keeps running for a similar item, includes strain naming and bundling, and builds the quantity of stock-keeping units (SKUs).

SUPPLY CHAIN FRAGMENTATION

The pharmaceutical esteem chain is extremely intricate and in a few sections even stances worries about item quality and wellbeing, causing numerous repercussions.

A Huge Number of Merchants

In the following five years, a pharma organization' dynamic supply base will twofold because of an expansion in fares and development of intermediates, excipients, and other crude materials. With organizations investigating new blend courses and new advances, crude material prerequisites are much more mind-boggling, and their accessibility is scattered. Different merchants with fluctuating prerequisites, the absence of clear order, the absence of vicinity to the producer, and varying degrees of value principles are clear difficulties. Subsequently, creation plan changes are getting to be plainly normal in view of poor provider benefit levels, additionally influencing the capacity of the store network to set aside a few minutes (Kim, 2005).

Various Assembling Offices

Vast organizations have somewhere in the range of 8 to 10 producing plants with particular capacities at separate areas. This has brought about complex multi-layer systems and material development that influences stock levels, as well as builds general production network costs.

Decentralized R&D Focuses

Organizations utilize numerous in-house focuses or outsider focuses at various phases of medical advancement. This makes many-sided quality in innovation exchange, stretching timetables for administrative endorsement and affecting the first-to-record framework. Likewise, there is a danger of business clump disappointment, which expands costs and lessens plant use.

Mind-Boggling and Unequipped Appropriation Arrange

Most outsider cool chain coordination suppliers do not have a satisfactory limit and temperature control frameworks to help the present medication stockpiling and taking care of necessities. In addition, pharma organizations lose control over the inventory network beyond the merchant. Organizations manage a great many merchants, which makes an absence of perceiving and problematic estimating and results in imperfect stock and poor administration levels.

SUPPLY CHAIN STRUCTURE

An extraordinary component of the pharmaceutical business is that it works two extremely diverse sorts of supply chains consistently. One supply chain underpins the medication improvement stage and the other one to offer a fruitful medication in the market. Clearly, the goals and imperatives dynamic in these two stages are extremely distinctive requiring altogether different sorts of production network abilities (Fein, 2003). While one supply chain is centeredon encouraging a brisk fulfillment of the clinical trials to get a brisk endorsement, the point of the other store network is to meet deals targets. Subsequently, the drivers inspiring the production network configuration are speed and high accessibility individually. Critical contemplations in the two cases incorporate safe authority and unique dealing with prerequisites. An essential assessment will, in any case, uncover that, as a rule, the pharmaceutical business lays little accentuation on its inventory network operational effectiveness (Woosley, 2009).

The Trial Supply Chain

The complexities in this stage emerge because of the trouble in anticipating the requirements of a trial prescription at various little destinations. Moreover, it is tough to know ahead of time if a site will be an overwhelming or a light patient enrollment. Since the trial meds are created in little groups, coordinating interest and supply is vital to guarantee accessibility as per quiet needs, which change at short notice. Given the laser-like concentrating of the trial on medicate endorsement, inventory network responsiveness is essential; buffering vulnerability with stock is not a reasonable alternative because of the time span of usability impediments and cost concerns. In this manner, the way to accomplishment in this stage is dexterity and availability to react to any possibility.

The Pharmaceutical Supply Chain

After a medication is propelled, a unique arrangement of targets, drivers, and requirements wind up plainly prevailing. Presently, the concentration shifts from nimbleness to high accessibility. Thus, there is a sensational move in the models and systems utilized to help this period of medication life cycle. In this stage, the multifaceted nature of the pharmaceutical production network comes about because of the inclusion of various huge autonomous associations of extremely assorted nature. The key partners in this inventory network incorporate various government offices, hospitals and centers, medicate makers, tranquilize merchants, drug store chains, and retailers, examine associations, and the FDA. To compound issues further, a similar production network is in charge of the dispersion of physician-recommended drugs, over-the-counter solutions, generics, and biologics having extraordinary taking care of requirements and operational goals (Gautrin, 2002).

Because of altogether different business targets, these associations influence the undertaking of overseeing supply to chain all the more troublesome. Besides, because of the central idea of the business and various merger and acquisitions to secure more R&D mastery, numerous pharmaceutical supply systems have developed in an uncontrolled manner as opposed to being made arrangements for ideal execution.

Most Recent Trends and Drivers

It is critical to recognize the pervasive patterns and critical drivers to acquire a better comprehension of the pharmaceutical store network structure. These powers handle the fundamental progression that characterize the connections between different store network constituents (Cachon & Lariviere, 2005).

Industry Issues

The pharmaceutical business is loaded with essential issues, which hinders its fast change. Because of its impossible to miss condition, these issues debilitating affect each part of the business, particularly the supply chain operations. So also, the issue of medication deficiencies is additionally on the ascent. This is an astonishing incline given the extremely sharp concentrate of the business on fill rates; an expressed target of the pharmaceutical business is to keep up high administration levels. However, in spite of industry's best exertion, comes about are bad (it is essential to review here that the present stock levels in store network are at an unsurpassed high).

REVERSE LOGISTICS

Overseeing item returns in the pharmaceutical business is substantially more than a primary coordination challenge. Because of the touchy idea of medications and their potential well-being and financial ramifications, administration of returned merchandise is a genuine business with legal consequences. Give us now a chance to investigate the two principle reasons for item return, to be specific medication review and medication lapse (Witmer & Deffenbaugh, 2004).

Drug Recall

Drugs can be reviewed either because of an impermanent issue with the item or a permanent expulsion of the medication from the market because of medication wellbeing related issues. In either case, tranquilize review is a unique occasion that makes various issues, not the minimum of which is the discolored notoriety of the organization. From operations outlook to it represents a huge test regarding coordinating the expulsion of each unsold thing from each point in the store network. Therefore, there are sudden moves in the volume of reviewed medicate in the system prompting limit issues - a lack coming about because of an impermanent review or an abundance because of a perpetual review - requiring prompt consideration.

Drug Lapse

It is typical to expect a little level of medications to remain unsold for quite a while and in the end lapse. An event that is exacerbated by the business-wide routine by conveying large amounts of completed products stock. Mostly, the terminated medications are expelled from the client areas and pulverized by authorized organizations. Much of the time, the maker will acknowledge the lapsed medication and discount a specific level of the cost back to the purchaser as well. It is critical for the medication producers to screen the amount and example of medication lapse painstakingly. An examination of this information can be utilized to assess and tune existing stock arrangements and figures.

SUPPLY CHAIN ORGANIZATION

The supply chain work falls under the domain of the assembling division. The key assembling procedure and production network hierarchical zones are as per the following key manufacturing strategy, which was shown in the figure (see Figure 3).

Figure 3. Key manufacturing strategy and supply chain authoritative regions
Source: (own elaboration)

Crude material quality and accessibility huge affect the capacity of a pharmaceutical organization to make drugs for the market. The pharmaceutical organizations, nonetheless, are interestingly restricted in their capacity to control these variables. As a rule, there is just a modest bunch of providers of basic crude materials and producers are the benevolence of their capacity to look after supply. A demonstration of nature or an administrative worry at a solitary plant can disable the supply of the crude material to the entire world for a long term (Wellman, 2001).

The pharmaceutical organizations react to this circumstance by keeping up huge supplies of such crude materials consistently. Since the cost of crude material is unimportantly contrasted with the open door cost of a lost deal, it is prudent for the pharmaceutical organizations to hold this arrangement. In addition, as portrayed prior, the pharmaceutical inventory network has long lead times, in this manner, in case of a crude material supply issue, the organization can realign its assets to exploit the time support and make vital alterations. Because of this particular circumstance, the part of crude material acquirement is direct when contrasted with different ventures. The provider base is regularly little and acquiring choices are straightforward.

SUPPLY CHAIN OPERATION

A review of the exercises attempted by the Purchasing and Operations gather is given underneath obtaining, additionally alluded to as Supply Chain Services Purchasing, is in charge of all key and operational exercises identified with acquiring including, merchant relationship administration, stock administration, returns administration, lapsed medication (funeral home) administration, and request preparing. For a medication wholesaler, a productive obtaining bunch is basic for different reasons, even more so in expansion based model. Of course, the obtaining part is experiencing a huge change because of the end of the expansion-based model. Presently, the concentration has moved from looking for purchasing chances to enhancing figure exactness and getting better rebates, where conceivable. Common obligations incorporate assignments, for example, accepting, arranging, putting away, pick, pack and sending (Miller, 2004).

Provider and Customer Management

Overseeing providers and clients is a testing recommendation in the marked medication fragment. Consider the provider side first. It is hard to deal with a provider since the provider has all the power and there is little that a wholesaler can do to affect this uneven relationship. In the meantime, it is less demanding to arrange, if the wholesaler has great clients, for example, huge healing facilities and government accounts. Given the idea of the business, it is imperative for the provider to work with the merchant to achieve patients at the earliest opportunity, particularly if the medication is not a first in class sedate. Likewise, at the appropriate time of time, the wholesalers end up plainly more grounded as they convey 30-35% of producers' aggregate deals, tilting the adjust to support them. The flow is altogether different for generics and OTC medications. The issues are extremely interesting on the client side too. In larger part of the cases, the clients have a tendency to be substantial and effective associations that request abnormal state of administration.

SUPPLY CHAIN PLANNING

Infrastructure Gaps

The pharmaceutical company faces many holes in its supply foundation, incorporating into transportation, stockpiling, and power supply. In transportation, fewer than 5 percent of streets are national thruways, and they handle more than 33% of the movement. The rail organize is correspondingly deficient, and the air arranges in underutilized. As far as capacity, the absence of a vigorous icy anchor system to help the inventory network speaks to a critical role in the present pharma framework. Medications have fluctuating capacity necessities to guarantee that strength is kept up all through their time span of usability. Moving claim to fame items and antibodies requires persistent checking at all stages of the esteem chain, yet with the present foundation, organizations are yet unfit to guarantee an item is put away at the required conditions all through its progress.

Lessen End-To-End Multifaceted Nature

Our examination demonstrates that overseeing intricacy is on the highest point of industry pioneers' plans. Nevertheless, most organizations presently cannot seem to dispatch organized endeavors.

First, pharmaceutical organizations must concentrate on combining and upgrading the system overall, likewise considering situations rising up out of the conceivable GST administration. The production network-working model should bolster consistent correspondence crosswise over providers, makers, wholesalers, and clients. Redundancies ought to be evacuated to enhance store network proficiency and discharge "sunk" limit. Combine abilities to adjust advantages for capacities and systems, prompting top-line change. For instance, Indian pharmaceutical organization Thus, it now has a decent grasp on multifaceted nature to help accomplish its coveted benefit and operational productivity levels.

Second, organizations require a customized perspective of their supply chains. As they wander into more specific items, division in light of buyers' needs, item sorts, item qualities, and markets will be critical to enhancing effectiveness. The industry has still not viably portioned the inventory network, which influences arrange execution and prompts decreased administration levels, more prominent strain on creation, and high production network costs. FMCG organizations, nevertheless, have rushed to receive division and have caught noteworthy esteem. For instance, a vast customer innovative gadgets maker in Asia with worldwide operations was adjusted topographically to its local markets. Once the distinctions in buyer desires and production network development wound up noticeably clear, the firm embraced two parallel store network portions. A productivity situated form to-stock model and administration level-arranged form to-request show were utilized to make premium portions. After division, year-on-year development expanded by around 14 percent (three-year CAGR). The figure shows a diminishing supply chain displaying (See Figure 4).

Third, the portfolio's many-sided quality ought to be taken care of both upstream (R&D portfolio multiplication) and downstream (item SKU expansion). There is an expanding pattern to designate more finances to R&D. Driving organizations are constantly justifying their R&D portfolio to line up with the general business methodology and streamline their R&D pipeline. Taking a gander at business SKUs, singular pharma locales produce 1,000 to 3,000 SKUs every month, taking into account numerous topographies. This can be decreased by enhancing limit and assets upstream and by murdering failing to meet expectations product offerings

Figure 4. Diminishing supply chain showcasing
Source: (own elaboration)

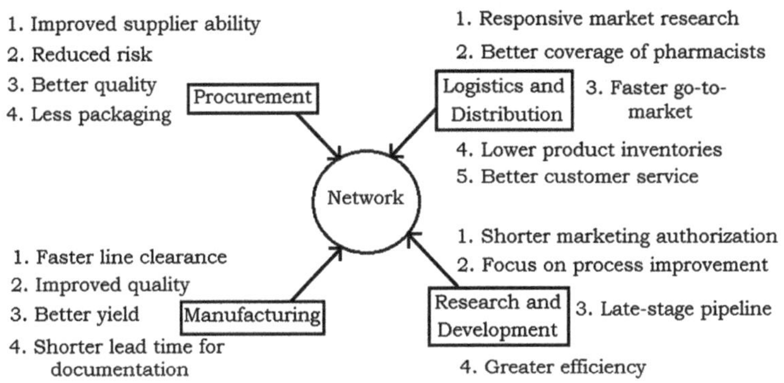

and SKUs. Subsequently, organizations can expect a prompt effect on the general adaptability of downstream procedures with a critical decrease in store network costs.

Make Nimbleness and Tracking in the Supply Chain

Notwithstanding market progression, for example, changing patient needs and moving ailment designs, the worldwide market is encountering huge medication deficiencies and more continuous flare-ups of transferable infections. To respond to these market changes and accomplish best-in-class execution levels, organizations require a store network-working model that is incorporated with their S&OP forms and their business methodologies.

New Advancement Advances

Formulations Those Are Simpler to Produce

Packed tablets containing a blend of dynamic fixings and excipients are yet the most widely recognized measurement shape. In any case, more refined medication conveyance procedures will furnish the methods with which to make definitions that are less demanding to fabricate – e.g., powder in vials and fluid beads on clear tablets. Specialists are additionally chipping away at the 'sacred chalice' of oral biologics, and industry specialists trust it will, in the end, be conceivable to create stable, pill-based forms of a few proteins. Utilizing plans that can be more effortlessly made will empower pharma sector to limit its interest in item and process improvement until the later stages of the item improvement lifecycle, when it is less demanding to appraise the potential estimation of new items. In addition, the improvement of oral biologics will dispose of the requirement for cold chain dispersion of such treatments (Yang & Chen, 2010).

Virtual Process Outline and Approval

In the interim, computational demonstrating will empower pharma sector to plan and approve fabricating forms for all intents and purposes, utilizing Quality by Design (QbD) standards. In-line process observing through process scientific advances (PAT) will create the information expected to approve these models and secure administrative endorsement. The FDA has effectively distributed a draft direction in which it proposes supplanting 'three-clump approval' with a three-arrange philosophy that includes planning a reasonable process, utilizing the information picked up being developed and scale-up; guaranteeing the procedure is able to do reproducibly fabricating business bunches; and approving it constantly amid routine generation. The traditional procedure of scaling up will additionally be supplanted by 'numbering up' – i.e., utilizing microreactors in parallel clusters. Numbering up has a few noteworthy focal points over customary procedures. It abstains from the requirement for exorbitant and tedious examinations to devise a procedure for scaling up synthetic responses, since the procedure that was utilized to deliver a couple grams of the item in the research center is the same one that is utilized to incorporate bigger amounts. Likewise, utilizing micro reactors makes it substantially simpler to control key parameters and in this manner enhance yields. The noteworthy open doors for enhancing the supply chain exist were shown in the figure (see Figure 5).

New Conveyance Advances

Similarly, as new advances are developing to help pharma organizations produce a more extensive and more perplexing scope of meds, so new advances are developing to enable them to convey those pharmaceuticals. Distributed computing will give the data stages they have to share information safely and financially with providers around the globe. They examine the information quickly and react to sudden changes in free market activity, as the industry makes more biologics with high unit esteems and authority conveyance requirements.

New Patient Interface Advances

New 'patient interface' innovations are similarly being produced, some of which will bring pharma organizations nearer to patients than at any other time. One case is the model chip and recipient formulated by Proteus Biomedical, which records precisely

Figure 5. Noteworthy open doors for enhancing the supply chain
Source: (own elaboration)

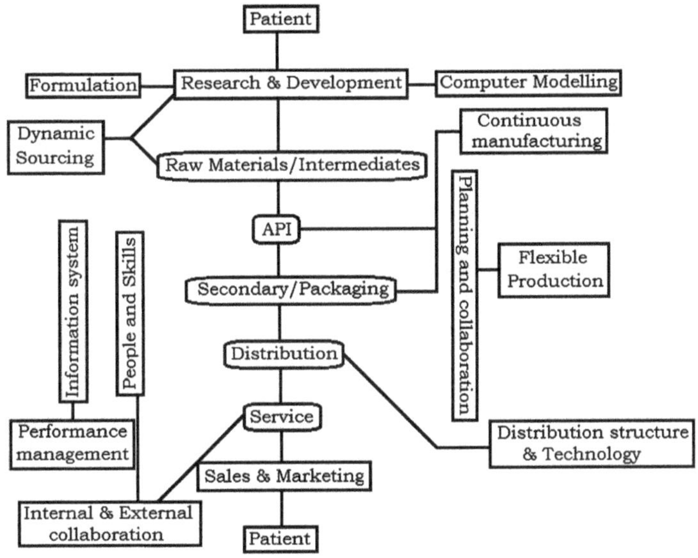

at the point when a tablet is used. There will be numerous such patient interface advancements available furthermore, the data they create will enable patients to deal with their wellbeing more viably, and additionally permitting human services suppliers to screen their consistence continuously. Nevertheless, they will likewise give pharma organizations with data they can utilize both to plan more hearty items and benefits, and to grow creation that is more exact and conveyance designs.

The Shifting Focus

Today, the effect of frameworks believing is unmistakable in each industry. Not to be cleared out behind, the pharmaceutical organizations to have been experiencing a progression of changes in the previous two decades to move far from the customary storehouse attitude. Organizations understand that colossal open doors exist to make noteworthy changes on the off chance that they think past enhancing a solitary capacity to incorporate all capacities in the esteem chain. Taking prompt from different ventures, pharmaceutical organizations have additionally begun regarding producing as a vital piece of association's plan of action.

Research and Development → Manufacturing → Sales and marketing

FUTURE PERSPECTIVES

The future difficulties around there are expensive and complex and will give fruitful ground to inquire about. They can be arranged under three headings:

- Upgrades to existing procedures;
- Upgrades to the vital basic leadership process and
- Future situations

Upgrades to Existing Procedures

The supply chain incorporates numerous operators, frequently with various goals. Their interior flow has a tendency to misrepresent the outside market elements and result in drawbacks in execution. This is a territory where community oriented estimating, arranging and stock administration will be extremely helpful. Here, the diverse operators in the inventory network will coordinate exercises over the chain. One of the principle explanations behind the present, more disseminated rehearse is the vast size of the operations, both as far as exercises and land traverse. Multisite arranging and booking apparatuses are required to help a communitarian arranging movement. The production network, for the most part, contains bigger measures of stock that may be essential if a more coordinated approach is taken after, with the correct supporting devices. Presumably, the most important metric to track and endeavour to enhance is that of the general inventory network process duration. As specified before, figures of 100– 300 days are a standard. The involvement in the business is that endeavours to decrease this are extremely compelling, yet they have been connected in a piecemeal manner to specific items, while the measure breaks down for others. A precise examination of the parts of the process duration ought to be attempted for an extensive variety of items. Plainly, expansive scale reproduction devices that assess both physical and business procedures would be valuable in this unique situation.

Upgrades to the Vital Basic Leadership Process

The present idea of the procedure innovation is one of the fundamental inventory network bottlenecks. There is a requirement for more dexterous gear, which will abbreviate process durations by a request of greatness and require insignificant time for cleaning and changeover. This will stay away from long crusades and should prompt "force"- based dynamic fixing producing, and hence more responsive supply chains. The necessary procedures should change too, with the emphasis being on planning forms that work at inherent rates (e.g. being restricted by response energy) as opposed to being constrained by hardware execution (e.g. warm exchange, mass exchange or blending attributes) of customary gear. On a basic level, the low tonnages included should prompt significantly less capital concentrated plants if this is accomplished. As a rule, huge upgrades to assembling innovation have not been of the most elevated need in this field to date. Procedures ought to be composed with a considerably more noteworthy level of unthinking understanding and controlled firmly if decreases in quality control exercises are to be conceivable. The effect of this has been exhibited before. The joining of advancement administration and limit and creation arranging will be imperative. As of now, limit issues regularly not considered at the improvement organization are:.

- Deficiencies of materials for pre-clinical investigations;
- Deficiencies of materials for clinical trials; and
- Delays to advertise—which is reliant on having material accessible, as well as on producing request at the late phases of improvement.

This is an extremely encouraging stage to treat the general pipeline/scope quantification issue, however it should be incorporated with an advanced treatment of hazard (e.g. using genuine alternatives hypothesis) and financial matters (e.g. assessing nearby tax assessment administrations, exchange estimating, obligation downsides, and so forth.) both of which have a huge effect on speculation choices. Besides, the demonstrating of testing and trials should be reached out to represent varieties in standard results, e.g. exceptionally fruitful trials bringing about short-circuiting of the endorsements procedure because of life-sparing medications. As a rule, the advancement of incorporated models of the life cycle, from disclosure through to utilization would significantly encourage vital basic leadership.

FUTURE SCENARIOS

Organizations have as of late moved far from item expansion and privately adjusted items. The basic bundling and naming norms in the European Union, for instance, have bolstered this. In any case, there has been much improvement in the field of "pharmacy financial aspects" which may create weights to invert this pattern. This settles on decisions in treatment choices by thought of expenses and results (clinical, monetary and humanistic). An imperative result of this kind of examination will be the emphasis on neighbourhood answers for nearby issues.

Another pattern, to some degree sometime later, will leave hereditary research and which will recognize target sub-populaces for various treatment administrations (the supposed "originator drugs"). These two drivers will offer ascent to extensive item and production network many-sided quality. The present assembling procedures and supply chains are not very much arranged to adapt to this. Essential assembling has a tendency to work in crusades; and auxiliary assembling cluster sizes are regularly 1– 4 million tablets. Plainly, the assembling procedures and supply chains should be re-planned if item customisation is to increment in accordance with these patterns. The producers should track store network execution measures precisely to comprehend the cost-to-serve for a varied client base. A growing region is that of quick reaction antibodies and different medications emerging out of conceivable crises (e.g. bioterrorism or quick creating plagues). Again, the customary inventory network (especially for immunizations) is moderate and lethargic. On the off chance that national governments are to actualize crisis readiness programs, the whole framework must be all around planned and tried through re-enactment. Choices, for example, where to make, in what amounts, where to hold stocks, where individuals should report, and so forth should be taken in a strong manner.

Organizations are putting resources into the improvement of yields that are outlined somehow to deliver pharmaceuticals; this will offer ascent to new research exercises in process (specifically recuperation steps) advancement, novel gear plan (e.g. supercritical divisions) and obviously in another kind of inventory network to streamline. There are additionally a few changes in progress in the business structure too—the development in therapeutic science, biotechnology and genomics will spread IP around and result in looser, virtual endeavours of joint endeavours, organizations together, and so forth. Counting to the general inclination towards outsourcing of assembling, this will offer ascent to complex expanded production network co-appointment. Lessons might be learnt from the car, PC and purchaser gadgets industries, where such supply chains as of now work.

CONCLUSION

The production of an incorporated, worldwide store network activity is no simple undertaking. There are numerous basic advances important to guarantee a deft, responsive, also, streamlined store network, and the examination challenges include different multilevel angles, for example, multiscale, multiactor, multilevel vulnerability, and multiobjective enhancement. This ought to enable the pharmaceutical business to make supply chains for various sorts of items and markets, to oversee sudden inversions of interest, and also, to diminish producing costs. The digitalization of medicinal services conveyance, with more prominent utilization of electronic wellbeing records, e-recommending and remote observing, will add to make a more ramified store network, with the dispersion of numerous more items to numerous more areas. The developing significance of the developing markets will likewise highlight these difficulties.

REFERENCES

Ballance, R., Pogany, J., & Forstner, H. (1992). *The world's pharmaceutical industries*. London, UK: Edward Elgar.

Booth, R. (1999). *The global supply chain. FT healthcare management report*. London: Financial Times Business Ltd.

Breiger, W. R., Osamor, P. E., Salami, K. K., Oladepo, O., & Otusanya, S. A. (2004). Interactions between patent medicine vendors and customers in urban and rural Nigeria. *Health Policy and Planning*, *19*(3), 177–182. doi:10.1093/heapol/czh021 PMID:15070866

Burns, L. (2002). Wharton school colleagues. In *The Health Care Value Chain Producers, Purchasers, and Providers*. San Francisco, CA: Jossey-Bass.

Butler, R. (2002). The end of the blockbuster. *Chemistry & Industry*, *9*, 9–10.

Cachon, G. P., & Lariviere, M. A. (2005). Supply Chain Coordination with Revenue-Sharing Contracts: Strengths and Limitations. *Management Science*, *51*(1), 30–44. doi:10.1287/mnsc.1040.0215

Fein, A. J. (2003). *Strategies for the unbundled supply chain*. Distributor's Link. Spring.

Gautrin, P. (2002). Challenges facing a pharmaceutical supply chain. *Logistics Quarterly, 8*.

Jarrett, P. (1998). Logistics in the health care industry. *International Journal of Physical Distribution & Logistics Management*, *28*(9/10), 741–742. doi:10.1108/09600039810248154

Kim, D. (2005). An integrated supply chain management system: A case study in healthcare sector. *Lecture Notes in Computer Science*, *3590*, 218–227. doi:10.1007/11545163_22

Miller, J. (2004), New Supply-Chain Dynamics Create a Distribution Services Sector. *Pharmaceutical Technology*.

Moser, M., Calderari, G., & Morini, P. (2000). Cleaning validation of a multipurpose plant for active pharmaceutical ingredient bulk production. *Chimia*, *54*, 731–733.

Pitta, D. A., & Laric, M. V. (2004). Value chains in health care. *Journal of Consumer Marketing*, *21*(7), 451–464. doi:10.1108/07363760410568671

Wellman, G.S. (2001) National supply-chain survey of drug manufacturer back orders. *American Journal of Health-Systems Pharmacy, 61*.

Witmer, D., & Deffenbaugh, J. (2004) The pharmaceutical supply chain: A perfect storm is brewing. *American Journal of Health-Systems Pharmacy, 61*.

Woosley, J. (2009). *Improving Healthcare Supply Chains and Decision Making in the Management of Pharmaceuticals* (Unpublished doctoral dissertation). Louisiana State University, Baton Rouge, LA.

Yang, F., Chen, P., He, W., Gu, N., Zhang, X., Fang, K., ... Tong, J. (2010). Bubble Microreactors Triggered by an Alternating Magnetic Field as Diagnostic and Therapeutic Delivery Devices. *Small*, *6*(12), 1300–1305. doi:10.1002mll.201000173 PMID:20486225

ADDITIONAL READING

Barbosa-Povoa, A. P. (2012). Progresses and challenges in process industry supply chains optimization. *Current Opinion in Chemical Engineering*, *1*(4), 446–452. doi:10.1016/j.coche.2012.09.006

Hansen, K. R. N., & Grunow, M. (2015). Planning operations before market launch for balancing time-to-market and risks in pharmaceutical supply chains. *International Journal of Production Economics*, *161*, 129–139. doi:10.1016/j.ijpe.2014.10.010

Papageorgiou, L. G., Rotstein, G. E., & Shah, N. (2001). Strategic supply chain optimization for the pharmaceutical industries. *Industrial & Engineering Chemistry Research*, *40*(1), 275–286. doi:10.1021/ie990870t

Perez-Escobedo, J. L., Azzaro-Pantel, C., & Pibouleau, L. (2011). New product development with discrete event simulation: Application to portfolio management for the pharmaceutical industry. *Industrial & Engineering Chemistry*, *50*(18), 10615–10629. doi:10.1021/ie200406s

Settanni, E., Harrington, T. S., & Srai, J. S. (2017). Pharmaceutical supply chain models: A synthesis from a systems view of operations research. *Operations Research Perspectives*, *4*, 74–95. doi:10.1016/j.orp.2017.05.002

Sundaramoorthy, A., & Karimi, A. (2008). Planning in pharmaceutical supply chain with outsourcing and new product introductions. *Industrial & Engineering Chemistry*, *43*(26), 8293–8306. doi:10.1021/ie0498571

Susarla, N., & Karimi, I. A. (2018). Chapter 22 - Integrated production planning and inventory management in a multinational pharmaceutical supply chain. *Computer-Aided Chemical Engineering*, *41*, 551–567. doi:10.1016/B978-0-444-63963-9.00022-1

Zhao, H., Xiong, C., Gavirneni, S., & Fein, A. (2012). Fee-for-service contracts in pharmaceutical distribution supply chains: Design, analysis, and management. *Manufacturing & Service Operations Management: M & SOM*, *14*(4), 685–699. doi:10.1287/msom.1120.0403

KEY TERMS AND DEFINITIONS

Drug Recall: A medication review happens when a remedy or over-the-counter solution is expelled from the market since it is observed to be either deficient or conceivably unsafe.

Inbound Logistics: Inbound logistics is a fundamental component of business tasks for an assembling firm, including the procedures of getting, putting away, and appropriating crude materials for use underway.

Supply Chain Management: It is the vital administration of exercises associated with the procurement and change of materials to completed items conveyed to the client.

Supply Chain Planning: Supply chain planning (SCP) is the forward-looking procedure of organizing resources for enhance the conveyance of merchandise, administrations, and data from provider to client, adjusting free market activity.

Chapter 9
Pharmaceutical and Life Sciences Supply Chain Management

Anbalagan Saravanan
Rajalakshmi Engineering College, India

ABSTRACT

The pharmaceutical industry quite broadly encompasses a large and varied number of logistics and supply chain activities. The industry, as a whole, relies on some standard benchmarking indicators such as months of on-hand inventory and inventory turns; however, the existing metrics do not allow for idiosyncrasies of the industry or provide adequately detailed insight into the key factors that make a pharmaceutical supply chain excellence. Over 75% of the markup on pharmaceutical products takes place at the manufacturer. This causes inventory-carrying costs to increase dramatically once the distribution segments of the supply chain purchase the product. Wholesalers and large pharmacy chains suffer high carrying costs on the final product. Inside pharmaceutical supply chains, companies must also face issues of product expiration and limited shelf lives. Seasonal and short shelf life products such as flu vaccines leave companies without the opportunity to redistribute or reallocate product in order to meet demand.

DOI: 10.4018/978-1-5225-5921-4.ch009

INTRODUCTION

The supply chain of the future will be built on the basis of flexibility, responsiveness and reliability shifting the supply paradigm from a stock-based model to an order-based model. It is imperative that organizations carefully balance operational and financial efficiencies when designing supply chains. Manufacturing operations continue to invest in new technologies targeting cost savings and flexibility, to address historically inefficient, low yield batch processes, with inconsistent quality outcomes. With the increase in biopharmaceutical research, the importance of climate controlled supply chains and faster response times will continue to increase. Inside pharmaceutical supply chains, companies must also face issues of product expiration and limited shelf lives. Seasonal and short shelf life products such as flu vaccines leave companies without the opportunity to redistribute or reallocate product in order to meet demand. In these instances the product placement must be accurate the first time; few second chances are available. With the increase in biopharmaceutical research, the importance of climate controlled supply chains and faster response times will continue to increase.

Supply Chain Management (SCM) has progressed toward becoming a key component of the present administration rehearses. Regularly, an inventory network comprises of various (creation) locales spread more than a few mainlands. Coordinating material streams among these locales is an extremely complex undertaking and for the most part, surpasses the "manual" limit of an individual (chief). Here, reasonable programming support is required, which is given by supposed Advanced Planning Systems (APS). A few exact investigations have been directed going for the disclosure of key achievement factors for a successful, prevalent store network. As one may expect, an extraordinary number of variables have been proposed and tried (Jayaram et al., 2004).There are diverse approaches to set up supply chains, each fit for accomplishing particular key and operational objectives of the organization. Update of associations and forms expands on key targets and on empowering data innovation. Execution Management needs to guarantee straightforwardness in operational control data, yet in addition, gives instruments and techniques to lead all workers to accomplish the vital objectives (Masteika & Cepinskis, 2015).

The endeavors of huge organizations and companies to outsource and globalize prompt a lasting change in calculated structures. Direct supplies anchors offer ascent to complex esteem chains with arranging attributes. Accomplices associated with the inventory network organize – providers, clients, and coordination specialist organizations – are incorporated more profoundly in the esteem including process. Alongside vertical coordination comes the accomplices' reliance upon each other. Unforeseeable bottlenecks in coordination methods – or even their entire disappointment – can notwithstanding bring the entire supply to fasten to its knees in outrageous cases. The results of such occasions are well known: Confirmed conveyance guarantees to clients either can't be kept or can just be kept at such a lopsidedly high cost, to the point that the initially proposed cost favorable position to be achieved from vertical combination rapidly turns into the correct insert. To limit the dangers of accessibility and disappointment alongside the subsequent danger of client disappointment, it is vital for coordination procedures to be guided productively. Or, on the other hand, to put it another way: Companies that globalize their business forms in entire or to some degree and at the same time outsource them to outside accomplices on the premise of out-entrusting models require to design all means steadily as well as additionally to screen their planned usage persistently. To deal with this, new strategies and apparatuses for Supply Chain Event Management (SCEM) can help to screen the advance of business procedures and report any deviations from plans in an auspicious form (Zahiri et al., 2017).

HISTORY OF SCM

Both modern building and operations explore their underlying foundations in coordination. While Industrial Engineering and Operations Research have each attempted to keep up particular personalities, huge numbers of their greatest triumphs have happened when utilized as a part of an incorporated system to address inventory network and coordination issues. Progressively this is alluded to by industry as "Inventory network Engineering." the concentrate of coordination look into was on the most proficient method to utilize motorization (e.g., beds and bed lifts) to enhance the very work escalated procedures of material dealing with and how to take better favourable position of room utilizing racking and better stockroom outline and design. The "unit stack" idea picked up prevalence and the utilization of beds ended up plainly far-reaching. In the mid-1950s, this idea was stretched out to transportation administration with the advancement of multi-purpose compartments together with boats, prepares, and trucks to deal with these holders (Rajeev et al., 2017).

This was essential for the production network globalization that was to come significantly later. Even though the expressions "warehousing" and "materials taking care of" were utilized to portray a significant number of these endeavours, this work could be seen as basic use of the mechanical building as opposed to as a teach of it claim. This developing relationship of store network administration with methodology is reflected in the Council of Logistics Management's changing its name to the Council of Supply Chain Management Professionals in 2005. They make the qualification that "Coordination is that piece of the production network process that designs, actualizes, and controls the proficient, compelling forward and turn around stream and capacity of merchandise, benefits, and related data between the purpose of beginning and the purpose of utilization so as to meet clients' prerequisites" while "Inventory network Management is the foundational, vital coordination of the customary business capacities and the strategies over these business capacities inside a specific organization and crosswise over organizations inside the store network for the motivations behind enhancing the long haul execution of the individual organizations and the production network in general."

The correspondence abilities have in a general sense changed the way we consider interchanges and data sharing. Notwithstanding, inventory network and coordination arranging are still basically in light of the conveyed models that came as the after-effect of PCs. There is no doubt that scholastic research can empower another age of inventory network and coordination arranging innovation in view of bringing together arranging with circulated joint effort. These innovation advances can give a colossal incentive in tending to conventional inventory network and coordination territories, for example, warehousing and circulation, transportation, and assembling coordination. Nevertheless, there are likewise numerous non-conventional ranges, for example, social insurance coordination and compassionate coordination that can get excellent incentive from expanding on the ideas and innovations that have effectively demonstrated fruitful in the customary store network and coordination zones. Finally, there are too great degree profitable experiences to be picked up by deliberately contemplating the store network and coordination execution of organizations over different ventures and nations (Zahiri et al., 2018).

CLASSES OF SUPPLY CHAINS

A supply chain is a magnificent device to break down, envision, and examine the structure of the store network, and to uncover redundancies and shortcomings. It empowers the definition of auxiliary changes and methodologies to enhance the execution of the production network as a whole. To have the capacity to distinguish the sort of choice issues confronting the store network, what's more, manage the determination of standard or specific modules, models and calculations for basic leadership. Two cases delineate the utilization of the typology so as to configuration arranging ideas fitting the specific necessities of these two sorts of supply chains. Most pharma companies have complex supply chains that are under-used, wasteful and poorly furnished to adapt to the kind of items descending the pipeline. This new report predicts that so as to meet the requests of a quick developing commercial centre and the move from patient to result, the pharma production network should experience a radical update (Stadtler et al., 2015). The figure shows that supply chain management technology (see Figure 1).

Figure 1. Supply chain management technology
Source: (own elaboration).

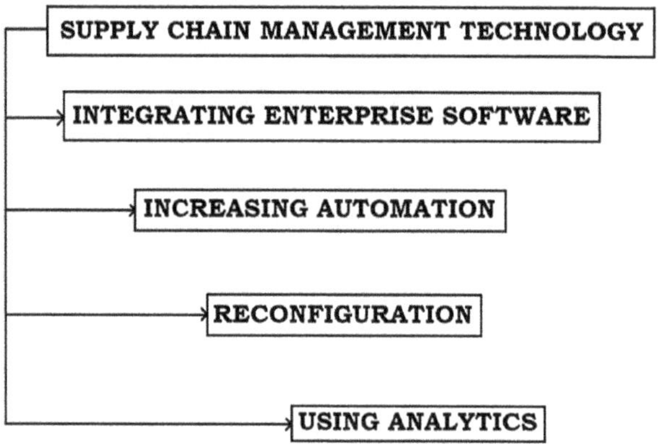

Inspiration and Basics

At the beginning of generation arranging and control a single idea and programming framework was connected in the industry — material necessities arranging (MRP) — regardless of the various necessities existing in different territories, for example, the generation of nourishments, pharmaceutical and automobiles. APS is considerably more flexible than MRP and ERP frameworks because of their displaying capacities and diverse arrangement strategies (notwithstanding for one module). Modules offered by a product seller may at present better fit one sort of store network than another. Characteristics may have ostensible properties (e.g. an item is storable or not), ordinal properties (e.g. an element's energy or, on the other hand, affect on fundamental leadership is respected higher or lower than standard) or cardinal properties (i.e. the trait can be tallied, similar to the quantity of lawfully isolated elements inside a production network) (Vonderembse et al., 2006).

Functional Attributes

The acquisition sort identifies with the number and kind of items to be acquired, the last one going from standard items to very particular items requiring extraordinary item know-how or generation process know-how (or gear). The accompanying quality portrays the sourcing sort, better known by its properties: single sourcing, twofold sourcing and various sourcing. Single sourcing exists if there is a one of a kind provider for a specific item to be acquired. In twofold sourcing there are two providers, each satisfying a bit of interest for the item to be obtained (e.g. 60% of the request is satisfied by the primary provider, 40% by the second provider). Many characteristics frame the generation sort. The two generally distinct properties are the association of the creation procedure and the reiteration of operations. Process association and streamlines speak to surely understood properties of the creation procedure. Process association requires that all assets prepared to do playing out an extraordinary undertaking be situated in a similar range. Usually, an item needs to go through a few shops to the point is done (Schneeweir, 2002).

The conveyance sort comprises the circulation structure, the example of conveyance, the organization of transportation means, and conceivable stacking limitations. The dissemination structure portrays the system of connections between the production line (distribution center) and the customer(s). A one-arrange conveyance structure exists if there are just immediate connections between a processing plant (stockroom) and its clients. On the off chance that the dispersion organizes has one middle layer (e.g. either central warehouses (CW) or, then again local stockrooms (RW)) a two-phase appropriation structure is given. A three organize appropriation structure fuses an extra layer (e.g. CW and RW). The example of conveyance is either cyclic or dynamic. In a cyclic example, merchandise is transported at settled interims of time (e.g. round-the-world ship takeoffs). A dynamic example is given if the conveyance is made relying upon request (for transportation). As respects, the arrangement of transportation implies one can recognize the organization of vehicles on courses (either standard courses or variable courses contingent upon request) and a given transportation limit on person interfaces in the conveyance arrange. It might even be conceivable to expect boundless transportation limits and to consider just a given cost work (e.g. because of an agreement with a huge outsider specialist organization). Stacking confinements (like the necessity of a full truck stack) may frame a further prerequisite.

The business kind of a substance in the inventory network to a great extent relies upon the connection to its clients. One outrageous might be a downstream substance in the inventory network (with some sort of "assertion" with respect to expected requests and an open data stream) while the other extraordinary might be an unadulterated market connection with numerous contenders (e.g. barters by means of Internet led by the acquiring branches of a substantial organization). This credit is firmly identified with the accessibility of future requests. These might be known (by contract) or must be estimated. The length of the estimate skyline best portrays the presence of (solid) request figures. Other than the general accessibility of interest data, the state of the request bend is of intrigue. Interest for a particular item may, for instance, be very static, sporadic, or, on the other hand regular. The run of the mill length and the present phase of an item's life cycle altogether impact proper promoting, generation arranging and budgetary techniques. As respects the items to be sold one should separate the number of item sorts offered and the level of customization (Silver et al., 1998).

Structural Attributes

Auxiliary qualities of a store network are assembled into the two classifications

- Topography of a store network
- Integration and coordination.

As respects, the geography of a store network the quality system structure depicts the material streams from upstream to downstream elements which are serial, concurrent, unique, or a blend of the three. Note that the system structure frequently matches with the BOM. The level of globalization ranges from supply chains working in a single nation to those with elements in a few countries. Worldwide supply ties not just need to consider duties and hindrances to exchange and trade rates differing after some time, yet additionally can benefit from them. Likewise, the area of the decoupling point(s) inside the store network has to be specified. Reconciliation and coordination concern the properties lawful position, adjust of energy, the course of coordination and kind of data traded. The legitimate position of substances has just been said. On the off chance that elements are legitimately isolated, a between authoritative inventory network exists, else it is called intra-organizational. For intra-authoritative supply chains, it will be considerably less demanding to arrange streams halfway than for between hierarchical supply chains. Likewise, the parity of energy inside a between authoritative store network assumes an imperative part for basic leadership. An overwhelming part in the store network can go about as a central firm. Then again, we have a production network of equivalents, named a polycentric supply chain (Dyckhoff & Finke, 1992).

SCM IN THE PHARMACEUTICAL SECTOR

Notwithstanding the regular store network outline choices; this model tends to the determination of future items from a pool of potential items and the time when they ought to be propelled. A few scientists have exhibited that the total pharmaceutical inventory network with essential and auxiliary generation. The figure shows that supply chain quality management system (see Figure 2). Supply chain management consolidates the ongoing displaying of applicable business forms with early cautioning frameworks. This implies SCM endeavours to enable the arrangements of interior and outside procedures to run much smoother all through the inventory network. Before concentrating on setting up individual SCM instruments for use in the pharmaceutical production network, we should investigate the store network overall and the potential for upgrading it. The concept of the supply chain in pharmaceutical sector was

Figure 2. Supply chain quality management system
Source: (own elaboration)

shown in the next figure (see Figure 3). The supply chains in the pharmaceutical business are regularly exceptionally coordinated and are described by long preparing circumstances (Marucheck et al., 2011).

Pharmaceutical production has been tormented for an extremely long time by an established creation process. This offer ascends to various shortcomings: the extension of creation limits was scarcely every conceivable in under four to five years (for instance multiplying the whole generation limit with respect to an item),

Figure 3. Supply chain management in the pharmaceutical sector
Source: (own elaboration)

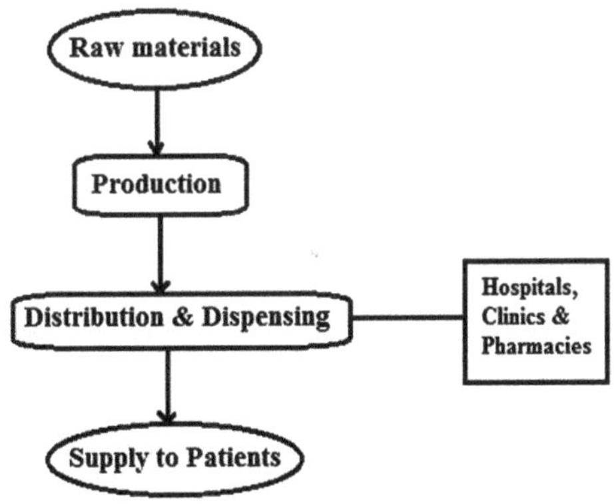

- Because of long handling circumstances and the challenges associated with limit adjustment, a limit cradle of at any rate half of the yearly necessities was presented between compound generation furthermore, pharmaceutical definition,
- The whole procedure of synthetic and pharmaceutical creation is generally massively mind-boggling, whereby the finished result of the substance/ microbiological union, for instance, was likewise dynamic element for a medication and the beginning material for assist compound/microbiological amalgamation,
- Dissemination happened regularly still happens by means of a multi-arrange retail course and was frequently joined with between time stockpiles that were not facilitated with each other.

The cost weight that has developed in light of statistic change on the one hand and because of advancing globalization on the other, has caused extensive changes in the zone of the creation of dynamic fixings. Pharmaceutical creation and conveyance are yet experiencing a procedure of change. Pharmaceutical creation, bundling and conveyance have progressed toward becoming locally unique ideas that should be acknowledged in a worldwide general methodology. In any case, when taken overall, clearly the cost weight in the pharmaceutical industry, similarly as in numerous other mechanical divisions, is causing thoughtfulness regarding be progressively centered on the administration of the production network.

Five supply chain capacities that triumphant pharmaceuticals should work to keep up upper hand:

Production

The pharmaceutical business generally has been obliged by unbending worldwide fabricating with specific creation gear, long lead times for materials and broad administrative prerequisites. This has prompted rigidity and powerlessness to respond rapidly to changes and offices that are either limit obliged or underutilized. Furthermore, rivalry and the race towards quality profiling for effective medications may well push huge pharmaceutical organizations into specialty drugs and littler clump generation. The whole of these patterns and qualities makes the medication fabricating condition ready for critical change.

Fulfillment

High levels of stock, low turns and late conveyances have tormented numerous pharmaceutical makers throughout the years. This execution has been endured in the past on drugs with secured licenses and where just a single source is accessible. With expanding rivalry, shorter selectiveness periods and littler clump creation, pharmaceutical organizations need to reposition satisfaction capacity to produce more precise execution and react to changing client request.

Changing Customer Demand: From Pallets to Packages

As beforehand specified, two patterns that will drastically influence the fate of pharmaceutical satisfaction are:

1. Littler bunch generation driven by genomics and client request
2. The expansion of retailer, supplier and purchaser direct to producers client base.

Customer Administration

The substance of the client is on a very basic level changing for medicate makers. In the first place, the concentration of choice power will move from that of essentially medicinal suppliers to a blend of restorative suppliers, drug specialists, drug store benefits administrators, oversaw mind suppliers and buyers. The advancement towards this expanding blend of choice influencers and producers for pharmacological medications won't be a direct way. Administrative bodies, strategies of drug stores and oversaw mind suppliers and the very phases of the item life cycle will influence who has the most noteworthy impact and who at last settles on the purchasing choice. Besides, the client base for medicate creators is evolving. Client base broadening from fundamentally wholesalers and GPOs to retailers, suppliers and shoppers presents open doors for makers to bring down general store network expenses and pick up deceivability to ongoing interest.

Forecasting and Planning

The obstacles to exact anticipating are various, including the absence of or postponed request deceivability, complex deals channels with setting up wholesalers, convenient and exact appropriation characteristically muddled by worldwide operations and consistency with the FDA's Current Good Manufacturing Practices (CGMP). At the point when the privilege anticipating techniques are tried, it can be just for nothing if a distributor acts in opposition to one's designs. The target of gauging and arranging is clear: to limit stock while meeting or surpassing client needs. Effectively accomplishing this goal requires the thought of four key segments: Approach, Quality Inputs, Methods and Tools and Structure.

Procurement

Over the previous decade, enhancing the obtaining capacity has turned into an essential and key piece of the objectives of most associations – fundamentally in light of the acknowledgement that expanded gainfulness can be similarly fulfilled by spending less. In the pharmaceutical business, e-obtainment has been vigorously grasped due to its relationship with lower exchange costs, bring down unit cost and a drive toward contract consistency. Frequently these concessions were accomplished with little respect to quality, add up to cost also, efficiency and brought about unassuming to negligible picks up in cost investment funds. There are altogether more prominent advantages to be picked up in the territory of acquirement. We will concentrate on two:

1. **Strategic Sourcing:** Key sourcing intrinsically concentrates on both immediate and roundabout material things that make up the lion's offer of expenses and efficiency issues. The more vital viewpoints incorporate into sourcing/outsourcing and the administration of agreement producing. Add up to cost administration assesses unit value, coordination and cargo costs, import/trade expenses, charges, benefit models and the cost of low quality. A pharmaceutical producer's way to deal with vital sourcing and speed of appropriation ought to be founded on the association many-sided quality and current level of process institutionalization.
2. **Supplier Management:** Provider administration programs proactively oversee provider connections furthermore, execution to guarantee supply targets are accomplished. The achievement of provider administration programs is very needy upon official sponsorship, cross-useful info, quantifiable execution measurements and process enablement. A considerable lot of the present production network administration and e-obtainment applications offer provider administration usefulness.

FUNDAMENTALS OF PHARMACEUTICAL SUPPLY CHAIN MANAGEMENT

SCM regarding Four Fundamentals, which are all key to the proceeding benefit of the organizations in all parts of the pharmaceutical store network. Fundamental 1 identifies with the general targets of SCM. These are concerned about

- Meeting or surpassing client benefit prerequisites in the market,
- Optimizing all out store network expenses and venture

Both are self-imperative. Customarily, inventory network costs (as an extent of aggregate cost base) have been bringing down in the pharma business than in others, bringing about a lower concentrate on SCM. Be that as it may, as with every single other part of the business descending weight now exists on store network costs, (for example, acquiring costs, creation costs, transport expenses and client benefit costs). At the same time, client benefit necessities are winding up increasingly requesting. Fundamental 2, identifying with SCM rationality, perceive that a production network is just as reliable as its weakest connection. This is as valid in the pharma business as it is in any industry. It requires that crude material providers, wholesalers, makers, retailers and others cooperate in new and inventive ways. It additionally requires that hindrances between internal capacities and exercises to be handled. Fundamental 3 is concerned about the proficient and viable administration of material, cash and data streams all through the store network. The last mentioned (i.e. administration of data streams) is of specific significance. Critical interest in data and interchanges innovation (ICT) in the pharma business as of late bears demonstration of this. Fundamental 4 requires organizations, especially in a situation where outsourcing of supply chain usefulness has turned out to be more typical, to re-evaluate both inside and outside client/provider connections (Uthayakumar & Priyan, 2013).

MODELS IN PHARMACEUTICAL SUPPLY CHAIN

Pharmaceutical creation must be seen more discriminately than synthetic creation on the grounds that here item separation happens inside the pharmaceutical store network. In the creation world that still wins to some degree today, a more grounded concentrate is set on the use of offices than on general improvement of expenses. Later on, it will be more critical to get the procedures "streaming". By and by, this implies short handling times – e.g. utilizing committed offices in compound creation; utilizing high synchronization and fast request changes in pharmaceutical generation or in certain cases through devotion also.

The explanations for the expanding interest for adaptability in the pharmaceutical creation inventory network are shifted. Most importantly, globalization has left its marks: the assortment of articles and additionally the quantity of bundles that must be particularly delivered for every nation at unified locales is expanding, while bunch sizes per arrange are diminishing. Likewise for instance in generics the benefit edges diminish caused by rivalry. Besides, pharmaceutical research is prompting a developing palette of items for more individualized treatment of something beyond furthermore, more diseases. The up to this point to a great extent homogeneous pharmaceutical market is being part into always heterogeneous littler sub-markets. The pattern towards person bundling is seeing a great extent of huge institutionalized bunches being supplanted with little, shopper situated or nation special bundles that fluctuate in shape, shading, measurements, rankle and pack estimate, print, cardboard, thwart, data flyer, and so forth. Bundles have new capacities, for instance

- Correspondence of the brand
- Security against duplicating
- Consistency bolster
- Senior agreeable
- Kids safety

Research is presently giving careful consideration to the relationships between Pharmaceutical Supply Chains (PSC) and the more extensive social insurance package. Coordination amongst performing specialists and stock administration are as yet seen to be the essential difficulties in reinforcing worldwide wellbeing pharmaceutical conveyance, be that as it may, the arrangement of complex stock models is considered lacking perse to enhance the present circumstance. Novel methodologies must be sent to accomplish more noteworthy ——end-to-end coordination along the PSC through innovation progresses in solutions assembling and more patient-driven conveyance models. After a medication is propelled, a totally unique arrangement of targets, drivers, and imperatives wind up plainly overwhelming.

Presently, the concentration shifts from nimbleness to high accessibility. Thusly, there is an emotional movement in the models and procedures utilized to help this period of medication life cycle. In this stage, the multifaceted nature of the pharmaceutical inventory network comes about because of the association of various extensive autonomous associations of extremely varied nature. The key partners in this production network incorporate various government offices, healing facilities, centers, sedate producers, medicate wholesalers, drug store chains, and retailers, inquire about associations, and the FDA. To compound issues further, a similar store network is in charge of the dispersion of physician endorsed drugs, over-the-counter (OTC) prescriptions, generics, and in addition biologics having unique taking care of necessities and operational targets. In fact, there are various separate associations, for example, insurance agencies, social insurance administration associations, and GPOs that further increment the multifaceted nature. Because of altogether different business destinations, these associations influence the undertaking of overseeing supply to chain all the more troublesome. Besides, because of the administrative idea of the business and various mergers also, acquisitions to obtain more R&D mastery, numerous pharmaceutical supply systems have developed in an uncontrolled manner instead of being gotten ready for ideal execution (Settanni et al., 2017).

PROCESS-BASED SCM

Supply chain Management process plays a tremendous hugeness in running key operations for practically every association. Without a fruitful store network, procedures could stop at the floor level and eventually cut down the outcomes. The process-based supply chain management system was shown in the figure (see Figure 4).

For such vast numbers of decades, supply chains have experienced their very own adventure from being as easy to as of late created calculation based ones. With regularly developing store network ideas, production network administration process has turned into a devoted capacity. Production network chiefs are given the duty to guarantee that inventory network, be it outer or inside, is both proficient and cost-effective.

- **Planning:** Planning is the vital piece of the inventory network administration process, to discover an ideal diagram of how to satisfy the end prerequisite. SCM chiefs ought to recognize a rundown of key segments like plant area and size, stockroom planning, conveyance models, IT arrangements' determination and so on. Not just this, the inventory network administration process would be fragmented if key lattices like transportation cost demonstrating, distribution center proficiency models and so forth are not created.
- **Basis:** At this phase of store network administration, the accentuation is on to learn the most dependable of providers for crude materials with the goal that the generation procedure could never damage. Be that as it may, testing conditions do emerge amid operations, store network directors must guarantee

Figure 4. Process- based supply chain management system
Source: (own elaboration)

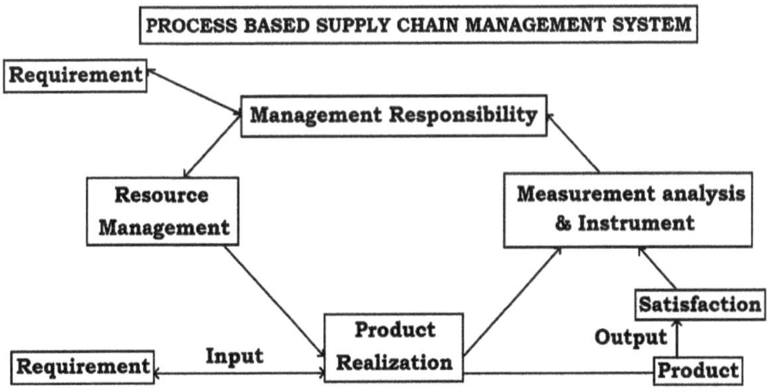

key torment purposes of supply cycle are continually being followed to keep the motor running. Holisol trusts that authoritative structure and in addition, choice of a competent provider is a certain something, however there ought to be a substantial framework set up for the consistent advancement of providers, which would support their productivity too.

- **Implement:** This is where very much outlined procedures are actualized with the goal that a detectable shape is given to existing plans as fabricated items that are prepared for testing, bundling, and conveyance. Not just this, comes about at this stage is measured so most extreme conceivable effectiveness is accomplished. Holisol's authorities' configuration financially savvies IT arrangements which empower clients in building brilliance and enhancing proficiency at the execution phase of the production network administration process.
- **Convey:** Supply chain when achieves this stage, the chiefs have a main job to convey the item/benefit in the correct amount, at the perfect place and ideal time by utilizing reasonable bearers. Production network directors ought to be completely furnished with present-day IT apparatuses to keep a track on warehousing systems, stock models and in addition, invoicing and instalment receipts.
- **Return:** Returns taking care of is the last advance of the inventory network administration process. It not just includes looking into returned items for quality purposes yet in addition, dealing with their stock. At the ground level, production network administrators ought to convey their assets supporting them with innovation for speedier pickups, faster substitutions and so forth. Returns administration ought to be an esteem upgrade measure according to production network administrators and they should guarantee each alluring measure is taken for most extreme conceivable productivity.

KEY AND CONFIGURATION ISSUES IN THE PHARMACEUTICAL SUPPLY CHAIN

The choices to be taken at this level include:

- **Pipeline and Improvement Administration:** This includes the determination of potential medications to grow further, and the arranging of the improvement action.
- **Process Improvement:** The examination of assembling courses and the age of assembling forms.
- Capacity arranging and plant and store network organization plan.

- **Plant Outline:** The determination and measuring of the significant gear also, capacity units. Vulnerability in the requests for existing medications (due to rivalry, vulnerability in the capacity to expand the ensured life through new definitions, and so forth.).
- **Uncertainty in the Pipeline of New Medications:** Specifically, which ones will be fruitful in trials, what kind of measurements and treatment administration will be ideal.
- **Process Advancement:** This is a perplexing issue, driven by science and yield streamlining. It regularly brings about wasteful procedures that are worked significantly more gradually than the inherent rates - offering ascend to group forms and long process durations in charge of a portion of the issues seen at the essential creation arranging stage.
- **Capacity Arranging:** The long lead times to make limit compelling imply that choices frequently should be taken at times of high vulnerability. Sitting tight for the vulnerabilities to be settled may defer an opportunity to advertise by an unsuitable sum.
- **Network Configuration:** Frequently impose suggestions outweigh everything else over coordination issues, these outcomes in monetary however possibly confused supply chains.
- **Plant Outline:** This tends to be exceptionally conventional, with no genuine change in assembling innovation for a long time (the workhorse of the essential assembling site is the glass-lined stainless steel clump reactor). There are noteworthy open doors for increased, consistent handling.

CHALLENGES IN THE PHARMACEUTICAL SUPPLY CHAIN

Pharma organizations need to oversee unimaginably complex supply chains and deal with the operational difficulties of working and associating with enormous quantities of providers contributing fixings and segments to sedate generation. What's more, now they have to meet track and follow mandates and consent to new serialization directions that expect the stock to be auditable as it travels through the store network (Prokop, 2017). Organizations getting to holds with serialization ought to consider if their current production network administration frameworks and procedures give:

- Precise data over the whole chain anytime and at any area
- Moment access to continuous updates and alarms if issues are identified
- Perceiving of all handovers in the store network
- Traceability back to the wellspring of all materials
- A consistent joint effort between all gatherings

OPERATIONAL ISSUES IN THE PHARMACEUTICAL SUPPLY CHAIN

Despite the fact that the procedures will shift between organizations, all significant pharmaceutical organizations will work ERP frameworks also, take after a business procedure along the accompanying lines (Wang et al., 2015):

- **Demand Administration:** In each topographical area, is produced, based on authentic information, advertise knowledge, and so forth. Tenders for fabricating may likewise be assessed and conceivably acknowledged at this stage.
- **Inventory Administration and Circulation Necessities Arranging:** The requests decided are accumulated and forced on the proper stockroom/ circulation focus. The effect on completed merchandise stock is surveyed and if essential, orders are put on upstream auxiliary producing destinations.
- **Secondary Creation Arranging and Planning:** The requests set on the optional destinations are arranged and afterwards planned for detail (commonly utilizing APS instruments). The effect of creating designs on dynamic fixing crude material stocks is assessed and on the off chance that vital, orders for AI are set on the upstream.
- **Primary Assembling Effort Is Arranging and AI Stock Administration:** Here, the requests put by auxiliary fabricating are fulfilled via cautious administration of stock also, creation arranging.

RISKS IN SUPPLY CHAIN MANAGEMENT

Pharmaceutical supply chain ought to give medications in the correct amount, with the adequate quality, to the ideal place and clients, at the opportune time and with ideal cost to be reliable with wellbeing framework's destinations and furthermore it should make benefits for its investors. Any dangers influencing the pharmaceutical inventory network not just can squander the assets yet additionally can undermine the patients' life by impeding access to medications. Hazard administration isn't just imperative in the pharmaceutical production network, yet in addition is a noteworthy player in different parts of pharmaceuticals, for example, solution and employments of prescription. Evaluating and executing the systems to oversee the dangers in the pharmaceutical production network is basic in wellbeing frameworks. The significance of the hazard administration is winding up more imperative since the solution is a profoundly directed item, which is under the controls and tight confinements of open administrative specialists. Likewise, supply of meds as key products in creating nations with much monetary, social and political precariousness is looked with more vulnerability.

Supply chain risk management (SCRM) is a vital and indissoluble piece of inventory network administrations to accomplish specified destinations. SCRM endeavours to limit store network weakness and vulnerabilities through relief designs. In this manner, it is basic to distinguish survey and organize all dangers to lessen and control the likelihood and effects of lamentable occasions. It is planned to dealing with the dangers in complex and dynamic free market activity systems. Different works have been accounted for with respect to various parts of inventory network dangers and dangers administration in the assembling segments. In pharmaceutical area, in spite of the fact that there are some surveys about in production network hazard administration with concentrate on fake, supply chain coordination, quality affirmation and endeavour chance administration. However there is not any methodical audit on the pharmaceutical hazard administration with point of view of makers' dangers. In the mean time, there are some orderly audits on SCRM in different ventures.

Production network with the buyer's prosperity approach, fake, calculated dangers, overall stock system, thing headway risks, normal peril organization, creation organize organization with prosperity course of action approach, store coordinate with association perspective and outcasts peril organization. The result of intrigue was characterized as pharmaceutical store network hazard administration from generation organization point of view. It infers articles with focus on customer security, regular peril organization, prosperity course of action and pariahs were barred effective overview in pharmaceutical generation arrange chance organization with perspective of creation associations is done; in spite of the way that there are some exact reviews with focus on vital, counterfeit, sedate security, quality danger organization and et cetera in the pharmaceutical business. For concentrating on the target of the investigation and averting decent variety, the catchphrases were restricted by master suppositions. So it could be said as a constraint of study. No complete examination, which is precisely coordinated with result of enthusiasm for this examination, was found with chosen catchphrases. At that point, none of the articles, which were included in this investigation, could cover all parts of the specified result of interests, and every one utilized and secured a few parts of store network chances in the pharmaceutical organizations. Albeit all creators achieved accord on barring a few investigations, yet it could be a hotspot for choice inclination.

Generally, there are two general sources of risk drivers:

- Internal Risk
- External Risk

Internal risks are chances under the immediate control of the association, counting broken machine, arranging, generation, and clients. However, external risks are chances past a company's control, including interest and supply dangers, fakes, fear mongering, direction and enactment, third-party relationship, cash and conversion scale changes. Since the interior dangers are preventable, this audit considers a portion of the critical outside dangers influencing pharmaceutical production network (Wildgoose, 2016).

Execution in the pharmaceutical organizations as a fundamental player in pharmaceutical store network has a noteworthy impact on store network administration effectiveness. Hazard ID, furthermore, alleviating them in pharmaceutical organizations not just can prompt process improvement, efficiency increment and limiting business hazard, yet additionally will offer assistance well-being frameworks to meet objectives of inventory network administration; Availability, Quality and Affordability. Many dangers announced in this examination are inside dangers because of procedures, individuals and capacities botch in a firm, which could be effectively overseen by reasonable alleviation procedures. Albeit just a couple of the dangers are outer ones however their effect on business interruption has not examined. Along these lines, distinguishing their hazard effects of dangers on business procedures and capacities and examining relief procedures to oversee them ought to be considered in future research.

CONCLUSION

As per this definition, an inventory network is magnificent on the off chance that it improves the business technique. In standard, subsequently, every effective organization is probably going to have an astounding inventory network. Despite the fact that the pharmaceutical business slacks different enterprises in the use of refined store network apparatuses and methods, driving pharmaceutical organizations have executed their business techniques viably by utilizing all around made store network hones. The most significant test looked by a protected medication producer is the vulnerability related to the dispatch of another medication. Therefore, anticipating request postures a noteworthy test for the store network organizers. To exacerbate the situation, including limit at short notice is not simple because of government controls which can take 2-4 years. Therefore, the scope organization takes an inside stage in handling the test of interest vulnerability. The pharmaceutical business is weak. Every part of the pharmaceutical production network is under strain to change. To make matters more terrible, the general sentiment is likewise extremely negative and condemning of the pharmaceutical industry. The real issues confronting the pharmaceutical business incorporate evaluating weights, the absence of R&D efficiency, an inadequacy of the blockbuster medicate model, and blast of generics. Also, the medication dissemination demonstrate is additionally under the flame. Thusly, the mainstays of the customary plan of action are deteriorating quickly. An essential parallel improvement that will muddle the circumstance is the developing enthusiasm for customized medication.

ACKNOWLEDGMENT

The author of the chapter would like to thank Dr. Senthil Kumar Ponussamy for his assistance in gathering and conducting research for the chapter and in providing guidance toward the publication.

REFERENCES

Dyckhoff, H., & Finke, U. (1992). *Cutting and packing in production and distribution: A typology and bibliography*. Heidelberg, Germany: Physica. doi:10.1007/978-3-642-58165-6

Marucheck, A., Greis, N., Mena, C., & Cai, L. (2011). Product safety and security in the global supply chain: Issues, challenges and research opportunities. *Journal of Operations Management*, *29*(7–8), 707–720. doi:10.1016/j.jom.2011.06.007

Masteika, I., & Cepinskis, J. (2015). Dynamic Capabilities in Supply Chain Management. *Procedia: Social and Behavioral Sciences*, *213*, 830–835. doi:10.1016/j.sbspro.2015.11.485

Prokop, D. J. (2017). Threats to Supply Chains. Global Supply Chain Security and Management, 41-63.

Rajeev, A., Pati, R. K., Padhi, S., & Govidan, K. (2017). Evolution of sustainability in supply chain management: A literature review. *Journal of Cleaner Production*, *162*, 299–314. doi:10.1016/j.jclepro.2017.05.026

Schneeweiss, C. (2002). *Einführung in die Produktionswirtschaft* (8th ed.). Berlin: Springer. doi:10.1007/978-3-642-59418-2

Settanni, E., Harrington, T. S., & Srai, J. S. (2017). Pharmaceutical supply chain models: A synthesis from a systems view of operations research. *Operations Research Perspectives*, *4*, 74–95. doi:10.1016/j.orp.2017.05.002

Silver, E., Pyke, D., & Peterson, R. (1998). *Inventory management and production planning and scheduling* (3rd ed.). New York: Wiley.

Stadtler, H., Kilger, C., & Meyr, H. (Eds.). (2015). *Supply Chain Management and Advanced Planning*. Berlin: Springer. doi:10.1007/978-3-642-55309-7

Uthayakumar, R., & Priyan, S. (2013). Pharmaceutical supply chain and inventory management strategies: Optimization for a pharmaceutical company and a hospital. *Operations Research for Health Care*, *2*(3), 52–64. doi:10.1016/j.orhc.2013.08.001

Vonderembse, M. A., Uppal, M., Huang, S. H., & Dismukes, J. P. (2006). Designing supply chains: Towards theory development. *International Journal of Production Economics*, *100*(2), 223–238. doi:10.1016/j.ijpe.2004.11.014

Wang, Y., Wallace, S. T., Shen, B., & Choi, T. M. (2015). Service supply chain management: A review of operational models. *European Journal of Operational Research*, *247*(3), 685–698. doi:10.1016/j.ejor.2015.05.053

Wildgoose, N. (2016). Supply Chain Risk Management. Enterprise Risk Management, 75-87.

Zahiri, B., Jula, P., & Moghaddam, R. T. (2018). Design of a pharmaceutical supply chain network under uncertainty considering perishability and substitutability of products. *Information Sciences*, *423*, 257–283. doi:10.1016/j.ins.2017.09.046

Zahiri, B., Zhuang, J., & Mohammadi, M. (2017). Toward an integrated sustainable-resilient supply chain: A pharmaceutical case study. *Transportation Research Part E, Logistics and Transportation Review*, *103*, 109–142. doi:10.1016/j.tre.2017.04.009

ADDITIONAL READING

Amaro, A. C. S., & Barbosa-Póvoa, A. P. F. (2008). Planning and scheduling of industrial supply chains with reverse flows: A real pharmaceutical case study. *Computers & Chemical Engineering*, *32*(11), 2606–2625. doi:10.1016/j.compchemeng.2008.03.006

Bravo, A. M. S., & de Carvalho, J. C. (2013). Understanding Pharmaceutical Sustainable Supply chains-A Case Study Application. *Independent Journal of Management & Production*, *4*(1), 228–247.

Carter, C. R., & Rogers, D. S. (2008). A framework of sustainable supply chain management: Moving toward new theory. *International Journal of Physical Distribution & Logistics Management*, *38*(5), 360–387. doi:10.1108/09600030810882816

Ding, B. (2018). Pharma Industry 4.0: Literature review and research opportunities in sustainable pharmaceutical supply chains. *Process Safety and Environmental Protection*. doi:10.1016/j.psep.2018.06.031

Enyinda, C. I., & Tolliver, D. (2009). Taking counterfeits out of the pharmaceutical supply chain in Nigeria: Leveraging multilayer mitigation approach. *Journal of African Business*, *10*(2), 218–234. doi:10.1080/15228910903187957

Gernaey, K. V., Cervera-Padrell, A. E., & Woodley, J. M. (2012). A perspective on PSE in pharmaceutical process development and innovation. *Computers & Chemical Engineering*, *42*, 15–29. doi:10.1016/j.compchemeng.2012.02.022

Klatte, S., Schaefer, H. C., & Hempel, M. (2017). Pharmaceuticals in the environment–A short review on options to minimize the exposure of humans, animals and ecosystems. *Sustainable Chemistry and Pharmacy*, *5*, 61–66. doi:10.1016/j.scp.2016.07.001

Settanni, E., Harrington, T. S., & Srai, J. S. (2017). Pharmaceutical supply chain models: A synthesis from a systems view of operations research. *Operations Research Perspectives*, *4*, 74–95. doi:10.1016/j.orp.2017.05.002

KEY TERMS AND DEFINITIONS

Process-Based Supply Chain Management: Appraisal underpins a procedure arranged view, and gives early cautioning signals.

Quality Management: Guarantees that an association, item, or administration is reliable. It has four primary parts: quality arranging, quality confirmation, quality control, and quality change.

Strategic Sourcing: Is a way to deal with inventory network administration that formalizes the way data is assembled and utilized so an association can use its united buying capacity to locate the most ideal qualities in the commercial center.

Supply Chain Management: Can be characterized as the outline, arranging, execution, control, and observing of production network exercises with the target of making net esteem, fabricating an aggressive foundation, utilizing overall coordination, synchronizing supply with request, and estimating execution all inclusive.

Supply Chain Risk Management: Is the execution of methodologies to oversee both regular and uncommon dangers along the production network in view of nonstop hazard appraisal with the target of decreasing weakness and guaranteeing congruity.

Chapter 10
Best Practices in the Pharmaceutical Supply Chain Management

Elumalai Gunasundari
SSN College of Engineering, India

ABSTRACT

The pharmaceutical industry is under severe pressure due to complex supply chains that are underutilized, inefficient, and ill-equipped to cope with the sort of products. The pharma supply chain must meet the demands of a fast-evolving marketplace and the shift from patient to an outcome to undergo a radical overhaul. Research and development (R&D) costs in the pharma industry are spiraling, development timelines are growing, and consumers are becoming increasingly knowledgeable about care options including drugs and treatment. The marketplace is fixed through the development cycle and increasing efficiency through rationalization or outsourcing of non-core activities. Recently, the pharma industry moved from the "one-size-fits-all" approach for the supply chain flexibility, responsiveness, and reliability. This chapter enables readers to understand the techniques for rapid commission and decommission new products and markets and alternate supply models, inventory tracking tools to eliminate counterfeiting and parallel-importing risks.

DOI: 10.4018/978-1-5225-5921-4.ch010

INTRODUCTION

In earlier years, the pharmaceutical industry is one of the most successful industries with various disciplines including research and development, production, sales and marketing (Amegashie-Viglo et al., 2014). Both sales and profits have been increased by continuing the top safety and quality standards in the pharmaceutical industries (Nakov et al., 2014; de Vries & Huijsman, 2011). However, nowadays, the pharma companies are facing more challenge made by an aging population, the increasing cost of healthcare, pressure from governments to reduce the price of drugs, barriers to entry in emerging markets and the wider adoption of generic drugs. Patients are demanding further personalized care over a multitude of various touch points. The modest intensity has improved with a rapid growth of generics. For the new market, the product portfolio has become more difficult with many niche products. Large drugstore chains for the over-the-counter products are commanding the high standards just like the consumer product companies. The increase of counterfeited drugs and the serialisation and quality regulation are imposing pharma companies to form their supply chains more strong to confirm full traceability (Abdallah, 2013). Therefore, the effective pharmaceutical supply chain management is extremely important to protect against these challenges successfully. The effective supply chain supplies drugs in the exact quantity and to consumers with the right quantity, with finest prices and at the correct time to provide profits for every stakeholder (Jaberidoost et al., 2015; Shou, 2013). The pharmaceutical supply chain is a major component of health organization including all procedures, data, resources, suppliers, manufacturers, intermediaries, third party service providers, merchandising and sales activity, logistics activities, financial and information technology. The application of supply chain management (SCM) systems in pharmaceutical companies is proposed towards rationalization the process of planning, production, distribution and storage of the final product before it comes to its final customer/user (Stadtler, 2004). The process of rationalization, via the introduction of standard SCM modules and systems in the pharmaceutical companies, then again permits reducing the cost of the final product, thus increasing its competitiveness compared to other related products formed by the competitive pharmaceutical companies. The main objective of this chapter is to study the challenges and their best practices in pharmaceutical supply chain management in the pharma industry. . The supply chain practices mentioned in this chapter can be used to maximize the revenue from the pharma products and industries can adopt themselves in the rapidly growing market price. The supply chain can be a best added value to the developing pharma industries.

BEST PRACTICES IN PHARMACEUTICAL SUPPLY CHAIN MANAGEMENT

Challenges in the Pharmaceutical Supply Chain

The major threat to the pharmaceutical industry still comes from the issues it has with its customers concerning quality issues. Presently the policy used to face such challenges is adding more tests throughout the supply chain. The end customers are mostly not interested in the complexities of the pharmaceutical supply chain or the challenges involved in managing multiple suppliers (Pelze, 2015). Generally, customers are required to get their medicine delivered on time, in the correct dosage, and at an affordable price. If a product delivery is delayed, or a medicine has been incorrectly labelled, the responsibility and consequences are inevitably borne by the pharmaceutical manufacturer listed on the product pack, even though the issue may have occurred somewhere in their supply chain. Top Challenges involved in pharmaceutical supply chain management in the pharma industry are explained as follows.

Lack of Coordination

Lack of coordination is a big challenge for the pharmaceutical industry. Generally, there are many links in the pharmaceutical supply chain that the most flexible, adaptable and successful supply chains should be well coordinated. However, this is not at all to be an easy task.

Temperature Control

Temperature failure of pharmaceutical products from exposure to hot or cold temperature is another major source of wastage in the pharmaceutical industry. Pharmaceutical products frequently need to be maintained at a constant temperature during its entire journey cycle to make sure usability for the patient. Various critical pharmaceuticals have strict temperature requirements. Especially, when a patient's health is at risk, supply chain visibility should be more important. In the pharmaceutical industry, controlled temperature cabinets are presented with pre-set temperature settings in the range of 2°Cto 8°C for cold or controlled room temperature ranging from 20°C to 25°C for storage. If a cabinet goes out of range, users immediately get alerts no need to worry about the location. Further, when the out-of-range incident occurred, users accurately identify what medication was there in the cabinet due to the complete inventory visibility the system provides. Therefore, inventory can be pulled as required.

Compliance

In the pharmaceutical supply chain, adherence to regulations worldwide is a must. With enhanced EU regulations coming into effect over the next few years, and the US stepping up its regulatory framework for the movement of medicines, keeping abreast of all compliance developments is needed.

Data

Probably the maximum opportunity and challenge simultaneously, the use of the data present across the pharma supply chain can frequently be a mostly untapped resource. The collection and sharing of information can attain a more efficient, effective and transparent process.

Scientific Progress

A pharmaceutical supply chain is an essential tool, which can make sure the significant efforts of research and development, as well as the manufacturing and production of a finished product. When science precedes a step move forward, the pharmaceutical supply chain cannot stand still. It is needed to respond consequently to the demands and advances of the industry.

Inventory and Warehouse Management

In pharmaceutical supply chains, managing inventory is a complex challenge, particularly for the lack of information and unique contextual challenges (Beier, 1995). Managing inventory comprises managing inventory levels, qualification, capacity, and replenishment decisions. These decisions would be formed together with exact data, however, even at the same time uncertainty can have dire effects. An off-site warehouse is also challenging, as it is not easy to track items beyond direct visibility and control. RFID system can give complete visibility to remote inventory, permitting better control and management (Bendavide et al., 2010). RFID-Enabled Controlled Temperature Cabinets are placed on-site at the distribution warehouse or other remote location. The solutions for managing inventory and warehouse are explained as follows:

- RFID-enabled controlled temperature cabinets are located on-site on the distribution warehouse or other remote location.

- Whenever the product is added or removed and the controlled temperature cabinet door is closed, simultaneously inventory details are updated without human intervention.
- Inventory tracking information consists of medication name, lot #, NDC#, and expiration date.
- Through a web-based client intelligence portal, real-time and accurate inventory details can be log on whichever time, from everywhere.
- Minute-by-minute product usage details can be observed, lacks against PAR noticed, and expirations tracked.
- For temperature out-of-range actions, low-stock thresholds or soon-to-expire inventory, customizable alerts are created.
- Usage information and analysis offer trending data to improved forecast demand, enhance inventory and minimize expenditure.

The grouping of on-site storage and real-time remote visibility lets for certain inventory management.

Shortage Avoidance

Exact, real-time visibility to remote inventory throughout the supply chain, combined with low-stock alerts and better long-term demand forecasting, all add to enhanced shortage avoidance.

- **Direct Real-Time Inventory Visibility:** The controlled temperature cabinets offer real-time visibility to cabinet inventory through a web-based portal. Inventory details comprise inventory count, medication name, lot number, and expiration date. The RFID-enabled system automatically updates inventory details upon the cabinet door closing and no need of manual intervention. Therefore, incorrect inventory counts are going to happen due to human error or workaround.
- **Low-Stock Alerts:** Item usually sets the customized PAR levels. When an item hits a low-stock threshold, alerts are generated that providing more time to re-order and avoid shortages. This facility as well as permits for improved inventory optimization and cost reduction in the long-term, as needless over-stock can be avoided.
- **Long-Term Demand Forecasting:** Usage of data is tracked every time an item is added to or removed from a temperature-controlled cabinet. Reports can be organized by item and date and still by the user when safe access is approved. The question should be addressed" what kind of medications are

used when, and by whom are deeply understand by using this detailed data to optimize inventory on an ongoing basis?

Expiration

Most effectively managing expirations over a complex supply chain once more comes down to visibility and requiring to identify where each individual item is in the chain, what is the expiration date of that exacting item, and somewhat to get advance reporting or notification that allows proactive removal of soon-to-expire items. The RFID system can be used to identify the place of each inventory all over the supply chain, with expiration date information.

Best Practices in the Supply Chain Management in the Pharmaceutical Industry

In worldwide, all companies in all market are having an aim to achieve the successful supply-chain management that including the procurement of raw materials, the change of those materials into ended products, inventory management, and the distribution of those products (Kumar & Jha, 2015). Effective supply chain management is essential as the industry particularly for pharmaceutical industry finds ways to decrease expenditure and sustains regulatory compliance and quality and safety standards. Even though the supply chain demands of companies utilize discrete manufacturing and make consumer or industrial products that may vary from pharmaceutical companies with process manufacturing, investigative best practices from outside the pharmaceutical industry is a useful tool to seek ways to optimize sourcing, procurement, inventory management, and distribution (Callender & Grasman, 2010). The pharmaceutical industry has been required to redefine the pharmaceutical supply chain management. The best practices required in the industries such as consumer goods and high-tech and pharma companies are explained as follows:

- Establishing procedures for initial supplier assessments and approval audits,
- Make quality and risk management a key element of supplier contracts,
- Ensure that supplier risk management is an on-going activity, not a one-time effort,
- Improve communication across the supply chain,
- Maintain comprehensive systems, metrics, and records,
- Understanding of true demand,
- Connect and collaborate using a business network,
- Quickly re-plan across the network,
- Better manage distribution,

- Control the quality at the Contract Manufacturing Organization (CMOs).

For decades, the old practices have detained control in many cases. Isolated decision makers follow transactional activities with their suppliers. There is minimal communication, little effort toward mutual improvement, and no real desire to track efficiency gains. Regulatory restraints and fortunate tax structures in a minimum number of manufacturing locations work in the industry's favour. Steady profits are resulting from captive customers that depend on the industry's products. Altogether, this has made altering the status quo unpalatable, or at least avoidable.

However, then a disruption arises. Possibly, it takes the form of breakthrough technology; or variations in customer demand patterns; or new, more nimble and innovative rivals. To respond, to cut expenditures and turn into more agile, industry leaders justify their sourcing and distribution and enhance operational effectiveness (Aronsson et al., 2011). Even though they are hesitant to make these moves initially, quickly companies determine that apparently modest shifts in supply chain strategy can change their industry and dramatically boost performance. Hesitant at first, and then in a great movement of an activity, the prevailing practices of the industry transformation. Nowadays, it has been happening in pharmaceutical companies.

In recent times, almost every major pharma company is challenging a far different and more troubling industrial environment than it handled even a few years back. Moreover, like companies in other industries before them, recognized pharmaceutical companies must handle this trouble in a way they identify as unaccustomed and unorthodox. They need to view their supply chain in a novel, strategic light, as a potential competitive advantage instead of an inevitable cost centre embedded in day-to-day processes. In the process, they must reject old attitudes that when drove nearly continuous success (Schneller & Schmeltzer, 2006).

In the earlier, for blockbuster drugs, multinationals faced little competition to ensure patent protection, which consecutively permitted the drug manufacturers to retain great expense points and margins on each pill, ointment, or liquid sold. However, nowadays, that is varying. Though over-the-counter and some other generic pharmaceuticals have been everywhere for several years, their effect now is more unyielding than it has been constantly, and it will develop still more noticeable in the following few years as big-name drug patents expire.

In the past, the pharmaceutical companies have answered to generics by emerging new blockbuster drugs; however, that will not be an option this time. Some of the drugs are left in the R&D pipeline, mainly as the science of drug development has turn into extremely complex. In the pharmaceutical industry, most of the low-hanging fruit are used as medicines that successfully address health problems for big markets, which have already been plucked. Furthermore, in many parts of the world, regulatory approval for new products has become greatly stricter and not as much of favourable to large pharmaceutical investments. The effect of this product development stoppage is revealed by inflating R&D costs and decreasing R&D productivity (Daniel et al., 2011). Worldwide, pharmaceutical companies expended about $130 billion on R&D in 2010, up from $54 billion 10 years before, however, the complete number of new drugs permitted by the U.S. Food and Drug Administration fell to 28 from 33, as said by market analyst Evaluate Pharma (Ehrhardt et al., 2012).

The rise of generics, joined with the high cost of drug development, places enormous price pressure on products formed by multinational pharmaceutical companies. The older distribution model is rather a simple chain made up of drug companies, wholesalers, and retailers and, in few locations, insurers challenges an invasion of new competitive systems in developed countries. Public and private health plans progressively depend on third-party pharmacy benefits managers or economic reimbursement policies to support low-cost generics over branded drugs. Simultaneously, more direct and more capable alternatives to traditional pharmacy dispensing choices including as the Internet and mail order, have been accepted with remarkable achievement. Furthermore, pharmacy combination and the grow of large chains have improved the negotiating power of the drug retailers, minimize the cost of a few medicines and forming generics come out to be an enhanced option in several categories. In the meantime, in growing markets, economically strapped consumers are attracted to incline toward less expensive drugs and generics and start-up local pharmaceutical companies are keenly aiming this demand.

Moreover, hospitals and other large purchasers, as well as payers and pharmacy chains, are more discussing contracts directly with pharmaceutical companies to buy drugs at set costs for a specific period of time. Worldwide, about 30 percent of all drugs, as well as 15 percent of on-patent drugs are currently bought through this so-called tender process. Not only does competitive bidding obtain prices, however, this approach also deeply influences the flexibility of supply chains and capacity management by driving the need for operational agility to deal with the fluctuating demand associated with tenders.

Herewith raft of industry disruptions, its modest surprise that profit margins at global pharmaceutical giants are coming under rising pressure.

Redefining Supply Chain Management

Redefining the supply chain is the best dominant approaches offered to global pharmaceutical companies in taking on these challenges. The majorities of pharmaceutical supply chains were initially recognized to produce items in bulk, in industrial unit not noted for agility. Therefore, supply chains were designed to avoid stock outs and to come across regulatory requirements, even though that meant retaining great inventory levels and carrying costs, and finally taking considerable write-offs.

As they face the issues that make threat to their future, global pharmaceutical companies must consciously change their supply chain to support revenue and profit growth. This indicates restructuring the supply chain and creating it more flexible; therefore, it can make and distribute drugs effectively to achieve the requirements of a range of product and market segments at modest cost levels. The supply chain must be constructed for various activities: to compare with generics at low price points for mature, off-patent products; to get the benefit of greater margins for critical drugs with lesser demand, and to manage the improved complexity of the new sales channels. These all depend on a company's present and future product portfolio and marketing strategy (Van Peteghem, 2015).

When a traditional pharmaceutical supply chain evolves into a flexible, cost-efficient, and functional system, an entirely new set of capabilities is needed. Formerly, pharmaceutical companies needed to focus their skills on research and development and on sales and marketing. For the most part, managing costs and operational quality is not a problem as much. Nevertheless, as the competitive landscape has shifted, so have the required operational capabilities. Today, operational capabilities arc critical, and these five strategic steps provide a path for developing them.

Following other industries, like high-tech and consumer goods, pharma companies essential to focus on the following best practice.

Connect and Collaborate Using a Business Network

Traditional ERP systems make sure not recommend a general and broad view of the production and transfer of goods from start to finish currently needed. By these traditional models, each link in the supply chain has its individual systems, which frequently not be able to connect into each other thus the level of visibility so desperately sought is challenging, if not painful, to complete. Logistics providers, networking suppliers, partners, and along the supply chain can provide a more broad view of activities. A cooperative system is needed for organizations that can be set with consistent information all over the supply chain. A digital business network is the base of a multi-enterprise supply chain that connecting each outside supply chain partners electronically through the cloud. Not like the old model of making point-to-point connections, this is a real, multi-tier network is connecting everyone, similar to the Internet does and letting all partners work in sync. This allows both end-to-end visibility and the collaboration looked-for to support business interactions between the dissimilar performers. Such a network is like an ERP system, but for the complete supply chain. This is virtually difficult to obtain the level of real-time visibility and coordination between every supply chain partners that are required (Lemoine, 2017).

Understand True Demand

Demand forecasts are only an educated guess of what future demand will be. For their OTC business, the many inventive pharma companies are following consumer products companies: taking more amounts of demand-related data that is at that point fed into sophisticated demand sensing solutions to greater guess true demand. This means working all the way to point-of-sale (POS) data or even using signals like weather forecasts or flu trends through social media. This enhanced demand picture is then broadcasted to each supply chain partners; make sure that the Pharma Company, suppliers and CMOs are entirely united. Demand sensing takes significantly greater on-shelf availability and minor inventories.

Control the Quality at the CMOs

Pharma companies are important to make sure end-to-end traceability. As external parties including CMOs, are gradually involved, pharma companies need to have visibility into partners' manufacturing operations to track product quality across the multi-tier, multi-enterprise supply chain. This means connecting to their CMO's manufacturing execution systems (MES) to capture appropriate information at each stage of production. This offers very granular factory transaction visibility to track material flows, lot genealogy, processing steps and associated parameters, such as yields or test results. These can be essential for any serialisation initiative.

Quickly Re-Plan Across the Network

In the pharmaceutical industry, quickly re-plan across the network that can be essential to detect and respond rapidly to variations in the demand and supply picture. Through business networks, companies can understand the end-to-end supply chain, not only in-house operations. Still, traditional planning systems lack the fast problem resolution and decision-support capabilities necessary to manage trade-offs and propose other scenarios presented by state-of-the-art planning applications. These tools let quick estimation of new data and simply compare different plans to choose the greatest option. Then, the new plan is communicated with every supply chain partners through the business network.

Better Manage Distribution

Pharma companies are more and more depends on external partners for transportation, warehousing and other value-added services. Confirming product availability denotes tightly managing distribution partners, which comprises getting complete downstream inventory visibility and sophisticated inventory strategies. Proactive management denotes assigning to the different channels too optimally and cost-effectively deliver the correct products to the correct customers and present reliable delivery commitments. This is important when challenging for shelf space at drugstore chains and pharmacies (Lemoine, 2017).

Adopt Tailored Business Streams

Today, big pharmaceutical companies tend to hold a one-size-fits-all approach to the supply chain, sustaining high levels of inventory and high service levels for almost all their drugs, no matter what the demand patterns may be (Ahmad et al., 2009). This can be a suitable model for high-margin products in a homogeneous market; however, it will not be enough in today's lower-margin segments and different environments. As an alternative, pharmaceutical company's necessity to employ a series of individual supply chains, each designed to its own product, market, and customer groups. For bulk products with the constant demand under deep pressure from generics, the supply chain should be built around cost competitiveness, which can be attained by manufacturing in low-wage countries and producing enough amounts for lean inventories based on historical and forecasted demand. With relative stability in demand planning, companies can weather long production lead times and enjoy significant savings from high utilization levels combined with low wages (Croom et al., 2000). By contrast, sales of high-margin drugs that are under patent protection or prepared for less-common medical conditions may be very hard to calculate, and the potential earnings rationalize a more favourable supply chain. These drugs may be produced in adequate volumes in factories near to their market, permitting small lead times so far keep away from costly stockouts in any markets. Additionally, a second source of production may be justified to make sure product stability in case of a disruption including fire, earthquake, or another natural disaster in the major industrial unit.

Add Flexibility to Product Design and Packaging

Pharmaceutical companies must control product demand volatility in low-margin drugs by performing pack-to-order strategies. This includes manufacturing, for example, one version of a pill that might be shipped effectively to abundant global markets, as an alternative of multiple versions, each for a separate region (as drug companies operate now with their less-than-efficient, widely dispersed factory and supply chain footprints). On the other hand, this approach could get the form of so-called postponement strategies, wherein drugs are packed to order in late stages of producing on the root of regional demand; this would decrease complete inventory levels and SKU complexity and also get better reaction time to market requirements and supply chain nimbleness (Ehrhardt et al., 2012). Better flexibility reduces inventory write-offs and working capital necessary for production.

Reconfigure the Supply Chain Footprint

In general, pharmaceutical production networks are categorized by large-scale factories and low productivity. Actually, average industry asset utilization levels are below 40 percent. Continuing that level of performance will only put pharmaceutical companies farther and farther behind in global markets. In its place, recognized drug makers must think about an entire overhaul of their factory footprint based on carefully constructed forecasts of regional and local customer demand and product requirements, as well as production and logistics cost and lead time trade-offs. Additionally, local rules must be taken into account. For example, in a few countries only domestically produced pharmaceuticals can come out on insurance reimbursement lists; in those cases, local manufacturing is de rigueur to stay away from a major competitive pricing drawback. There is no single blueprint for plant network design; the precise approach based on every company's existing footprint, its product portfolio, and its future growth strategy, for example, which types of products it plans to focus on and in which markets. Possible footprint designs are explained as follows:

- **Product Life-Cycle Model:** Production of items initially made in a particular launch plant is shifted to other, possibly lower-cost, factories as demand requires or as drugs lose patent protection.
- **Technological Model:** Manufacturing centres of excellence are created around new production or process technologies and innovative practices.
- **Geographic Model:** Plants are set up in numerous regions around the world on the basis of local demand for products.
- **Complexity Model:** A number of plants are committed to high-volume/low-complexity products and others to low-volume/high-complexity products, with resources allocated according to demand, competition, and whether high-margin pricing opportunities exist.

- **Product and Therapeutic Area Model:** Plants are planned for particular product groups or therapeutic areas to improve share R&D, manufacturing improvements, and strategic marketing efforts for related products and brands (Ehrhardt et al., 2012).

By reforming their factory footprint into it is largely well-organized and economical configuration, pharmaceutical companies can turn their supply chain into a source of ongoing competitive advantage, delivering mature products economically to compete head-to-head with makers of generics and manufacturing innovative drugs in manufacturing networks that can react rapidly to volatile market demands.

Create a Network of Third-Party Suppliers

To be ready for market dips, a wise make-versus-buy strategy is essential. If they outsource production of specific products, companies can better deal with slowdowns in demand by only dropping procurement from a supplier relatively than curtailing factory capacity utilization and taking on the expense of idle fixed assets. But drawing up a make-versus-buy strategy needs a set of clear product and market criteria to find out when third-party suppliers are more useful than, such as a streamlined and flexible factory footprint. Usually, if the volume is low and, significantly, if the drug is not a high-priority innovation that requires diligent intellectual capital safeguards having someone else make it is a popular choice. However, when manufacturing scale and efficiency are attainable, or the drug is a typical item in the company's portfolio, in-house production should be preferred.

Significantly Improve Planning Capabilities

Large-scale shifts in the competitive landscape have accelerated the significance of winning product launches and have better demand volatility and SKU proliferation. All of these conditions need strong planning capabilities to direct these shifts correctly. For example, a new product launch based on an accurate appraisal of expected demand so that adequate manufacturing capacity is obtainable to offer for the anticipated customer base and potential demand spikes. In addition, as generics go into the marketplace, company planners must accurately gauge their effect on individual branded drugs. This will lead the business side in managing inventory size, returns liabilities, and write-offs if sales go down. Moreover, as patents approach expiration, international businesses frequently attempt to expand their control of the drug's revenue stream by developing new forms and delivery approaches for the product, while generics attempt to keep pace with their own version of the drug. In turn, planners are the front line in analyzing the rash of new SKUs that will surely follow. To meet these challenges, pharmaceutical companies must arrange a well-organized business planning process that supports the company's portfolio management strategy and product transition plans. Input from sales, marketing, and finance departments is united with the most recent marketplace intelligence and historical demand data to make a consensus forecast for individual drugs and families of drugs. This process permits senior management to estimate different financial scenarios and business trade-offs. Companies with well-run planning processes experience substantial reductions in inventory levels, supply chain volatility, and manufacturing costs, and also see superior supply chain resilience. This is not a unique challenge for the pharmaceuticals sector; almost all industry these days has to think the form of its supply chain again in the get up of competitive transformation, and turn what were once regular operations into strategic capabilities (Hess & Rothaermel, 2011). However, for the reason that multinational pharmaceutical companies are coming to this challenge facing deep disruptions in their industry, the tactics they choose to use in remaking their supply chains could serve as a mainly valuable model for companies in other industries facing their own moment of truth.

New Product and Process Development

Matching supply with demand and implementing PAT in the parts of the manufacturing base where it can be applied are short-term measures. Long term, the pharmaceutical supply chain must gear up for a new pipeline that comprises products that are more difficult. The shift to biologics and the potential bundling of diagnostics, medical devices, and/or services will create the product of the future more complex to supply. To perform this effectively, pharmaceutical companies must consider manufacturing necessities when the product is still in the premature stages of development. Many companies in other sectors already combine the design, development, and production of their goods. This approach is called as product lifecycle management (PLM) that has equivalent potential in the pharmaceutical industry. PLM needs the manufacture of an integrated product and process data backbone spanning from premature development and discovery to marketing and sales. Constructing a collaborative design-supply chain that spans the complete product lifecycle has several benefits. Initial, it predicts updates in the manufacturing. It can also make simpler the transport of a product from one manufacturing site to another by applying a strategy based on preferred technology platforms. Moreover, for the reason that it decreases manufacturing delays and speeds up product transport, it can also speed up new product introductions. Thus, it gives an efficient channel for communicating feedback from the marketplace. This feedback can be used by manufacturers to improve the development and manufacturing of future products.

Extending Reach to the Customer

Nowadays, the pharmaceutical industry allows distribution to wholesalers and third-party logistics (3PL) providers and is less advanced regarding channel management match up to with the majority other sectors. This drawback in the pharmaceutical industry confines the amount of information about patient demand and product flow that is passed to the manufacturer supports parallel importing from cheaper to more costly regimes and prevents a company from being able to warranty the integrity of products after they depart the warehouse. Parallel trading expenses the pharmaceutical industry billions of dollars are spent every year, however, the majority of that money goes to the importers and pharmacy chains comparatively than healthcare payers and patients (Mustaffa & Potter, 2009). The majority of the imports are repackaged or relabeled that raises the risk of errors and forms it more complicated for pharmacists to differentiate reproduction from legitimate drugs. Specified these problems, it is significant that pharmaceutical companies take charge of their own distribution to exploit the potential of the various channels and to safeguard patients' from errors. One technique is to bring the majority inventive and costly products directly to retail pharmacies, hospitals, and specialist clinics exclusive of wholesalers. Actually, drug companies could still supply straightly to some patients with repeat prescriptions. Wholesalers would still have a major role in distributing mass-market drugs with bulk volumes and could form a far better contribution by assuming responsibility for packaging such products and managing their distribution on a regional, relatively than a national, basis. On the other hand, companies may decide to direct the funds used to maintain pharmaceutical distribution and channel management more efficiently (Enslow, 2017). By relying on wholesalers to distribute their products and using incentives and bonuses as motivation, pharmaceutical companies can manage the performance of their wholesalers and 3PL providers. To do so, pharmaceutical companies must generate stronger relationships with retail pharmacies and hospitals that distribute their products and focus on the needs of patients through channel-to-market innovations. If they create strong relationships, companies can wait for to channel control, observe margins recover, enjoy better market intelligence, accelerate the point at which sales peak, decrease planning inaccuracies, and control counterfeiting (Enyinda & Tolliver, 2009).

Time for Execution

There are no shortcuts, and there is no single solution when it comes to building a capable supply chain. The scale of change depends on the depth and length of the R&D productivity gap, the pace of technological progress, and the length of time needed for management to act.

The pharmaceutical supply chain can complicate or enable future growth. The supply chain can be used to accelerate time to market, maximize revenue from new products, block generic competition and protect patients from counterfeit drugs. By engaging in supply chain transformation and adopting an integrated approach to supply chain management, businesses will be able to position themselves to compete in the rapidly changing marketplace (Heninrich & Simchi-Levi, 2005). If appropriately managed, the supply chain can be a significant source of added value to any pharmaceutical company's bottom line.

Supply Chain Operating Network

New strategies utilize the experience of consumer product companies but get into account the specifics of the pharma industry. A cloud-based network to enable end-to-end visibility and collaboration between supply chain partners, joint with dedicated decision-support applications that leverage the data in this network is the most excellent set. The benefits are considerable and are up-to-date, end-to-end supply chain visibility 'one version of the truth' shared across all partners; full quality control of CMOs as required for traceability and serialisation; higher on-shelf availability, generally with lower inventories, through smarter channel allocations; better margins and ultimately higher market share; the early adopters are before now confine these benefits, placing themselves in front of their peers.

CONCLUSION

Pharmaceutical companies are only interested in continuing working with more suppliers and sub-suppliers in supply chain permitted to support their developing business while increasing end consumer demands and complex products. They is the necessity to implement new strategies that capitalize on the benefits of globalization and outsourcing while decreasing and controlling risks. As the supply chain raises more complex, there are suitable, effective controls and procedures in place to proactively manage and mitigate the potential risks to patient safety and compliance caused by improved complexity in supply chains. This chapter was clearly explained the challenges and best practices in the pharmaceutical supply chain.

ACKNOWLEDGMENT

The author of the chapter would like to thank Dr. Senthil Kumar Ponussamy for his assistance in gathering and conducting research for the chapter and in providing guidance toward the publication.

REFERENCES

Abdallah, A. A. (2013). Global Pharmaceutical Supply Chain: A Quality Perspective. *International Journal of Business and Management*, *8*(17), 62–70. doi:10.5539/ijbm.v8n17p62

Ahmad, N., Awan, M. U., Raouf, A., & Sparks, L. (2009). Development of a service quality scale for pharmaceutical supply chains. *International Journal of Pharmaceutical and Healthcare Marketing*, *3*(1), 26–45. doi:10.1108/17506120910948494

Amegashie-Viglo, S., Nikoi, & Kotei, J.A. (2014). Supply Chain Management of the Pharmaceutical Industry for Quality Health Care Delivery: Consumer Perception of Ernest Chemists Limited as a Pharmaceutical Service Provider in Ghana. *Journal of Information Engineering and Applications*, *4*(8), 15–39.

Aronsson, H., Abrahamsson, M., & Spens, K. (2011). Developing lean and agile health care supply chains. *Supply Chain Management*, *16*(3), 176–183. doi:10.1108/13598541111127164

Beier, F. J. (1995). The management of the supply chain for hospital pharmacies: A focus on inventory management practices. *Journal of Business Logistics*, *16*(2), 153–173.

Bendavide, Y., Boeck, H., & Philippe, R. (2010). Redesigning the replenishment process of medical supplies in hospitals with RFID. *Business Process Management Journal*, *16*(6), 991–1013. doi:10.1108/14637151011093035

Callender, C., & Grasman, S. E. (2010). Barriers and best practices for material management in healthcare sector. *Engineering Management Journal*, *22*(4), 11–17. doi:10.1080/10429247.2010.11431875

Croom, S. R., Romano, P., & Giannakis, M. (2000). Supply chain management: An analytical frame work for critical literature review. *European Journal of Purchasing and Supply Management*, *6*(1), 67–83. doi:10.1016/S0969-7012(99)00030-1 de Vries, J., & Huijsman, R. (2011). Supply chain management in health services: An overview. *Supply Chain Management*, *16*(3), 159–165. doi:10.1108/13598541111127146

Ehrhardt, M., Hutchens, R., & Higgins, S. (2012). Five Steps toward a Revitalized Pharmaceutical Supply Chain. *Spring*, (66).

Enslow, B. (2017). *Global Supply Chain Excellence: New Best Practices to Master*. Retrieved from http://www.supplychainbrain.com/content/sponsored-channels/amber-road-global-trade-mgmt/single-article-page/article/global-supply-chain-excellence-new-best-practices-to-master/

Enyinda, C. I., & Tolliver, D. (2009). Taking counterfeits out of the pharmaceutical supply chain in Nigeria: Leveraging multi layer mitigation approach. *Journal of African Business*, *10*(2), 218–234. doi:10.1080/15228910903187957

Heninrich, C.E., & Simchi-Levi, D. (2005). Do it Investments really change financial Performance. *Supply Chain Management Review*, 22-28.

Hess, A. M., & Rothaermel, F. T. (2011). When areas sets complementary? Star scientists, strategic alliances and innovation in the pharmaceutical industry. *Strategic Management Journal*, *32*(8), 895–909. doi:10.1002mj.916

Jaberidoost, M., Olfat, L., Hosseini, A., Kebriaeezadeh, A., Abdollahi, M., Alaeddini, M., & Dinarvand, R. (2015). Pharmaceutical supply chain risk assessment in Iran using analytic hierarchy process (AHP) and simple additive weighting (SAW) methods. *Journal of Pharmaceutical Policy and Practice*, *8*(1), 9. doi:10.118640545-015-0029-3 PMID:25838919

Kumar, N., & Jha, A. (2015). Quality Perspective of 'Good Distribution Practices' in Indian Pharmaceutical Industry. *IOSR Journal of Business and Management, 17*(11), 28-32.

Lemoine, P. (2017). *Best practice in pharma supply chain management*. Retrieved from https://pharmaphorum.com/views-and-analysis/best-practice-pharma-supply-chain-management/

Matlis, D.R., & Lennard, D.J. (2011). Improving Visibility of the Pharma Supply Chain: Best Practices and Technologies. *Pharmaceutical Technology, 4*.

Mustaffa, N. H., & Potter, A. (2009). Healthcare supply chain management in Malaysia: A case study. *Supply Chain Management*, *14*(3), 234–243. doi:10.1108/13598540910954575

Nakov, Z., Acevski, S., & Zareski, R. (2014). Implementation of Supply Chain Management (SCM) in pharmaceutical company, general principles and case study. *Macedonian Pharmaceutical Bulletin, 60*(2), 75 – 82.

Pelze, K. (2015). *What's Next for the Pharmaceutical Supply Chain?* Retrieved from https://www.allthingssupplychain.com/whats-next-for-the-pharmaceutical-supply-chain/

Schneller, E. S., & Schmeltzer, L. R. (2006). *Strategic management of the health care supply chain*. San Francisco, CA: Jossey-Bass.

Shou, Y. (2013). Perspectives on Supply Chain Management in the Healthcare Industry. In *2nd International Conference on Science and Social Research*. Atlantis Press. 10.2991/icssr-13.2013.144

Stadtler, H. (2004). Supply chain management- An overview. *Supply Chain Management and Advanced Planning, 3*, 9-24.

Van Peteghem, D. (2015). *Four Trends Redefining the Healthcare Supply Chain*. Retrieved from http://www.sustainablebrands.com/press/four_trends_redefining_healthcare_supply_chain

ADDITIONAL READING

Cachon, G., & Lariviere, M. (2005). Supply Chain Coordination with Revenue-Sharing Contracts: Strengths and Limitations. *Management Science, 51*(1), 30–44. doi:10.1287/mnsc.1040.0215

Henry, D., & Lexchin, J. (2002). The pharmaceutical industry as a medicines provider. *Lancet, 360*(9345), 1590–1595. doi:10.1016/S0140-6736(02)11527-3 PMID:12443614

Jaberidoost, M., Nikfar, S., Abdollahiasl, A., & Dinarvand, R. (2013). Pharmaceutical supply chain risks: A systematic review. *Daru: Journal of Faculty of Pharmacy, Tehran University of Medical Sciences, 21*(1), 69. doi:10.1186/2008-2231-21-69 PMID:24355166

Jayaram, J., Kannan, V., & Tan, K. (2004). Influence of initiators on supply chain value creation. *International Journal of Production Research, 42*(20), 4377–4399. doi:10.1080/00207540410001716516

Marucheck, A., Greis, N., Mena, C., & Cai, L. (2011). Product safety and security in the global supply chain: Issues, challenges and research opportunities. *Journal of Operations Management*, *29*(7), 707–720. doi:10.1016/j.jom.2011.06.007

Naraharisetti, P., & Karimi, I. (2010). Supply chain redesign and new process introduction in multipurpose plants. *Chemical Engineering Science*, *65*(8), 2596–2607. doi:10.1016/j.ces.2009.12.036

Shah, N. (2005). Process industry supply chains: Advances and challenges. *Computers & Chemical Engineering*, *29*(6), 1225–1235. doi:10.1016/j.compchemeng.2005.02.023

Sun, Q., Santoro, M. A., Meng, Q., Liu, C., & Eggleston, K. (2008). Pharmaceutical policy in China. *Health Affairs*, *27*(4), 1042–1050. doi:10.1377/hlthaff.27.4.1042 PMID:18607039

KEY TERMS AND DEFINITIONS

CMOs: A contract manufacturing organization (CMO) is a company that provides other companies in the pharmaceutical industry on a contract basis to offer comprehensive services from drug growth during drug manufacturing.

Demand: It is a multifaceted arrangement of push- and pull-driven demand and regulatory and pricing pressures.

Drug Manufacturing: It is the process of industrial-scale production of pharmaceutical drugs in pharmaceutical companies.

Network: It is the process of developing a mutually valuable relationship with other business people and potential clients and/or customers.

Packaging: It can be defined as the economical way of providing presentation, protection, identification, information, convenience, compliance, integrity, and stability of the product.

Pharmaceutical: A compound, which is manufactured for use as a medicinal drug.

Product Design: It is basically the efficient and effective creation and development of ideas all the way through a process that directs to new products.

Supply Chain: It is a scheme of organizations, people, information, activities, and resources in the process of transferring a product or service from supplier to customer.

Chapter 11
Distributed Trust Using Blockchain for Efficient Pharmaceutical Supply Chain

Arun Kumar Nageswar
VTU Extenstion Centre, India

Siva Yellampalli
VTU Extension Centre, India

ABSTRACT

With traditional ERP systems, there is a lack of networking among suppliers, partners, and logistics providers. So, there is a need to have a holistic view of production and movement of goods from production to last mile delivery. The physical and digital supply chains need to be integrated to ensure secure supply chains that promote business excellence, collaboration among stakeholders, and reduce costs. The high-level view over their supply chains allows them to function better in a multi-channel world. It also helps them identify where to reduce stock without compromising customer service. Otherwise, it leads to a delay in delivery, counterfeit products, thefts, fraud, and cyberpiracy, which may lead to lawsuits and losing of brand image. The tacit function of supply chain management is to provide tracking of specific goods in the supply chain. So, it is imperative to leverage the blockchain technology stack to map multi-enterprise value networks and enable connected multi-modal networks.

DOI: 10.4018/978-1-5225-5921-4.ch011

INTRODUCTION

This chapter provides an overview of vulnerabilities in the security of the pharma supply chain, transportation constraints related to pharma products and compliance challenges. It also explains the blockchain technology and its application to pharma supply chain to overcome the challenges. The objective of this chapter is to provide an overview of blockchain as a technology to streamline a heterogeneous systems into a homogenous systems so as to ensure secure digital pharma supply chain. It also provides a high-level architecture in order to institutionalize blockchain as a backbone for the secure digital supply chain. There are multiple scenarios in pharma manufacturing and supply chain management where the blockchain can help clear bottlenecks, ensure greater GMP/GDP compliance, and reduce operational expenses. The blockchain is being applied in supply chains, insurance, payments, audits and customs brokerage. This chapter also provides a brief introduction about AR and RFID technology and vulnerabilities in the security of RFID technology and how to overcome it.

BACKGROUND

The blockchain is a digital database using blocks that are linked and secured by cryptography and can be used to keep a record of any information or assets. This includes physical assets, like transportation containers, or virtual assets, like digital currencies. It is a digital ledger system (DLT) used to record and log transactions, grouping them into 'blocks'. In each step of the distribution process in the pharma supply chain, a network of computers will vouch for the provenance and authenticity of a drug shipment. Each participant controls a node on the network, and transactions require a consensus. The permission-based nature of the node system is a superior way for companies to share information with partners and customers without "leaking key business information". So private blockchain is preferred over public blockchain. One use is to register the transfer of goods between two parties, identified as two addresses in the blockchain. The transaction logged in the blockchain would include relevant supply chain information such as location, date, price, temperature, humidity and quantity, which would be available in the distributed ledgers. This makes it possible for anyone involved in this transaction to trace every ingredient or component to its place of origin. The decentralized ledger makes it impossible for anyone to manipulate this data, giving regulators such as food standards agencies or drugs regulators the ability to determine who is responsible for contamination or other breaches of compliance. Blockchain could provide significant benefits, with barcode-tagged drugs scanned and entered into secure digital blocks whenever they change hands. This ongoing real-time record could be viewed anytime by authorized parties and even customers at the far end of the supply chain.

Blockchain promises to be the ultimate trust machine. It can transform the role of the traditional intermediaries. It consists of two parts of the business ecosystem namely application and infrastructure. It creates institutional trust, reduction of grey markets and patient safety for the society. It increases interoperability, waste reduction, and better visibility of the supply chain for the industry. It increases ROI and optimizes resource allocation for the organization. (Srivastava & Mahlum, 2017).

Suppose a user requests a transaction, it is broadcast to a network consisting of computers known as nodes. This network of nodes validates the transaction and the user's status using known algorithms. A verified transaction may involve cryptocurrency, contracts, records or other information. Once verified the transaction is combined with other transactions to create a new block of data for the ledger. The new block is added to the existing blockchain, in a way that is permanent and unalterable. Distributed ledgers may be private or public and can vary in structure and size. In public blockchain, each user has a copy of the ledger and participate in confirming transactions. Where as in private blockchain, permission is required for users to have a copy of the ledger and to participate in confirming transactions (Sabogal, 2017)

Supply chain security is one aspect that has recently won attention when the DSCSA has been implemented in the U.S under Obamacare to, amongst others, fight the counterfeit drug problem and to ensure the traceability of the medicinal product along the supply chain. After successful implementation, the act enables verification of the legitimacy of a drug, enhance detection of illegal drugs and facilitate recalls of a drug. The supply chain in the pharmaceutical industry is complex, with drugs changing ownership from manufacturers to distributors, repackagers, and wholesalers before reaching the customer. There is little to no visibility for manufacturers throughout the supply chain to track authenticity. Consequences include the counterfeit drug problem and inefficient processes for conducting recalls and returns processing. These inefficiencies result in financial losses and loss of trust with consumers.

The blockchain could be an opportunity platform to increase trust and transparency, with customers being able to track pharmaceutical products throughout the supply chain. The packaging of a drug could be scanned by a barcode anytime the drug changes ownership. Only trusted parties are granted access to write on the blockchain. The record is delivered on the blockchain in real time. Manufacturers and end customer can scan the barcode and see the history. Optimally, the platform ensures drug identification, tracing, verification and notification in case an illegitimate drug is found. Blockchain solution brings integrity, traceability, and transparency to the global drug supply chain (Schöner, Kourouklis, Sandner, Gonzalez & Förster, 2017).

Due to the challenges of batch manufacturing, especially when it comes to monitoring the logistical journey of pharmaceuticals, industry players continually face issues related to product degradation and recalls, compliance with best practices for manufacturing and distribution. IoT applications for manufacturing and supply chain management have become popular investment areas for many industries. Connected equipment, men and material tracking, sample lifecycle management, smart packaging and cold chain monitoring are among the IoT applications that are particularly well suited to the pharmaceuticals industry. IoT technologies allow companies to connect and extend visibility into shop-floor activities, which can significantly increase productivity and assure GMP compliance (Saboo, Chourey & Suranglikar, 2017).

Blockchain is a digital technology that combines cryptographic, data management, networking, and incentive mechanisms to support the checking, execution, and recording of transactions between parties. A blockchain ledger is a chain of blocks of transactions. Parties proposing a transaction may add it to a pool of transactions intended to be recorded on the ledger. Processing nodes within that blockchain community take some of those transactions, check their integrity, and record them in new blocks on the ledger. The contents of the blockchain ledger are replicated across many geographically-distributed processing nodes. These processing nodes jointly operate the blockchain system, without the central control of any single trusted third party. Nonetheless, the blockchain system ensures that all nodes eventually achieve consensus about the integrity and shared contents of the blockchain ledger (Staples et al., 2017).

In a public blockchain, anyone can become a processing node called miner. Whereas in private blockchain the admittance of processing nodes is controlled by the regulatory body. Most public blockchains use Nakamoto consensus, where processing nodes by convention treat the longest history of blocks as the authoritative history. On private blockchains, conventional replication algorithms such as practical Byzantine fault tolerance can be used instead of Nakamoto consensus. This can provide stronger guarantees about the completion of transactions and may be more performant, but only support a smaller number of processing nodes which must be more trusted (Staples et al., 2017).

Blockchain includes stakeholders like users of the blockchain, software developers who manage code base, miners or processing nodes of the blockchain and regulators of the pharma industry. Supply chains involve physical movements of goods, the latency for information transfer should be minimal. During points of handover, there may be a low latency requirement for confirmation of receipt of goods. Blockchain commit times are likely to be too long for this, but it may be possible to instead provide cryptographically-signed receipts off the chain, with the delivery agent able to lodge those to the blockchain at a later time. If all participants publish all event data for item movements, this might become a bottleneck. There are two options to address that: filtering to only publish events that are relevant for other parties or limiting the range of participants that can use a particular aggregation server. In the latter case, it may be subsequently possible to define a way to federate data access across multiple aggregation servers. Extending the supply chain to a new participant requires integration of that participant's system with all participants that need to exchange documents directly with the new participant. The collaborative process requires the same amount of integration initially: the data formats used during its execution need to be agreed upfront. However, any new participant needs to integrate their systems with the given process, and thus the integration burden for the remaining participants is reduced. This methodology may as such also increase the uptake of standards for supply chain documents, since there is a central medium, the collaborative process, which makes the adoption of standards particularly beneficial (Staples et al., 2017)

RFID is a method of identifying unique items using radio waves. Typical RFID systems are made up of three components: readers (interrogators), antennas and tags (transponders) that carry the data on a microchip. RFID tags are further broken down into two categories. Active RFID tags and Passive RFID tags. Active RFID tags arc battery powered. They broadcast a signal to the reader and can transmit over the greatest distances (100+ feet). Typically, they can cost $20.00 or more and are used to track high-value goods like vehicles and large containers of goods. Shipboard containers are a good example of an active RFID tag application.

Passive RFID Tags do not contain a battery. Instead, they draw their power from the reader. The reader transmits a low power radio signal through its antenna to the tag, which in turn receives it through its own antenna to power the integrated circuit (chip). The tag will briefly converse with the reader for verification and the exchange of data. As a result, passive tags can transmit information over shorter distances (typically 10 feet or less) than active tags. They have a smaller memory capacity and are considerably lower in cost ($1.00 or less) making them ideal for tracking lower cost items.

There are two basic types of chips available on RFID tags, read-only and read-write. Read-only chips are programmed with unique information stored on them during the manufacturing process. The information on read-only chips can never be changed. With read-write chips, the user can add information to the tag or write over existing information when the tag is within range of the reader. Read-write chips are more expensive than read-only chips. Another method used is something called a "WORM" chip (Write Once Read Many). It can be written once and then becomes "Read Only" afterwards. This is a desirable format since companies will be able to write an EPC (electronic product code) to the tag when the product is produced and packaged.

While choosing the RFID tag following issues need to be considered:

1. Tag cost
2. Tag size
3. Infrastructure cost
4. Read distances
5. Government regulation
6. Anti-collision

RFID promises to provide huge advantages to manufacturers by offering the tools to better plan production and respond more quickly to market demand. It will facilitate automation of inventory counts and speed shipping and receiving at the distribution level. For retailers, it will help to reduce stock-outs, enable product tracking and potentially reduce theft and streamline the POS function. RFID will also open other merchandising opportunities and help with the overall consumer buying experience. Due to the current cost of the technology (both tags and infrastructure), it is expected that the initial phase of adoption will be aimed at carton and pallet marking applications. As the cost of tags and readers comes down, a wider adoption at the item marking level will develop. In order for RFID to grow quickly, it is important that standards be developed so that the technology providers are working toward a common goal of providing low cost and compatible technologies. Not only will it drive down costs, but standards will also help users to reap the greatest benefit from their investment by providing value throughout the whole supply chain.

MAIN FOCUS OF THE CHAPTER

The pharma supply chain may be broadly classified as drug discovery, development, manufacturing, warehousing and distribution. This chapter leverages the advantages of both IoT and blockchain to build secure pharma supply chain in the distribution phase. Blockchain may be applied in clinical trials to increase transparency. It can also be used to increase the shop floor visibility, equipment monitoring and inventory management in manufacturing. It can be used to increase real-time visibility by tracking products in warehouse operations. It can also be used to perform patient health monitoring. However, this scope of this chapter is restricted to monitoring cold conditions on shipping vehicles by managing temperature spikes in the distribution phase. This chapter explores how pharmaceuticals companies can employ the blockchain to control cold conditions, which augment, enrich, automate and revitalize distribution and supply chain management. A brief description is made about RFID and AR with their limitations and solutions to overcome security vulnerabilities.

Issues, Controversies, Problems

In the existing supply chain infrastructure, there are disparate data sources and each stakeholder has separate client-server technologies to process the transaction. Therefore, there is a lack of uniform infrastructure backbone to provide visibility of transaction to all stakeholders and a formal handshake during the transfer of assets. Since each stakeholder does not trust another stakeholder system. In this case, blockchain is a right choice because the intent is to enable trust among stakeholders, provide data transparency and gain efficiency in the supply chain. Suppose the transactions are within a single organization or organization unit then, it is not advisable to adopt the blockchain technology. Following listed issues need to be addressed by blockchain.

1. **Biologics:** They have a larger proportion of high-value active ingredients with shorter shelf lives
   a. Storage.
      i. Temperature sensitive
      ii. Humidity controlled.
2. **Challenges in the Supply Chain:** In the distribution phase as the stakeholders increase the supply chain is vulnerable with poor visibility.
   a. **Vulnerabilities:**
      i. Drug ownership transfer
      ii. Efficiency in last mile delivery
      iii. Counterfeit drugs entering the supply chain
      iv. Existing manual process is paper heavy
   b. **Visibility of Supply Chain:** Pharma manufactures, other stakeholders and patients have little visibility to track the authenticity of drugs
      i. Traceability
      ii. Transparency
      iii. Meeting regulatory compliance
      iv. Integrity
      v. Demurrage
      vi. Lost sales
      vii. Expediting cost
3. **Stakeholders:** Multiple stakeholders with the mishmash of disparate databases.
   a. Applicable to distribution phase.
      i. Carriers
      ii. Brokers
      iii. Vendors
      iv. Consumers

v. Exporter
vi. Importer
vii. Customs
viii. Government Authorities
ix. Freight forwarders
x. Custom House Agent
xi. Insurer
xii. Reinsurer
xiii. Bank
xiv. Transshipment parties
xv. Shipping carrier

4. **Compliance:** Adherence to local, country and international regulations and quality control
   a. Applicable to full pharma supply chain.
      i. PMDA
      ii. GMP
      iii. DSCSA.
      iv. GDP 2013/C 343/01
5. **Documentation:** Multiple artifacts listed below are being shared with multiple parties
   a. Applicable to full pharma supply chain.
      i. Purchase order
      ii. Sales contract
      iii. Commercial invoice
      iv. Shipment bill
      v. Certificate of origin
      vi. Bill of lading /AW bill
      vii. Customer duty paid documents
      viii. Bill of entry
      ix. Letter of credit
      x. Bank payment advice
      xi. HSN codes book
      xii. Licenses
      xiii. Test report
      xiv. Adhoc exemptions
      xv. Freight invoice
      xvi. Insurance declaration
6. **Non Functional Requirements:** The new proposed digital pharma supply chain need to address the following core issues to connect the stakeholders seamlessly.

a. Applicable to full pharma supply chain.
    i. Interoperability
    ii. Latency
    iii. Integrity
    iv. Confidentiality
    v. Availability
    vi. Anonymity
    vii. Non-Repudiability
    viii. Ease of adding stakeholders

SOLUTIONS AND RECOMMENDATIONS

Blockchain technology-based smart contracts can be used to track and trace the products in the supply chain and validate the same on a real-time basis. This expedites the process of transactions. In the traditional database approach, the validation process is manual and it requires intermediaries, whereas, in the blockchain, each stakeholder event and action shall be captured and validated as per the smart contract and hence reducing manual intervention for verification and counter verification. The shipment tracking involves tracking the cross-border shipment from purchase order to receipt to the buyer. Blockchain shall be able to create, update and inform the different parties when any of the events in the supply chain occur. The objective is to track the shipment and inform all the involved stakeholders regarding the changes. The goal is to minimize rechecking, revalidation, reverification, and automate the process.

IoT devices are used to leverage the blockchain technology to achieve data immutability, visibility of health of shipments to all stakeholders and while reducing operating cost in the pharma supply chain.

In order to avoid late deliveries and spoilage, it is imperative to track the storage conditions of sensitive drugs. IoT devices collect data from temperature-controlled containers to track drugs in environmental conditions. Consequently, it is compared with thermostability tables to generate alerts in the event of temperature excursions. It helps in less drug expiration and degradations from temperature spikes. Every shipment shall be associated with a smart contract in order to ensure compliance with respect to temperature constraints. Smart contracts are self-enforcing and self-executing since it can verify for its correctness and enforce predefined rules. Blockchain provides the required infrastructure for smart contracts to run, execute and verify these smart contracts. A smart contract can be used for financials like Bitcoin or general services like Ethereum. Thus, smart contracts may be viewed as protocol mandating a contractual clause, which is also visible to third-party agency. Every block in blockchain has a reference to the predecessor and hence the term blockchain. As evident in the pharma supply chain, there are many stakeholders and automation shall reduce operating cost. The temperature data of each block can be used for audits by external agencies and it is tamper-proof. The whole framework is a decentralized and initial cost involved in setting up the system is low.

As per GDP compliance, it is mandatory for pharmaceutical companies to insist with logistics providers to record the temperature of every shipment at all times and to intimate the sender and recipient of any variations. A consensus is reached by both parties namely sender and recipient regarding the allowed temperature variations by ensuring it in a smart contract. The data in the block is visible to any third party agency for regulation thus avoiding any intermediaries and reducing cost. Thus blockchain is a decentralized system with trusted consensus between the parties by using smart contracts. The GDP compliance is ensured by the self-enforcing and self-executing smart contracts thereby reducing the intermediaries and cost. The data in the block is visible to any third party agency for any compliance thus reducing any manual intervention.

So in the digital supply chain, every shipment shall be associated with smart contract ID. Based on the shipment having specific temperature constraints or attributes a new smart contract is created and mapped with the shipment. The server hosts a node, which can participate in a network of nodes and can create the smart contract and monitors it for any changes and calls contract related functions. During the transfer of ownership of drugs among stakeholders, a new transaction is submitted to a network of computers known as nodes. It shall be verified for compliance by reading the historical temperature or humidity data or attributes of the product with the associated smart contract data. Thus smart contracts ensure compliance. On successful verification, this transaction is combined with other transactions to create a new block of data for the ledger. This new block is then added to the existing blockchain. Consequently, this block of data is immutable and publicly accessible to sender, recipient and verifiable by any third party. In the near future, this data shall be made available to the customer so that he/she is empowered to ascertain the quality of the product before using.

IOT device with GSM (GPRS enabled) with required sensors with a control board will be fixed into the vehicle as shown in Fig 1. This device will be powered from the vehicle's battery. IOT capabilities provided include GPS, Temperature and Humidity of the vehicle. It shall have a battery in it for the failsafe mechanism if the vehicle battery has been disconnected or drained. The device shall be able to store the IOT Sentences in case of non-availability of the GSM network and the same shall be pushed to the Cloud in the First In First Out basis (FIFO). The device shall provide OTA (Over the Air) based firmware upgrades. The device configuration settings like Cloud address and other details should be configurable by SMS. The device shall be configured to send IOT Sentences as Web Requests. The HTTP based

Figure 1. Architecture Diagram
Source: (Disruptive Innovation for Auto Insurance ..., 2018)

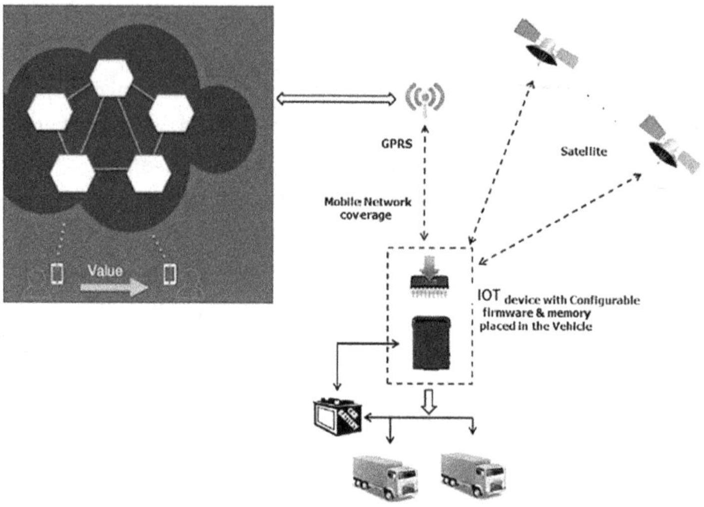

Web Requests will be received by Cloud. The device shall directly talk to Cloud Server, which shall aggregate the telematics data. The IOT data shall be collected using mobile services of Azure.

Smart contracts not only define the rules and penalties around an agreement in the same way that a traditional contract does, but also automatically enforce those obligations. An option contract between parties is written as code into the blockchain.

Figure 2. Smart Contract and Stakeholders
Source: (own elaboration)

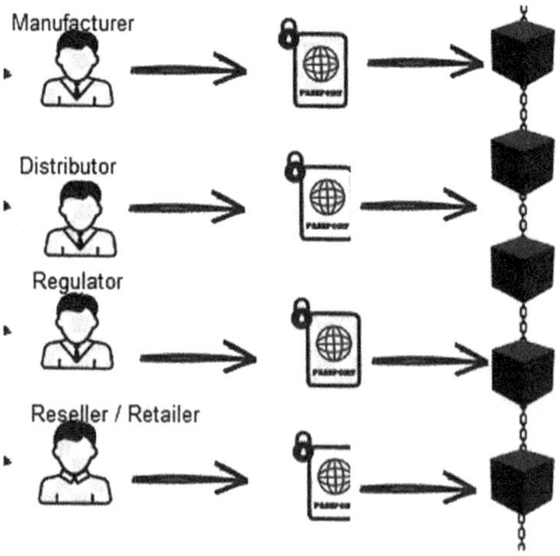

The individuals involved are anonymous, but the contract is the public ledger. A triggering event like an increase in temperature/humidity above the specified limit is hit and the contract executes itself according to the coded terms. Regulators can use the blockchain to understand the activity in the market while maintaining the privacy of individual actor's positions. Smart contracts provides autonomy since agreement is made by stakeholder and executed automatically by the network rather than by any third party individual, trust is established since the documents are encrypted in the shared ledger, backup is taken since the documents are duplicated many times over, safety is ensured since cryptography of documents is used, speed is better compared to paperwork done manually, savings are substantial since intermediaries are avoided and it is accurate since the manual process is eliminated.

The smart contract can enforce the process as follows. First, it can reject messages if they arrive at the wrong point in the process. Second, messages are only accepted from the participant who is authorized to send them. For instance, customs clearing can only be granted by customs. Third, conditions can be specified on the process model level and executed in smart contract code directly, so that e.g. a particular process branch automatically gets activated when certain conditions are met or certain events are observed

Smart contracts can be processed by blockchains like Bitcoin, Side Chains, NXT and Ethereum. Smart contracts are created with the elements of data that would be tracked in a verifiable manner as shown in fig 3. The event alerts like

Figure 3. Smart Contract processing based on event
Source: (Blockchain in supply chain)

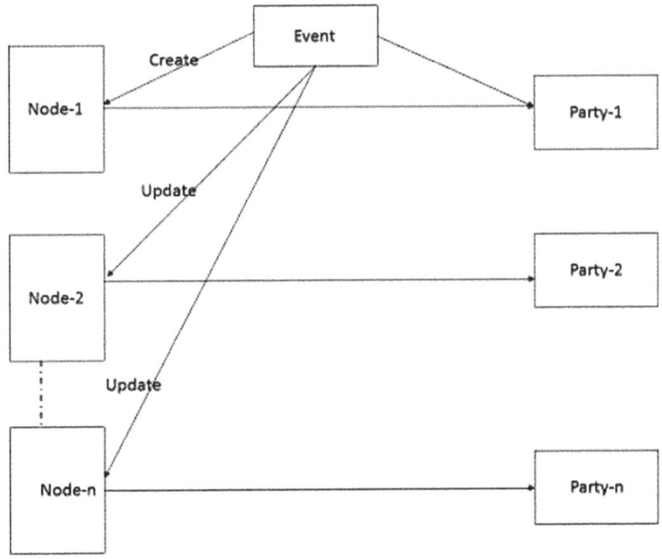

temperature or humidity variations shall be generated. The documents and payments get released automatically when the events get verified against the smart contracts. The information would be verified and reconciled by the various nodes. Based on the blockchain verified event, the next event can be triggered. For example, when the event for temperature/humidity takes place, which can be verified by sensor/ IOT data, linked to that shipment, the bank can be instructed to release the payment.

The Azure platform enables stakeholders in the supply chain to connect, store, analyze and derive deep insights regarding the quality of the shipments as shown in fig 4. In this device-centric solution, private cloud implementation is used. The objective of Azure services is to enable flow of information between the connected devices and business assets like mobile phones, personal computers, tablets and cloud backend systems for the purpose of analysis and visibility of supply chain shipments. Devices may be connected directly or indirectly through a gateway. A cloud gateway provides endpoints for device connectivity and facilitates bi-directional communication with the backend system. The back end comprises multiple components to provide device registration and discovery, data collection, transformation, and analytics, as well as business logic and visualizations. Azure services ensure vast hardware and software heterogeneity, security and privacy measures, including device and user identity, authentication and authorization, data protection for data at rest and data in motion, hyper-scale deployments involving

Figure 4. Azure Cloud services
Source: (Microsoft Corporation, 2016)

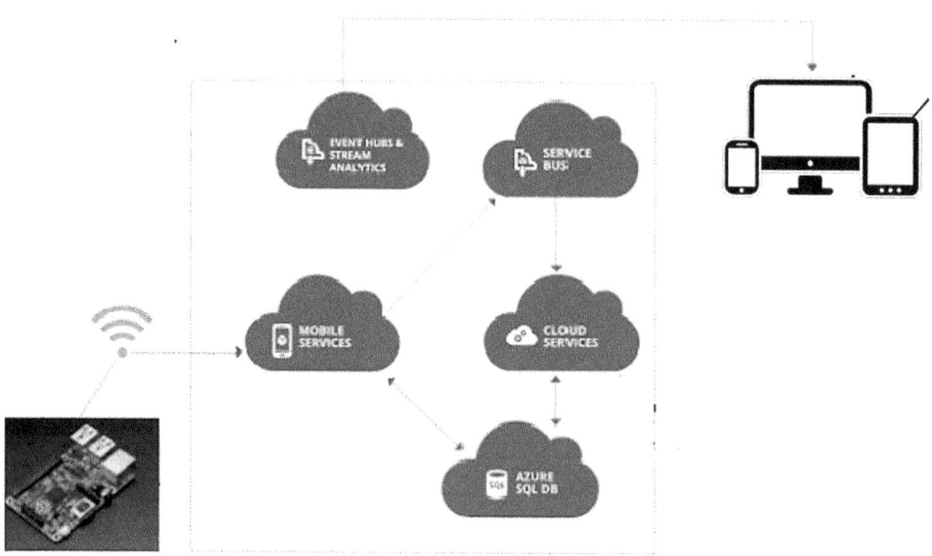

millions of connected devices, flexibility built upon a principle of composability to allow for a number of extension points and to enable the usage of various first-party or third-party technologies for the individual conceptual components. In order to deploy the cloud following steps need to be followed.

1. Create an IoT hub that will receive data from devices and send commands back to it
2. Create an Event hub into which we will post alerts
3. Create a Stream Analytics job that will read data from the IoT hub and post alerts into the Event hub
4. Create a Storage account that will be used by the worker role
5. Deploy a simple worker role that will read alerts from the Event hub and forward alerts to devices through the IoT hub.

Dashboards using cloud computing, IoT integration, cryptographic key management shall be combined off-chain with blockchain. In order to support scalability of the blockchain, confidentiality and backward compatibility with legacy systems all other databases are stored off-chain. Regulators should be aware of risks and limitations of the blockchain and need to provide guidance in framing the smart contracts so as to set the expectation for evidence in order to meet the requirements for approval. Regulators should be neutral in framing the specifications for smart contracts and should not impose restrictions and prohibitions for private blockchain. They should embrace non-blockchain technology.

RFID is used extensively in the context of SCM for item tagging and multi-pack tagging for track and trace. A RFID chip or tag is a passive antenna that can be activated when it is close to an energy source. When the RFID device is scanned by a reader, the chip delivers a set of data that can be verified against a database. The real value of such a device is to have a low price (from a few cents up to $1) for standard product. This is a simple solution that is easy to install and well known by customers. The primary use of this solution is to track products across the logistics chain. New applications have been used since the introduction of RFID tags for anti-counterfeiting purposes. The idea is to check, during the RFID tag reading process, that the information contained on the chip is the same as that stored in a centralized database. If it matches, then the product is a genuine one. However, this is not a fully secure process. Indeed, several articles and demonstrations have revealed that it is possible to view the memory content of the RFID tag. It is then a rather simple task to create a new RFID tag containing exactly the same data information. So the technical tradeoffs in the communication stack and also vulnerabilities associated with RFID tags need to be understood. More complex RFID tags are available and are based on Physical Unclonable Functions (PUF). But the price, the real value added of the tags, is definitively less competitive due to the addition of new security features.

Cloud makes products smart and trackable. Each product interaction can be captured in real time and generate valuable data (analytics). RFID tags are used in the reader/writer mode. Read and write permissions of tags are important. The unauthorized read or write functions are unwelcome. Physical security of the tags, unwitting actions weakening the system, as well as threats aiming to damage the system are potential risks of RFID tag security. The aim of an attacker is to potentially find a way to manipulate the data stored on the tag such as overwriting malicious data onto the original one, deleting the content of the tag, or even cloning the tag and impersonating it thereafter. An attacker may inject a worm-URL into the tag, eventually causing the smartphone that reads tag to become infected. Denial of Service (DoS) attack is another risk for the tags

As a prevention mechanism, read and write privileges can be defined for the tags, so that only the authorized users can make use of the service. Recent studies have examined authentication and encryption on tags. One of these demonstrated a cryptographic challenge-response protocol is executed between the reader and the tag that is based on Public Key Cryptography (PKC) and Public Key Infrastructure (PKI). The protocol successfully detects illegal modification and cloned tag cases. In another recent study, a security-enabled passive RFID tag is designed and implemented which supports authentication using symmetric cryptography. The tag is also able to digitally sign the data using asymmetric cryptography.

Augmented Reality in Logistics, its importance and its application in logistics' element execution is also discussed in this book chapter. It is well-known fact that in warehouses, workers are prone to stress, fatigue and depression due to monotonous routines. This leads to errors during object selection and decision making. Augmented reality (AR) is a visualization solution where the user is immersed in the natural environment and manage the situation and the object. AR can be used for item visualization in the warehouse to decrease the object pick up time, reduce the errors and make the process more humane. Additional checking of items could diminish the number of potential errors. The advantages of using computer-generated visualizations and 3D model projections instead of text and image-based guides, which shall reduce damages and losses.

FUTURE RESEARCH DIRECTIONS

One of the key challenges of blockchain-based IoT applications is the limited computing power of many IoT devices. Encryption and verification of blockchain transactions can require considerable processing power, which may not be available in low-end devices. In addition, the use of more processing power can increase both the energy consumption and the cost of the solution.

Transaction processing on a blockchain is slow. In order to arrive at a consensus, all the network nodes should come to an agreement before ascertaining that the transaction is valid. This may be a slower process compared to traditional computing. Until the block in which transaction is made has been verified it is marked as untrustworthy. During the time, the transaction is submitted and block settles any attacker may tamper the transaction. So further study is needed to avoid this security vulnerability.

All nodes in the blockchain do not perform distributed computing, instead, they perform identical operations for each transaction based on the same rules. They write the same transaction result to the blockchain. Every node has an identical history. It implies that blockchain is less efficient as duplication of the single instance of the node is performed. The size of the blockchain grows based on the transactions. Therefore, some blockchains may grow faster in size. The health of the blockchain is partially based on the number of nodes in the network. The sufficient advancement in HDD capacity should overcome the storage space issue. Some users trust the server and connect to the blockchain online. So further study is needed in understanding the access time, storage space and efficiency of the blockchains as transactions increase.

It is not suitable to store large volumes or high-velocity data called big data. Since there is an inherent limitation in the blockchain, because of high redundancy prevalent in the blockchain where every processing node obtains a copy of the distributed ledger. So there is a need to store just the hash or meta-data of the large data in the blockchain. The performance of such an architecture needs to be evaluated.

The bandwidth of the blockchain is the same as the bandwidth of one network node. The maximum number of transactions processed during a second determines the processing capacity of the blockchain. After processing a certain amount of latency is involved in recording the transaction result to the node. The duration of the time taken to record a single transaction result also determines the processing capacity of the blockchain. Compared to existing supply chain transactions, the scalability of the blockchain as new active users are added is minimal. The maximum throughput of the blockchain compared to conventional transaction processing systems is lower. So further study is needed to understand the effectiveness of the scalability of the blockchain by adopting other techniques like sharding, state channels, and reduced inter-block time.

In case someone in the network controls more than half of the computing power being used for mining, then blockchain is prone to a 51% attack. Then that person can write alternative history and it becomes reality. However, traditional systems are immune to these attacks. Further study is needed to establish the probability of a 51% attack as the number of miners increase. Likewise, the impact of network security by excessive mining needs to be studied.

Since blockchain replicates the full content of its distributed ledger to all the processing nodes, the data is transparent to all the stakeholders in the supply chain. So data privacy and confidentiality are hard to establish using public blockchain since any member of the public can access the whole history of the transaction and use it without any restriction. The disclosure of the commercially sensitive data to all stakeholders like customers, suppliers, retailers may have an adverse effect on the companies keeping in mind the competitiveness in the market. So further study is needed to restrict the visibility of the sensitive data in the blockchain by using specific techniques such as encryption, or holding data off-chain, must be used to achieve Confidentiality.

An individual holds the power over data in the supply chain they want to verify in the blockchain. If the transaction goes sour after it has been verified, then the only feasible way of returning the transaction is if the stakeholders agree to reverse it. Compared to the traditional system where the third-party mediator is used to settling the transaction, there is no arbiter in the blockchain. So further study is required to add an impartial moderator in the technology stack of the blockchain.

Blockchains which use Nakamoto consensus do not offer immutability because a transaction may be thought of as being on a longer chain which means it is committed. Consequently, it may be on a shorter chain which means it is no longer committed. So participants prefer to move to longer chains and when a transaction has been committed to blockchain for a long time then it immutable. It is recommended to use other consensus mechanisms like Practical Byzantine Fault Tolerance that can offer stronger, more conventional immutability properties. If blockchain contains some illegal content or the court orders some content to be removed, then it is difficult to remove.

Governance of the blockchain and blockchain based systems is a challenge when there are no central owner and stakeholders have different purposes. Stakeholders influence the software upgrade and infrastructure changes are not defined. The software upgrade may include defect fixes, new enhancements or migration to new environments or contexts. Smart contracts cannot be changed however, the state of the variables within the smart contract can be modified. So this kind of changes should be provisioned before ahead of time.

Further research is needed to draft formal specification and verification standards for smart contracts and protocols. Functional and non-functional prosperities of blockchain based solutions need to analyzed using different architectures.

The reasons for not embracing AR by the industries need to be studied. The pros and cons of existing AR platforms need to be studied.

Applications for RFID within the supply chain can be found at multiple frequencies and different RFID solutions may be required to meet the varying needs of the marketplace. Many of today's RFID technologies cannot reliably cover areas wider than 4 to 5 feet, making them unsuitable for wide openings that are the norm in manufacturing, distribution and store receiving dock environments. Since UHF can cover portals up to 9 feet wide it is gaining industry support as the choice bandwidth for inventory tracking applications including pallets and cases. Technology providers are developing readers that work with multiple system protocols and frequencies so that users will be able to choose the RFID products that work best for their market and products.

CONCLUSION

Blockchain was introduced to support the digital currency. But now it is evolved to as a foundation for transactions in the industry. It is both a database storing transaction history and computational platform to process smart contracts as transactions. It is a distributed database which is replicated across different locations as nodes and operated collectively based on consensus. Currently, the pharma supply chain is dependent on third parties for services like logistics, tracking, customs clearance and other services. By using blockchain-based solution the need for intermediaries is avoided and it can be operated collectively by the processing nodes. Compared to conventional centralized databases and computational platforms (on-premises or cloud), blockchains can reduce third parties and operational risks by providing neutral ground between stakeholders. Blockchain technologies may provide advantages for integrity and non-repudiation. However, they also currently have limitations with regard to confidentiality, privacy, and scalability. For latency and availability, reading is improved but writing is worsened. Public blockchains provide very low restrictions to the entry of new stakeholders in the pharma supply chain that can facilitate productivity. However, it does not mandate the authentication of new stakeholders, which creates challenges for regulation. Private blockchains can provide security in terms of authentication and access to address the concerns of regulation. Nevertheless, it may not be private enough to provide normal levels of confidentiality for business operations in the pharma supply chain. Blockchain may involve other components like dashboards, cryptographic key management, off-chain databases, protocols and processing of nodes. By integrating other components the business risk and regulatory acceptance may be addressed and likewise leveraging the opportunities of the blockchain.

Blockchain may be considered as an economic overlay in the world of seamlessly connected devices like IoT sensors, wearable computing and other multi devices. The foundation of blockchain is based on the assumption not to trust anyone. It overcomes traditional client-server architecture wherein each transaction need to trust the server. Instead, the peer-to-peer blockchain architecture is used by having identical nodes. By providing trusted, automated transactions without the need for third parties, blockchain enables efficiency and agility wherever products, information, ownership, location or payments change hands. Improved visibility, reduced risk and greater automation will drive down costs, improve timely delivery of goods, reduce wastage, and enable new financial models that could eliminate intermediaries.

It is called a distributed trust mechanism since it removes the dependency on a single third party to maintain the ledger. In a blockchain-based system it does not remove the trust, instead, the trust boundaries are wider. The smart contract is not a legal contract. It is a means for executing the provisions of the contract or some kind of evidence for the agreement. The massive redundancy in a large number of processing nodes in a blockchain system shall require more electricity than in a centralized non-replicated database. This is an inevitable trade-off for the distributed trust and increased availability offered by a blockchain compared to conventional client-server technology.

The distributed trust shall be critical in supporting the heterogeneous variety of participants in the supply chain. The blockchain shall act as a kind of logically centralized database of supply chain data, it can be geographically and organizationally distributed to match the real-world supply chains. Data integrity in the historical log of events is key for creating provenance about individual shipments and shall improve the efficiency. Logistics efficiency shall also be improved by providing greater transparency on the status of shipments and processes, which are currently often opaque and lack visibility. However, the rigor to have greater transparency need to be weighed in order to protect commercial confidentiality. Commercial supply chain documentation and visibility of logistics help in managing risks and facilitate trade, finance and insurance applications.

Supply chains are a highly promising domain for the application of blockchain technology. Blockchains hold potential not just to integrate transaction exchange and improve operational efficiencies across a diverse industry, but also to improve supply chain quality, facilitate provenance for pharmaceutical goods, and reduce the cost of regulatory approvals. It shall reduce cost and time for remittances but to achieve the acceptance of regulators internationally is a challenge. This book chapter helps the managers in decision making with respect to technology choices like AR or RFID or cloud computing for each of the problem statement in warehouse structuring or planning and in supply chain visibility.

REFERENCES

Sabogal, J. (2017). *Integrating IoT then Blockchain into your Drug Supply Chain*. Rockville, MD: IEEE Standards Association.

Saboo, M., Chourey A., & Suranglikar M.. (2017). *The Internet of Things:The New Rx for Pharmaceuticals Manufacturing & Supply Chains*. Cognizant.

Schöner, M. M., Kourouklis, D., Sandner, P., Gonzalez, E., & Förster, J. (2017). *Blockchain Technology in the Pharmaceutical Industry*. Frankfurt, Germany: Frankfurt School Blockchain Center.

Srivastava, A., & Dave, M. (2017). *Is Blockchain A Pipe Dream Or Right Fit For Pharma Supply Chain*. Rockville, MD: IEEE Standards Association.

Staples, M., Chen, S., Falamaki, S., Ponomarev, A., Rimba, P., Tran, A. B., ... Zhu, J. (2017). *Risks and opportunities for systems using blockchain and smart contracts. Data61*. CSIRO.

ADDITIONAL READING

Bocek, T., Rodrigues, B. B., Strasser, T., & Stiller, B. (2016). *Blockchains Everywhere - A Use-case of Blockchains in the Pharma Supply-Chain*. Zurich, Switzerland: University of Zurich.

Cirulisa, A., & Gintersa, E. (2013). *Low cost augmented reality and RFID application for logistics items visualization*. Valmiera, Latvia: ICTE in Regional Development.

KEY TERMS AND DEFINITIONS

AR: Augmented reality.

Bitcoin: It is a peer-to-peer payment system invented by an unidentified programmer, or group of programmers, under the name of Satoshi Nakamoto.

DLT: Digital ledger system.

DSCSA: Drug supply chain security act. It is a more uniform drug tracking system to institute full, unit-level track-and-trace systems for products as they move through the supply chain.

Ethereum: It is a public blockchain-based distributed computing platform, featuring smart contract functionality. It provides a decentralized virtual machine, the Ethereum virtual machine (EVM), which can execute peer-to-peer contracts using a token called ether.

GDP: Good distribution practice of medicinal products for human use.

GMP: Good manufacturing practice.

GPRS: General packet radio service. It is a packet-oriented mobile data service on the 2G and 3G cellular communication system's global system for mobile communications (GSM).

GPS: Global positioning system. It is a network of orbiting satellites that send precise details of their position in space back to earth.

GSM: Global system for mobile communications. It is a standard developed by the European Telecommunications Standards Institute (ETSI) to describe the protocols for second-generation digital cellular networks used by mobile devices.

IoT: Internet of things.

PDMA: Prescription drug marketing act.

POS: Point of sale.

RFID: Radio frequency identification. It is a method of identifying items uniquely using radio waves. Radio waves do not require line of site and can pass through materials like cardboard and plastic but not metals and some liquids.

ROI: Return on investment.

TAG: The generic term for a radio frequency identification device. Sometimes referred to as smart labels.

UHF: Ultra-high frequency (UHF; 850 to 950 MHz). Ultra-high frequency radio band allocated for RFID use. UHF RFID can send information faster and farther than high and low frequency tags. UHF RFID is gaining industry support as the choice bandwidth for inventory tracking applications including pallets and cases. UHF RFID features larger tags and readers with the longest read distances (2-3 feet with handheld readers and more than 9 feet with portal readers).

Chapter 12
Knowledge Sharing Barriers Affecting Pharmaceutical Supply Chain Performance

Anirban Ganguly
O. P. Jindal Global University, India

Debdeep Chatterjee
Concordia University, Canada

Asim Talukdar
O. P. Jindal Global University, India

ABSTRACT

The pharmaceutical supply chain is one of the most complex supply chains in the world. The primary objective of this chapter is to analyze the role of knowledge sharing barriers in supply chain performance. The chapter will explore significant knowledge sharing barriers that might deter the performance of a pharmaceutical supply chain. This chapter is expected to provide the twofold contribution to the academicians and practitioners. Firstly, it will socialize the importance of knowledge sharing barriers and the role they can play in deterring the performance of a pharmaceutical supply chain, and secondly, the prioritized ranking of the identified knowledge sharing barriers is expected to aid the policymakers and managers to understand the relative importance of the knowledge sharing barriers and design their knowledge management strategies accordingly.

DOI: 10.4018/978-1-5225-5921-4.ch012

INTRODUCTION

The pharmaceutical industry can be stated as a systemic network of a set of complex processes, operations and organizational structure which is involved in the discovery, development, and manufacturing of medications. It comprises the part of the healthcare sector that deals with medications and comprises of drug manufacturers, drug marketers, and biotechnology companies (Benson, 2015). Over the years, the pharmaceutical industry has played a vital role in facilitating business operations and societal growth of a country. The origin of the pharmaceutical industry stems from two important sources – the apothecaries and that moved into wholesale production of drugs and the chemical companies that established research labs and discovered medical applications for their products starting in the late nineteenth center (Chemical and Engineering News). With time, the pharmaceutical industry had undergone major transformation and innovations, and have become one of the leading revenue generating sectors of business. The global pharmaceutical industry was worth an estimated $1 trillion in 2014 and currently, the worldwide pharmaceutical sales have amounted to $963 billion (Statista, 2018). Additionally, the value of the global prescription drug market was estimated to be $816 billion in 2016 and the US market, which was a key driver of the growth, accounted for $320 billion in 2016 (Hardman&Co, 2017). Therefore, the importance of pharmaceutical industry had been acknowledged by academicians and practitioners alike, and have highlighted the need for further investigation in this sector.

In spite of its heightened importance, globalization, the complexity of new pharmaceutical drugs and equipment, and diminishing protection by patents have affected all stages of the business value chain – from drug development till distribution and networking (Papageorgiou et al., 2001). This, therefore, has compelled the pharmaceutical organizations to revisit their business model and often come up with new business strategies. Furthermore, the complexity of the pharmaceutical industry and healthcare, in general, has highlighted the need for efficient management of its supply chain. However, in spite of the utmost importance of supply chain in the manufacturing (and service) domain, the pharmaceutical industry was one of the late adopters in the application of modern supply chain and practices. A possible reason for this can be the fact that the profitable heritage of the pharmaceutical industry, coupled with the low cost of goods sold (COGS), might have been responsible for its lack of impetus on designing and managing efficient supply chain (Singh, 2005). However, during the past decade, the pharmaceutical supply chain has started gaining rapid prominence in the market, mainly as a weapon to combat the huge complexity and heterogeneity associated with it. This situation has been further complicated by the interplay of fundamentally different types of key stakeholders, such as drug manufacturers, wholesale distributors, retail pharmacies, hospitals, managed care organizations, and insurance companies (Singh, 2005), thereby elevating the importance of pharmaceutical supply chain in the process.

Over the years, it has been observed that the operational process of the pharmaceutical industry has been twofold – a part that is involved in discovery and developments of the pharmaceutical drugs and equipment, and the second one that is involved in the distribution and selling of the same. Therefore, equal emphasis needs to be placed on both the aspects in order to develop an efficient pharmaceutical supply chain. A supply chain can be defined as "a network of independent or independent business entities collectively responsible for procurement, manufacturing, and distribution activities associated with the manufacturing of a product" (Swaminathan et al., 1998, p. 607). Supply chain management, which includes an effective coordination between supply and demand and involves sourcing of raw materials and work in progress inventories, manufacturing and assembly, logistics (and reverse logistics) and distribution, and inventory management, among others, currently form the backbone of any manufacturing and service industry alike. As a result, the pharmaceutical industry has started comprehending the importance of having an efficient supply chain in their system. Procurements, logistics, inventory management and distribution had become important ingredients for the pharmaceutical industry to strive and survive in the market. Furthermore, an emerging interest in reverse logistics and the vast number of product recalls over the years has elevated the importance of supply chain among the pharmaceutical organization (Narayana et al., 2014). Additionally, recycling, disposal, scheduling, and planning have been studied in the context of designing effective distribution networks and healthcare logistics (Narayana et al., 2014), thereby making it utmost important for the pharmaceutical industry to design and develop efficient supply chain.

Like any other industry, information regarding demand patterns and flow of inventory (and materials) are intrinsically connected. The pharmaceutical supply chain is a rich example of information flows to many stakeholders and since the information regarding demand and flow of materials are intrinsically connected, speed and accuracy are among the major concerns on managing information (Pedroso & Nakano, 2009). According to Pedroso and Zwicker (2008), the pharmaceutical supply chain can harbor structured, unstructured, controlled and uncontrolled knowledge dissemination, so it could be important for the pharmaceutical organizations to map those knowledge flows. Furthermore, since the decision making in the case of a pharmaceutical supply chain is especially significant since shortage of necessary medicines and improper use of pharmaceutical products is not only lead to a financial loss for the organization, but also can lead to a loss in human life (Uthayakumar & Priyan, 2013), a superior management and sharing of information/knowledge can aid in mitigating this uncertainty (and the consequent loss arising out of it). However, in spite of the utmost importance of knowledge sharing ineffective performance of the supply chain, it has been observed that certain barriers to knowledge sharing can act as a major roadblock to effective flow of knowledge, thereby deterring the overall supply chain performance, which in turn can lead to increased cost and ultimately customer dissatisfaction. It is therefore important that organizations become aware of barriers to knowledge sharing and implement necessary steps to overcome those. The current chapter tries to shed some light on this important issue of knowledge sharing barriers affecting supply chain performance.

The purpose of this chapter is to explore the significant knowledge sharing barriers that might hinder the performance of a pharmaceutical supply chain. Beginning with an overview of pharmaceutical supply chains and the role that knowledge sharing can play in facilitating its performance, the chapter goes to identify a set of important knowledge sharing barriers that might act as a stumbling block in the functioning and management of pharmaceutical supply chains. The chapter will also orient the readers on the role that the identified knowledge sharing barriers can play in preventing a streamlined management of the supply chain. Additionally, through a survey conducted on the Indian pharmaceutical sector, this chapter will also determine a relative ranking of the identified knowledge sharing barriers to access their relative criticality. The chapter will also draw inferences based on the discussions and direct the readers to possible areas of further development and research. This chapter is expected to contribute to the body of knowledge in the domain of pharmaceutical supply chain by (a) socializing the importance of knowledge sharing barriers in deterring the performance of the pharmaceutical supply chain and (b) the prioritized ranking of the identified knowledge sharing barriers is expected to aid the policy makers and managers to understand the relative importance of the knowledge sharing barriers and in turn design their knowledge management strategies.

PHARMACEUTICAL SUPPLY CHAIN: AN OVERVIEW

A pharmaceutical supply chain can be defined as *a socio-technical system aimed to align firms in enabling the achievement of improved health status through medicines provisions. Complementary and alternative products and process technologies may coexist within such a system* (Settanni et al., 2017). It typically consists of primary and manufacturing organizations, distribution and warehousing, logistics, wholesalers, retailers/hospitals/health centers and last but not the least, the patients (Shah, 2004; Yu et al., 2010). A pharmaceutical supply chain, therefore, is primarily concerned with the correct pharmaceutical drugs and equipment reaching the right patients at the right time. Furthermore, the pharmaceutical companies at the upstream source of the products need to minimize their integrated total cost in supply chain and inventory management without compromising with customer satisfaction (Uthayakumar & Priyan, 2013).

Therefore, it is essential that a pharmaceutical supply chain needs to have perfect coordination among their channel members in order to ensure that both cost and service objectives are successfully met. Figure 1 provides the readers with a simple schematic of a pharmaceutical supply chain.

Figure 1 provides the readers with a basic framework of the pharmaceutical supply chain. A typical pharmaceutical supply chain starts with the suppliers of raw materials and other inventories to the manufacturers who in turn manufactures the pharmaceutical drugs. The manufacturers are generally grouped into two types the branded drug manufacturers and the generic ones. The manufacturers in turn either sell the finished product either directly (Government, Hospitals etc.) or through an intermediary like a distributor, who in turn sales it to the retailers. Ultimately, the pharmaceutical drugs and equipment reach the patients, either directly or through an intermediary. Therefore, as we can see, the key stakeholders for a supply chain comprises of multiple entities like suppliers, manufacturers, distributors, hospital, pharmacies and last but not the least, the patients. Furthermore, according to Singh (2005), to add to the existing complexity of the supply chain, it is further made complex by adding other entities like insurance companies, healthcare management organizations, and regulatory bodies, among others. Additionally, one of the most important drivers of the pharmaceutical industry is the time-to-market and organizations, who are successful in following this gains significant returns in the early life of a successful drug (Shah, 2004). Therefore, it is advisable to restructure the supply chain along local and global avenues, which is expected to lead to a reduction in capacity, and an increase in the time to delivery and in turn will be beneficial for both the organization and the patients alike.

Figure 1. The pharmaceutical supply chain
Source: (own elaboration)

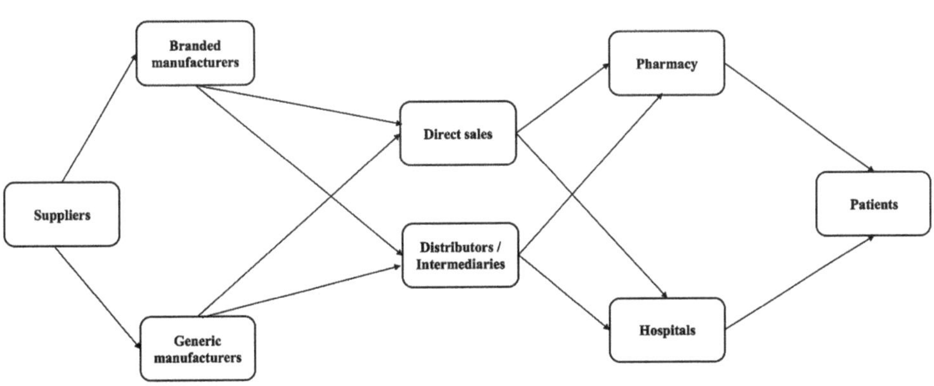

One of the key drivers of effective supply chain management is a proper flow of information. An effective flow of information from the source to the destination and vice versa can ensure that the activities and decisions throughout the supply chain are coordinated (Lee and Whang, 2000), thereby improving the overall performance of the supply chain. An effective sharing of information/knowledge among the pharmaceutical supply chain members can lead to effective inventory management, operationally efficient logistics and distribution, optimization of warehousing and reverse logistics and successful demand forecasting, among others. Furthermore, extant literature in knowledge sharing has repeatedly indicated the importance of the application of the same in the context of supply chains due to the fragmented knowledge across complex supply chains (Mara et al., 2012). Although the concepts of knowledge management and sharing have been mostly discussed in the context of outsourcing, decision support, new product development, (Al-Mutawaha et al., 2009), there is still a dearth of literature in addressing this issue in the context of the pharmaceutical supply chain. Furthermore, the barriers to knowledge sharing, which has proved to be the downfall of many organizations and their supply chain, has also not been discussed in the context of the pharmaceutical supply chains. The current chapter tries to bridge this gap in the extant literature by addressing this important but rarely discussed topic.

KNOWLEDGE SHARING IN SUPPLY CHAIN

Over the years, knowledge management and sharing have become key determinants of the competitive advantage of supply chains. In order to improve inter-organizational coordination and product quality, manufacturing firms often require sharing process knowledge (Cheng et al., 2008). Knowledge sharing within a supply chain has thus become a common practice because it enhances the competitive advantage of the supply chain as a whole (Cheng et al., 2008; Holland, 1995). Since supply chains are designed for achieving competitive advantage, it is important for the organization (pharmaceutical organization, in the current context) to have a good understanding of the factors affecting knowledge sharing, and also possibly, the barriers affecting the same. In this context, Zhou and Benton (2007) have identified the quality of information, the content of the information and the technological support felicitating the information/knowledge sharing process as the key drivers of information/knowledge sharing in supply chains. Additionally, they also emphasized the role of effective information sharing in enhancing supply chain practice and dynamism.

According to Rashed et al. (2010), a knowledge sharing in supply chains are more valuable as they are nothing but a more valuable and actionable information. Since knowledge is a collection of information presented in a useful fashion, it allows for making decisions regarding a particular decision, unlike information, which simply gives us the fact (Rasheed et al., 2010). Knowledge sharing, which can comprise of both explicit (knowledge that is documented) and tacit (knowledge which is not documented but mostly gathered from experience, etc.) knowledge, is expected to vastly improve the operational effectiveness and performance of a supply chain. Therefore, firms need to share knowledge both internally and externally with their customers, suppliers, and partners (Shih et al., 2012) in order to derive superior profits and gain competitive advantage. Furthermore, since the current day supply chains are often dispersed across the globe, sharing of knowledge and information among the various nodes of the supply chain has become even more paramount. Therefore, by coordinating different parties along the supply chain network, or establishing business partnerships, supply chain management creates a win-win situation for all members, thereby bringing about a great advance in gaining a firm foothold in the market (Yu et al., 2001). Therefore, as various researchers have repeatedly indicated, knowledge sharing, in various forms and entities, can go a long way in ensuring the success of a supply chain. However, having said this, researchers have also pointed towards the failure of supply chains due to the lack of proper sharing and transfer of knowledge, which has been termed as knowledge sharing barriers by Reige (2005). The current research expects to shed some light on this issue and the subsequent sections of the chapter will be devoted towards identifying and analyzing a set of critical knowledge sharing barriers associated with the performance of a supply chain – in particular, a pharmaceutical supply chain.

KNOWLEDGE SHARING BARRIERS

Over the years, knowledge sharing has become an important ingredient for an organization's knowledge management strategy and practice. However, despite the importance of knowledge sharing in achieving competitive advantage, it has been observed that several barriers often make the knowledge sharing process extremely difficult to achieve, thereby compromising in the performance of the organization and deliver a positive return on investment (Reige, 2005). This is also true for an organization's supply chain, which requires a harmonious functioning among all their members for its successful performance. Knowledge sharing barriers can be termed as a set of factors that might deter the transfer of knowledge (Szulanski, 2003), thereby making it difficult for the organizations to achieve the goals and deliver a positive return on investment (Ganguly et al., 2018). Knowledge sharing barriers can, therefore, lead to a delay in product introduction, increased cost and ultimately, a fall in customer satisfaction (Barson et al., 2000), all of which can lead to a severe dent in competitive advantage. Additionally, knowledge sharing barriers might also refrain employees from sharing knowledge with colleagues and other external/internal entities (Titi Amayah, 2013), which might lead to a reduction in the dissemination of knowledge, leading to the failure of a supply chain in the process.

It can be stated that organizational climate and culture, coupled other factors such as individual motivation, teams, technology and so on might prove to be a barrier in the effective transfer of knowledge (Sun & Scott, 2005). Furthermore, knowledge sharing barriers can be both external (originating from external knowledge and sources) as well as internal (originating from within an organization) in nature (Ganguly et al., in press), as well as 'driving' and 'dependent' barriers, with the driving barriers being the leading, independent barriers while the dependent barriers are influenced by others, which hinders KS (and KM in general) in the process (Sharma et al., 2012). Furthermore, knowledge sharing barriers have broadly been classified into three major groups - organizational, individual and technology (Riege, 2005). While organizational factors include organizational structure and culture, individual barriers are related to the internal being of the individual, such as motivation and cultural background and the technical factors include the unavailability of the required technological resources to assist in the implementation of knowledge sharing activities (Vajjhala & Vucetic, 2013). Researchers have also argued that identified culture (both organizational and individual), leadership, efforts vs. reward, knowledge complexity and the influence of social factors such as level of trust among employees could influence the perceptions of KS (McDermott and O'Dell, 2001; Vajjhala & Vucetic, 2013). While Okoroafor (2014) identified trust, culture and knowledge fit as three of the major barriers to knowledge sharing, Rivera-Vazquez et al. (2009) identified the cultural barriers as one of the foremost ones for knowledge sharing activities in an organization. Additionally, lack of top management commitment and incentives to encourage sharing of knowledge, in addition to individual and social barriers that often prevent effective knowledge sharing have also been identified as major barriers to knowledge sharing in an organization (Bureš, 2003; Sensky, 2002; Singh & Kant, 2008).

IDENTIFYING THE KNOWLEDGE SHARING BARRIERS IN A PHARMACEUTICAL SUPPLY CHAIN

Over the years, researchers on supply chain management have repeatedly stressed the importance of knowledge sharing in its effective and efficient performance. Along with the positive effect of knowledge sharing, possible barriers to knowledge sharing in supply chains has also been a subject of previous research activities (Aziz & Sparrow, 2011; Bandopadhyay & Pathak, 2007; Cheng et al, 2008; Gunasekaran & Ngai, 2004; Natti & Ojasalo, 2008; Patil & Kant, 2014). The major issue with most supply chains is that the philosophy of knowledge management and sharing is not embedded in their system and business processes. As a result, the participation level of knowledge management and sharing is very low and often neglected, the top management not committed enough to support the process, as well as the funds allocated towards this process is often insufficient (Natti & Ojaslo, 2008;.Zhao et al., 2012). Furthermore, lack of trust among supply chain members, coupled with low data and information security, makes knowledge sharing even more difficult in the supply chains and opportunistic behavior of certain supply chain members has the strongest negative influence on trust and knowledge sharing (Cheng et al., 2008; Patil & Kant, 2014). Finally, lack of technological infrastructure to adapt knowledge management and sharing in the supply chain has also proven to be a significant barrier to knowledge sharing in supply chains (Wong & Wong, 2011).

Based on the literature review of knowledge sharing barriers affecting supply chains, coupled with discussions with the subject matter experts and industry professionals in the field of pharmaceutical supply chain, the authors identified a set of fourteen important knowledge sharing barriers that might affect the performance of a pharmaceutical supply chain. These are provided to the readers in table 1, along with the related literature.

Table 1 presents in front of the readers a set of fourteen critical knowledge sharing barriers (B1 to B14) that might serve as a roadblock to the effective performance of a pharmaceutical supply chain. Literature reviews, discussions and interviews comprised the main techniques used to arrive at the research results. The authors' had multiple formal and informal discussions with the subject matter experts, in addition to referring to the extant literature on the role of knowledge sharing and knowledge management in pharmaceutical supply chains in order to arrive at the initial set of barriers. The initial set was then discussed with the subject matter experts to validate their authenticity and also to separate the vital few from the trivial many. The subject matter experts were identified after careful consideration and consisted of highly experienced industry professionals from the Indian pharmaceutical sector and having experience in dealing with pharmaceutical supply chains. In addition, their knowledge regarding knowledge management / knowledge sharing was also taken into account. The discussions and interviews with subject matter experts were conducted formally and informally by the authors' themselves through telephone, Skype and face to face and the salient points arising out of the discussion were carefully noted and subsequently used to finalize the set of KS barriers illustrated in table 1.

The data gathered based on the discussions and the interviews were analyzed with the objective of determining any underlying pattern or trend in the identification process of the knowledge sharing barriers. It was noted that although the subject matter experts were involved in individual (and separate) interviews/discussion sessions,

Table 1. Critical knowledge sharing barriers affecting pharmaceutical supply chain performance

#	Knowledge Sharing Barriers	Source
B1	Lack of trust and commitment of supply chain members	Shih et al. (2012), Samuel et al. (2011), Spekman et al. (2002)
B2	Lack of information security within the supply chain	Gunasekaran and Ngai (2004)
B3	Opportunistic behavior of the supply chain members for their own motive and purpose	Cheng et al. (2008)
B4	Lack of willingness to share knowledge among the different members of the supply chain	Natti and Ojasalo (2008), Shih et al. (2012), Hutzschenreuter and Horstkotte (2010)
B5	Lack of technology support and infrastructure	Wong and Wong (2011)
B6	Lack of proper organizational structure	Ahmad and Daghfous (2010), Natti and Ojasalo (2008),
B7	Lack of reciprocity of knowledge	Hong et al. (2011), Wasko and Faraj (2005)
B8	Lack of top management commitment, including financial commitment	Bandyopadhyay and Pathak (2007), Reige (2005), Oliva (2014)
B9	Lack of rewards and incentives, thereby leading to a loss in motivation to share knowledge	Hutzschenreuter and Horstkotte (2010)
B10	Loss of intellectual property ownership	Chou and Passerini (2009)
B11	Lack of technical assistance to the suppliers	Hutzschenreuter and Horstkotte (2010)
B12	Difficulty in understanding and codifying tacit knowledge	Simonin (2004)
B13	Lack of formal and informal interaction among the supply chain members, thereby leading to a lack of knowledge sharing	Bartol and Srivastava (2002), Reige (2005),
B14	Unclear definition of roles and responsibilities of supply chain members	Natti and Ojasalo (2008)

Source: (own elaboration based on sources mentioned in the table)

there emerged a distinct pattern in them in filtering out the vital ones from the initially identified set of barriers. The interview/discussion notes exhibited fourteen barriers associated with a knowledge sharing in the performance of a pharmaceutical supply chain process and were considered as the final set for further analysis.

RESULT ANALYSIS: RANKING THE BARRIERS

Once the final set of risks was identified based on discussions/interviews with the subject matter experts, the next stage was to design a self-administered survey that was used for further analysis of the barriers. Research on self-administered surveys has suggested that the design of the instrument is extremely important in obtaining unbiased answers from respondents (Couper et al., 2001; Fink, 2008). Since the survey formed a very important component of the overall objective of the research it was designed with careful accuracy. The survey respondents selected were industry professionals having considerable experience in the pharmaceutical industry and who was well conversant with the operations of their supply chain. The number of industry professionals surveyed was 50 and the data were gathered in the form of a survey questionnaire was designed for prioritization of the identified knowledge sharing barriers. In this context, it should be mentioned that before the survey was sent out to the targeted respondents, a pilot survey was conducted on a group of four to five experts from the pharmaceutical industry with considerable experience in supply chain management. The purpose of the pilot study was to reveal deficiencies in the design of the survey before it was deployed within the main study. It also aided the authors' to reduce the number of unanticipated problems regarding the study, as well as providing them with clearer ideas and approaches that enhanced the chances of getting clearer findings in the main study. Some of the issues that were revealed by the pilot study (for example, some of the questions were restructured with the intention of reducing ambiguity) were subsequently resolved prior to sending out the final survey questionnaire. Once the responses were gathered, the next step was to analyze the responses to arrive at the final conclusion, as discussed in the following paragraph.

As a part of the survey responses, the respondents were asked to rate the impact of the knowledge sharing barriers on a 7 point Likert scale. The 7-point Likert was used as it tends to be a good balance between having enough points of discrimination without having to maintain too many response options. Once the responses were obtained, the next stage was to determine the mean and standard deviation of the identified barriers with the objective of looking at their relative criticality for the performance of the pharmaceutical supply chain. This is illustrated in table 2.

Table 2 exhibits the identified barriers along with their mean and standard deviation. Based on their mean values, the knowledge sharing barriers were ranked and the ranks were provided in the last column. Figure 2 exhibits the knowledge sharing barriers to the readers in the descending order of their criticality.

Table 2. Relative criticality of the identified knowledge sharing barriers affecting pharmaceutical supply chain performance

	Knowledge Sharing Barriers	Mean	Standard Deviation	Rank
B1	Lack of trust and commitment of supply chain members	6.47	0.997	1
B2	Lack of information security within the supply chain	6.07	1.002	4
B3	Opportunistic behavior of the supply chain members for their own motive and purpose	6.14	1.101	3
B4	Lack of willingness to share knowledge among different members of the supply chain	6.22	0.986	2
B5	Lack of technological support and infrastructure	5.44	0.885	8
B6	Lack of proper organizational structure	5.84	0.976	6
B7	Lack of reciprocity of knowledge	6.01	0.879	5
B8	Lack of top management commitment, including financial commitment	5.61	0.923	7
B9	Lack of rewards and incentives, thereby leading to a loss in motivation to share knowledge	4.78	0.891	9
B10	Loss of intellectual property ownership	4.59	1.004	10
B11	Lack of technical assistance to the suppliers	4.16	0.971	12
B12	Difficulty in understanding and codifying tacit knowledge	3.13	0.897	14
B13	Lack of formal and informal interaction among the supply chain members, thereby leading to a lack of knowledge sharing	4.32	1.005	11
B14	Unclear definition of roles and responsibilities of supply chain members	3.68	0.788	13

Source: (own elaboration)

As seen from Figure 2 (and Table 1), lack of trust and commitment among the supply chain members emerged to be the most important knowledge sharing barriers affecting the performance of a pharmaceutical supply chain. This was followed by lack of willingness to share knowledge among the supply chain members (which once again can be deduced to stem from the lack of trust) and the opportunistic behavior of the supply chain members. Furthermore, lack of information security and

Figure 2. Relative criticality of the knowledge sharing barriers
Source: (own elaboration)

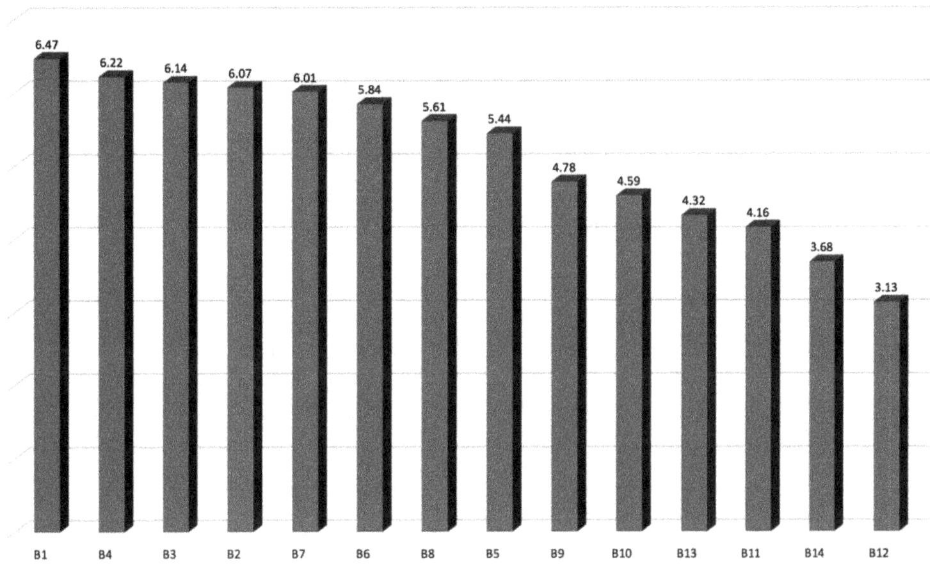

reciprocity of knowledge also proved to be significant barriers to knowledge sharing affecting the performance of a pharmaceutical supply chain. However, it was also observed that unclear definitions of roles and responsibilities of the supply chain members, lack of formal and informal meetings, difficulty in understanding tacit knowledge, among others, although considered as important barriers, but was not given as much priority by the supply chain professionals in the Indian pharmaceutical industry, as the other barriers.

Once the barriers were identified and ranked, the next stage of the research was to consolidate them into important groups with the objective of developing a theory for the barriers. The statistical technique of Factor Analysis (FA), which involves the goal of representing the interrelationships among a set of variables by a set of broad reference variables called factors, was used to achieve this objective. These group of variables (which are also known as factors) are by definition highly inter-correlated and are assumed to represent dimensions within the data (Hair et al., 2010). Once the number of factors was determined, the following step was to select a rotation method with the objective of having a better understanding of the groups. The rotation technique used in this study was the 'varimax rotation', which led to a proper representation of the relationship between the barriers and the rotated components, called factor loadings. This is provided to the readers in Table 3.

Table 3. Factors representing the KS barriers affecting pharmaceutical supply chain performance

KS Barriers and Factors	Loading Coefficients	Reliability (Cronbach's α)
F1. Organizational Barriers		
B2. Lack of information security within the supply chain	0.903	0.725
B6. Lack of proper organizational structure	0.702	
B8. Lack of top management commitment	0832	
B9. Lack of rewards and incentives	0.876	
B10. Loss of intellectual property ownership	0.709	
B13. Lack of formal and informal interaction among the supply chain members, thereby leading to a lack of knowledge sharing	0.793	
B14. Unclear definition of roles and responsibilities of supply chain members	0.683	
F2. Individual Barriers		
B1. Lack of trust and commitment of supply chain members	0.802	0.714
B3. Opportunistic behavior of the supply chain members for their own motive and purpose	0.697	
B4. Lack of willingness to share knowledge among different members of the supply chain	0.736	
B7. Lack of reciprocity of knowledge	0.702	
B12. Difficulty in understanding and codifying tacit knowledge	0.643	
F3. Technology Barriers		
B5. Lack of technological support and infrastructure	0.712	0.687
B11. Lack of technical assistance to the supplier	0.681	

Source: Authors' own research and findings

Table 3 exhibits the identified barriers along with their factors, loading coefficient and the reliability measure (Cronbach's α). According to the literature on statistics, reliability analysis is generally conducted to check the internal consistency of a summated scale where several items are summed to form a total score (Ganguly et al., 2018). In the context of this research, the value of Cronbach's Alpha (α) for the scales ranged from 0.687 to 0.725, suggesting that the items have relatively acceptable internal consistency for this type of exploratory research (Hair et al., 2010). The following section of the chapter will be devoted towards a detailed discussion of the findings derived from the survey of the knowledge sharing barriers.

DISCUSSING THE MAJOR FINDINGS

Knowledge management and sharing have often been considered as one of the most important ingredients for the proper functioning of a supply chain. The purpose of this chapter was to familiarize the academicians and practitioners alike regarding the important role that barriers to knowledge sharing might play in achieving the desired success of a pharmaceutical supply chain. Once the result from the study was collected and analyzed, the authors thought it to be worthwhile to discuss the result as obtained above in the light of other research made in the similar areas and to contextualize it thereby highlighting the similarities and differences observed. A review of extant literature of knowledge sharing barriers affecting supply chain performance indicated that individual factors play a very important role in preventing proper harnessing of knowledge, along with the organizational factors. This was in conformance with the current study (table 2), where individual factors related came out to be the most important ones and the lack of trust turned out to be the most important one. A possible reason for this might be the highly complex and often unstructured nature of pharmaceutical supply chains in India. Additionally, cutthroat competition among a plethora of supply chains, in both the branded and the generic sector, might also lead to the lack of trust arising out of the fear of losing competitive ground. This was in conformance with the previous studies by Shih et al. (2012), Samuel et al. (2011) and Spekman et al. (2002), among others, who indicated that the lack of trust is one of the major deterrents of supply chain performance. Additionally, the lack of trust is assumed to lead to a reluctance in knowledge sharing among the supply chain members, which came out to be the second most important barrier. Furthermore, due to the highly complex and unstructured nature of the Indian pharmaceutical supply chain, coupled with lack of information security, makes it extremely difficult for a proper exchange and sharing of knowledge, which also emerged as one of the major barriers to knowledge sharing. This supports the findings of Gunasekaran and Ngai (2004). Additionally, the lack of reciprocity of knowledge as well as the opportunistic behavior of the supply chain members also acted as important knowledge sharing deterrent in the Indian pharmaceutical sector.

In addition to the individual knowledge sharing behavior, it was also observed from the study that the organization also plays a role in deterring knowledge sharing among supply chain members. Among those, lack of proper organization structure, top management commitment, and unclear definition of roles and responsibilities of the supply chain members evolved as the most important ones. This, once again, can be attributed to the unstructured nature of the Indian pharmaceutical sector, especially for the organizations specializing in selling generic brands, where the entire operations are often conducted in a less than systematic fashion. In those cases, top management is not entirely devoted towards ensuring an efficient knowledge flow among the supply chain members, in addition to the organization structure not being able to facilitate the same. On top of this, since ensuring proper supply chain activities are often considered as routine jobs for the supply chain members, they are not rewarded for coming up with a new idea that might improve the efficiency of the supply chain. The lack of rewards and incentives was highlighted in previous studies (Hutzschenreuter & Horstkotte, 2010; Lekhawipat et al., 2018), and once again proved to be an important knowledge sharing barriers in the context of the current investigation.

Finally, it was also observed that certain technological issues also played a role in acting as knowledge sharing barriers in the Indian pharmaceutical industry. Lack of technical assistance to the suppliers (Hutzschenreuter & Horstkotte, 2010) and the lack of technological support and infrastructure (Wong & Wong, 2011) proved to be the most important ones. In spite of India making rapid progress in the domain of information and technology, there is still a long way to go in reaching the technological infrastructure provided by the developed nations. This is also evident in the supply chain performance, where technical glitches can often result in a delay in information transfer, which in turn can bullwhip into a substantial financial loss to the organizations – especially so in the case of the pharmaceutical industry, which itself is highly complex and delicate in nature.

The Factor analysis conducted on the identified barriers resulted in three clear factors – Organizational, Individual and Technology related. These findings confirmed to the previous findings from the domain of knowledge sharing, which emphasized the importance of the abovementioned three major categories of knowledge sharing barriers. As observed from table 3, Organizational and Individual Barriers came out to be the two most important ones, followed by the Technological barriers as determined by the Indian pharmaceutical SMEs., and the findings reflect the ones observed through generalized studies.

CONCLUSION AND FUTURE RESEARCH DIRECTIONS

Although the body of literature on knowledge management and knowledge sharing has substantially expanded over the years, there is still a noticeable dearth of literature on identifying and analyzing knowledge sharing barriers (apart from the seminal work by Riege, 2005), especially in the domain of pharmaceutical sector. The study conducted in this research has identified a set of important knowledge sharing barriers that might hinder the performance of a pharmaceutical supply chain. The identified knowledge sharing barriers are expected to serve as a roadmap to the practitioners involved in designing and managing the supply chain of a pharmaceutical organization. The information provided in this paper should aid the policy makers to understand the critical knowledge sharing barriers associated with the performance of a pharmaceutical supply chain and the relative criticality would help them to develop mitigation strategies accordingly. It would enable practitioners engaged in the pharmaceutical supply chain to understand the similarities and dissimilarities between supply chains of other industries. For example, the supply chain entities in a pharmaceutical supply chain are diverse and special attention should be paid to build trust and motivate inter-entity knowledge sharing. This could be made possible by organizing more field visit days, early supplier integration, however, there are more stringent regulation and patent laws which thus restraint needs to be exercised beyond a certain point. Moreover, there is a flow of technical information among certain entities of the supply chain and rich information requires high capacity channels and it is much more effectively delivered by personal contact. (Pedroso & Nakano, 2009). There is also scope to further integrate technological capabilities into downstream pharmaceutical supply chain, for example, CVS, a major US pharmacy chain. CVS allows customers to place prescription orders on the CVS Web site and pick up their orders at their local store, eliminating waiting time in the process (Lee & Whang, 2001).

Pharmaceutical industry offers certain unique features when compared to other industries. It has a very stable demand for generic products while there is no purchasing decision power with the final consumers. There are visibly imposing challenges in the upstream pharmaceutical supply chain where there is a need for technical knowledge dissemination among supply chain partners in a timely and confidential manner. We expect as technologies like RFID and specialized inventory management theories like VMI system develop different nodes of supply chain performance in the chain will be significantly improved. An emerging area is that of rapid response group who operate in emergency situations but and it will definitely broaden the horizon of the pharmaceutical supply chain. From researchers' point of view, the addition of e-commerce in the pharmaceutical supply chains would demand a renewed examination of restructured contractual relationships between manufacturers, suppliers, and consumers. All these fluxes in the pharmaceutical supply chain also mean that knowledge sharing mechanism and scope will also be readjusted. However, in the current day business environment, where the success of an organization often rests on the success of its supply chain, knowledge sharing barriers can serve as a roadblock towards its success, which in turn might end up lowering the bottom line of the organization. So, organizations need to be wary about the changes in the industry and the implications in knowledge sharing activity inside their supply chains.

REFERENCES

Ahmad, N., & Daghfous, A. (2010). Knowledge sharing through inter-organizational knowledge networks Challenges and opportunities in the United Arab Emirates. *European Business Review*, *22*(2), 153–174. doi:10.1108/09555341011023506

Al-Mutawah, K., Lee, V., & Cheung, Y. (2009). A new multi-agent system framework for tacit knowledge management in manufacturing supply chains. *Journal of Intelligent Manufacturing*, *20*(5), 593–610. doi:10.100710845-008-0142-0

Aziz, N., & Sparrow, J. (2011). Patterns of gaining and sharing of knowledge about customers: A study of an Express Parcel Delivery Company. *Knowledge Management Research and Practice*, *9*(1), 29–47. doi:10.1057/kmrp.2011.3

Bartol, K. M., & Srivastava, A. (2002). Encouraging knowledge sharing: The role of organizational reward systems. *Journal of Leadership & Organizational Studies*, *9*(1), 64–76. doi:10.1177/107179190200900105

Benson, M. (2015, January 22). *An easier way to understand the pharma industry*. Retrieved from: https://marketrealist.com/2015/01/easier-way-understand-pharma-industry

Bureš, V. (2003). Cultural Barriers in Knowledge Sharing. E+M Ekonomics and Management, Liberec, 6, 57-62.

Chemical & Engineering News. (n.d.). Retrieved from https://pubs.acs.org/cen/coverstory/83/8325/8325future.html

Cheng, J. H., Yeh, C. H., & Tu, C. W. (2008). Trust and knowledge sharing in green supply chains. *Supply Chain Management*, *13*(4), 283–295. doi:10.1108/13598540810882170

Chou, P., & Passerini, K. (2009). Intellectual property rights and knowledge sharing across countries. *Journal of Knowledge Management*, *13*(5), 331–344. doi:10.1108/13673270910988141

Couper, M. P., Traugott, M. W., & Lamias, M. J. (2001). Web survey design and administration. *Public Opinion Quarterly*, *65*(2), 230–253. doi:10.1086/322199 PMID:11420757

Fink, A. (2012). *How to Conduct Surveys: A Step-by-Step Guide*. Sage Publications.

Ganguly, A., Chatterjee, D., & Farr, J. V. (2018). Evaluating Barriers to Knowledge Sharing affecting New Product Development team performance. *International Journal of Innovation Management*, *1850048*. doi:10.1142/S1363919618500482

Gunasekaran, A., & Ngai, E. W. T. (2004). Information systems in supply chain integration and management. *European Journal of Operational Research, 159*(2), 269–295. doi:10.1016/j.ejor.2003.08.016

Hair, J. P., William, C., Black, W. C., Babin, B. J., & Anderson, R. E. (2010). *Multivariate Data Analysis*. Pearson.

Hardman & Co. (2017, March 2). *Global Pharmaceuticals. 2016 Industry Statistics*. Retrieved from: http://www.hardmanandco.com/docs/default-source/sector-docs/life-sciences-documents/02.03.17-global-pharmaceutical-industry-2016-statistics.pdf

Holland, C. P. (1995). Cooperative supply chain management: The impact of interorganizational information systems. *The Journal of Strategic Information Systems*, *4*(2), 117–133. doi:10.1016/0963-8687(95)80020-Q

Hong, D., Suh, E., & Koo, C. (2011). Developing strategies for overcoming barriers to knowledge sharing based on conversational knowledge management: A case study of a financial company. *Expert Systems with Applications*, *38*(12), 14417–14427. doi:10.1016/j.eswa.2011.04.072

Hutzschenreuter, T., & Horstkotte, J. (2010). Knowledge transfer to partners: A firm level perspective. *Journal of Knowledge Management*, *14*(3), 428–448. doi:10.1108/13673271011050148

Lee, H. L., & Whang, S. (2000). Information sharing in a supply chain. *International Journal of Manufacturing Technology and Management*, *1*(1), 79–93. doi:10.1504/IJMTM.2000.001329

Lee, H. L., & Whang, S. (2001). E-business and supply chain integration. *Standford Global Supply Chain Management Forum, 2*.

Lekhawipat, W., Wei, Y. H., & Lin, C. (2018). How internal attributions affect knowledge sharing behavior. *Journal of Knowledge Management*, *22*(4), 867–886. doi:10.1108/JKM-02-2017-0081

McDermott, R., & O'Dell, C. (2001). Overcoming cultural barriers to sharing knowledge. *Journal of Knowledge Management*, *5*(1), 76–85. doi:10.1108/13673270110384428

Narayana, S. A., Pati, R. K., & Vrat, P. (2014). Managerial research on the pharmaceutical supply chain–A critical review and some insights for future directions. *Journal of Purchasing and Supply Management*, *20*(1), 18–40. doi:10.1016/j.pursup.2013.09.001

Natti, S., & Ojasalo, J. (2008). Loose coupling as an inhibitor of internal customer knowledge transfer: Findings from an empirical study in B-to-B professional services. *Journal of Business and Industrial Marketing*, *23*(3), 213–223. doi:10.1108/08858620810858472

Okoroafor, H. (2014). The barriers to tacit knowledge sharing in franchise organizations. *Knowledge Management Research and Practice*, *12*(1), 97–102. doi:10.1057/kmrp.2013.30

Oliva, F. L. (2014). Knowledge management barriers, practices and maturity model. *Journal of Knowledge Management*, *18*(6), 1053–1074. doi:10.1108/JKM-03-2014-0080

Papageorgiou, L. G., Rotstein, G. E., & Shah, N. (2001). Strategic supply chain optimization for the pharmaceutical industries. *Industrial & Engineering Chemistry Research*, *40*(1), 275–286. doi:10.1021/ie990870t

Patil, S. K., & Kant, R. (2014). A fuzzy AHP-TOPSIS framework for ranking the solutions of Knowledge Management adoption in Supply Chain to overcome its barriers. *Expert Systems with Applications*, *41*(2), 679–693. doi:10.1016/j.eswa.2013.07.093

Pedroso, M. C., & Nakano, D. (2009). Knowledge and information flows in supply chains: A study on pharmaceutical companies. *International Journal of Production Economics*, *122*(1), 376–384. doi:10.1016/j.ijpe.2009.06.012

Pedroso, M. C., & Zwicker, R. (2008). Product information management: Basis for relationships in the supply chain. *JISTEM-Journal of Information Systems and Technology Management*, *5*(1), 109–134.

Rashed, C. A. A., Azeem, A., & Halim, Z. (2010). Effect of information and knowledge sharing on supply chain performance: A survey based approach. *Journal of Operations and Supply Chain Management*, *3*(2), 61–77.

Riege, A. (2005). Three-dozen knowledge-sharing barriers managers must consider. *Journal of Knowledge Management*, *9*(3), 18–35. doi:10.1108/13673270510602746

Samuel, K. E., Goury, M. L., Gunasekaran, A., & Spalanzani, A. (2011). Knowledge management in supply chain: An empirical study from France. *The Journal of Strategic Information Systems*, *20*(3), 283–306. doi:10.1016/j.jsis.2010.11.001

Settanni, E., Harrington, T. S., & Srai, J. S. (2017). Pharmaceutical supply chain models: A synthesis from a systems view of operations research. *Operations Research Perspectives*, *4*, 74–95. doi:10.1016/j.orp.2017.05.002

Shah, N. (2004). Pharmaceutical supply chains: Key issues and strategies for optimisation. *Computers & Chemical Engineering*, *28*(6), 929–941. doi:10.1016/j.compchemeng.2003.09.022

Sharma, B. P., Singh, M. D., & Neha. (2012). Knowledge sharing barriers: An approach of interpretive structural modeling. *IUP Journal of Knowledge Management, 10*(3), 35 - 52.

Shih, S. C., Hsu, S. H., Zhu, Z., & Balasubramanian, S. K. (2012). Knowledge sharing—A key role in the downstream supply chain. *Information & Management*, *49*(2), 70–80. doi:10.1016/j.im.2012.01.001

Simonin, B. L. (2004). An empirical investigation of the process of knowledge transfer in international strategic alliances. *Journal of International Business Studies*, *35*(5), 407–427. doi:10.1057/palgrave.jibs.8400091

Singh, M. (2005). *The Pharmaceutical Supply Chain: a Diagnosis of the State-of-the-Art (Master thesis)*. Boston: Massachusetts Institute of Technology.

Singh, M. D., & Kant, R. (2008). Knowledge management barriers: An interpretive structural modeling approach. *International Journal of Management Science and Engineering Management*, *3*(2), 141–150.

Spekman, R. E., Spear, J., & Kamauff, J. (2002). Supply chain competency: Learning as a key component. *Supply Chain Management*, *7*(1), 41–55. doi:10.1108/13598540210414373

Statista. (2018). *Global pharmaceutical sales from 2015 to 2017, by region (in billion U.S. dollars)*. Retrieved from: https://www.statista.com/statistics/272181/world-pharmaceutical-sales-by-region/

Swaminathan, J. M., Smith, S. F., & Sadeh, N. M. (1998). Modeling Supply Chain Dynamics: A Multiagent Approach. *Decision Sciences*, *29*(3), 607–632. doi:10.1111/j.1540-5915.1998.tb01356.x

Szulanski, G. (2003). *Sticky knowledge: barriers to knowing in the firm*. London: Sage Publications.

Titi Amayah, A. (2013). Determinants of knowledge sharing in a public sector organization. *Journal of Knowledge Management*, *17*(3), 454–471. doi:10.1108/JKM-11-2012-0369

Uthayakumar, R., & Priyan, S. (2013). Pharmaceutical supply chain and inventory management strategies: Optimization for a pharmaceutical company and a hospital. *Operations Research for Health Care*, *2*(3), 52–64. doi:10.1016/j.orhc.2013.08.001

Vajjhala, N. R., & Vucetic, J. (2013). Key barriers to knowledge sharing in medium-sized enterprises in transition economies. *International Journal of Business and Social Science*, *4*(13), 90–98.

Wasko, M. M., & Faraj, S. (2005). Why should I share? Examining social capital and knowledge contribution in electronic networks of practice. *Management Information Systems Quarterly*, *29*(1), 35–57. doi:10.2307/25148667

Wong, W. P., & Wong, P. S. (2011). Supply chain management, knowledge management capability, and their linkages towards firm performance. *Business Process Management Journal*, *17*(6), 940–964. doi:10.1108/14637151111182701

Yu, X., Li, C., Shi, Y., & Yu, M. (2010). Pharmaceutical supply chain in China: Current issues and implications for health system reform. *Health Policy (Amsterdam)*, *97*(1), 8–15. doi:10.1016/j.healthpol.2010.02.010 PMID:20307912

Yu, Z., Yan, H., & Edwin Cheng, T. C. (2001). Benefits of information sharing with supply chain partnerships. *Industrial Management & Data Systems*, *101*(3), 114–121. doi:10.1108/02635570110386625

Zhao, J., Pablo, P., & Qi, Z. (2012). Enterprise knowledge management model based on China's practice and case study. *Computers in Human Behavior*, *28*(2), 324–330. doi:10.1016/j.chb.2011.10.001

Zhou, H., & Benton, W. C. Jr. (2007). Supply chain practice and information sharing. *Journal of Operations Management*, *25*(6), 1348–1365. doi:10.1016/j.jom.2007.01.009

ADDITIONAL READING

Drakulich, A. (2011). Special Report Preventing And Troubleshooting Manufacturing Deviations Industry Experts Offer Their Best Practices For Dealing With Deviations. *Pharmaceutical Technology*, *35*(1), 44.

Haque, M., & Islam, R. (2013). Effects Of Supply Chain Management Practices On Customer Satisfaction: Evidence From Pharmaceutical Industry Of Bangladesh. *Global Business And Management Research*, *5*(2/3), 120–136.

Liebman, M. (2001). E-Impact On The Pharmaceutical Industry. *Medical Marketing & Media*, *36*(10), 40–40.

Lilleoere, A. M., & Hansen, E. H. (2011). Knowledge-Sharing Practices In Pharmaceutical Research And Development—A Case Study. *Knowledge and Process Management, 18*(3), 121–132. doi:10.1002/kpm.379

Mangan, J., & Christopher, M. (2005). Management Development And The Supply Chain Manager Of The Future. *International Journal of Logistics Management, 16*(2), 178–191. doi:10.1108/09574090510634494

Ponis, S. T., & Koronis, E. (2012). A Knowledge Management Process-Based Approach To Support Corporate Crisis Management. *Knowledge and Process Management, 19*(3), 148–159. doi:10.1002/kpm.1390

Qureshi, A. M. A., & Evans, N. (2015). Deterrents To Knowledge-Sharing In The Pharmaceutical Industry: A Case Study. *Journal of Knowledge Management, 19*(2), 296–314. doi:10.1108/JKM-09-2014-0391

Wouters, M. J., & Van Donselaar, K. H. (2000). Design Of Operations Management Internships Across Organizations—Learning Om By Doing Om. *Interfaces, 30*(4), 81–93. doi:10.1287/inte.30.4.81.11645

KEY TERMS AND DEFINITIONS

Knowledge Management: The process of efficiently gathering, sharing, using, and managing knowledge among a set of individual and/or groups in an organization.

Knowledge Sharing: A formal or informal exchange/dissemination of knowledge among individuals or groups.

Knowledge Sharing Barriers: A single factor or a set of factors that has a significant negative influence on the knowledge sharing process.

Pharmaceutical Industry: Industry related to manufacturing, supplying, and dealing with pharmaceutical medicines and equipment.

Supply Chain: A system comprising of organizations, personnel, information, logistics, distribution, and other resources involved in the movement of products and services from the manufacturer to the end customers.

Supply Chain Management: Managing the activities across the supply chain from the point of origin to the point of consumption.

Section 5

Pharmaceutical Supply Chain Characteristics:

Case Studies

The last section contains a detailed description of the current issues in the pharmaceutical sector: one chapter about national issues and one from a company's perspective.

Chapter 13
Sustainable Supply Chain as a Part of CSR Strategy:
The Example of Polpharma, Poland

Katarzyna Osiecka-Brzeska
Higher School of Administration and Business in Gdynia, Poland

ABSTRACT

Corporate social responsibility policies have become an important management strategy in companies. This sector tries to respond to stakeholders' needs while developing socially responsible business activities and sustainable values. A sustainable supply chain is an integral part of CSR strategy in a pharmaceutical industry. Purchased goods and services have to present high standards and quality. As international companies have many suppliers and contractors, it is important to conduct and promote worked out values among all business partners. The aim of this chapter is to investigate the corporate social responsibility values of Polpharma Group. The chapter describes the long-term strategy of sustainability in Polpharma and the responsibilities of Polpharma in all business sectors. The most essential part will be the description of the process of sustainable supply chain formation. The chapter will describe the implementation of a code of conduct among suppliers. The case study in this chapter will be based on Polpharma, one of the largest Polish pharmaceutical companies.

DOI: 10.4018/978-1-5225-5921-4.ch013

INTRODUCTION

Recent years have brought a higher interest in terms of protection of the environment. As a derivative, the interest in the international standards of Sustainable Development (SD) and Corporate Social Responsibility (CSR) is growing and rules of sustainability are becoming operational standards in many enterprises. The popularity of sustainability principles has a positive impact on companies, which, asides from their size or field of activity, are implementing policies that take into account not only the economic aspects of companies activity but social and environmental as well.

Porter and Kramer (2006) prove that for modern companies sustainable management is a broad term, used in all areas of company's activity. One of the integral elements of the sustainable production process is a sustainable supply chain (SSC), which meets the requirements of producers, suppliers, and clients at the same time. When comparing the traditional and sustainable supply chain, on will easily notice, that the proper functioning of SSC is more likely to depend on the preferences and behavior of the customer. It is directly connected to the products flowing through the SSC and the fact that they are usually made in the recycling process. It may happen, that recycled products are characterized by non-plain features, this means that they may differ from their original counterparts. As a result, clients may occur disaffected (Nowakowska-Grunt, 2005). Following consumer needs and keeping them close to the company is one of the main targets of modern sells strategies. This is why many companies started to analyze their supply chains widely – taking into consideration the flow of goods into and outside the company. The result of the analyzes was a Sustainable Supply Chain which integrates economic, social and environmental values as a part of CSR policy (Olejniczak & Koch, 2015).

The paper is going to introduce the topic of Sustainable Supply Chain and show the main values of SSC management. In the second part, the paper will focus on the case of Polpharma Group, a polish pharmacy company. The paper will give a little place for Polpharma's CSR strategy, and then highlight the main areas of SSC. The aim of this chapter is to prove that sustainable actions taken in a supply chain may contribute positively to the company's reputation as well as social and economical operations.

BACKGROUND: SUSTAINABLE SUPPLY CHAIN IN THEORY

A supply chain is an essential part of every modern enterprise. A supply chain should be integrated with the strategy of a company, as it has an impact on a number of actions taken by the company, among which one can mention: level of costs, quality of production, a flow of information, materials and finances between a company and main stakeholders. Moreover, the supply chain should respond to the needs of present and future customers and should be designed to service the customers as good as possible. One should remember that modern customers are much more educated in terms of responsible consumption and therefore, their requirements towards ecological and social effects of a production process, including supply chain, are growing. Basing on those facts, companies compete to design as an effective supply chain as possible, that would ensure the efficient flow of goods from and towards the enterprise. The introduction of Sustainable Supply Chain (SSC) can be considered as an ecological awareness of managers and their desire of bringing company's CSR policy to a higher level, but it also should be considered as a strategy of making long-term contracts with customers. When analyzed in this way, the SSC becomes a compromise between profit, needs of stakeholders (inc. customers) and eco-efficiency of the enterprise (Olejniczak & Koch, 2015).

The economic aspect of SSC is understood mainly as an integration of development management and supply management to raise the efficiency of the enterprise. The effectiveness in ecological and social terms should lead to lower costs and shorter times of delivery. They should also lower the number of defective products and mistakes in the whole delivery chain. This should have a positive impact on the economic results of the enterprise. To achieve this, the enterprise needs to harmonize all economic, social and ecological aspects of the supply chain. The most important economic, social and ecological aspects that can be managed in a supply chain are mentioned in Table 1 (Jastrzębska, 2011). Yet, one needs to remember that social and ecological issues have to match economical matters in such a way that they can become a basis for a longtime efficiency of supply chain without lowering financial results.

Table 1. Sustainable supply chain management issues

Sustainable Supply Chain Management Issues		
Economical	**Social**	**Ecological**
• The financial condition of suppliers, • The reliability of suppliers, • The level of dependence on suppliers, • Fair contract terms, • Timely payments, • Regular orders, • Adequate prices, not using the economic advantage to negotiate • Unfair contract terms, • The diversity of suppliers, • Prevention of corruption	• Freedom of association and collective bargaining, • The prohibition of forced labor, • Prohibition of child labor, • Counteracting discrimination, • Fair wages, • Compliance with working hours and paid overtime, • Working conditions, • Social security, • Minimizing adverse impact on the local community and supporting its development	• Managing the whole product life cycle (from design to recycling), • Incidental environmental pollution, • Minimizing pollutant emissions, • Limiting threats to biodiversity, • Rationalization of water and other raw materials consumption, • Energetic efficiency, • Waste management

Source: (Jastrzębska, 2011)

Basing on a synergy of economic, social and environmental issues it is possible to indicate that managing a sustainable supply chain is a consistent part of corporate social responsibility (CSR) policy. Just as CSR, the sustainable supply chain should have three main pillars: economic, social and ecological effectiveness, which will join and balance the risk management in a co company and will be observing the law, standards, and regulations. Those three pillars should be further used to create corporate's culture, the basis for IT alignment and a unified strategy of development of a supply chain. The importance of social, economic and environmental pillars for the development of SSC is shown in Figure 1.

Among the main economic benefits of introducing a SSC one can mention (Zailani, Jeyaraman, Vengadasan & Premkumar, 2012):

- A better reputation of the company,
- The loyalty of suppliers and customers,
- Lower costs of:
  - Occupational health and safety,
  - Recruitment and job rotation: Resulting from safe storage in transport,
  - Personnel: better working conditions can increase motivation and productivity or reduce staff absenteeism,
- Shorter supply time,
- Better product quality,
- Increasing the competitive advantage,
- Savings due to the reduction of waste.

Figure 1. House of Sustainable Supply Chain Management
Source: (Teuteberg & Wittstruck, 2010)

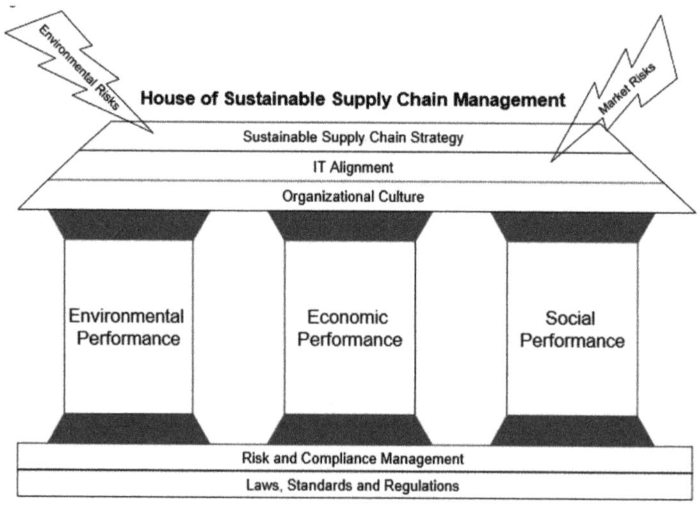

A modern economy is clearly changing into more environmentally friendly and it has started to expect from its participants, enterprises among them, to involve in the non-material sphere of the business reality. It means that companies should start covering both social and environmental relations that fuse with the concept of sustainability (see Figure 2). Global, Internet-based economy allows companies to purchase goods from suppliers from all over the world. Those suppliers usually represent different business models, corporate values, and cultures. It is extremely hard to build a stable base of suppliers, sub-contractors and business partners when they operate on different values and goals. To gain profits from the diversity of partners in a SSC, the company must include social and ecological issues in the system of a supply chain. The introduction of high common standards for the suppliers may be connected to the fact that the company or customers negatively perceive some of the suppliers' business behaviors. This is the reason why companies should expect from the participants of the supply chain the reliable information about the production technologies, work standards and influence on the environment. As a result of such proceeding, the company should check and control the action of the suppliers and other participants of SSC to have an influence on parties creating its supply chain. As a further action, the company should provide a public report on its SSC, in which the information about the main aspects of SSC should be enclosed. The report should contain the information about the contractors of the product, production conditions, delivery of raw materials, conditions of transportation and utilization of products (Olejniczak & Koch, 2015).

The responsible and sustainable company needs to take the responsibility for all the decisions taken in a supply chain. Those decisions should not only consider the economic aspects and benefits of the company, but also the environmental and social ones. Those aspects should be respected on each and every stage of building the company's strategies, what includes the sustainable supply chain as well. The stages of building the sustainable supply chain are shown in Figure 3.

Usually, management of sustainable supply chain is defined as the management of three dimensions of the chain, which includes such issues as human rights, law and employee's duties, occupational safety and health, prohibition of child labor and prevention of discrimination. Those issues should not depend on the company's location, laws, culture or economy. Therefore, the goal of a SSC is to create, protect and increase long-term values for all stakeholders involved in the presence of products and services on the market. In other words, one can say that a sustainable supply chain is inseparably connected with sustainable products (Mesjasz-Lech, p.31). This means those products are pro-ecological and prosocial at every stage - from extraction through distribution, to delivery. In practice, enterprises can undertake a number of pro-social activities in the environment, thus taking responsibility for their decisions – the examples of such actions in a supply chain can be found in table 2.

Figure 2. Sustainable Supply Chain
Source: (Olejniczak & Koch,2015)

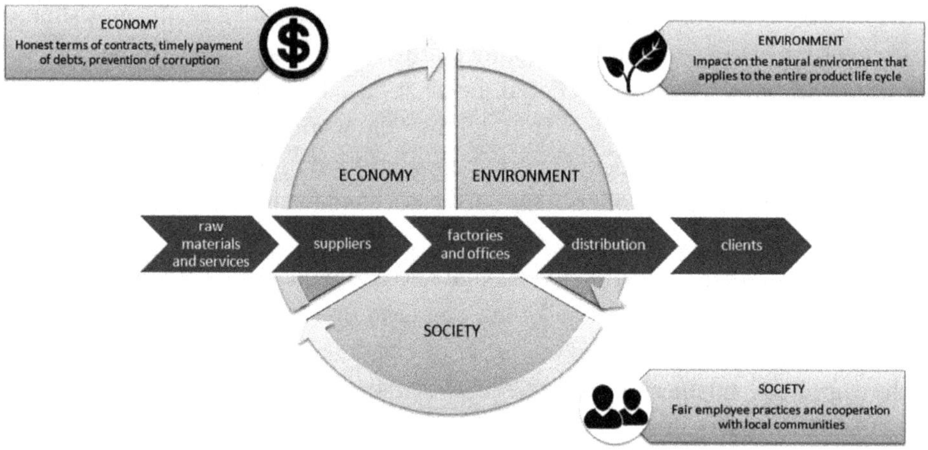

Figure 3. Stages of Sustainable Supply Chain
Source: (CSRinfo, 2012)

On the one hand, it is important that companies undertake simultaneous activities in all three dimensions of the sustainable supply chain. On the other hand, enterprises should undertake only those actions that are possible and real to be done. This is the result of the fact that every company or industry will undertake a number of its own activities and initiatives. Managers need to remember that the complex and length of the SSC depends on the size of the company, the field of business, corporate culture, financial possibilities and many other factors. This is why one should be aware that initiatives organized as a part of the sustainable supply chain may differ between companies and industries (Olejniczak & Koch, 2015). Table 3 presents the exemplary activities in three areas of the SSC in the pharmaceutical industry - supply of raw materials and semi-finished products, own production and cooperation, sales and distribution.

It can be stated that the modern enterprise faces a real challenge regarding the creation of a sustainable supply chain. Taking actions that may seem unprofitable may bring significant non-financial benefits to all parties, both in the short and long

Table 2. Activities in the supply chain for sustainable development

Actions Recommended in a Sustainable Supply Chain				
Design and Product Development	**Purchase Process**	**Logistics**	**Productions**	**Marketing**
• Reduction of raw materials consumption, • Use of more environmentally friendly materials, • Searching for local alternatives to raw materials, • Use of recycled raw materials, • Designing energy-saving, low-cost and water-saving products, • Product planning for recycling, cradle-to-cradle, and eco-design	• Applying ecological and social criteria in the selection of suppliers, • Risk analysis and environmental and social impacts, • Building long-lasting relationships with suppliers, • Open circulation of product information, • Determining an adequate price for expectations, • Transparency of activities	• Low-carbon transport, • Consolidation of distribution (e.g. Size of deliveries, directions of deliveries), • Achieving scale effects in distribution, • Strengthening cooperation between suppliers, • Distribution and delivery planning taking into account the improvement of their efficiency	• Location activities and the selection of suppliers, • Analysis of environmental and social standards applicable to regional • Suppliers, • Taking into account a wide range of environmental protection (fuel and coal consumption, • Greenhouse gas emissions), • Study of the company's impact on the local labor market, • The use of cleaner production technologies, • Application of environmental management systems, • Implementation of industrial ecology principles, • Closing the water and energy cycle, • Rational waste management	• Reliable information on origin, composition, and impact on the environment, • The use of eco-tags, • Eco-marketing, • Introduction of pickup of used products, • Extension of maintenance services - an extension of product life cycle

Source: (Olejniczak, & Koch, 2015)

term. Depending on the type of activities undertaken by individual stakeholders, these benefits may be of a different nature.

THE CHARACTERISTICS OF THE POLPHARMA GROUP

The Polpharma Group is the largest manufacturer of medicines in Poland. The company is also a leader in the Polish pharmaceutical market. The company was

Table 3. Desired actions in the most important areas of the supply chain

Areas of Actions	Examples of Action
Supply of raw materials and semi-finished products	Caring about: • quality and adherence to technological and ethical regimes by suppliers, • minimization of packaging weight and volume, use of recyclable packaging, • local sources of supply, • education in environmental and ethical standards of production, good relations with other participants in the production, subsidy and consumption chain, Supporting: • national packaging recycling systems, • delivery systems applying practices in line with the principles of sustainable development
Production and cooperation	Caring for natural resources as well as a reduction: • water and energy consumption, • losses in the production and transport process at every stage of the functioning of the product, and: • optimization of supply, storage, sales logistics, • innovative activities that improve the efficiency of production processes
Sales and distribution	Caring about: • building offers made of products produced in accordance with the principles of responsible production, and: • creating the opportunity for consumers to choose products that are appropriate for their health, environmental protection and ethical principles, • educating the consumer about the possibility of choosing products conducive to adequate consumption and waste management after consumption, promoting products manufactured in accordance with the principles of ethics, providing local suppliers, producers, and employees with decent working and pay conditions,- implementing responsible management of trade, energy, and auxiliary waste

Source: (Olejniczak & Koch, 2015)

established in Starogard Gdański (the north of Poland) in 1935. During the last 80 years, Polpharma has built a reliable brand by producing high-quality products and building trust among patients, doctors and business partners. Nowadays, the company belongs to the 20 largest generic companies in the world. It has seven production facilities in Poland, Russia and Kazakhstan and seven Research and Development centers. Polpharma has over 7,000 employees in Poland and abroad. In the beginning, the company operated mainly in the Central and Eastern Europe market, but it has expanded in the Caucasus and Central Asia market. Its marketing and sales structures can be found in the Czech Republic, Slovakia, Bulgaria, Romania, Lithuania, Latvia, Ukraine, Belarus, Russia, Azerbaijan, Uzbekistan, Kazakhstan and Vietnam (Polpharma, 2018).

The Polpharma Group offers around 600 products, which can be bought in 50 countries all around the world. The product portfolio covers prescription and restricted medical prescription drugs. It specializes in cardiology, neurology, and gastroenterology. A major part of the product portfolio take Over the Counter drugs (OTC). This significant portfolio is the reason why the company has a leading share in Polish key therapeutic areas. The product range is extended by dietary supplements, cosmetics, medical devices, and phytopharmaceuticals. The latest novelty of Polpharma is the investment into the development of biological medicines, which are thought to be the future of contemporary pharmacotherapy, the treatment of cancers or autoimmune diseases. Last, but not least, the company is the largest Polish manufacturer of pharmaceutical substances which are successfully implemented in highly developed markets of the European Union and the United States (Polpharma, 2018).

The Polpharma Group's field of action has a great meaning for human health and the level of living in many European and Asian countries. The effect of this is a mission, which says that the Group aims to "*constantly strive for excellence in delivering high-quality pharmaceuticals*". The company claims that their highest values are human life and health, this is why the company takes care of the quality of products and harmonious coexistence with the natural environment. As the patients are the main stakeholders of Polpharma, the company wants to ensure their wellbeing and propagate the rules of preventive medicine. As the development of medical and biotechnological science determinates the development of Polpharma and its products, the company helps physicians by supporting them with the newest medical knowledge. The Group also supports the Polish science and numerous social undertakings. One cannot forget that Polpharma is an important actor on the business scene – to act as good as possible, the company respects the needs of employees, business partners, local communities and social organizations. In everyday business relations, the workers of Polpharma have to follow the rules of honesty and professional ethics. "*Everything we do is driven by integrity and professionalism*" – has become the keynote of Polpharma's actions (Polpharma, 2017).

The Polpharma Group took patterns of corporate social responsibility (CSR) since the very beginning of the company. With the rapid growth of sustainability action in Poland, the company intensified their actions in this field after 2000. The great meaning in the development of CSR actions at Polpharma had a fact, that the company was privatized mostly with the use of Polish capital. Since then, the company has been proving the value of sustainable development by harmoniously reconciling business objectives with the needs of stakeholders[1]. In 2014 it was decided to systematize the CSR initiatives and select three key areas: serving patients and society, ethical business conduct and innovations, the advancement of knowledge. To fulfill those areas with coordinated CSR actions, the company follows high ethical standards and cares for the natural environment. It also takes into account the needs of main stakeholders: employees, patients, the medical and scientific community, customers, suppliers, local communities and other participants of the healthcare sector (Polpharma, 2015).

Corporate Social Responsibility at Polpharma

The Polpharma Group has been operating on a Polish market for the last 80 years and it has respected the rules of corporate social responsibility for most of the time, even when the CSR policy was not known in the Polish business reality. The begging of the Polpharma's social responsibly was connected more to the sponsorship than to the CSR we know nowadays. In 1999, the company for the first time decided to create the Environmental Report, which was used only for internal use of managers. In 2000, the company decided to sponsor Polpharma Starogard Gdański team - a men's basketball team. Later on, the same year, the company was privatized – the privatization was based on Polish capital and it began a shift in the company's mindset on its role in the society.

In 2001, The Polpharma Group decided to establish the Foundation for the Development of Polish Pharmacy and Medicine (later called: the Polpharma Scientific Foundation). The foundation runs a competition for funding of research projects in pharmaceutical and medical sciences. The competition is announced every year. In 2002, the European Educational Program was launched. The program's goal is to provide doctors and pharmacists with the knowledge of the latest advancements in medicine and pharmacy. In the same year, Polpharma inaugurated the Polscreen: the Polish Program for the Prevention of Coronary Disease. It was the largest population-based study in the world, examining almost 730,000 patients in years from 2002 to 2005. In 2003, the Polish Cardiac Society awarded to Polpharma with the title of the Friend of Polish Cardiology. One year later, in 2004, the Polpharma Group obtained the 'integrated permit – a document that confirms the company's adjustment to EU requirements on integrated pollution prevention and control. To fallow the further requirements of EU, in 2007, the company obtained the ISO 14001 environmental certificate and OHSAS 18001 occupational health and safety certificate. 2008 was another milestone year for Polpharma's sustainability and it was full of socially responsible actions, among which one can mention (Polpharma, 2015):

1. A publication of the first Polish monograph on therapeutic compliance and doctor-patient cooperation in chronic diseases by the Polpharma Scientific Foundation;

2. A launch of an education campaign addressed to pregnant women and those planning to start a family, called "It's a Shame not to Ask – Pregnancy without Herpes";
3. The calling and the first edition of the "Green Process": a competition rewarding environmental initiatives of Polpharma's employees;
4. The implementation of the "Green Chemistry" policy: a commitment to consider the environmental aspects at the beginning of production process, which includes the early stage of design of products and manufacturing technologies;
5. The launch of an innovative education program, which aims at breaking taboos in sexual health. The program is called the National Sexual Health Program;
6. The initiation of the "Knowledge Pharm": a program for medicine and pharmacy students from Polish universities;

The enormous number of CSR actions in 2008 made that year very special, but 2008 was also an important year for one another reason – in 2008 the first official Environmental Report of the Polpharma Group was published. In 2009 Polpharma launched the "Solution to Forgetfulness", a campaign addressed to people whose loved ones are starting to have memory problems. This campaign aimed to widen the group's social responsibility. The year 2011 brought for Polpharma an establishment of a cooperation with the European Blood Donor Foundation. According to the assumptions of the program, a part of sale revenue from one of Polpharma's products supported campaign promoting voluntary blood donation called the Blood Relatives (*pl.: Krewniacy*). The year 2012 was started by another social action called "Pressure for Life" (pl.: Ciśnienie na życie), which became the largest education campaign on hypertension in Poland. In the same year, the "Let's Go Cycling" (*pl.: Wszyscy na rowery*) program was implemented. The purpose of this program was to promote bike commuting among polish citizens. 2012 was also a year of the first edition of the "Stop Accidents Program" (*pl.: Stop Wypadkom*), which promotes safety attitudes and encourages reporting of near misses among company's workers (Polpharma, 2014).

2013 was a year of the Publication of the first Corporate Social Responsibility Report created accordingly to GRI guidance. Later that year, a Polpharma Group's Employee Volunteering Program was launched. Workers taking part in this program receive a chance to undertake social action in their local communities. In the same year, a "Get Ready for a Shock" (*pl.: Przygotuj się na wstrząs*) was also launched. This campaign aimed to educate about anaphylaxis and anaphylactic shock. Another important footstep taken in 2013 was joining the Responsible Business Forum and becoming a strategic partner for the development and promotion of CSR in Poland (Polpharma, 2014).

In 2014 Polpharma received two awards important from the CSR port of view: the "Social Campaign of the Year 2013 Award" for the Pressure for Life campaign and the "Employee-Friendly Employer Award". In 2014, the Polpharma Group completed the first milestone in the development of the Ethics Program Adoption. The same year, the company contributed to the establishment of the Ethics Officers Coalition, which was done under the auspices of the Global Compact Initiative of the UN Secretary-General in Poland. Later the same year, the Polpharma Group joined, the Development Initiatives Forum (FIR) and the FIR Grants Fund as a partner. The company's objective was to develop transversal cooperation in Pomerania area, Poland. 2014 was a very important year, as it brought strategic changes to the CSR management at Polpharma. It was decided to structure all CSR initiatives taken within the Group. The reorganization of the CSR policy was supposed to show what else may be done to better respond to stakeholder needs while developing value-based business activities at the same time. To find a solution, the Polpharma Group appointed the first stakeholder panel. Key stakeholders and decision-makers of the most important business areas took part in a long process of development of the CSR strategy. As a result of the stakeholder panel, the three main pillars of social responsibility were selected (Polpharma, 2015):

1. Serving the patients and the community,
2. Ethical conduct of business and innovation
3. Advancing knowledge.

Basing on those three interlaced areas, the Polpharma made 14 commitments to fulfill 6 out of 17 Sustainable Development Goals (CSRConsulting, 2017):

- SDG: 3. Human health and wellbeing
- SDG: 5. Gender equality
- SDG: 8. Economic growth and decent work
- SDG: 9. Innovation and infrastructure
- SDG: 12. Responsible consumption and manufacturing
- SDG: 16. Peace, justice, and strong institutions

The CSR activities specified in 2014 were supposed to pursue until 2018. While specifying the main areas of Group's CSR policy, the company decided to sign the Declaration of Polish Businesses for Sustainable Development. The Declaration was signed during the initiation of the 3rd stage of Vision 2050 – the New Agenda for Business in Poland. Systematized CSR strategy and all the other important events of 2014, led the Polpharma Group to the announcement of Social Responsibility Strategy in 2015 (Polpharma, 2018).

2015 was a year of another award - Award of the CSR Golden Leaf by "Polityka" weekly, the third place in the Responsible Business Ranking and title of industry CSR leader in the Pharmacy & Medicine category. This was connected to the publication of the first university textbook on patient compliance in Poland. The textbook was prepared and published by the Polpharma Scientific Foundation. In 2015, the Polpharma Group celebrated its 80th anniversary. Especially on that occasion, Polpharma held the POLRUN relay – a race during which more than 700 employees run 960 km. Owing to that the Group sent 524 children from Children's Homes to summer camps. At the same year, the Polpharma decided to sign the Diversity Charter, what was supposed to highlight the fact, that the company is a high-quality employer. Development of the new corporate social responsibility strategy of Polpharma Group for the years from 2015 to 2018 (Polpharma, 2018).

Polpharma's Sustainable Supply Chain

Polpharma Group has made the sustainability of a supply chain a crucial component of a comprehensive approach to CSR. The fact that the Group is present in many international markets puts on Polpharma a great pressure on the quality of a supply chain. As both a purchaser of goods and services and supplier of medicines and pharmaceutical substances for other entities, Polpharma recognizes the importance of having high standards within the supply chain. This is why Polpharma has made sustainable supply chain an integral and essential part of the business.

The company strives to make its products with the highest quality and safety. The construction of a sustainable supply chain is an important element of a comprehensive approach to the social responsibility of the Polpharma Group. Care for the Suppliers to meet additional requirements regarding the respect for human rights, employee practices or environmental protection is considered to be a duty of the Polpharma Group, which wants to base its operations on an ethical foundation. This is the reason why Polpharma searches for the best suppliers who meet our strict quality standards and can confirm it by current audit results. The company puts the requirements on themselves when it acts as a supplier of products and services for other companies. Polpharma Group wants to build a sense of shared responsibility within the supply chain. The members of Polpharma's SSC should take the responsibility not only for a final product but also for the highest ethical standards and harmonious development of all actors participating in the life cycle of products. All of those assumptions built the basis for a new co-operation system with suppliers - a balanced strategy of a sustainable supply chain. An important part of it is the Supplier Code of Conduct of Polpharma Groups. The first works on the project began in the autumn of 2014 and the final work was announced in 2015 (Polpharma, 2017).

When working on the sustainability of its supply chain, Polpharma made sure it the action was related to company's strategy. Building a responsible supply chain, defined on the basis of three strategic goals, is one of the 14 commitments of the Corporate Social Responsibility Strategy. They were presented in the three-year strategy of Sustainable Supply Chain (SSC) and grouped in 4 areas: employee involvement and education, educational activities addressed to suppliers, impact and real change in the supply chain, and internal system solutions. The first and important stages of a continuous improvement of a supply chain is a creation of the Supplier Code of Conduct for Polpharma Group. The Polpharma Group's Code of Conduct for Suppliers is the policy that points Polpharma's workers and suppliers how to improve business practices within the supply chain. The document describes the most important requirements for suppliers which would like to start or continue the cooperation with Polpharma. The Code of Conduct includes the strict rules in such fields of running a business as ethical and fair business conduct, respect for human rights, occupational health and safety and last but not least the responsibility for product quality and the environment. Code's clarity is an important condition for the assessment and selection of partners for cooperation. One of the first steps of the development of the Code was the analysis of suppliers in terms of potential risks in the area of corporate social responsibility. When taking the first steps in the development of the Supplier Code of Conduct, the Polpharma Group assessed the total of 1572 suppliers. The suppliers could be divided into 11 main categories (Polpharma, 2015):

1. Manufacturers of machines, equipment and raw materials for the production of packaging,
2. Logistic centers,
3. Transport companies,
4. Manufacturing plants,
5. Sales offices,
6. Suppliers of non-productive, marketing and engineering services,
7. Wholesales pharmaceuticals,
8. Patients,
9. Hospital applicants,
10. Pharmacies,
11. Weighting companies.

All of the supplying companies were assessed from the perspective of current and potential risks. Chosen suppliers were invited to the circle of companies that set the standards of ethics and responsibility within the Group's SSC. The Group continuously improves its standards of conduct, and promote them among its business partners to raise standards in this field in Poland.

All suppliers that want to or already do cooperate with Polpharma Group are expected to adhere to the rules of the Suppliers' Code of Conduct. The Code of Conduct of the Polpharma Group is the expression of a strategic attitude to a responsible supply chain.

One of the main prerequisites for cooperation with our Group is a confirmation of compliance with the Code of Conduct. A supplier has also to proceed in accordance

Figure 4 Sustainable Supply Chain in Polpharma
Source: (Polpharma,2015)

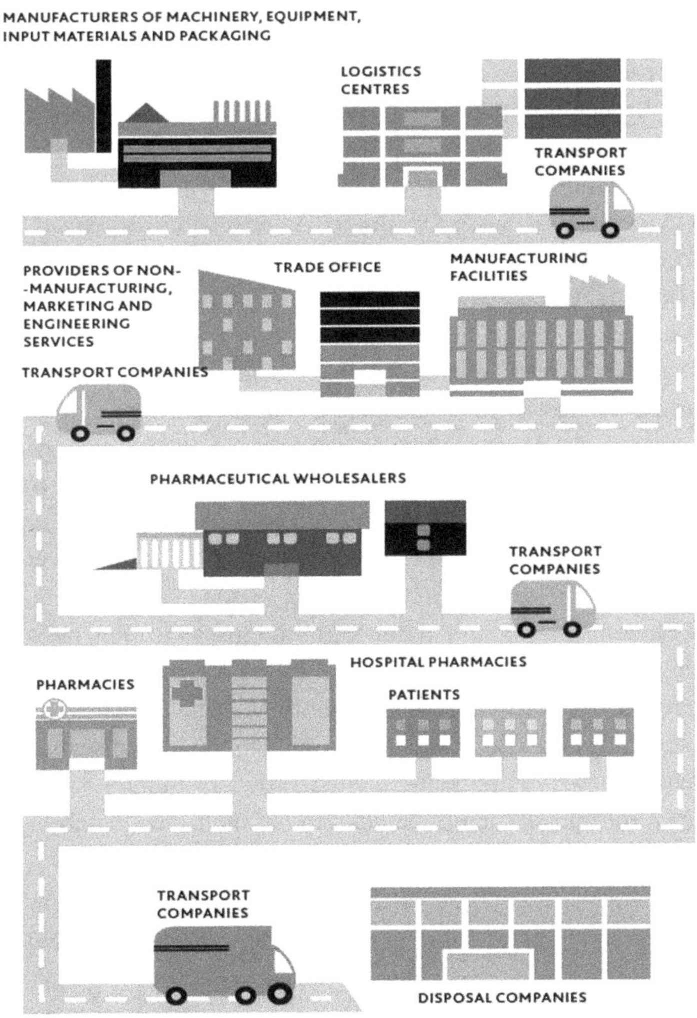

with Code's provisions. The Group's suppliers can find in the Code the most important requirements in the fields of (Polpharma, 2018):

- Management and ethics,
- Health and safety at work,
- Employment conditions and rights of employees
- Studies and experiments involving humans and animals,
- Safety and quality of products,
- Impact on the natural environment.

The Polpharma Group also expects suppliers to be active in the promotion of the awareness of the idea of sustainable development among its stakeholders. Suppliers should verify all actions taken by their employees and sub-suppliers to make sure those actions have adjusted the idea of sustainability.

During the process of the creation of the sustainable supply chain strategy and the Code, Polpharma Group Suppliers participated in the functioning of various departments of the company - from quality, health, and safety, to the environment and compliance. Polpharma also invited its suppliers from Poland and abroad to the dialogue about the shape of planned solutions. An interesting element of SSC creation was the screening of companies cooperating with Polpharma from all shopping areas - materials and raw materials used for production, non-productive materials, and services as well as technical and engineering purchases. The analysis allowed the Polpharma Group to estimate the actual and potential risks in various CSR areas at its suppliers. On those bases, a sustainable supply chain strategy was developed. It was announced in 2015 to the company's employees and business partners. From the beginning, Polpharma was planning long-term effects to achieve. Among them, one can find improvement in the quality of management at suppliers, minimalization of the risks in the supply chain through tool available on the www page of the company. Therefore, the very important aspect of SSC was highlighted: building an awareness among suppliers and educating them in the field of sustainability. What is interesting, Polpharma did not want to impose the standards on suppliers but invited them to cooperate and implement the Code's standards by themselves. To help the suppliers understand and implement the SSC, Polpharma, just after the announcement of new requirements, invited suppliers to take part in workshops and educational meetings. The implementation of the Code, which began in 2015, involved the following stages (Suppliers Polpharma, 2017):

1. Providing information to suppliers and signing a statement regarding Code of Conduct

2. Education of suppliers (workshops in a fixed or online form, information materials, and training, creation of the knowledge portal for suppliers),
3. Self-assessment: in the form of an online survey that allows suppliers to assess the level of implementation of the principles contained in the Code of Conduct in their companies,
4. Improvement and verification: internal and external audits of suppliers.

The Polpharma Group expects that its suppliers will undertake relevant efforts in the process of adjusting their production and business actions to the requirements of the Code. The minimal standers and action that are expected from suppliers are (Suppliers Polpharma, 2017):

- The communication of all requirements under the Code of Conduct to supplier's employees and suppliers,
- The assurance of compliance with the rules of the Code of Conduct by all actors in the supply chain,
- The verification of compliance with the assumptions of the Code and implementation of a system for their supervision,
- The promotion and dedication to increasing the awareness the idea of sustainable development.

The Polpharma Group, being aware that Suppliers need time to ensure that some organizational changes and operations are in compliance with the Code of Conduct. This is why the Code's implementation process was divided into several stages. The first stage was called "Communicating the information and signing the code of conduct". In 2015, all Polpharma's suppliers received the Code of Conduct with information about the principles of the Sustainable Supply Chain. They were also told what are expectations with regard to the implementation of the Code of Conduct in the Polpharma Groups. Since 2015 all suppliers are required to sign ethical clauses in their contracts or agreements (Suppliers Polpharma, 2017).

The next step was an education of suppliers. Since 2015 Polpharma launched a dedicated platform which provides basic knowledge on SSC and is a tool for communication with suppliers. Once a year, the Polpharma Group organizes in-house workshops for polish Suppliers. The online e-learning courses are available in two languages and might be translated into more languages. Polpharma's suppliers are encouraged to share good practices, which are also presented online (Suppliers Polpharma, 2017).

The third step of encouraging suppliers to introduce SSC is a self-assessment. Polpharma asks demands from suppliers to conduct self-assessment in which they have to specify the degree to which they meet the basic sustainable development and corporate social responsibility criteria. The self-assessment questionnaire is also presented online on the platform provided by Polpharma. Self-assessment results are not only a tool for Polpharma to evaluate its suppliers. It is also a feedback for Suppliers that shows them the level of their implementation of the principles of the Code and their good practices. The self-assessment also highlights the key areas for improvement along with recommendations on further actions. What is important is the fact that a negative result of the self-assessment questionnaire does not exclude supplier from further cooperation. Yet, the supplier should improve his actions to continue cooperation (Suppliers Polpharma, 2017).

The last step in achieving a common sustainability is a verification and constant improvement. Polpharma's goal is to continuously improve supply chain and the ethical should play the most important part of it. This is why the company plans technical audits among all of their Suppliers. The pilot of the ethical audit programme was run in 2017, but the proper programme will be launched in 2018. Audits will not concern all of the suppliers but cover selected ones (Suppliers Polpharma, 2017).

Polpharma's Achievements in the Implementation of the SSC

As the Polpharma Group's goal is to achieve the supply chain of best quality. To do so, the Group introduced a measurement and implemented a strategy, which is based on 4 key areas: education and involvement of employees, education, and involvement of suppliers, impact and real change in the supply chain and systemic solutions supporting the implementation of the strategy.

One of the pillars of Polpharma's SSC strategy is the involvement of employees. The Group has kept its employees involved in the strategy since the beginning of work on it. A cycle of training sessions was prepared and addressed to the purchasing departments' employees. Coordinators from other key Departments were also invited to take part in those trainings as it was crucial for the company to include a wide range of porkers as possible. Thanks to this the company has achieved results which would have been impossible to achieve only for the Purchasing Department (Rzeszotalska & Musiał, 2016).

The second integral part of SSC strategy is education and involvement of Suppliers – all of the suppliers received the Polpharma Group Supplier Code of Conduct. In the beginning, the Code was sent to 1,572 suppliers. As next step of Polpharma's cooperation with suppliers was including the Code as an integral part of the contract and the ethical clause as a part of agreements. Polpharma has already organized 4 workshops on SSC, which were attended by 151 suppliers. The positive information is the fact that most of the suppliers, that took part in pieces of training, claim to have changed the awareness of SSC. Satisfactory is the fact that many supplying companies are open to changes related to SSC and are keen to

Figure 5. Polpharma Group's Sustainable Supply Chain Strategy 2015 – 2018
Source: (Polpharma, 2017)

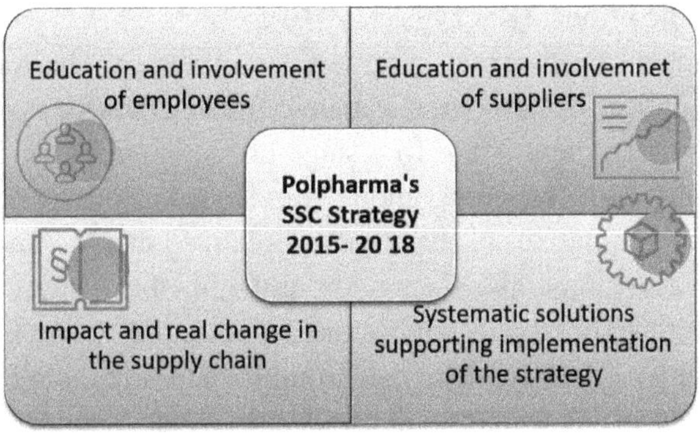

implement it. Basing on feedback from suppliers, Polpharma noticed elements of support and strengthening of relationships (Polpharma, 2018).

Polpharma has also based its strategy on influencing and introducing real changes in the supply chain. This part of the SSC strategy includes a programme of ethical audits among cooperating companies. The pilot programme started in 2017, but one still has to wait for the results. The launch of the full audit programme is expected to take place in 2018. To ensure the proper development of the SSC strategy the Polpharma Group decided to introduce the systematic solutions supporting the implementation of the strategy. A number of internal measures which support the implementation of the strategy are taken into consideration. The measures are taken to improve supply chain sustainability and to make it more matched to customers' expectations. During the process of ethical audit, measures that relate to sustainable supply chain were acknowledged. The ethical audit project has become the reason for deepening relations with suppliers. What can be recognized as a positive effect of it is the fact that not only the straight relations of supplied products and services are developed, but also business management on both sides (Polpharma, 2018).

RESULTS AND EFFECTS

A dedicated website www.dostawca.polpharma.pl WWW has been launched, in order to make it easier for Suppliers to access the knowledge. The website is a basic source of knowledge about the Polpharma's Sustainable Supply Chain project. The WWW platform also includes e-learning which introduces the Suppliers the requirements of the Code of Conduct and CSR aspects of doing business with Polpharma Group. On-line training is available in two language versions - Polish and English. The Polpharma Group meets with the Suppliers in Poland during educational workshops - over 150 suppliers have participated in the project since the beginning of the project (Kaczyńska, 2016).

In 2017, once again, Polpharma's suppliers were assessed. The evaluation process covered 3,900 Suppliers, almost twice as many as during the first assessment carried out in 2015. The assessment is the first stage of preparations, which precede the launch of the ethics audit program among suppliers. From the very beginning of the project, the representatives of the company realized that the implementation of the Code of conduct cannot take place without the involvement of suppliers. They were fully aware that social and environmental standards cannot be imposed on Suppliers from above. That was why the Group invited Suppliers from Poland and abroad to work on the shape and guidelines of the Code. From the earliest stages of the project implementation, one had to remember about the long-term effects that the company wanted to achieve. Those goals were: to improve the quality of management at Suppliers and to minimize the risks in the supply chain on Group's side. Hence, the very important aspect was the building of awareness and education of Suppliers (Polpharma, 2018).

The activities are undertaken as a part of the project resulted in a change in thinking about the importance and the role of risk in the supply chain. They also had a positive effect on raising awareness on this subject among employees, suppliers and the environment of the Polpharma Group. The Group is convinced that in the long term it will have an impact on raising standards in the supply chain by minimizing risks in the field of human rights, ecology and security. In addition, this project has become the starting point for building relationships with Suppliers. The relations were widened from the context of the quality of products and services provided to the management of businesses on both sides. The activities carried out by the company are also a response to the expectations of Groups' customers. Polpharma is a supplier for international partners and as so, it has to carry out audits. During one of the last ethical audits, carried out by a large customer, Polpharma's Sustainable Supply Chain activities have been noticed. In the final summary of the audit, the SSC has been communicated as a distinction against the companies from the region.

REFERENCES

Brudlak, H., Duliniec, E., & Gołębiowski, T. (2011). *Współpraca w łańcuchach dostaw a konkurencyjność przedsiębiorstw i kooperujących sieci*. Warszawa: OW SGH.

CSRConsulting. (2017). *SDGs w Praktyce. Kampania 17/17 - Popharma.* Retrieved from http://www.sdgs.pl/polpharma-2/

Jastrzębska, E. (2011). Zarządzanie odpowiedzialnym łańcuchem dostaw jako element wdrażania koncepcji rozwoju zrównoważonego. In Współpraca w łańcuchach dostaw a konkurencyjność przedsiębiorstw I kooperujących sieci. Warszawa: OW SGH.

Kaczyńska, G. (2016). *Strategiczne podejście do ochrony środowiska w Grupie Polpharma.* Retrieved from. http://www.gridw.pl/images/documents/geo6/Grazyna_Kaczynska_Polpharma.pdf

Majesz-Lech, A. (2014). Przesłanki rozwoju koncepcji zielonego łańcucha dostaw. *Przegląd Organizacji, 5.*

Nowakowska-Grunt, J. (2005). Strategie logistyczne organizacji sieciowych w zapewnianiu dostępności polskich produktów spożywczych na rynku UE. In *Strategie i logistyka organizacji sieciowych.* Wrocław: Wydawnictwo Akademii Ekonomicznej im. Oskara Langego we Wrocławiu.

Olejniczak, K. (2015). Zarządzanie zrównoważonym łańcuchem dostaw – cz. 2. Zintegrowana postawa wobec odpowiedzialności. *ABC Jakości Badania. Certyfikacja. Notyfikacja, 82.*

Olejniczak, K., & Koch, P. (2015). Zrównoważony rozwój w łańcuchu dostaw – Cz. 1. Zarys problematyki. *ABC Jakości Badania. Certyfikacja. Notyfikacja, 82.*

Polpharma. (2017). *Raport Społecznej Odpowiedzialności Grupy Polpharma 2015-2016.* Retrieved from: https://www.polpharma.pl/upload/2017/12/raport-spolecznej-odpowiedzialnosci-polpharmy-2015-201665.pdf

Polpharma. (2018). *Polpharma Group: Information, History, CSR, Sustainable Supply Chain, code of Conduct.* Retrieved from https://www.polpharma.pl

Popharma. (2014). *Raport Społecznej Odpowiedzialności Grupy Polpharma 2011-2013.* Retrieved from: https://www.polpharma.pl/aktualnosci-odpowiedzialnosc/polpharma-opublikowala-raport-spoleczny/

Popharma. (2015). *Raport Społecznej Odpowiedzialności Grupy Polpharma 2013-2014.* Retrieved from: https://www.polpharma.pl/upload/2016/01/polpharma-raport-spoleczny-2013-2014-lekki.pdf

Porter, M. E., & Kramer, M. R. (2006). Strategy and society: The link between competitive advantage and corporate social responsibility. *Harvard Business Review, 84*, 78–92. PMID:17183795

Rzeszotalska, M., & Musiał, M. (2016). Etyczny i odpowiedzialny biznes. *Harvard Business Review Polska*. Retrieved from https://www.hbrp.pl/b/etyczny-i-odpowiedzialny-biznes/PpnAtTRUO

Skandynawsko-Polska Izba Gospodarcza. CSRinfo. (2012). CSR w łańcuchu dostaw I w partnerstwie biznesowym – doświadczenia firm skandynawskich. Warszawa: CSRinfo.

Suppliers Polpharma. (2017). *Suppliers Code of Conduct*. Retrieved from: dostawca.polpharma.pl

Teuteberg, F., & Wittstruck, D. (2010). A Systematic Review of Sustainable Supply Chain Management Research. What is there and what is missing? Osnabruck: University of Osnabruck: Betriebliches Umwelt- und Nachhaltigkeitsmanagement.

Witkowski, J. (2005). *Strategie i logistyka organizacji sieciowych*. Wrocław: Wydawnictwo Akademii Ekonomicznej im. Oskara Langego we Wrocławiu.

Zailani, S., Jeyaraman, K., Vengadasan, G., & Premkumar, R. (2012). Sustainable Supply Chain Management (SSCM) in Malaysia: A survey. *International Journal of Production Economics*, *140*(1), 330–340. doi:10.1016/j.ijpe.2012.02.008

ADDITIONAL READING

Ahi, P., & Searcy, C. (2013). A comparative literature analysis of definitions for green and sustainable supply chain management. *Journal of Cleaner Production*, 52.

Benton, W. C., & Maloni, M. (2005). The influence of power driven buyer/seller relationships on supply chain satisfaction. *Journal of Operations Management*, 23.

Carr, A. S., & Pearson, J. N. (1999). Strategically managed buyer-supplier relationships and performance outcomes. *Journal of Operations Management*, 17.

Das, T. K., & Teng, B. S. (1997). Sustaining strategic alliances: Options and guidelines. *Journal of General Management*, 22.

De Toni, A., & Nassimbeni, G. (1999). Buyer-supplier operational practices, sourcing policies and plant performance: Results of an empirical research. *International Journal of Production Research*, 37.

Duffy, R., & Fearne, A. (2004). The impact of supply chain partnerships on supplier performance. *International Journal of Logistics Management*, 15.

Harland, C. M. (1996). Supply Chain Management: Relationships, Chains and Networks. *British Journal of Management*, 7.

Lambert, D. M., Emmelhainz, M. A., & Gardner, J. T. (1996). Developing and Implementing Supply Chain Partnerships. *International Journal of Logistics Management*, 7.

KEY TERMS AND DEFINITIONS

Corporate Social Responsibility (CSR): A concept in which a company is able to limit its external costs by taking social and environmental aspects into economic actions.

Supplier's Code of Conduct: A company's core document that outlines expectations regarding workplace standards and business practices which suppliers are required to adhere.

Suppliers' Good Practices: A set of best managerial practices provided by company's suppliers, which are treated as an example of cost, production, and time optimization for other suppliers.

Sustainability: The approach to balance economic, social, and environmental aspects of development.

Sustainable Development Goals (SDGs): A collection of 17 sustainability goals created by the United National in 2015, for stable and balanced development of the Earth.

Sustainable Supply Chain Strategy (SSCS): A strategy of long-term management and development of a supply chain, in which environmental risk, waste costs, and ethical values are taken into consideration.

ENDNOTE

1 As the main stakeholder ware mentioned: employees, patients, the medical and scientific community, customers, suppliers, and local communities.

Chapter 14 Collaboration in the Mexican Pharmaceutical Industry: An Analysis Within the Institutional Framework

José G. Vargas-Hernández
University of Guadalajara, Mexico

Alma Isela Rodríguez Hernández
University of Guadalajara, Mexico

ABSTRACT

The objective of this chapter is to analyze the collaboration networks of the Mexican pharmaceutical industry from an institutional approach. The pharmaceutical sector at a global level is characterized by a high dynamism in innovation and collaboration. One could say that the high value recorded by the industry is due to this. However, in Mexico, the lack of efficient institutions that ensure the appropriation of profits for investment in research within the industry is not perceived; this situation leads us to the next question, What are the dynamics of collaboration between pharmaceutical companies in Mexico? To answer this question, a database was created that identifies the alliances of the companies belonging to the Canifarma. Finally, a comparison of the number of registrations and patent applications between eight of these companies is made to measure the results of this situation.

DOI: 10.4018/978-1-5225-5921-4.ch014

INTRODUCTION

The pharmaceutical industry in Mexico has been consolidated by its high competitiveness and growth. This industry contributes 1.2% of the Gross Domestic Product (GDP). In addition to the fact that in recent years it has registered a steady increase in its market value, placing it in the eleventh position of the markets with the highest value according to data from the Federal Commission for Protection against Health Risks (Cofepris, 2013). However, the number of Mexican companies in the sector that manage to enter into strategic alliances and cooperation networks that allow them to acquire sustainable competitive advantages are few.

This can be verified by reviewing patent applications by Mexican pharmacists compared to foreign ones. In this industry, it is common for large multinational companies to acquire smaller Mexican companies. The purpose of this paper is to perform an institutional analysis of the pharmaceutical industry in Mexico and to identify the reasons why companies lack innovation and development to create a proposal for improvement.

In this way the work is composed in its first section of the literature review on collaboration networks, followed by the empirical review that shows case studies similar to the present. The third part presents a brief description and analysis of the current situation of the existing networks within the industry with data obtained from the Canifarma. Also included are the registers of the eight companies chosen randomly from the list of Canifarma members. Finally, the conclusions are presented and some suggestions are made to improve the activity of collaboration between the companies of the sector in Mexico. It is recognized that the limitations of the document are based on the limited information available on the collaborative activities of the chosen companies.

BACKGROUND OF THE PROBLEM

The pharmaceutical sector at a global level has been characterized by its high investment in research and development (R&D) which has made it one of the most innovative. Precisely this - innovation - is the pillar on which the rapid growth of this sector is based (KPMG, 2006, p.6). However, there are a number of factors that threaten the growth of this sector. These threats include counterfeiting (piracy), theft, smuggling, and the alteration or adulteration of pharmaceutical products that represent a loss of billions around the world, representing 10% of world trade (AMECE, 2006).

Another factor, that while not illegal but competing ironically with pharmaceutical laboratories, is known as generic drugs. These types of drugs arise when the patent, document issued by the State granting the exclusive right to use or commercially exploit someone an invention, loses its capacity for protection. The aim of the patent is for laboratories to recover development costs before making a profit, but when the right of exploitation ends, any laboratory can manufacture the drug and its prices decrease. In the United States and the European Union, patent protection is 17 and 10 years respectively, while in Mexico it is 20 years. The alternatives that, according to KPMG (2006), have the laboratories that develop and patent medicines are:

1. request for new patents for new applications of a drug that already exists. In this way the life of the patent is lengthened and cannot be used by generic laboratories; and
2. on patents that are about to expire, the laboratory itself can enter the generic market and compete with laboratories dedicated to this.

There is also the protection of trademarks and this consists of an authorization granted by the State to individuals the use of a denomination that distinguishes a product for commercial purposes. The right to use a trademark lasts for 10 years. The main difference between patents and trademarks is that trademarks can be renewed for equal periods indefinitely. In Mexico, the sector has to face all these problems, although some of these tend to be acuter than others due to the conditions in the country (KPMG, 2006, p. 5-6).

In relation to the above it can be said that, although competition with generic drugs discourages innovation in the sector, this is not the biggest problem. The lack of compliance with the laws in our country makes way for unfair and illegal drug competition. Mexico has the largest pharmaceutical market in Latin America, contributing 1.2% of the country's GDP in 2011 and 3.2% of manufacturing GDP in 2014 (Cofepris, 2013; INEGI, 2017). In 2006, there were 224 drug laboratories in the country that belonged to 200 companies, of which 46 were part of corporations with a majority foreign capital (KPMG, 2006, p.18-19). Drug piracy losses in the country were around 700 million USD, according to the Mexican Association of Pharmaceutical Research Industries (AMECE, 2006).

This problem undoubtedly discourages the investment of large pharmaceutical companies, but it is also a public health problem. The high costs of medicines favor the increase in the commercialization of counterfeit drugs (estimated to be about 80% from Asian countries) and expired drugs, which endangers the health of the user (KPMG, 2006, p. 7).

In order to combat the problem of theft and/or falsification of medicines, the government and pharmaceutical companies have taken measures ranging from satellite tracking of products to avoiding that drivers know what they carry (especially when it comes to of psychotropic drugs) to inhibit the theft of the loading units. Another way to combat drug counterfeiting is to use Radio Frequency Identification (RFID). RFID is a method of remote data storage and retrieval that uses tags or RFID tags. These contain antennas that allow it to receive and respond to RF requests from an RFID transceiver (AMECE, 2006).

The purpose of RFID tags is to identify the product within the production and distribution process. With these labels, counterfeiting, theft, smuggling, copying, alteration and adulteration of pharmaceutical products are avoided or diminished. The cost of these RFID tags is extremely high. In the case of Mexico, pharmaceutical companies cannot sustain the cost of their use in each of their products, this would make them lose profitability. Farmacias del Ahorro is one of the main distributors in Mexico and believes that investing in the use of these RFID tags in pharmaceuticals would be a great advance for the country. It would provide greater security to the industry concerned with the problem of counterfeiting and would generate economic benefits for companies in the long term. However, there must be cooperation on the part of all the companies in the industry (AMECE, 2006).

Although these measures seek to counteract the advance of the black market for medicines, it will not have the expected effect without the collaboration and good functioning of the institutions that the State has created for the same purpose. "The Ministry of Health (SSA) is responsible for granting registration to medicines that they intend to produce, sell, distribute and / or dispose of" (Am AMECE, 2006, p. 18).

The organisms that represent the industry are the National Association of Manufacturers of Medicines (ANAFAM), Canifarma, the Mexican Association of Pharmaceutical Research Industries (AMIIF) and Cofepris. In this sense, the Canifarma can be considered as the main representative body of the industry since it concentrates approximately 90% of the companies. Among its functions is to define the general interests of the member companies (national and foreign) and create commissions or bodies necessary to create harmony between the interests of industry and the public.

Within this body operates the Council of Ethics and Transparency of the Pharmaceutical Industry in Mexico (CETIFARMA) whose purpose is to achieve the development of a socially responsible industry to contribute to the welfare of society in general. La Canifarma operates under the supervision of the Ministry of Economy (SE). Cofepris is another agency created by the government to improve the situation of the Mexican pharmaceutical industry. It is a decentralized agency of the SSA and its functions are regulation, control and health promotion, hoping to preserve the health of the Population (AMECE, 2006; KPMG, 2006).

To have a broader picture, a brief description of the composition of the health system in Mexico should be made. There are three sectors: private, public and social security. Within the public, the SSA is the highest authority and has under its responsibility institutes, health centers and hospitals directed primarily at the low-income population. The DIF (Integral Family Development) provides this service to children and their families who do not have social security. In this sector - social security - the Mexican Social Security Institute (IMSS) and the Institute of Social Security and Social Services of State Workers (ISSSTE) are the main providers of health services, covering 13.2 and 10.4 million people in 2006.

In the private sector, Hospital Ángeles is the group with the largest presence in the country. Finally, it is necessary to mention the importance of the distributors since the pharmaceutical companies in the country do not have their own distribution. For 2006 there were more than 100 companies dedicated to distribution. The most important were: Casa Marzam, Casa Saba, Farmacias Benavides, National Drug and Provider of Medications (KPMG, 2006).

The industry in Mexico is full of actors interested in the growth of the sector for the benefit of companies, but also of consumers. The Mexican market is regulated by a wide range of institutions that regulate the activity. However, the lack of forcefulness in applying the laws opens the door for unfair competition to undermine the competitiveness of these companies. This, as already mentioned, increases the costs of companies and inhibits investment in the country.

REVIEW OF LITERATURE

This section discusses the importance of strategic alliances, the benefits of being involved in some, and, above all, the conditions that must exist for them to develop properly. On the subject of inter-organizational relationships and collaboration networks there is a wide range of literature, but here it is used only the one that allows to analysis what happens in the Mexican pharmaceutical sector.

This business sector is representative on the subject mainly for the rapid advances in technology and innovation that exist in its interior. The companies belonging to it are immersed in a dynamic of high competitiveness, but also of collaboration. The objective of these alliances is to generate joint capabilities and maintain leadership in the face of competition.

In general, "alliances are seen as a way to leverage the specific skills and competencies of companies in order to compete more effectively in the marketplace" (Rao & Reddy, 1995, p.502). In addition, it seeks to acquire resources and/or skills that are not possible to produce internally and when the risks of cooperation are estimated as tolerable. This type of collaboration is carried out in order to reduce the risks associated with implementing a new project, access new markets and technologies, accelerate the entry of a product to the market, take advantage of economies of scale (internal and external and pooling complementary competences.

Also, alliances facilitate complex intra- and inter-organizational coordination, resulting in a pool of trust, reciprocity, and mutual dependence. In an industry so changing in these respects, firms that enjoy an advantageous position against the competition could lose it quickly (Rao & Reddy, 1995). This is why companies are forced to enter into this dynamic of cooperation.

Likewise, the conditions that must exist for these agreements to be carried out should be mentioned. The decision to ally depends heavily on resource constraints, the position of each partner in the value chain, the level of technological sophistication required, and previous experiences with alliances (Powell et al., 1996). Other elements to be considered according to Camargo (2011) in relation to the partners of the alliance are:

1. Shareholders' equity;
2. Their orientation towards learning;
3. Orientation towards the learning of the alliance; and
4. Social networking of the alliance.

However, there are barriers that inhibit the formation of alliances between companies. Among them we find: 1) lack of trust between the parties; 2) difficulty to give up control; 3) the complexity of the project as a whole and 4) differential capacity to learn new skills. With regard to this last aspect, it should be noted that the "absorptive capacity" of a company will allow it to benefit more from an alliance. The internal and external capacities are not substitutes; they can be cataloged as complementary. Thus, the first ones support the evaluation of the advances in research abroad and the second ones are a good support to be aware of what happens abroad, besides providing resources that cannot be created internally (Powell et al., 1996).

In this sense, it can be affirmed that the creation of knowledge occurs in a context of a community that is fluid and changing. This, in the same way, could be cataloged as a network that serves as a space for innovation and a means of access to resources that otherwise are not available. It is important for organizations to identify their position in the organization in order to know the direction in which they are headed and the role they can play (Powell et al., 1996). The business alliances are then immersed in a system of networks that link them with other companies, but also within their internal organization (Castells, 2001).

Gulati (1998) defines a social network as a set of nodes (people or organizations) united by a set of social relations. It is considered that the economic actions of the members of the network are affected by the social context itself and the position of each member within the network. He adds that the generation of networks of inter-organizational alliances is due to the exogenous dependence of resources that drives the companies to cooperate and the insertion in an endogenous dynamic that, in a progressive way, guides the choice of partners.

In general, networks can be considered as the links and interactions that make it possible for information and knowledge to be transferred to companies, business chains, organizations and the institutional frameworks of each society to produce innovation and at the same time generate learning in the society. An important part of the networks between companies are the shocks, the impacts generated in the networks by the changes that affect them. An important feature of shocks is the intensity and pace of the process of change, and shocks are imposed by reforms in competitive processes and market structures (Cimoli, 2007).

Thus, a major change occurs in information and telecommunication technologies that allow companies to operate in networks more easily. For example, companies currently participate in various alliances and therefore carry out geographical movements of their research and production centers which are positioned in countries with an advanced economy. In this way, information and telecommunications technologies allow the exchange of information faster and easier, although this does not necessarily imply the creation and diffusion of knowledge (Cimoli, 2007). This scenario is called technological shock. Finally, it should be noted that this whole system of exchange and production of knowledge and innovation is framed by the institutional systems that exist in a society.

The type of collaboration, as well as its intensity, is conditioned by institutions or, rather, by the institutional configuration of a society. The conceptualization of institutions describes them as the rules or norms that shape human interaction. There is also another approach that sees them as the behavior that results from the norms that society itself imposes over time (North, 1990, Schotter, 1981, cited by Hollingsworth, 2000).

Following this order of ideas, Hollingsworth (2000) proposes a multilevel institutional analysis to understand the type of innovation that emerges in each society. The first level recognizes the rules, conventions, habits and values of a society. These change slowly over time and are the ones that shape the preferences of individuals. It is said that the greater the pluralism and complexity of a society, the more ambiguity there is about the rules and norms of society.

Continuing, the second level identifies institutional arrangements. These "are involved in the coordination of the various economic agents: producers, suppliers of raw materials, knowledge, etc., raw material processors, information; workers; customers of raw materials, finished goods and information "(Hollingsworth, 2000, p. 605). At the next level of analysis are the institutional sectors, these include all the organizations in a society that provide a particular service or product. This also includes education systems, businesses, financial markets, the legal system and the state.

The fourth level raises the effect that the regulatory framework has on organizations that tend to conform to institutional norms and rules. It can be seen how the changes that the organization undergoes in its structure and organizational culture as it forms the evolution of the institutional environment. Finally, the fifth and final level of analysis focuses on the results of such institutional configurations. This can be measured by the degree of innovation, education, and distribution of resources within a society compared to others (Hollingsworth, 2000).

The institutional framework can be affected by changes related to the interactions of individuals. Based on this assumption, Campbell (as quoted in Hollingsworth, 2000) considers two types of changes, the radical and the gradual. The first consists of the changes generated during the interaction of actors with different norms, such as cultures, rituals of action, etc., thus maintaining an intense relationship. The second is when there are small changes during the interaction of agents.

Finally, the institutional framework determines the variation in the innovative style of societies. By conducting an institutional analysis of a society, one can begin to understand in what type of organizations the production of certain types of knowledge is carried out and how this is related to certain types of innovation (Hollingsworth, 2000). As a consequence, it can be determined why some societies have a greater technological, innovative and economic development, and why other societies do not produce such development.

EMPIRICAL REVIEW

This section presents the different studies carried out on the pharmaceutical industry in order to contextualize it in greater detail. Orsenigo et al. (2001) carried out a study on the evolution of companies in this industry based on a database created by the University of Siene that contains a sample of more than 14,000 R&D projects. Pharmaceutical companies of which 5056 are agreements and 9785 research projects represented by 2297 companies and institutions.

The classification of companies consists of 3 categories: Established firms, new biotechnology companies and institutions, and the quantity represented by each is 651, 1372 and 274 respectively (Orsenigo et al., 2001). In addition, two types of time are considered to classify the R&D projects that are the micro level that considers the difference between the original and developed projects, while the macro level includes all new industry networks and new agreements.

As a result of this study, Orsenigo, et al. (2001) found that knowledge growth is positively related to the structure of the pharmaceutical network. Thus, it was identified that the organization of R&D, the patterns of division of labor and the dynamics of the industry are involved in the growth of knowledge, thus generating very complex network structures. In addition, it is found that the existence of the network has correspondence with the appearance of new technologies and that the older companies enjoy greater benefits since they have known to frame the knowledge has a high level of generality.

On the other hand, Dong and Yang (2015) perform an analysis of the pharmaceutical industry of the United States of America from 4 variables that are the experience of the alliance, the knowledge network, the knowledge investment and the investment in information technology (IT). The first variable has two alternatives to be measured, either by considering the number of successful alliances and the intensity of the alliance that was measured by dividing the number of successful alliances among the number of drugs approved by the Food and Drug Administration Drug Administration) in a focal year between 2003 and 2005 which are the years of analysis. The second variable is measured considering all patents available in the industry. For the third variable, the number of inventors and co-inventors in a specific year is taken into account. Finally, the investment in IT was obtained using various computer tools such as the IBM computer, non-IBM, mini-computer, PC and LAN.

The sample used by Dong and Yang (2015) was based on the public data of the US pharmaceutical industry using the SIC 2834 code from the Standard and Poor's Compustat database. The result of this research was that the intensity measures of the alliance's investors and co-inventors are significantly related to the knowledge of organizations in the pharmaceutical industry (Dong & Yang, 2015). Also, the interaction between the variables of the experience in an alliance with the investment in IT demonstrated a positive relation with the creation of knowledge in the organizations.

In 2005, Gay and Dousset developed a study on the industry network in biotechnology from a static model. What characterizes the study is the type of analysis model since in other studies each particular partnership is studied. Spatial and temporal limits were considered for this study. The former is defined by data obtained from the Security Data Company's online database of financial transactions", Thomson Financials, provided by LEREPS, University Research Center in Toulouse, France with a specialization in internet sites, new media and annual reports SEC files (Gay & Dousset, 2005). The sample consisted of 739 alliances carried out by 557 companies from the database identified as antibody-related treatments. The second limitation is the time period and for this study is from 1990 to 2004 presented in two periods of 7 years each.

Gay and Dousset (2005) found a relationship between the number of nodes, that is, the number of relationships between one company and another and the number of patents that the organization has. In this sense, they deduce that intellectual property is used to describe the relationship between the intangible, the associations with the innovations of the companies. Medarex (Medx), Abgenix (Abgx) and Cambridge Antibody Technology (CAT) are the companies with the most nodes in this entry, therefore the largest generators of patents on antibodies. In addition, 50% of the companies in the study have some patent which demonstrates the strength of the companies in biotechnology to discover new drugs.

The study also points out that 5% of the companies analyzed are not related to technology and are related to another organization (Gay & Dousset, 2005). This case is interesting because these companies may be about to disappear or think of creating innovation strategies because otherwise they would die.

Gay and Dousset (2005) emphasize the fact that central nodes are limited by technological changes in the market. Such centralization of the nodes can be interpreted as an indicator of obtaining patents and dissemination of knowledge. There is also an important relationship between the number of alliances and the number of products, mainly in the seven best pharmaceutical companies in the world. Finally, it is concluded that soon the market will only be made up of innovative companies and market leaders, while small ones will have a hard time staying on.

THEORETICAL ASSUMPTION

The institutions implemented by the Mexican government have not been adequate to improve the situation of the pharmaceutical industry in terms of innovation and development.

Methodology and Results

The collection of the data of the pharmaceutical industry was carried out directly from the page of the Canifarma. Data were also obtained directly from the websites of each of the companies registered in this chamber. In order to identify the relationships between these companies, the Ucinet and NetDraw programs were used, graphically showing the connections in the form of nodes and arcs.

The eight companies chosen to compare their activity in terms of patent application and registration were chosen randomly from the list of Canifarma members. The data of its patents were obtained from the Mexican Institute of Industrial Property (IMPI) and the United States Patent and Trademark Office (USPTO).

According to the 97 pharmacists considered to do the network analysis of the industry, it was found that there is little collaboration between these as shown in the figure (see Figure 1). Only pharmaceuticals Novartis, Alpharma, Glaxo, Healthcare and Aspen are distinguished by their collaborations with other companies in the industry.

The direction of the bows shows the recognition of the relationship or alliance of one company with another. While red nodes identify companies with more alliances. These companies are at the heart of the network and you can say that they are the creators of synergy in the industry. It should be mentioned that the companies that do not have a relationship with another do not appear in Figure 1.

It should be noted that these companies are mostly foreign companies that found conditions conducive to producing in Mexico as specialized and cheap labor, especially in the Mexico City (Tejada, 2014). This is why the largest production volume in the country is in that state as shown in Figure 2.

Analysis of Eight Companies in the Sector

This section presents the results of the analysis of the companies Probiomed, Pfizer, Fresenius, Ferring, Genomma, Rayere, Exakta and Pro-Ventas (see Figure 3). The purpose of this is to make a more specific description of the networks that exist

Figure 1. Network of the pharmaceutical industry in Mexico.
Source: (own elaboration based on data collected from each of the websites of the pharmacies registered in CANIFARMA)

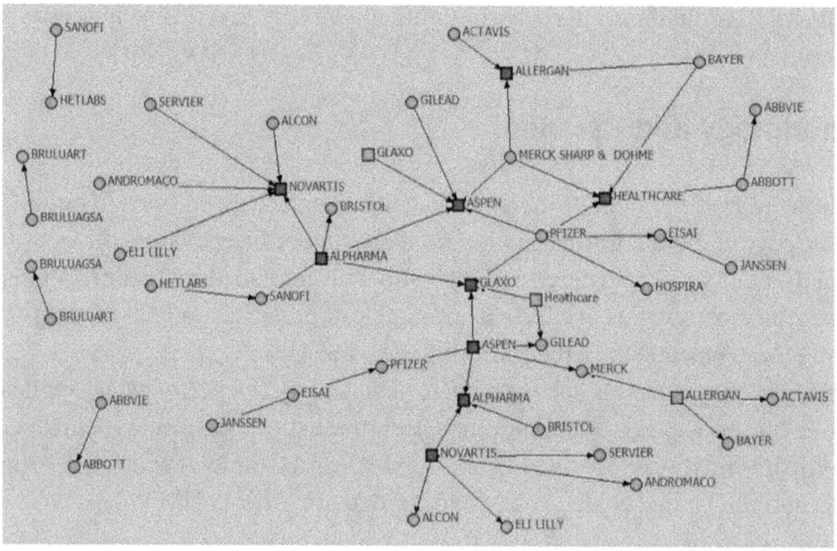

Figure 2. Production of the pharmaceutical industry by federative entity
Source: (INEGI, Economic Census, 2014)

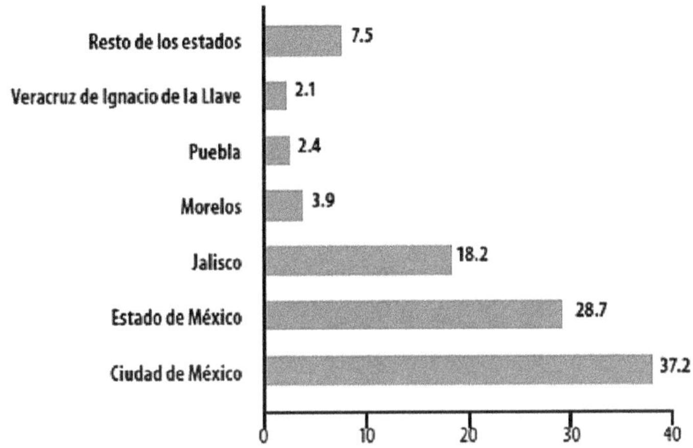

between the companies of the industry. The eight companies carry out activities in the state with the largest production of medicines in the country (Mexico City), in addition Fresenius has a presence in the State of Mexico, Nuevo León, Jalisco and Aguascalientes. While Probiomed also has presence in Jalisco and Nuevo León. Pfizer in Nuevo león. Rayere in Aguascalientes, Baja California and Campeche. Exakta in Puebla (INEGI, 2017).

Figure 3. Network of the eight selected companies
Source: (own elaboration)

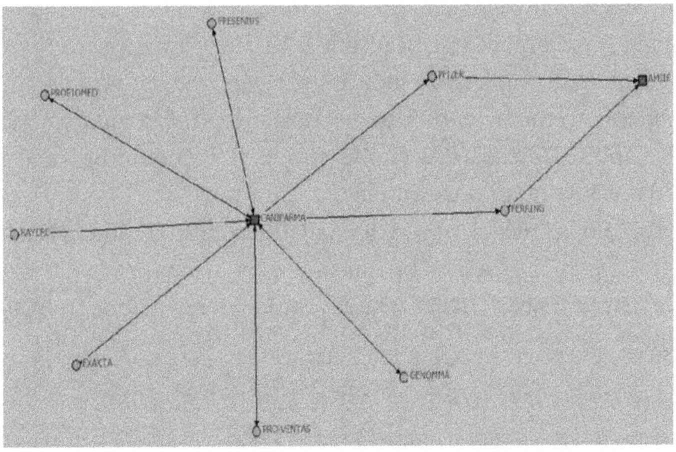

From these companies it is deduced that there is a lack of direct relation between them and that the only connection that is presented is through the Canifarma and AMIIF business organizations.

Tables show the number of trademarks and patents applied for and registered with the IMPI and the USPTO, respectively (see Table 1, see Table 2. From this information the existence of the great difference between the Mexican companies (Exakta, Pro-Ventas, Rayere, Genomma and Probiomed) and the foreign companies (Pfizer, Fresenius, Ferring) in terms of Innovation and Development is considered. While Mexican companies are on a par with trademark registration, in the field of patents they are far below foreign companies. With only four records Rayere is the Mexican company with the highest number of patents registered in the IMPI. We can see that Mexican companies, besides not cooperating with others, have a low activity in the production of patents.

CONCLUSION AND RECOMMENDATIONS

The pharmaceutical industry in Mexico is one of the main generators of income that attract foreign investment. The main cause of the investment decision is based on the quality of the labor that can be obtained in the country at a relatively low cost, mainly in Mexico City.

However, the problem of insecurity in the country is decisive for reducing the investment incentive in Mexico and, above all, the lack of institutional capacity of the Mexican government to punish it. Problems like theft, piracy, adulteration and smuggling are not punished. It is therefore necessary to consider reforming the institutional framework in such a way as to punish violators heavily in order to generate confidence in investors.

The Mexican government must build a regulatory framework that encourages the production of medicines to reduce its price in the market and that families have greater access to them. In this sense, designing the regulatory framework to restrict similar and OTC can be a viable option. This could prevent people from self-medication or low-quality medicines.

Another problem is the lack of Mexican institutions that foment the formation of strategic alliances, which is a new business strategy to improve the ties with other companies and to obtain benefits that alone could not have done or would have cost them more time.

Table 1. Trademarks and patents registered with the IMPI

	Pfizer S.A. DE C.V. (HARMACIA & UPJHON/ WYETH, S. DE R.L. DE C.V.	Pharmacos Exakta S.A. de C.V.	PROVENTAS, S.A. DE C.V.	PROBIOMED, S.A. DE C.V.	FARMACEUTICOS RAYERE, S.A.	FERRING, S.A. DE C.V.	FRESENIUS KABI MEXICO, S.A. DE C.V.	GENOMMA LABORATORIES MEXICO, S.A. DE C.V.
Number of trademarks	2598	130	18	177	111	76	122	46
Number of patent applications	2013	5	0	1	5	74	50	0
Number of patents	1582	0	0	0	4	45	41	0
Patents in medicine	152	0	0	0	0	0	0	0

Source: (own elaboration based on IMPI data)

Table 2. Trademarks and patents registered with the USPTO

	Pfizer S.A. DE C.V. (HARMACIA & UPJHON/WYETH, S. DE R.L. DE C.V.	Pharmacos Exakta S.A. de C.V.	PROVENTAS, S.A. DE C.V.	PROBIOMED, S.A. DE C.V.	FARMACEUTICOS RAYERE, S.A.	FERRING, S.A. DE C.V.	FRESENIUS KABI MEXICO, S.A. DE C.V.	GENOMMA LABORATORIES MEXICO, S.A. DE C.V.
Number of patents	4047	0	0	0	0	133	716	0

Source: (own elaboration based on USPTO data)

As it was seen in the section on methodology and results, the companies that compete in the Mexican pharmaceutical industry are mostly of foreign origin and the few nationals present little innovation. The reason why the nationals are not on a par with the larger ones. It is because they do not learn from them. While foreign companies have a long history of collaborating with other companies in other countries with better-designed institutions, in Mexico, no alliances or networks are developed, thus the difference in innovation.

In this sense, the creation of programs, conventions, and reform of the regulatory framework in Mexico is necessary so that the companies of this industry can create knowledge and innovations in an accelerated way. The culture of constant innovation must persist since it is the only way for companies to remain in the pharmaceutical industry, which will be reflected in the increase of applications for patents and trademarks.

REFERENCES

AMECE. (2006). *Diagnóstico del sector farmacéutico en México, para la aplicación de la Tecnología de Identificación por Radio Frecuencia (RFID) en los Medicamentos*. University of La Salle.

Camargo, F. (2011). Factores de éxito de las alianzas estratégicas: El caso de las empresas integradoras mexicanas. *Estudios Gerenciales*, *27*(120), 105–126. doi:10.1016/S0123-5923(11)70171-1

Castells, M. (2001). *La ciudad de la Nueva Economía.* Retrieved from: http://www.redalyc.org/articulo.oa?id=11202708

Cimoli, M. (2007). Evaluación de un programa de innovación y sistemas de producción en América Latina: Estudio sobre la dinámica de redes. *CEPAL-Serie desarrollo productive, 184*, 1-42.

COFEPRIS. (2013), Gestión de la salud pública en México. Secretaría de salud, México.

Dong, J. Q., & Yang, C.-H. (2015). Information technology and organizational learning in knowledge alliances and networks: Evidence from U.S. pharmaceutical industry. *Information & Management*, *52*(1), 111–122. doi:10.1016/j.im.2014.10.010

Exakta. (2017). *Exakta*. Retrieved from: http://www.exakta.mx/

Ferring. (2017). *Ferring*. Retrieved from: http://ferring.com.mx/

Fresenius. (2017). *Fresenius*. Retrieved from: http://www.freseniuskabi.com.mx/portal/Portal.nsf?Open

Gay, B., & Dousset, B. (2005). Innovation and network structural dynamics: Study of the alliance network of a major sector of the biotechnology industry. *Science Direct*, *34*, 1457–1475.

Genomma Lab. (2017). *Genomma Laboratories*. Retrieved from: http://www.genommalab.com/es/ index.html

Gulati, R. (1998). Alliances and Networks. *Strategic Management Journal*, *19*(4), 293–317. doi:10.1002/(SICI)1097-0266(199804)19:4<293::AID-SMJ982>3.0.CO;2-M

Hollingsworth, R. (2000). Doing institutional analysis: Implications for the study of innovations. *Review of International Political Economy*, *7*(4), 595–644. doi:10.1080/096922900750034563

IMPI. (2017). *Instituto Mexicano de la Propiedad Industrial*. Retrieved from: http://www.impi.gob.mx/

INEGI. (2016). *Estádisticas a propósito de... la industria farmacéutica*. Aguascalientes: Instituto Nacional de Estádistica y Geografía.

INEGI. (2017). *Directorio Estadístico Nacional de Unidades Económicas*. National Statistical Directory of Economic Units. Retrieved from: http://www.beta.inegi.org.mx/app/mapa/denue/

KPMG. (2006). *La Industria Farmacéutica en México*. KPMG.

Orsenigo, L., Pammolli, F., & Riccaboni, M. (2001). Technological change and network dynamics lessons from the pharmaceutical industry. *Research Policy*, *30*(3), 485–508. doi:10.1016/S0048-7333(00)00094-9

Pfizer. (2017). *Pfizer*. Retrieved from: https://www.pfizer.com.mx/

Powell, W. W., Koput, K., & Smith-Doerr, L. (1996). Interorganizational Collaboration and the Locus of Innovation: Networks of Learning in Biotechnology. *Administrative Science Quarterly*, *14*(1), 116–145. doi:10.2307/2393988

Probiomed. (2017). *Probiomed*. Retrieved from: http://www.probiomed.com.mx/

Proventas. (2017). *Proventas*. Retrieved from: http://www.proventas.com.mx/

Rao, B. P., & Reddyt, S. (1995). A Dynamic Approach to the Analysis of Strategic Alliances. *International Business Review*, *4*(4), 499–518. doi:10.1016/0969-5931(96)81750-1

Rayere. (2017). *Rayere*. Retrieved from: http://www.rayere.com.mx/fr_frameset.htm

USPTO. (2017). *United States Patent and Trademark Office*. Retrieved from: http://www.uspto.gov/

ADDITIONAL READING

Anónimo (2001). Informe: Los OTCs y las nuevas farmacias. *Merchandising News* Octubre 2001 p. 1-4

Ascione, F., Manifold, C., & Parenti, M. (1997). Principles of drug information and scientific literature evaluation. American Pharmaceutical Association. 2nd Edit. Washington DC. 1997.

British National Formulary (BNF) *(1995). British Medical association and the Royal pharmaceutical society of Great Britain,* 30.

Chetley, A. (1990). *A healhy business? World health and the pharmaceutical industry* (1st ed.). Zed Book- London.

Cruzado L. R. (1996). Análisis Comparativo de la Información de Medicamentos. *Medicamentos y Salud Popular. 32*.

Durán Gracia, E., & .... (1999). Calidad en farmacoterapia: Un proceso integral. *Medicine*, *7*(134), 6361–6366.

Hartog R. & Schulte –Sasse (1990). *German and Swiss drug supplies to the third world: Survey and evaluation of pharmacological rationality* - Buko Pharma -Kampagne . HAI 1990.

Heineck, I., Schenckel, E. P., & Vidal, X. (1998). Medicamentos de Venta Libre en el Brasil. *Revista Panamericana de Salud Pública*, *6*, 385–391. PMID:9734218

Lopez - Linares, R. (1998). *Promoviendo la Salud o los Negocios*. Encuentro AIS Sudamérica -Enero 1998.

Peretta, M., & Ciccia, B. (2008). *Graciela Reingeniería de la práctica farmacéutica*. Manuscrypt.

Valladares, G. (2001). Situación y medicamentos en el País: Mercado y acceso a medicamentos. *Revista de Salud y Medicamentos*, *54*, 11–21.

Vermengo, M. J. (1998). *Control Oficial de Medicamentos*. Organización Panamericana de la Salud – PAME 1998.

KEY TERMS AND DEFINITIONS

Alliance: It is an agreement made by two or more parties to achieve a set of objectives desired by each party independently.

Collaboration: The action and effect of collaborating to work together with another or other people to carry out a work or achieve an objective.

Institution: Institutions are "the rules of the game" supported by stable, valued, recurring patterns of behavior. As structures or mechanisms of social order, they govern the behavior of a set of individuals within a given community.

Interinstitutional: The coordination of actors, to the interaction of institutions through joint action mechanisms around projects common, to the formulation, construction, and collective execution of programs, projects, and actions that involve initiatives, resources, potentialities, and shared interests.

Mexican: From Mexico or relative to this American country.

Network: Organization formed by a set of establishments of the same branch, and sometimes under the same address, which are distributed by several places in a locality or geographical area to provide a service.

Pharmaceutical Industry: The pharmaceutical industry is a business sector dedicated to the manufacture, preparation, and commercialization of medicinal chemicals for the treatment and also the prevention of diseases.

Compilation of References

5 ways the digital supply chain drives success for life sciences. (2016). Retrieved from: https://assets1.dxc.technology/life_sciences/downloads/DXC_Digital_Supply_Chain_Drives_Success_for_Life_Sciences.pdf

A report from PWC entitled From Vision to Decision Pharma 2020. (n.d.). Retrieved from: www.pwc.in

Abdallah, A. A. (2013). Global Pharmaceutical Supply Chain: A Quality Perspective. *International Journal of Business and Management*, *8*(17), 62–70. doi:10.5539/ijbm.v8n17p62

Abraham, J. (2009). Global health challenges in the pharmaceutical world. *Health Economics, Policy, and Law*, *4*(01), 115–127. doi:10.1017/S174413310800457X PMID:19099620

Adobor, H. (2012). Ethical Issues in Outsourcing: The Case of Contract Medical Research and the Global Pharmaceutical Industry. *Journal of Business Ethics*, *105*(2), 239–255. doi:10.100710551-011-0964-0

Ahmad, N., Awan, M. U., Raouf, A., & Sparks, L. (2009). Development of a service quality scale for pharmaceutical supply chains. *International Journal of Pharmaceutical and Healthcare Marketing*, *3*(1), 26–45. doi:10.1108/17506120910948494

Ahmad, N., & Daghfous, A. (2010). Knowledge sharing through inter-organizational knowledge networks Challenges and opportunities in the United Arab Emirates. *European Business Review*, *22*(2), 153–174. doi:10.1108/09555341011023506

Akbar, Z. (1994). Determinants of Electronic Integration in the Insurance Industry: An Empirical Test. *Management Science*, *40*(5), 549–566. doi:10.1287/mnsc.40.5.549

Albuquerque, B. R., Prieto, M. A., Barreiro, M. F., Rodrigues, A., Curran, T. P., Barros, L., & Ferreira, I. C. F. R. (2017). Catechin-based extract optimization obtained from *Arbutus unedo* L. fruits using maceration/microwave/ultrasound extraction techniques. *Industrial Crops and Products*, *95*, 404–415. doi:10.1016/j.indcrop.2016.10.050

Al-Mutawah, K., Lee, V., & Cheung, Y. (2009). A new multi-agent system framework for tacit knowledge management in manufacturing supply chains. *Journal of Intelligent Manufacturing*, *20*(5), 593–610. doi:10.100710845-008-0142-0

Amami, M., & Brimberg, J. (2004). *Technology Diffusion: The role of Web Systems, Environment and Organizational Factors*. AIM.

AMECE. (2006). *Diagnóstico del sector farmacéutico en México, para la aplicación de la Tecnología de Identificación por Radio Frecuencia (RFID) en los Medicamentos*. University of La Salle.

Amegashie-Viglo, S. (2014). Supply Chain Management of the Pharmaceutical Industry for Quality Health Care Delivery: Consumer Perception of Ernest Chemists Limited as a Pharmaceutical Service Provider in Ghana. *Journal of Information Engineering and Applications*, *4*(8).

Amegashie-Viglo, S., Nikoi, & Kotei, J.A. (2014). Supply Chain Management of the Pharmaceutical Industry for Quality Health Care Delivery: Consumer Perception of Ernest Chemists Limited as a Pharmaceutical Service Provider in Ghana. *Journal of Information Engineering and Applications*, *4*(8), 15–39.

An interview with Jacques Mulder. (2015). *Cross-Sector Convergence in Health*, 1-8.

Anderson, D. L., & Lee Hau, L. (2001). New Supply Chain Business Models – The Opportunities and Challenges. *The ASCET Project.*.

Anderson, A. C. (2003). The Process of Structure-Based Drug Design. *Chemistry & Biology*, *10*(9), 787–797. doi:10.1016/j.chembiol.2003.09.002 PMID:14522049

Andes, D., Diekema, D. J., Pfaller, M. A., Prince, R. A., ... Jou, J. (2008). In vivo pharmacodynamic characterization of anidulafungin in a neutropenic murine canddiasis model. *Antimicrobial Agents and Chemotherapy*, *52*(2), 539–550. doi:10.1128/AAC.01061-07 PMID:18070979

Andreas & Kotzab. (2003). Does supply chain management really pay? Six perspectives to measure the performance of managing a supply chain. *European Journal of Operational Research*, *144*, 306–320.

Angerhofer, J., & Angelides Marios, C. (2006). A model and a performance measurement system for collaborative supply chains Bernhard. *Decision Support Systems*, *42*(1), 283–301. doi:10.1016/j.dss.2004.12.005

Applied Product Marketing. (n.d.). Retrieved from: http://www.AppliedProductMarketing.com

Aronow, W. S., & Wilbert, S. A. (2014). Indications for Implantable Cardioverter-Defibrillator Therapy and Recommendations for Implantable Cardioverter-Defibrillator Therapy in Patients not Included or not Well Represented in Clinical Trials. *Journal of Cardiovascular Diseases & Diagnosis*.

Aronsson, H., Abrahamsson, M., & Spens, K. (2011). Developing lean and agile health care supply chains. *Supply Chain Management*, *16*(3), 176–183. doi:10.1108/13598541111127164

Ashish, A., & Shankar, R. (2006). Modeling the metrics of lean, agile and agile supply chain: An ANP-based approach. *European Journal of Operational Research*, *173*(1), 211–225. doi:10.1016/j.ejor.2004.12.005

aus der Beek, T., Weber, F. A., Bergmann, A., Hickmann, S., Ebert, I., Hein, A., & Küster, A. (2016). Pharmaceuticals in the environment—global occurrences and perspectives. *Environmental Toxicology and Chemistry*, *35*(4), 823–835. doi:10.1002/etc.3339 PMID:26666847

Aziz, N., & Sparrow, J. (2011). Patterns of gaining and sharing of knowledge about customers: A study of an Express Parcel Delivery Company. *Knowledge Management Research and Practice*, *9*(1), 29–47. doi:10.1057/kmrp.2011.3

Baines, D. A. (2011). *Thesis on Problems Facing the Pharmaceutical Industry and Approaches to Ensure Long Term Viability*. University of Pennsylvania Scholarly Commons. Retrieved from: (http://repository.upenn.edu/od_theses_msod/33

Baker, M. (2013). Fragment-based lead discovery grows up. *Nature Reviews. Drug Discovery*, *12*(1), 5–7. doi:10.1038/nrd3926 PMID:23274457

Bakos, J. Y., & Treacy, E. T. (1986, June). Information technology and corporate strategy; A research perspective. *Management Information Systems Quarterly*, *10*(2), 107–119. doi:10.2307/249029

Baldi, A. (2010). Computational Approaches for Drug Design and Discovery: An Overview. *Systematic Reviews in Pharmacy*, *1*(1), 99–105. doi:10.4103/0975-8453.59519

Ballance, R., Pogany, J., & Forstner, H. (1992). *The world's pharmaceutical industries*. London, UK: Edward Elgar.

Baller, R. (2008). *Komplexitätsmanagement logistischer Prozesse. Studienarbeit an der Dresden International University MBA in Logistics Management vorgelegt von Lehrstuhl für BWL*. Ingolstadt: Verlag fuer oekonomische Texte.

Barki, H., & Pinsonneault, A. (2003). *The Construct of Organizational Integration: A Research Framework and Its Application to Enterprise Systems Research*. Cahier du Geris no 03-04 Février.

Barney Jay, B. (2001). Resource-based theories of competitive advantage: A ten year retrospective on the resource-based view. *Journal of Management*, *27*(6), 643–650. doi:10.1177/014920630102700602

Barney Jay, B., & Arikan Asli, M. (2001). The Resource-based View: Origins and Implications. *Strategic Management Journal*.

Bartol, K. M., & Srivastava, A. (2002). Encouraging knowledge sharing: The role of organizational reward systems. *Journal of Leadership & Organizational Studies*, *9*(1), 64–76. doi:10.1177/107179190200900105

Baumgarten, H., & Walter, S. (2011). Trends und Strategien in der Logistik. In H. Baumgarten, H. Wiendahl, & J. Zentes (Eds.), *Logistikmanagement. Strategien-Konzepte,-Praxisbeispiele* (pp. 13–21). Berlin: Springer.

Beamon Benita, M. (1998). Supply Chain Design and Analysis: Models and Methods. *International Journal of Production Economics*, *55*(3), 281–294. doi:10.1016/S0925-5273(98)00079-6

Begg, D., Fischer, S., & Dornbusch, R. (2007). *Makroekonomia*. Warszawa: PWE.

Beier, F. J. (1995). The management of the supply chain for hospital pharmacies: A focus on inventory management practices. *Journal of Business Logistics*, *16*(2), 153–173.

Bendavide, Y., Boeck, H., & Philippe, R. (2010). Redesigning the replenishment process of medical supplies in hospitals with RFID. *Business Process Management Journal*, *16*(6), 991–1013. doi:10.1108/14637151011093035

Benjamin, R. I., de Long, D. W., & Morton, M. S. (1990). Electronic data interchange: How much competitive advantage? *Long Range Planning*, *23*(1), 29–40. doi:10.1016/0024-6301(90)90005-O

Benson, M. (2015, January 22). *An easier way to understand the pharma industry*. Retrieved from: https://marketrealist.com/2015/01/easier-way-understand-pharma-industry

Berkman, H., & Eugster, M. (2017). Short on drugs: Short Selling during the Drug Development Process. *Journal of Financial Markets*, *33*, 102–123. doi:10.1016/j.finmar.2017.02.001

Biffi, M., Ziacchi, M., Bertini, M., Sangiorgi, D., Corsini, D., Martignani, C., ... Giuseppe, B. (2008). Longevity of implantable cardioverter-defibrillators: Implications for clinical practice and health care systems. *Europace*, *10*(11), 1288–1295. doi:10.1093/europace/eun240 PMID:18772164

Blaik, P. (2001). *Logistyka. Koncepcja zintegrowanego zarządzania*. Warszawa: PWE.

Blaik, P., Bruska, A., Kauf, S., & Matwiejczuk, R. (2013). *Logistyka w systemie zarządzania przedsiębiorstwem*. Warszawa: PWE.

Boonstra, A., & de Vries, J. (2005). Analyzing inter-organizational systems from a power and interest perspective. *International Journal of Information Management*, *25*(6), 485–501. doi:10.1016/j.ijinfomgt.2005.08.006

Booth, R. (1999). *The global supply chain. FT healthcare management report*. London: Financial Times Business Ltd.

Borgstrom, B., & Hertz, S. (2011). Supply Chain Strategies: Changes in Customer Order-Based Production. *Journal of Business Logistics*, *32*(4), 361–373. doi:10.1111/j.0000-0000.2011.01031.x

Brdulak, H. (Ed.). (2012). *Logistyka przyszłości*. Warszawa: PWE.

Breiger, W. R., Osamor, P. E., Salami, K. K., Oladepo, O., & Otusanya, S. A. (2004). Interactions between patent medicine vendors and customers in urban and rural Nigeria. *Health Policy and Planning*, *19*(3), 177–182. doi:10.1093/heapol/czh021 PMID:15070866

Brenda, M., & Zmud, R. W. (1996). Measuring the Extent of EDI Usage in Complex Organizations: Strategies and Illustrative Examples. *Management Information Systems Quarterly*, *20*(3), 331–345. doi:10.2307/249659

Bruce, L. (2003). Defending value and maximizing profitability of innovative pharmaceuticals over their entire life cycles. *International Journal of Medical Marketing*, *3*(3), 195–197. doi:10.1057/palgrave.jmm.5040119

Brudlak, H., Duliniec, E., & Gołębiowski, T. (2011). *Współpraca w łańcuchach dostaw a konkurencyjność przedsiębiorstw i kooperujących sieci*. Warszawa: OW SGH.

Burchart-Korol, D., Czaplicka-Kolarz, K., & Witkowski, K. (2013). Metody oceny ekoefektywności w zarządzaniu łańcuchem dostaw. *Logistyka*, *5*, 258–263.

Bureš, V. (2003). Cultural Barriers in Knowledge Sharing. E+M Ekonomics and Management, Liberec, 6, 57-62.

Burns, L. (2002). Wharton school colleagues. In *The Health Care Value Chain Producers, Purchasers, and Providers*. San Francisco, CA: Jossey-Bass.

Business health care group, Towers Watson/National Business Group on Health. (2014). *Trends in Benefit Design Evolution & National Employer Initiative on Specialty Pharmacy*. Business health care group, Towers Watson/National Business Group on Health, 2014. The New Health Care Imperative.

Butler, R. (2002). The end of the blockbuster. *Chemistry & Industry*, *9*, 9–10.

Cachon, G. P., & Lariviere, M. A. (2005). Supply Chain Coordination with Revenue-Sharing Contracts: Strengths and Limitations. *Management Science*, *51*(1), 30–44. doi:10.1287/mnsc.1040.0215

Callender, C., & Grasman, S. E. (2010). Barriers and best practices for material management in healthcare sector. *Engineering Management Journal*, *22*(4), 11–17. doi:10.1080/10429247.2010.11431875

Camargo, F. (2011). Factores de éxito de las alianzas estratégicas: El caso de las empresas integradoras mexicanas. *Estudios Gerenciales*, *27*(120), 105–126. doi:10.1016/S0123-5923(11)70171-1

Cancer Drugs Fund: The bigger picture. (n.d.). . doi:10.1136/bmj.i5090

Castells, M. (2001). *La ciudad de la Nueva Economía*. Retrieved from: http://www.redalyc.org/articulo.oa?id=11202708

Chaberek, M. (2010). Praktyczne i teoretyczne aspekty kontaminacji i atomizacji logistyki i informatyki ekonomicznej. In Informatyczne narzędzia procesów logistycznych (pp. 13-24). Warszawa: Wyd. CeDeWu.

Chaberek, M. (1999). Logistyka - dawne i współczesne płaszczyzny jej praktycznego stosowania. *Pieniądze i Więź*, *3*, 140–145.

Chaberek, M. (2002). *Makro-i mikroekonomiczne aspekty wsparcia logistycznego*. Gdańsk: Wyd. UG.

Chaberek, M. (2014). Theoretical, regulatory and practical implications of logistics. *LogForum*, *10*(1), 3–12.

Chaberek, M. (2015). Logistyczne aspekty bezpieczeństwa. *Zeszyty Naukowe Uniwersytetu Gdańskiego. Ekonomika Transportu i Logistyka, 56*, 21–36.

Chang, S.-L., Reay-Chen, W., & Shih-Yuan, W. (2007). Applying a direct multi-granularity linguistic and strategy-oriented aggregation approach on the assessment of supply performance. *European Journal of Operational Research, 177*(2), 1013–1025. doi:10.1016/j.ejor.2006.01.032

Chemical & Engineering News. (n.d.). Retrieved from https://pubs.acs.org/cen/coverstory/83/8325/8325future.html

Cheng, J. H., Yeh, C. H., & Tu, C. W. (2008). Trust and knowledge sharing in green supply chains. *Supply Chain Management, 13*(4), 283–295. doi:10.1108/13598540810882170

Chen, I. J., & Antony, P. (2004). Towards a theory of supply chain management: The constructs and measurements. *Journal of Operations Management, 22*(2), 119–150. doi:10.1016/j.jom.2003.12.007

Chiung, M., Hae, L. Y., & Seok, J. C. (2008). Integrated process planning and scheduling in a supply chain. *Computers & Industrial Engineering, 54*(4), 1048–1061. doi:10.1016/j.cie.2007.06.018

Choon. (2001). A framework of supply chain management literature. *European Journal of Purchasing & Supply Management, 7*, 39-48.

Chou, P., & Passerini, K. (2009). Intellectual property rights and knowledge sharing across countries. *Journal of Knowledge Management, 13*(5), 331–344. doi:10.1108/13673270910988141

Chow, W. S., Madu, C. N., Kuei, C.-H., Lu, M. H., Lin, C., & Tseng, H. (2008). Supply chain management in the US and Taiwan: An empirical study. *The International Journal of Management Science Omega, 36*(5), 665–679. doi:10.1016/j.omega.2006.01.001

Christopher, M. (1998). *Logistics and Supply Chain Management: Strategies for reducing cost and improving service*. London: Financial Times Pitman Publishing.

Christopher, M. (1998). *Logistics and supply chain management: Strategies for reducing costs and improving service*. London: Financial Times - Prentice Hall.

Ciesielski, M. (1998). *Strategie logistyczne przedsiębiorstw*. Poznań: Wyd. AE w Poznaniu.

Ciesielski, M. (Ed.). (2002). *Sieci logistyczne*. Poznań: Wyd. AE w Poznaniu.

Cimoli, M. (2007). Evaluación de un programa de innovación y sistemas de producción en América Latina: Estudio sobre la dinámica de redes. *CEPAL-Serie desarrollo productive, 184*, 1-42.

Clemens, L., Leonard, F., & Marc, W. (2004). Designing a performance measurement system: A case study. *European Journal of Operational Research, 156*(2), 267–286. doi:10.1016/S0377-2217(02)00918-9

Clemons & Row. (1991). Sustaining IT Advantage: The Role of Structural Differences. *MIS Quarterly, 15*(3), 275-292.

Closs , & Mollenkopf, . (2004). A global supply chain framework. *Industrial Marketing Management, 33*(1), 37–44. doi:10.1016/j.indmarman.2003.08.008

COFEPRIS. (2013), Gestión de la salud pública en México. Secretaría de salud, México.

Cokky, H., & Smits, M. (2004). *A resource based and real options perspective on IT infrastructure investments aiming for strategic flexibility.* Center for Research on Information Systems Management.

Couper, M. P., Traugott, M. W., & Lamias, M. J. (2001). Web survey design and administration. *Public Opinion Quarterly, 65*(2), 230–253. doi:10.1086/322199 PMID:11420757

Cozzella, L., Simonetti, C., & Spagnolo, G. S. (2012). Drug packaging security by means of white-light speckle. *Optics and Lasers in Engineering, 50*(10), 1359–1371. doi:10.1016/j.optlaseng.2012.05.016

Croom, S. R., Romano, P., & Giannakis, M. (2000). Supply chain management: An analytical frame work for critical literature review. *European Journal of Purchasing and Supply Management, 6*(1), 67–83. doi:10.1016/S0969-7012(99)00030-1

CSRConsulting. (2017). *SDGs w Praktyce. Kampania 17/17 - Popharma.* Retrieved from http://www.sdgs.pl/polpharma-2/

Cunningham, C., & Tynan, C. (1993). Electronic Trading, Inter-organizational Systems and the nature of Buyer-seller Relationships: The need for a network Perspective. *International Journal of Information Management, 13*(1), 3–28. doi:10.1016/0268-4012(93)90044-5

Daems, R., Maes, E., Mehra, M., Carroll, B., & Thomas, A. (2014). MD3, Pharmaceutical Portfolio Management: Global Disease Burden and Corporate Performance Metrics. *Value in Health, 17*(6), 732–738. doi:10.1016/j.jval.2014.07.005 PMID:25236997

Daly, R., & Kolassa, M. (2004). Start early, sell more, sell longer. *Pharmaceutical Executive, 1*, 8–20.

Das, M. K., & Chakraborty, T. (2016). ANN in Pharmaceutical Product and Process Development. Artificial Neural Network for Drug Design, Delivery and Disposition, 277-293.

de Castro, L. A. B. (2011). Partnering Brazilian biotech with the global pharmaceutical industry. *Nature Biotechnology, 29*(3), 210–211. doi:10.1038/nbt.1801 PMID:21390019

De la Fuente, M., Ros, L., & Cardós, M. (2008). Integrating Forward and Reverse Supply Chains: Application to a metal-mechanic company. *International Journal of Production Economics, 111*(2), 782–792. doi:10.1016/j.ijpe.2007.03.019

de Vries, J., & Huijsman, R. (2011). Supply chain management in health services: An overview. *Supply Chain Management, 16*(3), 159–165. doi:10.1108/13598541111127146

Delivering at the Speed of Business: Digital Supply Networks in Life Sciences. (2016). Accenture. *Life Sciences*, 1–12.

Deng, J., Xu, Z., Xiang, C., Liu, J., Zhou, L., Li, T., ... Ding, C. (2017). Comparative evaluation of maceration and ultrasonic-assisted extraction of phenolic compounds from fresh olives. *Ultrasonics Sonochemistry*, *37*, 328–334. doi:10.1016/j.ultsonch.2017.01.023 PMID:28427640

Dennis, Z. K. (2008). Product lifecycle management: Marketing strategies for the pharmaceutical industry. *Journal of Medical Marketing: Device Diagnostics Pharmaceutical Market*, *8*(4), 293–301. doi:10.1057/jmm.2008.23

Deshpande, P. B., Kumar, G. A., Kumar, A. R., Shavi, G. V., Karthik, A., Reddy, M. S., & Udupa, N. (2011). Supercritical fluid technology: Concepts and pharmaceutical applications. *PDA Journal of Pharmaceutical Science and Technology*, *65*(3), 333–344. doi:10.5731/pdajpst.2011.00717 PMID:22293238

Dingemanse, J., & Krause, A. (2017). Impact of pharmacokinetic-pharmacodynamic modelling in early clinical drug development. *European Journal of Pharmaceutical Sciences*, *109*, S53–S58. doi:10.1016/j.ejps.2017.05.042 PMID:28535992

Docteur, E. (2009). *Ensuring Efficiency in Pharmaceutical Expenditure*. Achieving Better Value for Money in Health Care.

Dong, J. Q., & Yang, C.-H. (2015). Information technology and organizational learning in knowledge alliances and networks: Evidence from U.S. pharmaceutical industry. *Information & Management*, *52*(1), 111–122. doi:10.1016/j.im.2014.10.010

Droppert, H., & Bennett, S. (2015). Corporate social responsibility in global health: An exploratory study of multinational pharmaceutical firms. *Globalization and Health*, *11*(15), 1–8. PMID:25886175

Dunlap-Hinkler, D., Kotabe, M., & Mudambi, R. (2010). A story of breakthrough versus Incremental innovation: Corporate entrepreneurship in the global pharmaceutical industry. *Strategic Entrepreneurship Journal*, *4*(2), 106–127. doi:10.1002ej.86

Duperon, W. O., & Cinar, E. M. (2010). Global Competition Versus Regional Interests: FDI and Pharmaceuticals in India. *Journal of International Commercial Law and Technology*, *5*(4), 181–200.

Dyckhoff, H., & Finke, U. (1992). *Cutting and packing in production and distribution: A typology and bibliography*. Heidelberg, Germany: Physica. doi:10.1007/978-3-642-58165-6

Ehrhardt, M., Hutchens, R., & Higgins, S. (2012). Five Steps toward a Revitalized Pharmaceutical Supply Chain. *Spring*, (66).

Embracing Innovation. (2017). Driving Growth Across Healthcare Continuum.

Embracing the change: An Introduction to Multichannel Marketing. (2014). *Eye for Pharma*, 1-3. Retrieved from: www.eyeforpharma.com/multichannelreport

Enslow, B. (2017). *Global Supply Chain Excellence: New Best Practices to Master*. Retrieved from http://www.supplychainbrain.com/content/sponsored-channels/amber-road-global-trade-mgmt/single-article-page/article/global-supply-chain-excellence-new-best-practices-to-master/

Enyinda, C. I., & Tolliver, D. (2009). Taking counterfeits out of the pharmaceutical supply chain in Nigeria: Leveraging multi layer mitigation approach. *Journal of African Business*, *10*(2), 218–234. doi:10.1080/15228910903187957

EPA. (2000). *The Lean and Green Supply Chain: A Practical Guide for Materials Managers and Supply Chain Managers to Reduce Costs and Improve Environmental Performance*. Retrieved from: https://www.epa.gov/p2/lean-and-green-supply-chain-practical-guide-materials-managers-and-supply-chain-managers-reduce

Exakta. (2017). *Exakta*. Retrieved from: http://www.exakta.mx/

Feasibility Study Measuring the Economic Footprint of the Pharmaceutical Industry. (2013). Retrieved from: https://www.ifpma.org/wp-content/uploads/2016/02/wifor_feasibility_study_2013.pdf

Fein, A. J. (2003). *Strategies for the unbundled supply chain*. Distributor's Link. Spring.

Ferring. (2017). *Ferring*. Retrieved from: http://ferring.com.mx/

Fielden, M. R., & Kolaja, K. L. (2008). The role of early in vivo toxicity testing in drug discovery toxicology. *Expert Opinion on Drug Safety*, *2*(2), 107–110. doi:10.1517/14740338.7.2.107 PMID:18324874

Fink, A. (2012). *How to Conduct Surveys: A Step-by-Step Guide*. Sage Publications.

France-Anne Gruat, L. F., & Vale'rie Botta, G. (2007). A framework to analyse collaborative performance. *Computers in Industry*, *58*(7), 687–697. doi:10.1016/j.compind.2007.05.007

Fresenius. (2017). *Fresenius*. Retrieved from: http://www.freseniuskabi.com.mx/ portal/Portal.nsf?Open

Friemann, F., & Schönsleben, P. (2013). *Global Logistics Excellence and Best Practices in Pharma: Results from an interview series with 11 large, multinational pharmaceutical companies*. Retrieved from: https://www.research-collection.ethz.ch/

Friemann, F., & Schönsleben, P. (2016). Reducing Global Supply Chain Risk Exposure of Pharmaceutical Companies by Further Incorporating Warehouse Capacity Planning into the Strategic Supply Chain Planning Process. *Journal of Pharmaceutical Innovation*, *11*(2), 162–176. doi:10.100712247-016-9249-6

Gaisford, S. (2017). 8 – 3D printed pharmaceutical products. In 3D Printing in Medicine (pp. 155-166). Woodhead Publishers.

Gallo, M., Formato, A., Ianniello, D., Andolfi, A., Conte, E., Ciaravolo, M., ... Naviglio, D. (2017). Supercritical fluid extraction of pyrethrins from pyrethrum flowers (*Chrysanthemum cinerariifolium*) compared to traditional maceration and cyclic pressurization extraction. *The Journal of Supercritical Fluids*, *119*, 104–112. doi:10.1016/j.supflu.2016.09.012

Galović, T. (2015). The international competitiveness of the pharmaceutical industry within 21 OECD countries. *Ekonomski Vjesnik*, *28*(1), 225–241.

Ganguly, A., Chatterjee, D., & Farr, J. V. (2018). Evaluating Barriers to Knowledge Sharing affecting New Product Development team performance. *International Journal of Innovation Management, 1850048*. doi:10.1142/S1363919618500482

Gassmann, O., & Oliver, G. (2002). Global Corporate R&D to and from Emerging Economies. In *Global Corporate R&D to and from Emerging Economies*. Retrieved from: http://www.glorad.org

Gautam, A., Pan, X., & Ajay, G. (2016). The changing model of big pharma: Impact of key trends. *Drug Discovery Today*, *21*(3), 379–384. doi:10.1016/j.drudis.2015.10.002 PMID:26477304

Gautrin, P. (2002). Challenges facing a pharmaceutical supply chain. *Logistics Quarterly, 8*.

Gay, B., & Dousset, B. (2005). Innovation and network structural dynamics: Study of the alliance network of a major sector of the biotechnology industry. *Science Direct*, *34*, 1457–1475.

Genomma Lab. (2017). *Genomma Laboratories*. Retrieved from: http://www.genommalab.com/es/ index.html

Gernaey, K. V., Cervera, A. E., & Woodley, J. M. (2011). PSE in Pharmaceutical Process Development. *Computer-Aided Chemical Engineering*, *29*, 1628–1632. doi:10.1016/B978-0-444-54298-4.50104-5

Giunipero, L. C., & Brand, R. R. (1996). Purchasing's role in supply chain management. *International Journal of Logistics Management*, *7*(1), 29–38. doi:10.1108/09574099610805412

Global Life Sciences Outlook Thriving in today's uncertain market. (2017). Retrieved from: https://www2.deloitte.com/global/en/pages/life-sciences-and-healthcare/articles/global-life-sciences-sector-outlook.html

Gray, J. V., Roth, A. V., & Leiblein, M. J. (2011). Quality risk in offshore manufacturing: Evidence from the pharmaceutical industry. *Journal of Operations Management*, *29*(7-8), 737–752. doi:10.1016/j.jom.2011.06.004

Grean & Shaw. (2000). *Supply-Chain Integration through Information Sharing: Channel Partnership between Wal-Mart and Procter & Gamble*. Center for IT and e-Business Management, University of Illinois at Urbana-Champaign.

Grosse, A. (2013). *Pharmaceutical Patents, Global Health and the TRIPS Agreement* (Unpublished seminar paper). University of Vienna, Austria.

Grover, A., Citro, B., Mankad, M., & Lander, F. (2012). Pharmaceutical companies and global lack of access to medicines: Strengthening accountability under the right to health. *The Journal of Law, Medicine & Ethics*, *40*(2), 234–250. doi:10.1111/j.1748-720X.2012.00661.x PMID:22789043

Grudzień, Ł. (2012). Koncepcja oceny jakości informacji o procesach w systemach zarządzania. In R. Knosala (Ed.), *Materiały XV Konferencji Innowacje w zarządzaniu i inżynierii produkcji* (pp. 633–644). Opole: Wyd. AE w Opolu.

Guidance for Industry Best Practices in Developing Proprietary Names for Drugs. (2014). Food and Drug Administration, Drug Safety. Retrieved from: http://www.regulations.gov/

Gulati, R. (1998). Alliances and Networks. *Strategic Management Journal, 19*(4), 293–317. doi:10.1002/(SICI)1097-0266(199804)19:4<293::AID-SMJ982>3.0.CO;2-M

Guler, I., & Nerkar, A. (2012). The impact of global and local cohesion on innovation in the pharmaceutical industry. *Strategic Management Journal, 33*(5), 535–549. doi:10.1002mj.957

Gunasekaran, A., & Ngai, E. W. T. (2004). Information systems in supply chain integration and management. *European Journal of Operational Research, 159*(2), 269–295. doi:10.1016/j.ejor.2003.08.016

Gunasekaran, A., Patel, C., & McGaughey Ronald, E. (2004). A framework for supply chain performance measurement. *International Journal of Production Economics, 87*(3), 333–347. doi:10.1016/j.ijpe.2003.08.003

Gunnarsson, C., & Jonsson, S. (2003). Charge the relationships and gain loyalty effects: Turning the supply link alert to IT opportunities. *European Journal of Operational Research, 144*(2), 257–269. doi:10.1016/S0377-2217(02)00392-2

Hagelaar G., &Van Der Vorst J. (2001). *Environmental Supply Chain Management: using Life Cycle Assessment to structure supply chains.* Paper IAMA, Sydney, Australia.

Hair, J. P., William, C., Black, W. C., Babin, B. J., & Anderson, R. E. (2010). *Multivariate Data Analysis.* Pearson.

Haleem, R. M., Salem, M. Y., Fatahallah, F. A., & Abdelfattah, L. E. (2015). Quality in the pharmaceutical industry – A literature review. *Saudi Pharmaceutical Journal, 23*(5), 463–469. doi:10.1016/j.jsps.2013.11.004 PMID:26594110

Haralambos, S., Panagiotis, P., Tarantilis, C. D., & Kiranoudis, C. T. (2008). Dynamic modeling and control of supply chain systems: A review. *Computers & Operations Research, 35*(11), 3530–3561. doi:10.1016/j.cor.2007.01.017

Harbir, K. (2012). Processing technologies for pharmaceutical tablets: A Review. *International Research Journal of Pharmacy, 3*(7), 20–23.

Hardman & Co. (2017, March 2). *Global Pharmaceuticals. 2016 Industry Statistics.* Retrieved from: http://www.hardmanandco.com/docs/default-source/sector-docs/life-sciences-documents/02.03.17-global-pharmaceutical-industry-2016-statistics.pdf

Harrington, T. S., Phillips, M. A., & Singh Srai, J. (2017). Reconfiguring global pharmaceutical value networks through targeted technology interventions. *International Journal of Production Research, 55*(5), 1471–1487. doi:10.1080/00207543.2016.1221541

Harrison, A., & van Hoek, R. (2010). *Zarządzanie logistyką*. Warszawa: PWE.

Hassan, B. A. R. (2012). Overview on Pharmaceutical Formulation and Drug Design. *Pharmaceutica Analytica Acta*, *3*(10).

Heninrich, C.E., & Simchi-Levi, D. (2005). Do it Investments really change financial Performance. *Supply Chain Management Review*, 22-28.

Hentschel, B. (2012). Green Logistics – a call for sustainability in logistics chains. *Logistyka*, *6*, 15–17.

Hess, A. M., & Rothaermel, F. T. (2011). When areas sets complementary? Star scientists, strategic alliances and innovation in the pharmaceutical industry. *Strategic Management Journal*, *32*(8), 895–909. doi:10.1002mj.916

Heydari, J. (2014). Lead time variation control using reliable shipment equipment: An incentive scheme for supply chain coordination. *Transportation Research Part E, Logistics and Transportation Review*, *63*, 44–58. doi:10.1016/j.tre.2014.01.004

Hodgon, V. M., & Hoque, M. E. (2017). The growth strategies of a global pharmaceutical company: a case study of Aspen Pharmacare Holdings Limited. *Problems and Perspectives in Management, 15*(1), 248-259.

Holland, C. P. (1995). Cooperative supply chain management: The impact of inter-organizational information systems. *The Journal of Strategic Information Systems*, *4*(2), 117–133. doi:10.1016/0963-8687(95)80020-Q

Holland, C. P., & Geoffrey, L. A. (1997). Mixed Mode Network Structures: The Strategic Use of Electronic Communication by Organizations. *Organization Science*, *8*(5), 475–48. doi:10.1287/orsc.8.5.475

Hollingsworth, R. (2000). Doing institutional analysis: Implications for the study of innovations. *Review of International Political Economy*, *7*(4), 595–644. doi:10.1080/096922900750034563

Hollinshead, G. (2017). The tortuous ascent of global value chains – the case of pharmaceutical R&D in China. *Critical Perspectives on International Business*, *13*(3), 244–262. doi:10.1108/cpoib-09-2016-0032

Holweg, M., Disney, S., Holmstrom, J., & Smaros, J. (2005). Supply Chain Collaboration: Making Sense Of The Strategy Continuum. *European Management Journal*, *23*(2), 170–181. doi:10.1016/j.emj.2005.02.008

Hong Ilyoo, B. (2002). A new framework for inter-organizational systems based on the linkage of participants' roles. *Information & Management*, *39*(4), 261-270.

Hong, D., Suh, E., & Koo, C. (2011). Developing strategies for overcoming barriers to knowledge sharing based on conversational knowledge management: A case study of a financial company. *Expert Systems with Applications*, *38*(12), 14417–14427. doi:10.1016/j.eswa.2011.04.072

Horner, R. (2016). Pharmaceuticals and the Global South: A Healthy Challenge for Development Theory? *Geography Compass*, *10*(9), 363–377. doi:10.1111/gec3.12277

Hsu, J. C., & Lu, C. Y. (2015). The evolution of Taiwan's National Health Insurance drug reimbursement scheme. *DARU Journal of Pharmaceutical Sciences, 23*(15).

Hu, Y., Scherngell, T., Man, S. N., & Wang, Y. (2013). Is the United States Still Dominant in the Global Pharmaceutical Innovation Network? *PLOS ONE, 8*(11), e77247, 1-7.

Hughes, J. P., Rees, S., Kalindjian, S. B., & Philpott, K. L. (2010). Principles of early drug discovery. *British Journal of Pharmacology*, *162*(6), 1239–1249. doi:10.1111/j.1476-5381.2010.01127.x PMID:21091654

Hulbert, M. H., Feely, L. C., Inman, E. L., Jophnson, A. D., ... Zour, E. (2008). Risk Management in Pharmaceutical Development Process. *Journal of Pharmaceutical Innovation*, *3*(4), 227–248. doi:10.100712247-008-9049-8

Hutzschenreuter, T., & Horstkotte, J. (2010). Knowledge transfer to partners: A firm level perspective. *Journal of Knowledge Management*, *14*(3), 428–448. doi:10.1108/13673271011050148

Iacovou, C. L., Benbasat, I., & Dexter, A. S. (1995). Electronic Data Interchange and Small Organizations: Adoption and Impact of Technology. *Management Information Systems Quarterly*, *19*(4), 465–485. doi:10.2307/249629

IMPI. (2017). *Instituto Mexicano de la Propiedad Industrial*. Retrieved from: http://www.impi.gob.mx/

INEGI. (2016). *Estádisticas a propósito de... la industria farmacéutica*. Aguascalientes: Instituto Nacional de Estádistica y Geografía.

INEGI. (2017). *Directorio Estadístico Nacional de Unidades Económicas*. National Statistical Directory of Economic Units. Retrieved from: http://www.beta.inegi.org.mx/app/mapa/denue/

Inkpen, A. C., & Julian, B. (1994). International Joint Ventures and Performance: An Inter-organizational Perspective. *International Business Review*, *3*(3), 201–217. doi:10.1016/0969-5931(94)90002-7

Isaksen, A., & Kalsaas, B. T. (2009). Suppliers and Strategies for Upgrading in Global Production Networks: The Case of a Supplier to the Global Automotive Industry in a High-cost Location. *European Planning Studies*, *17*(4), 569–585. doi:10.1080/09654310802682131

Itkar, S. (2007). Pharmaceutical management. Pune. *Nirali Prakashan*, *3*, 12–17.

Jaberidoost, M., Olfat, L., Hosseini, A., Kebriaeezadeh, A., Abdollahi, M., Alaeddini, M., & Dinarvand, R. (2015). Pharmaceutical supply chain risk assessment in Iran using analytic hierarchy process (AHP) and simple additive weighting (SAW) methods. *Journal of Pharmaceutical Policy and Practice*, *8*(1), 9. doi:10.118640545-015-0029-3 PMID:25838919

Jagersma, P. K. (2011). Competitive information logistics. *Business Strategy Series, 12*(3), 136–145. doi:10.1108/17515631111130103

Jarrett, P. (1998). Logistics in the health care industry. *International Journal of Physical Distribution & Logistics Management, 28*(9/10), 741–742. doi:10.1108/09600039810248154

Jastrzębska, E. (2011). Zarządzanie odpowiedzialnym łańcuchem dostaw jako element wdrażania koncepcji rozwoju zrównoważonego. In Współpraca w łańcuchach dostaw a konkurencyjność przedsiębiorstw I kooperujących sieci. Warszawa: OW SGH.

Jedliński, M. (2009). In pursuit of the essence of logistic potential of an enterprise. *LogForum, 5*(8), 1–7.

Jedliński, M. (2015). Dynamic logistics strategies in the company logistics potential management. *Russian Journal of Logistics and Transport Management, 2*(1), 3–10. doi:10.20295/2313-7002-2015-1-3-10

Jovanovic, A. A., Dordevic, V. B., Zdunic, G. M., Pljevljakusic, D. S., Savikin, K. P., Godevac, D. M., & Bugarski, B. M. (2017). Optimization of the extraction process of polyphenols from *Thymus serpyllum L.* herb using maceration, heat- and ultrasound-assisted techniques. *Separation and Purification Technology, 179*(31), 369–380. doi:10.1016/j.seppur.2017.01.055

Kaczyńska, G. (2016). *Strategiczne podejście do ochrony środowiska w Grupie Polpharma.* Retrieved from. http://www.gridw.pl/images/documents/geo6/Grazyna_Kaczynska_Polpharma.pdf

Kaplan & Duchon. (1988). Combining qualitative and quantitative methods in information systems research: A case study. *Management Information Systems Quarterly*, 571–586.

Kassie, G.M., & Mammo, S. (2014). Assessment of pharmaceutical store management in woreda health offices of westhararghe zone, Ethiopia. *International Research Journal of Pharmacy, 5*(8), 642-645.

Kawabata, Y., Wada, K., Nakatani, M., Yamada, S., & Onoue, S. (2011). Formulation design for poorly water-soluble drugs based on biopharmaceutics classification system: Basic approaches and practical applications. *International Journal of Pharmaceutics, 420*(1), 1–10. doi:10.1016/j.ijpharm.2011.08.032 PMID:21884771

Kesic, D. (2011). Pharmaceutical Industry in Strategic Development. *International Journal of Economics and Research, 2*(6), 29–37.

Ketchen Jr David, J., Hult, G., & Tomas, M. (2007). Bridging organization theory and supply chain management: The case of best value supply chains. *Journal of Operations Management, 25*(2), 573–580. doi:10.1016/j.jom.2006.05.010

Khawaja, S. A., Malhotra, M., & Grover, V. (2005). Examining the Impact of Inter-organizational Systems on Process Efficiency and Sourcing Leverage in Buyer-Supplier Dyads. *Decision Sciences, 36*(3), 365.

Kim, H. R. (2014, January). Formulation of a Success Model in Pharmaceutical R&D: Efficient Innovation Model. *SAGE Open*, 1–9.

Kim, D. (2005). An integrated supply chain management system: A case study in healthcare sector. *Lecture Notes in Computer Science*, *3590*, 218–227. doi:10.1007/11545163_22

Kish, L. (2012). *The Blockbuster Drug of the Century: An Engaged Patient*. Retrieved from http://www.hl7standards.com/blog/2012/08/28/drug-of-the-century/

KMPG. (n.d.). *Pharma 2030: From evolution to revolution*. Retrieved from: https://assets.kpmg.com/content/dam/kpmg/xx/pdf/2017/02/pharma-outlook-2030-from-evolution-to-revolution.pdf

Kontoravdi, C., Samsatli, N. J., & Shah, N. (2013). Development and design of bio-pharmaceutical processes. *Current Opinion in Chemical Engineering*, *2*(4), 435–441. doi:10.1016/j.coche.2013.09.007

KPMG. (2006). *La Industria Farmacéutica en México*. KPMG.

Kramarz, W., & Kramarz, M. (2013). Wspomaganie sterowania przepływami materiałowymi w sieciowych łańcuchach dostaw - zakłócenia i odporność. *Logistyka*, *5*, 315–319.

Kumar, N., & Jha, A. (2015). Quality Perspective of 'Good Distribution Practices' in Indian Pharmaceutical Industry. *IOSR Journal of Business and Management, 17*(11), 28-32.

Kumar, K., & van Dissel, H. G. (1996). Sustainable collaboration: Managing Conflict and cooperation in inter-organizational Systems. *Management Information Systems Quarterly*, *20*(3), 279–300. doi:10.2307/249657

Lai, K., Ngai, E. W. T., & Cheng, T. C. E. (2002). Measures for evaluating supply chain performance in transport logistics. *Transportation Research Part E, Logistics and Transportation Review*, *38*(6), 439–456. doi:10.1016/S1366-5545(02)00019-4

Lambert Douglas, M., & Cooper Martha, C. (2000). Issues in Supply Chain Management. *Industrial Marketing Management*, *29*(1), 65–83. doi:10.1016/S0019-8501(99)00113-3

Lamia, B., & Vincent, C. (2007). Towards an aggregation performance measurement system model in a supply chain context. *Computers in Industry*, *58*(7), 709–719. doi:10.1016/j.compind.2007.05.012

Langley, C. J. Jr, & Morice, W. D. (1982). Strategies for Logistics Management: Reactions to a Changing Environment. *Journal of Business Logistics*, *3*(1), 1–16.

Lee, H. L., & Whang, S. (2001). E-business and supply chain integration. *Standford Global Supply Chain Management Forum, 2*.

Lee, H., & Whang, S. (2001). *E-business and Supply Chain Integration*. Stanford Global Supply Chain Management Forum, SGSCMF-W2-2001.

Lee, H. L. (2007). Sekret najbardziej efektywnych łańcuchów dostaw. In *Zarządzanie łańcuchem dostaw* (pp. 99–108). Gliwice: Helion.

Lee, H. L., & Billington, C. (1992). Supply Chain Management: Pitfalls and Opportunities. *Sloan Management Review*, *33*(Spring), 65–73.

Lee, H. L., & Whang, S. (2000). Information sharing in a supply chain. *International Journal of Manufacturing Technology and Management*, *1*(1), 79–93. doi:10.1504/IJMTM.2000.001329

Lee, M., & Choi, M. (2015). Analysis on Time-Lag Effect of Research and Development Investment in the Pharmaceutical Industry in Korea. *Osong Public Health and Research Perspectives*, *6*(4), 241–248. doi:10.1016/j.phrp.2015.07.001 PMID:26473091

Lekhawipat, W., Wei, Y. H., & Lin, C. (2018). How internal attributions affect knowledge sharing behavior. *Journal of Knowledge Management*, *22*(4), 867–886. doi:10.1108/JKM-02-2017-0081

Lemoine, P. (2017). *Best practice in pharma supply chain management*. Retrieved from https://pharmaphorum.com/views-and-analysis/best-practice-pharma-supply-chain-management/

Levi, Kaminsky, & Levi. (2002). Designing and managing the supply chain, Concepts, strategies and Case studies (2nd ed.). McGraw-Hill/Irwin.

Light, D. L., Donald, W. L., Warburton, R., & Rebecca, W. (2011). Demythologizing the high costs of pharmaceutical research. *Biosocieties*, 1–17. Retrieved from www.palgrave-journals.com/bioso/

Li, S., Ragu-Nathan, B., Ragu-Nathan, T. S., & Subba Rao, S. (2006). The impact of supply chain management practices on competitive advantage and organizational performance. *Omega*, *34*(2), 107–124. doi:10.1016/j.omega.2004.08.002

Li, S., Rao, S., Ragunathan, T., & Ragunathan, B. (2005). Development and validation of a measurement instrument for studying supply chain management practices. *Journal of Operations Management*, *23*(6), 618–641. doi:10.1016/j.jom.2005.01.002

Little, A. D. (2016). *Presentation on Trends in the pharmaceutical industry*. Retrieved from: http://i3health.eu/wp-content/uploads/2016/01/Presentation-E.Croufer-.pdf

Longest & Young. (2000). *Health care management*. New York: Delmar.

Lummus, R. R., & Vokurka, R. J. (1999). Defining supply chain management: A historical perspective and practical guidelines. *Business Process Management Journal*, *6*(2), 11–17.

Lu, X.-H., Huang, L.-H., & Heng, M. S. H. (2005). Critical success factors of inter-organizational information systems; A case study of Cisco and Xiao Tong in China. *Information & Management*.

Macpherson, A. (2001). *Corporate directions in supply chain management: Implications for SME competences and inter-organizational relations*. working paper022.

Majesz-Lech, A. (2014). Przesłanki rozwoju koncepcji zielonego łańcucha dostaw. *Przegląd Organizacji, 5.*

Malone Thomas, W. (1988). What is Coordination Theory? *National Science Foundation Coordination Theory Workshop*.

Malone, Thomas, & Yates. (1986). *Electronic Markets and Electronic Hierarchies: Effects of Information Technology on Market Structures and Corporate Strategies*. Center for Information Systems Research.

Management Centre Europe. (2017). Retrieved from: www.mce.eu

Mańkowski, C. (n.d.). *Synergia w logistyce*. Gdańsk: Wyd. UG.

Marczyk, J., Czarnota, J., & Gliński, J. (2014). *Trend: Wzrost złożoności jako sygnał ostrzegawczy*. Retrieved from: https://www.hbrp.pl/b/trend-wzrost-zlozonosci-jako-sygnal-ostrzegawczy/flU42RBp

Marucheck, A., Greis, N., Mena, C., & Cai, L. (2011). Product safety and security in the global supply chain: Issues, challenges and research opportunities. *Journal of Operations Management*, *29*(7–8), 707–720. doi:10.1016/j.jom.2011.06.007

Masoumi, A. H., Yu, M., & Nagurney, A. (2012). A supply chain generalized network oligopoly model for pharmaceuticals under brand differentiation and perishability. *Transportation Research Part E, Logistics and Transportation Review*, *48*(4), 762–780. doi:10.1016/j.tre.2012.01.001

Masteika, I., & Cepinskis, J. (2015). Dynamic Capabilities in Supply Chain Management. *Procedia: Social and Behavioral Sciences*, *213*, 830–835. doi:10.1016/j.sbspro.2015.11.485

Matlis, D.R., & Lennard, D.J. (2011). Improving Visibility of the Pharma Supply Chain: Best Practices and Technologies. *Pharmaceutical Technology, 4*.

McDermott, R., & O'Dell, C. (2001). Overcoming cultural barriers to sharing knowledge. *Journal of Knowledge Management*, *5*(1), 76–85. doi:10.1108/13673270110384428

McLaren, T. S., Head, M. M., & Yuan, Y. (2004). Supply chain management information systems capabilities. An exploratory study of electronics manufacturers. *Information Systems and e-Business Management*, *2*(2), 207–222. doi:10.100710257-004-0035-5

Measuring Pharmaceutical Quality through Manufacturing Metrics and Risk-Based Assessment. (2014). Engelberg Centre for Healthcare Reform at Brookings.

Meier, J. (1995). The importance of relationship management in establishing successful inter-organizational systems. *Journal of Strategic Information Systems*, *4*(2), 135-148.

Mentzer, J. T., DeWitt, W., Keebler, J. S., Min, S., Nix, N. W., Smith, C. D., & Zacharia, Z. G. (2001). Defining supply chain management. *Journal of Business Logistics*, *22*(2), 1–25. doi:10.1002/j.2158-1592.2001.tb00001.x

Mesjasz, C. (2014). Zalety i wady koncepcji złożoności systemów organizacyjnych. In Współczesne kierunki rozwoju nauk o zarządzaniu w kontekście dokonań naukowych Profesora Adama Stabryły (pp. 129-150). Kraków: Mfiles.pl.

Michael, W., & Hulland, J. (2004). Review: The Resource-Based View And Information Systems Research: Review, Extension, And Suggestions For Future Research. *Management Information Systems Quarterly*, *28*(1), 107–142. doi:10.2307/25148626

Miller, J. (2004), New Supply-Chain Dynamics Create a Distribution Services Sector. *Pharmaceutical Technology.*

Moser, M., Calderari, G., & Morini, P. (2000). Cleaning validation of a multipurpose plant for active pharmaceutical ingredient bulk production. *Chimia*, *54*, 731–733.

Mousazadeh, M., Torabi, S. A., & Zahiri, B. (2015). A robust possibilistic programming approach for pharmaceutical supply chain network design. *Computers & Chemical Engineering*, *82*, 115–128. doi:10.1016/j.compchemeng.2015.06.008

Mustaffa, N. H., & Potter, A. (2009). Healthcare supply chain management in Malaysia: A case study. *Supply Chain Management*, *14*(3), 234–243. doi:10.1108/13598540910954575

Nakov, Z., Acevski, S., & Zareski, R. (2014). Implementation of Supply Chain Management (SCM) in pharmaceutical company, general principles and case study. *Macedonian Pharmaceutical Bulletin, 60*(2), 75 – 82.

Narayana, S. A., Pati, R. K., & Vrat, P. (2014). Managerial research on the pharmaceutical supply chain – A critical review and some insights for future directions. *Journal of Purchasing and Supply Management*, *20*(1), 18–40. doi:10.1016/j.pursup.2013.09.001

Natti, S., & Ojasalo, J. (2008). Loose coupling as an inhibitor of internal customer knowledge transfer: Findings from an empirical study in B-to-B professional services. *Journal of Business and Industrial Marketing*, *23*(3), 213–223. doi:10.1108/08858620810858472

Nault Barrie, R., & Dexter Albert, S. (1995). Added Value and Pricing with Information Technology. *Management Information Systems Quarterly*, *19*(4), 449–464. doi:10.2307/249628

Neely, A., Adams, C., & Kennerley, M. (1995). *The Performance Prism: The Scorecard for Measuring and Managing Business Success.* Financial Times Prentice Hall.

Nematollahi, M., Hosseini-Motlagha, S. M., & Heydari, J. (2017). Economic and social collaborative decision-making on visit interval and service level in a two-echelon pharmaceutical supply chain. *Journal of Cleaner Production*, *142*, 3956–3969. doi:10.1016/j.jclepro.2016.10.062

Ning, Y. M., & Maher, V. E. (2015). Food and Drug Administration Process for development and approval of drugs radiopharmaceuticals: Treatment in urologic oncology. *Urologic Oncology: Seminars and Original Investigations*, *33*(3), 137–142. doi:10.1016/j.urolonc.2014.12.008 PMID:25613202

Norman, J., Madurawe, R. D., Moore, C. M. V., Khan, M. A., & Khairizzaman, A. (2017). A new chapter in pharmaceutical manufacturing: 3D-printed drug products. *Advanced Drug Delivery Reviews*, *108*, 39–50. doi:10.1016/j.addr.2016.03.001 PMID:27001902

Novel Drugs Summary. (2016). U.S. Food and Drug Administration. Retrieved from: www.fda.gov

Nowakowska-Grunt, J. (2005). Strategie logistyczne organizacji sieciowych w zapewnianiu dostępności polskich produktów spożywczych na rynku UE. In *Strategie i logistyka organizacji sieciowych.* Wrocław: Wydawnictwo Akademii Ekonomicznej im. Oskara Langego we Wrocławiu.

Nugraha, A. S. (2007). Global pharmaceutical industries, drugs exploration and patenting: Impact on developing countries. *Pharmaceutical Journal of Indonesia, 5*(2), 1–8.

Nurmilaakso, J. M., & Kotinurmi, P. (2004). A review of XML based supply chain integration. *Production Planning and Control, 15*(6), 608–621. doi:10.1080/09537280412331283937

Nurmilaakso, J.-M. (2007). Adoption of e-business functions and migration from EDI-based toXML-based e-business frameworks in supply chain integration. *International Journal of Production Economics.*

OECDC. (2017). *World Drug Report 2017.* Retrieved from: https://www.unodc.org/wdr2017/index.html

Okoroafor, H. (2014). The barriers to tacit knowledge sharing in franchise organizations. *Knowledge Management Research and Practice, 12*(1), 97–102. doi:10.1057/kmrp.2013.30

Olejniczak, K. (2015). Zarządzanie zrównoważonym łańcuchem dostaw – cz. 2. Zintegrowana postawa wobec odpowiedzialności. *ABC Jakości Badania. Certyfikacja. Notyfikacja, 82.*

Olejniczak, K., & Koch, P. (2015). Zrównoważony rozwój w łańcuchu dostaw – Cz. 1. Zarys problematyki. *ABC Jakości Badania. Certyfikacja. Notyfikacja, 82.*

Oliva, F. L. (2014). Knowledge management barriers, practices and maturity model. *Journal of Knowledge Management, 18*(6), 1053–1074. doi:10.1108/JKM-03-2014-0080

Orsenigo, L., Pammolli, F., & Riccaboni, M. (2001). Technological change and network dynamics lessons from the pharmaceutical industry. *Research Policy, 30*(3), 485–508. doi:10.1016/S0048-7333(00)00094-9

Osorio, J. G., & Muzzio, F. J. (2016). Effects of processing parameters and blade patterns on continuous pharmaceutical powder mixing. *Chemical Engineering and Processing, 109,* 59–67. doi:10.1016/j.cep.2016.07.012

Pandey, P., Bharadwaj, R., & Chen, X. (2017). Modeling of drug product manufacturing processes in the pharmaceutical industry. *Predictive Modeling of Pharmaceutical Unit Operations,* 1-13.

Paolo, G., Nicola, S., & Lucrezia, S. (2007). Performance measurement of the after-sales service network—Evidence from the automotive industry. *Computers in Industry, 58*(7), 698–708. doi:10.1016/j.compind.2007.05.008

Papageorgiou, L. G., Rotstein, G. E., & Shah, N. (2001). Strategic supply chain optimization for the pharmaceutical industries. *Industrial & Engineering Chemistry Research, 40*(1), 275–286. doi:10.1021/ie990870t

Pareek, V., & Khunteta, A. (2014). Pharmaceutical packaging: Current trends and future. *International Journal of Pharmacy and Pharmaceutical Sciences*, *6*(6), 480–485.

Parekh. (2001). *It's Not Just About Software: A Holistic View on Supply Chain Management in the Connected Economy.* Plan Central Inc.

Park, Y., Goto, D., Yang, K. F., Downton, K., Lecomte, P., Olson, M., & Mullins, C. D. (2016). A Literature Review of Factors Affecting Price and Competition in the Global Pharmaceutical Market. Value in Health. *The Journal of The International Society for Pharmacoeconomics and Outcomes Research*, *19*(3), A265.

Patil, H., Tiwari, R. V., & Repka, M. A. (2016). Hot-Melt Extrusion: From Theory to Application in Pharmaceutical Formulation. *AAPS PharmSciTech*, *17*(1), 20–42. doi:10.120812249-015-0360-7 PMID:26159653

Patil, S. K., & Kant, R. (2014). A fuzzy AHP-TOPSIS framework for ranking the solutions of Knowledge Management adoption in Supply Chain to overcome its barriers. *Expert Systems with Applications*, *41*(2), 679–693. doi:10.1016/j.eswa.2013.07.093

Paul, F., & Jim, B. (2005). A review of performance measurement: Towards performance management. *Computers in Industry*, *56*(7), 663–680. doi:10.1016/j.compind.2005.03.001

Pedroso, M. C., & Nakano, D. (2009). Knowledge and information flows in supply chains: A study on pharmaceutical companies. *International Journal of Production Economics*, *122*(1), 376–384. doi:10.1016/j.ijpe.2009.06.012

Pedroso, M. C., & Zwicker, R. (2008). Product information management: Basis for relationships in the supply chain. *JISTEM-Journal of Information Systems and Technology Management*, *5*(1), 109–134.

Pelze, K. (2015). *What's Next for the Pharmaceutical Supply Chain?* Retrieved from https://www.allthingssupplychain.com/whats-next-for-the-pharmaceutical-supply-chain/

Petkov, V., Petkova, O., Andrew, T., & Nepal, T. (2007). Mixing Multiple Criteria Decision Making with soft systems thinking techniques for decision support in complex situations. *Decision Support Systems*, *43*(4), 1615–1629. doi:10.1016/j.dss.2006.03.006

Pfeffer, J., & Salanick, G. R. (1978). *The External Control of Organizations: A Resource-dependence Perspective*. New York: Harper & Row.

Pfizer. (2017). *Pfizer*. Retrieved from: https://www.pfizer.com.mx/

Pharma Processing. (n.d.). Retrieved from http://www.pharmpro.com

Phelps, K. (2011). Repositioning to enhance a product's lifecycle. *Drug Discovery Today. Therapeutic Strategies*, *8*(3-4), 97–101. doi:10.1016/j.ddstr.2011.09.006

Pitta, D. A., & Laric, M. V. (2004). Value chains in health care. *Journal of Consumer Marketing*, *21*(7), 451–464. doi:10.1108/07363760410568671

PoliticIndia Research. (2015). *Market analysis of global pharmaceutical industries and trend estimation*. Report Sample. Retrieved from: http://www.politicindia.com/reports.php?rid=13

Polpharma. (2017). *Raport Społecznej Odpowiedzialności Grupy Polpharma 2015-2016*. Retrieved from: https://www.polpharma.pl/upload/2017/12/raport-spolecznej-odpowiedzialnosci-polpharmy-2015-201665.pdf

Polpharma. (2018). *Polpharma Group: Information, History, CSR, Sustainable Supply Chain, code of Conduct*. Retrieved from https://www.polpharma.pl

Popharma. (2014). *Raport Społecznej Odpowiedzialności Grupy Polpharma 2011-2013*. Retrieved from: https://www.polpharma.pl/aktualnosci-odpowiedzialnosc/polpharma-opublikowala-raport-spoleczny/

Popharma. (2015). *Raport Społecznej Odpowiedzialności Grupy Polpharma 2013-2014*. Retrieved from: https://www.polpharma.pl/upload/2016/01/polpharma-raport-spoleczny-2013-2014-lekki.pdf

Porter, M. E., & Kramer, M. R. (2006). Strategy and society: The link between competitive advantage and corporate social responsibility. *Harvard Business Review*, *84*, 78–92. PMID:17183795

Powell, T. C., & Dent-Micallef, A. (1997). Information Technology as Competitive Advantage: The Role of Human, Business, and Technology Resources. *Strategic Management Journal*, *18*(5), 375–405. doi:10.1002/(SICI)1097-0266(199705)18:5<375::AID-SMJ876>3.0.CO;2-7

Powell, W. W., Koput, K., & Smith-Doerr, L. (1996). Interorganizational Collaboration and the Locus of Innovation: Networks of Learning in Biotechnology. *Administrative Science Quarterly*, *14*(1), 116–145. doi:10.2307/2393988

Prajapati, V., & Dureja, H. (2012). Product Lifecycle management in pharmaceuticals. *Journal of Medical Marketing*, *12*(3), 150–158. doi:10.1177/1745790412445292

Probiomed. (2017). *Probiomed*. Retrieved from: http://www.probiomed.com.mx/

Prokop, D. J. (2017). Threats to Supply Chains. Global Supply Chain Security and Management, 41-63.

Proventas. (2017). *Proventas*. Retrieved from: http://www.proventas.com.mx/

Qureshi, A. J., Gericke, K., & Blessing, L. (2014). Stages in Product Lifecycle: Trans-disciplinary Design Context. *Procedia CIRP*, *21*, 224–229. doi:10.1016/j.procir.2014.03.131

Rai, A., Bhargava, R., & Mohanty, B. (2016). Simulation of supercritical fluid extraction of essential oil from natural products. *Journal of Applied Research on Medicinal and Aromatic Plants*, *5*, 1–9. doi:10.1016/j.jarmap.2016.09.005

Rajeev, A., Pati, R. K., Padhi, S., & Govidan, K. (2017). Evolution of sustainability in supply chain management: A literature review. *Journal of Cleaner Production*, *162*, 299–314. doi:10.1016/j.jclepro.2017.05.026

Rantanen, J., & Khinast, J. (2015). The Future of Pharmaceutical Manufacturing Sciences. *Journal of Pharmaceutical Sciences*, *104*(11), 3612–3638. doi:10.1002/jps.24594 PMID:26280993

Rao, B. P., & Reddyt, S. (1995). A Dynamic Approach to the Analysis of Strategic Alliances. *International Business Review*, *4*(4), 499–518. doi:10.1016/0969-5931(96)81750-1

Rashed, C. A. A., Azeem, A., & Halim, Z. (2010). Effect of information and knowledge sharing on supply chain performance: A survey based approach. *Journal of Operations and Supply Chain Management*, *3*(2), 61–77.

Ratajczak, M., Kubicka, M. M., Kaminska, D., Sawicka, P., & Długaszewska, J. (2015). Microbiological quality of non-sterile pharmaceutical products. *Saudi Pharmaceutical Journal*, *23*(3), 303–307. doi:10.1016/j.jsps.2014.11.015 PMID:26106278

Rayere. (2017). *Rayere*. Retrieved from: http://www.rayere.com.mx/fr_frameset.htm

Reddy, J., & Rao, M. (2014). Opportunities for Indian pharmaceutical companies in the era of globalization. *Journal of Global Trends in Pharmaceutical Sciences*, *5*(2), 1567–1575.

Rehman, M. S. U., Rashid, N., Ashfaq, M., Saif, A., Ahmad, N., & Han, J.-I. (2015). Global risk of pharmaceutical contamination from highly populated developing countries. *Chemosphere*, *138*, 1045–1055. doi:10.1016/j.chemosphere.2013.02.036 PMID:23535471

Ren, C., Ren, S., Chai, Y., Liu, Y., & Tian, C. (2002). Modeling agile supply chain dynamics: A complex adaptive system perspective. In *Proceedings of the IEEE International Conference on Systems, Man and Cybernetics* (vol. 3, pp. 1-6). IEEE.

Report, M. T. (2016). *Pulse of the industry*, 1-62.

Riege, A. (2005). Three-dozen knowledge-sharing barriers managers must consider. *Journal of Knowledge Management*, *9*(3), 18–35. doi:10.1108/13673270510602746

Riggins, F. J., Kriebel, C. H., & Mukhopadhyay, T. (1994). The Growth of Inter-organizational Systems in the Presence of Network Externalities. *Management Science*, *40*(8), 984–998. doi:10.1287/mnsc.40.8.984

Robb David, J. (2008). Supply chain and operations practice and performance in Chinese furniture manufacturing. *International Journal of Production Economics*, *112*(2), 683–699. doi:10.1016/j.ijpe.2007.04.011

Rosińska-Bukowska, M. (2012). *Rozwój globalnych sieci biznesowych jako strategia konkurencyjna korporacji transnarodowych*. Łódź: Wyd. UŁ.

Rousseaux, C. G., & Bracken, W. M. (2013). Overview of Drug Development. Haschek and Rousseaux's Handbook of Toxicologic pathology, 647-685.

Ruppel, C. (2004). An information systems perspective of supply chain tool compatibility: The roles of technology fit and relationships. *Business Process Management Journal*, *10*(3), 311–324. doi:10.1108/14637150410539713

Russell, J. H., & Vitale, M. R. (1988). Creating Competitive Advantage with Inter-organizational Information Systems. *Management Information Systems Quarterly*, *12*(2), 153–165. doi:10.2307/248839

Rutkowski, K. (2004). Zarządzanie łańcuchem dostaw – próba sprecyzowania terminu i określenia związków z logistyką. *Gospodarka Materiałowa i Logistyka*, *12*, 2–8.

Rzeszotalska, M., & Musiał, M. (2016). Etyczny i odpowiedzialny biznes. *Harvard Business Review Polska*. Retrieved from https://www.hbrp.pl/b/etyczny-i-odpowiedzialny-biznes/PpnAtTRUO

Saaksvuori, A., & Immonen, A. (2004). Product lifecycle management systems. In *Product Lifecycle Management*. Berlin: Springer. doi:10.1007/978-3-540-24799-9_3

Sabogal, J. (2017). *Integrating IoT then Blockchain into your Drug Supply Chain*. Rockville, MD: IEEE Standards Association.

Saboo, M., Chourey A., & Suranglikar M.. (2017). *The Internet of Things:The New Rx for Pharmaceuticals Manufacturing & Supply Chains*. Cognizant.

Safdar, M. N., Kausar, T., Jabbar, S., Mumtaz, A., Ahad, K., & Saddozai, A. A. (in press). Extraction and quantification of polyphenols from kinnow (*Citrus reticulate* L.) peel using ultrasound and maceration techniques. *Journal of Food and Drug Analysis*. PMID:28911634

Samaranayake, Y. H., Ye, J., Yau, J. Y. Y., Cheung, B. P. K., & Smaranayake, L. P. (2005). In vitro method to study antifungal perfusion in Candida biofilms. *Journal of Clinical Microbiology*, *43*(2), 818–825. doi:10.1128/JCM.43.2.818-825.2005 PMID:15695686

Sampata, B. N., & Shadlen, K. C. (2017). Secondary pharmaceutical patenting: A global perspective. *Research Policy*, *46*(3), 693–707. doi:10.1016/j.respol.2017.01.005

Samuel, K. E., Goury, M. L., Gunasekaran, A., & Spalanzani, A. (2011). Knowledge management in supply chain: An empirical study from France. *The Journal of Strategic Information Systems*, *20*(3), 283–306. doi:10.1016/j.jsis.2010.11.001

Sangjae, L., & Gun, L. G. (2003). The impact of partnership attributes on EDI implementation success. *Information & Management*, *42*, 503–516.

Schneeweiss, C. (2002). *Einführung in die Produktionswirtschaft* (8th ed.). Berlin: Springer. doi:10.1007/978-3-642-59418-2

Schneider, J., & Jennifer, S. (2004). *Thesis on Integrated sustainability in the pharmaceutical industry*. Rochester Institute of Technology RIT Scholar Works. Retrieved from: http://scholarworks.rit.edu/article

Schneller, E. S., & Schmeltzer, L. R. (2006). *Strategic management of the health care supply chain*. San Francisco, CA: Jossey-Bass.

Schöner, M. M., Kourouklis, D., Sandner, P., Gonzalez, E., & Förster, J. (2017). *Blockchain Technology in the Pharmaceutical Industry*. Frankfurt, Germany: Frankfurt School Blockchain Center.

Settanni, E., Harrington, T. S., & Srai, J. S. (2017). Pharmaceutical supply chain models: A synthesis from a systems view of operations research. *Operations Research Perspectives*, *4*, 74–95. doi:10.1016/j.orp.2017.05.002

Shafaat, K., Hussain, A., Kumar, B., Hasan, R. U., Prabhat, P., & Yadav, V. K. (2013). *World Journal of Pharmacy and Pharmaceutical Sciences*, *2*(5), 2499–2515.

Shah, N. (2004). Pharmaceutical supply chains: Key issues and strategies for optimisation. *Computers & Chemical Engineering*, *28*(6), 929–941. doi:10.1016/j.compchemeng.2003.09.022

Shanmugam, S. (2015). Granulation techniques and technologies: Recent progresses. *BioImpacts*, *5*(1), 55–63. doi:10.15171/bi.2015.04 PMID:25901297

Shapiro, J. F. (2001). *Beyond Supply Chain Optimization to Enterprise Optimization*. Enterprise Optimization, Academic Research.

Sharma, B. P., Singh, M. D., & Neha. (2012). Knowledge sharing barriers: An approach of interpretive structural modeling. *IUP Journal of Knowledge Management, 10*(3), 35 - 52.

Shaw, B., & Whitney, P. (2016). Ethics and compliance in global pharmaceutical industry marketing and promotion: The role of the IFPMA and self-regulation. *Pharmaceuticals Policy and Law*, *18*(1-4), 199–206. doi:10.3233/PPL-160443

Shih, S. C., Hsu, S. H., Zhu, Z., & Balasubramanian, S. K. (2012). Knowledge sharing—A key role in the downstream supply chain. *Information & Management*, *49*(2), 70–80. doi:10.1016/j.im.2012.01.001

Shih-Yuan, W., Chang, S.-L., & Wang, R.-C. (2006). Assessment of supplier performance based on product-development strategy by applying multi-granularity linguistic term sets. *Omega*.

Shijaku, R., Larraza-Kintana, M., & Urtasun-Alonso, A. (2016). Organizational dynamic embeddedness and external shocks: The impact of financial and recession crises in strategic networks of the global pharmaceutical industry. *Complexity*, *21*(S1), 602–621. doi:10.1002/cplx.21776

Shirai, H., Prades, C., Vita, R., Marcatili, P., Popovic, B., Xu, J., ... Ikeda, K. (2014). Antibody informatics for drug discovery. *Biochimica et Biophysica Acta (BBA) -. Proteins and Proteomics*, *1844*(11), 2002–2015. doi:10.1016/j.bbapap.2014.07.006

Shou, Y. (2013). Perspectives on Supply Chain Management in the Healthcare Industry. In *2nd International Conference on Science and Social Research*. Atlantis Press. 10.2991/icssr-13.2013.144

Shyh-Rong, F., Jyh-Jeng, W., Shih-Chieh, F., Chang, Y.-S., & Chao, P.-W. (2008). Generating effective inter-organizational change: A relational approach. *Industrial Marketing Management*, *37*(8), 977–991. doi:10.1016/j.indmarman.2007.08.004

Siau, K., & Tian, Y. (2004). Supply chains integration: Architecture and enabling technologies. *The Journal of Computer Information Systems*, *44*(3), 67.

Silva, R. P. F. F., Rocha-Santosa, T. A. P., & Duarte, A. C. (2016). Supercritical fluid extraction of bioactive compounds. *TrAC Trends in Analytical Chemistry*, *76*, 40–51. doi:10.1016/j.trac.2015.11.013

Silver, E., Pyke, D., & Peterson, R. (1998). *Inventory management and production planning and scheduling* (3rd ed.). New York: Wiley.

Simonin, B. L. (2004). An empirical investigation of the process of knowledge transfer in international strategic alliances. *Journal of International Business Studies*, *35*(5), 407–427. doi:10.1057/palgrave.jibs.8400091

Singh, M. (2005). *The Pharmaceutical Supply Chain: a Diagnosis of the State-of-the-Art (Master thesis)*. Boston: Massachusetts Institute of Technology.

Singh, M. D., & Kant, R. (2008). Knowledge management barriers: An interpretive structural modeling approach. *International Journal of Management Science and Engineering Management*, *3*(2), 141–150.

Sinha, S., & Vohora, D. (2018). Drug Discovery and Development: An Overview. Pharmaceutical Medicine and Translational Clinical Research, 19-32.

Siqueira, S., Falcao-Silva, V. D. S., Agra, M. D. F., Dariva, C., Siqueira-Junior, S. P. D., & Fonseca, M. J. V. (2011). Biological activities of Solanum paludosum Moric. extracts obtained by maceration and supercritical fluid extraction. *The Journal of Supercritical Fluids*, *58*(3), 391–397. doi:10.1016/j.supflu.2011.06.011

Skandynawsko-Polska Izba Gospodarcza. CSRinfo. (2012). CSR w łańcuchu dostaw I w partnerstwie biznesowym – doświadczenia firm skandynawskich. Warszawa: CSRinfo.

Sliwoski, G., Kothiwale, S., Meiler, J., & Lowe, E. W. Jr. (2014). Computational methods in drug discovery. *Pharmacological Reviews*, *66*(1), 334–395. doi:10.1124/pr.112.007336 PMID:24381236

Smith, R., & Van De Ven, A. H. (1992). Structuring Cooperative Relationships between Organizations. *Strategic Management Journal*, *13*(7), 483–498. doi:10.1002mj.4250130702

So Young, S., & Michael, L. (2008). The effect of forecasting and information sharing in SCM, for multi-generation products. *European Journal of Operational Research*, *186*(1), 276–287. doi:10.1016/j.ejor.2007.01.034

Soliman, K. S., & Janz, B. D. (2004). An exploratory study to identify the critical factors affecting the decision to establish Internet-based inter-organizational information systems. *Information & Management*, *41*(6), 697–706. doi:10.1016/j.im.2003.06.001

Sousa, R. T., Liu, S., Papageorgiou, L. G., & Shah, N. (2011). Global supply chain planning for pharmaceuticals. *Chemical Engineering Research & Design*, *89*(11), 2396–2409. doi:10.1016/j.cherd.2011.04.005

Spekman, R. E., Spear, J., & Kamauff, J. (2002). Supply chain competency: Learning as a key component. *Supply Chain Management*, *7*(1), 41–55. doi:10.1108/13598540210414373

Spigarelli, F., & Wei, H. (2012). *The rising Chinese pharmaceutical industry: local champions vs global players*. c.MET Working paper 06/2012.

Srinivasan, K., Kekre, S., & Mukhopadhyay, T. (1994). Impact of Electronic Data Interchange Technology on JIT Shipments. *Management Science*, *40*(10), 1291–1304. doi:10.1287/mnsc.40.10.1291

Srivastava, A., & Dave, M. (2017). *Is Blockchain A Pipe Dream Or Right Fit For Pharma Supply Chain*. Rockville, MD: IEEE Standards Association.

Srivastava, R. (2016). How Indian Pharmaceutical Companies Are Building Global Brands: The Case of the Himalaya Herbal Brand. *Thunderbird International Business Review*, *58*(5), 399–410. doi:10.1002/tie.21827

Stadtler, H. (2004). Supply chain management- An overview. *Supply Chain Management and Advanced Planning, 3*, 9-24.

Stadtler, H. (2008). Supply Chain Management - An Overview. In H. Stadtler & C. Kilger (Eds.), *Supply Chain Management and Advanced Planning. Concepts, Models, Software and Case Studies* (4th ed.; pp. 3–28). Berlin: Springer.

Stadtler, H., Kilger, C., & Meyr, H. (Eds.). (2015). *Supply Chain Management and Advanced Planning*. Berlin: Springer. doi:10.1007/978-3-642-55309-7

Staples, M., Chen, S., Falamaki, S., Ponomarev, A., Rimba, P., Tran, A. B., ... Zhu, J. (2017). *Risks and opportunities for systems using blockchain and smart contracts. Data61*. CSIRO.

Statista. (2017). *Medicine Spending Worldwide*. Retrieved from: https://www.statista.com/statistics/280572/medicine-spending-worldwide/

Statista. (2018). *Global pharmaceutical sales from 2015 to 2017, by region (in billion U.S. dollars)*. Retrieved from: https://www.statista.com/statistics/272181/world-pharmaceutical-sales-by-region/

Subramani Mani, R. (2003, September). How suppliers benefit from IT use in supply chain relationships? *MIS Quarterly*.

Suppliers Polpharma. (2017). *Suppliers Code of Conduct*. Retrieved from: dostawca.polpharma.pl

Susarla, N., & Karimi, I. A. (2012). Integrated supply chain planning for multinational pharmaceutical enterprises. *Computers & Chemical Engineering*, *42*, 168–177. doi:10.1016/j.compchemeng.2012.03.002

Swaminathan, J. M., Smith, S. F., & Sadeh, N. M. (1998). Modeling Supply Chain Dynamics: A Multiagent Approach. *Decision Sciences*, *29*(3), 607–632. doi:10.1111/j.1540-5915.1998.tb01356.x

Szmelter, A. (2017). *Determinanty kształtowania strategii logistycznych w światowym przemyśle motoryzacyjnym* (Unpublished doctoral dissertation). University of Gdańsk, Sopot, Poland.

Szmelter, A. (2012). Wykorzystanie koncepcji Six Sigma w logistyce zaopatrzenia. *Roczniki Naukowe Wyższej Szkoły Bankowej w Toruniu, 11*(11), 391–402.

Szmelter, A. (2014). *Synergy phenomenon in supply logistics*. Saarbrücken: LAP Lambert Academic Publishing.

Szulanski, G. (2003). *Sticky knowledge: barriers to knowing in the firm*. London: Sage Publications.

Szymczak, M. (2004). *Logistyka w procesie internacjonalizacji przedsiębiorstw*. Poznań: Wyd. AE w Poznaniu.

Teker, S. C. (2017). The Implementation of Analytic Hierarchy Process in Pharmaceutical Industry for Selection Process of 3rd Party Logistics Service Provider. *Öneri, 12*(48), 107-124.

Tempest, B. (2010). A structural change in the global pharmaceutical marketplace. *Journal of Genetic Medicine*, *7*, 113–117.

Teuteberg, F., & Wittstruck, D. (2010). A Systematic Review of Sustainable Supply Chain Management Research. What is there and what is missing? Osnabruck: University of Osnabruck: Betriebliches Umwelt- und Nachhaltigkeitsmanagement.

Thomas Douglas, J., & Griffin Paul, M. (1996). Invited Review Coordinated supply chain management. *European Journal of Operational Research*, *94*(1), 1–15. doi:10.1016/0377-2217(96)00098-7

Thomé, A. M. T., Hollmann, R. L., & do Carmo, L. S. (2014). Research synthesis in collaborative planning forecast and replenishment. *Industrial Management & Data Systems*, *114*(6), 949–965. doi:10.1108/IMDS-03-2014-0085

Titi Amayah, A. (2013). Determinants of knowledge sharing in a public sector organization. *Journal of Knowledge Management*, *17*(3), 454–471. doi:10.1108/JKM-11-2012-0369

Toma, S.-G., & Marinescu, P. (2012). Business Models Based on Corporate Social Responsibility: The Case of Global Pharmaceutical Companies. Ovidius University Annals. *Economics Sciences Series*, *XII*(1), 1221–1225.

Torreya. (2017). *Global Pharma Industry Study*. Retrieved from: https://torreya.com/publications/torreya_global_pharma_industry_study_october2017.pdf

Toru, S., Clay, D. C., & Nicovich Stefan, G. (2002). Development of an integrated supply chain model. *Eighth Americas Conference on Information Systems*.

Tracey, M., & Tan, C. L. (2001). Empirical analysis of supplier selection and involvement, customer satisfaction, and firm performance. *Supply Chain Management*, *6*(3–4), 174–188. doi:10.1108/EUM0000000005709

Trevor, W. (1997). Strategic Information systems Interorganisational Information Systems: Issues affecting interorganisational cooperation. *The Journal of Strategic Information Systems*, *6*(3), 231–250. doi:10.1016/S0963-8687(97)00018-8

Tridas, M., Sunder, K., & Suresh, K. (1995). Business Value of Information Technology: A Study of Electronic Data Interchange. *Management Information Systems Quarterly*, *19*(2), 137–156. doi:10.2307/249685

Trkman, P., McCormack, K., de Oliveira, M. P. V., & Ladeira, M. B. (2010). The impact of business analytics on supply chain performance. *Decision Support Systems*, *49*(3), 318–327. doi:10.1016/j.dss.2010.03.007

Tung-Lai, H., & Jiuh-Biing, S. (2005). Relationships of channel power, noncoercive influence strategies, climate, and solidarity: A real case study of the Taiwanese PDA industry. *Industrial Marketing Management*, *34*(5), 447–461. doi:10.1016/j.indmarman.2004.10.005

Twiss, B. C. (1984). Forecasting Market Size and Market Growth Rates for New Products. *Journal of Product Innovation Management*, *1*(1), 19–29. doi:10.1016/S0737-6782(84)80039-9

U.S. Congress, Office of Technology Assessment (OTA), Innovation and Commercialization of Emerging Technology, OTA-BP-ITC-165. (1995). Washington, DC: U.S. Government Printing Office.

USPTO. (2017). *United States Patent and Trademark Office*. Retrieved from: http://www.uspto.gov/

Uthayakumar, R., & Priyan, S. (2013). Pharmaceutical supply chain and inventory management strategies: Optimization for a pharmaceutical company and a hospital. *Operations Research for Health Care*, *2*(3), 52–64. doi:10.1016/j.orhc.2013.08.001

Vajjhala, N. R., & Vucetic, J. (2013). Key barriers to knowledge sharing in medium-sized enterprises in transition economies. *International Journal of Business and Social Science*, *4*(13), 90–98.

Van Peteghem, D. (2015). *Four Trends Redefining the Healthcare Supply Chain*. Retrieved from http://www.sustainablebrands.com/press/four_trends_redefining_healthcare_supply_chain

Verma, R., & Pullman, M. E. (1998). An analysis of the supplier selection process. *Omega*, *26*(6), 739–750. doi:10.1016/S0305-0483(98)00023-1

Verniers, I., Stremersch, S., & Croux, C. (2011). The global entry of new pharmaceuticals: A joint investigation of launch window and price. *International Journal of Research in Marketing*, *28*(4), 295–308. doi:10.1016/j.ijresmar.2011.05.008

Vonderembse, M. A., Uppal, M., Huang, S. H., & Dismukes, J. P. (2006). Designing supply chains: Towards theory development. *International Journal of Production Economics*, *100*(2), 223–238. doi:10.1016/j.ijpe.2004.11.014

Wagenknecht, C. (2001). *Logistik - Planung und Steuerung von umfassenden Geschäftsprozessen.* Retrieved from: http://www.uni-kl.de/MISP/vortrag_wagenknecht.pdf

Wang, Y., Wallace, S. T., Shen, B., & Choi, T. M. (2015). Service supply chain management: A review of operational models. *European Journal of Operational Research*, *247*(3), 685–698. doi:10.1016/j.ejor.2015.05.053

Warkentin, Sugumaran, & Bapna. (2001). E-knowledge networks for inter-organizational collaborative e-business. *Logistics Information Management*, *14*(1-2), 149-162.

Wasielewska-Marszałkowska, I. (2015). Rozwój oferty usług i zadań usługodawców logistycznych i jego wpływ na zarzadzanie współczesnymi łańcuchami dostaw. *Zeszyty Naukowe Uniwersytetu Gdańskiego. Ekonomika Transportu i Logistyka*, *56*, 177–190.

Wasko, M. M., & Faraj, S. (2005). Why should I share? Examining social capital and knowledge contribution in electronic networks of practice. *Management Information Systems Quarterly*, *29*(1), 35–57. doi:10.2307/25148667

Weiland, D. (2016). Omnichannel as a new challenge for logistics. *Torun Business Review*, *15*(4), 69–78.

Wellman, G.S. (2001) National supply-chain survey of drug manufacturer back orders. *American Journal of Health-Systems Pharmacy, 61*.

Wenna. (2002). *The transforming power of Business to Business Electronic Business*. Next Generation Business Publishing.

Werner, J., & Gerald, R. (2007). Performance improvement of supply chain processes by coordinated inventory and capacity management. *International Journal of Production Economics*, *108*(1-2), 183–190. doi:10.1016/j.ijpe.2006.12.047

Westphal, R. (2000). Komplexitätsmanagement in der Produktionslogistik. *Diskussionsbeiträge aus dem Institut für Wirtschaft und Verkehr*, *4*, 1–61.

Wildgoose, N. (2016). Supply Chain Risk Management. Enterprise Risk Management, 75-87.

William, D., & McCarthy, J. E. (1997). *Product Life Cycle: "Essentials of Marketing"*. Richard D Irwin Company.

Williams, C. T. (2015). Food and Drug Administration Drug Approval Process: A History and Overview. *The Nursing Clinics of North America*, *51*(1), 1–11. doi:10.1016/j.cnur.2015.10.007 PMID:26897420

Williamson Oliver, E. (1981). The economics of organization: The transaction cost approach. *American Journal of Sociology*, *87*(3), 548–577. doi:10.1086/227496

Wilson, M., Williams, M. A., Jones, D. S., & Andrews, G. P. (2012). Hot-melt extrusion technology and pharmaceutical application. *Therapeutic Delivery*, *3*(6), 787–797. doi:10.4155/tde.12.26 PMID:22838073

Witkowski, J. (1995). *Strategia logistyczna przedsiębiorstw przemysłowych*. Wrocław: Wyd. AE we Wrocławiu.

Witkowski, J. (2005). *Strategie i logistyka organizacji sieciowych*. Wrocław: Wydawnictwo Akademii Ekonomicznej im. Oskara Langego we Wrocławiu.

Witkowski, J. (2010). *Zarządzanie łańcuchem dostaw. Koncepcje, procedury, doświadczenia*. Warszawa: PWE.

Witmer, D., & Deffenbaugh, J. (2004) The pharmaceutical supply chain: A perfect storm is brewing. *American Journal of Health-Systems Pharmacy, 61*.

Witty, A. (2011). New Strategies For Innovation In Global Health: A Pharmaceutical Industry Perspective. *Health Affairs*, *30*(1), 118–126. doi:10.1377/hlthaff.2010.0933 PMID:21209447

Wong, W. P., & Wong, P. S. (2011). Supply chain management, knowledge management capability, and their linkages towards firm performance. *Business Process Management Journal*, *17*(6), 940–964. doi:10.1108/14637151111182701

Woosley, J. (2009). *Improving Healthcare Supply Chains and Decision Making in the Management of Pharmaceuticals* (Unpublished doctoral dissertation). Louisiana State University, Baton Rouge, LA.

Yang, F., Chen, P., He, W., Gu, N., Zhang, X., Fang, K., ... Tong, J. (2010). Bubble Microreactors Triggered by an Alternating Magnetic Field as Diagnostic and Therapeutic Delivery Devices. *Small*, *6*(12), 1300–1305. doi:10.1002mll.201000173 PMID:20486225

Yannis & Erik. (1992). *When Quality Matters: Information Technology And Buyer-Supplier Relationships*. Center for Coordination Science Technical Report.

Yao, X., Ding, J., Liu, Y., & Li, P. (2017). The New Drug Conditional Approval Process in China: Challenges and Opportunities. *Clinical Therapeutics*, *39*(5), 1040–1051. doi:10.1016/j.clinthera.2017.03.016 PMID:28431767

Yeung, Lo, Yeung, & Cheng. (2008). Specific customer knowledge and operational performance in apparel manufacturing. *International Journal of Production Economics*.

Yu, X., Li, C., Shi, Y., & Yu, M. (2010). Pharmaceutical supply chain in China: Current issues and implications for health system reform. *Health Policy (Amsterdam)*, *97*(1), 8–15. doi:10.1016/j.healthpol.2010.02.010 PMID:20307912

Yu, Z., Yan, H., & Edwin Cheng, T. C. (2001). Benefits of information sharing with supply chain partnerships. *Industrial Management & Data Systems*, *101*(3), 114–121. doi:10.1108/02635570110386625

Zadbuke, N., Shahi, S., Gulecha, B., Padalkar, A., & Thube, M. (2013). Recent trends and future of pharmaceutical packaging technology. *Journal of Pharmacy & Bioallied Sciences*, *5*(2), 98–110. doi:10.4103/0975-7406.111820 PMID:23833515

Zahiri, B., Jula, P., & Moghaddam, R. T. (2018). Design of a pharmaceutical supply chain network under uncertainty considering perishability and substitutability of products. *Information Sciences*, *423*, 257–283. doi:10.1016/j.ins.2017.09.046

Zahiri, B., Zhuang, J., & Mohammadi, M. (2017). Toward an integrated sustainable-resilient supply chain: A pharmaceutical case study. *Transportation Research Part E, Logistics and Transportation Review*, *103*, 109–142. doi:10.1016/j.tre.2017.04.009

Zailani, S., Jeyaraman, K., Vengadasan, G., & Premkumar, R. (2012). Sustainable Supply Chain Management (SSCM) in Malaysia: A survey. *International Journal of Production Economics*, *140*(1), 330–340. doi:10.1016/j.ijpe.2012.02.008

Zannou, E. A., Li, P., & Tong, W. Q. (2009). Chapter 40 – Product Lifecycle Management (LCM). In Developing Solid Oral Dosage Forms, Pharmaceutical Theory and Practice (pp. 911-921). Academic Press.

Zhao, J., Pablo, P., & Qi, Z. (2012). Enterprise knowledge management model based on China's practice and case study. *Computers in Human Behavior*, *28*(2), 324–330. doi:10.1016/j.chb.2011.10.001

Zheng, Y., Tice, C. M., & Singh, S. B. (2017). Conformational control in structure-based drug design. *Bioorganic & Medicinal Chemistry Letters*, *27*(13), 2825–2837. doi:10.1016/j.bmcl.2017.04.079 PMID:28479196

Zhou, H., & Benton, W. C. Jr. (2007). Supply chain practice and information sharing. *Journal of Operations Management*, *25*(6), 1348–1365. doi:10.1016/j.jom.2007.01.009

About the Contributors

Hamed Nozari was born in Iran, in 1984. He received the BS. Degree in Mechanical engineering (fluid mechanic) in 2009, and continued his educations in Industrial Engineering (production planning and Socioeconomics engineering) in MSc and PhD levels. He has taught various courses in the field of Industrial Engineering and has published many books and papers as well. Now he is a researcher in the field of operations research and metaheuristic algorithms.

Agnieszka Szmelter, PhD, is a research assistant at the Chair of Logistics, Faculty of Economics, University of Gdańsk since 2012. She is an author of over 20 scientific papers in English and Polish. Her book "Synergy phenomenon in supply logistics" was awarded by The Polish Centre for Analyses in Transport and Infrastructure. Her major scientific interests are logistics strategies and mobility cultures. She is a Lean Six Sigma Black Belt, ISO 9001 and 14001 internal auditor, SAP Certified Application Associate and Design Thinking Moderator.

* * *

Mokhtar Amami (PhD) is a Professor of Strategic Management of Technology at Royal Military College of Canada. His researches have been published in management journals and some books of micro-economy. His research interests include information systems use and supply chain management.

Debdeep Chatterjee is currently a graduate student in Supply Chain Management at John Molson School of Business, Concordia University, Canada. He is a graduate of Jadavpur University, Calcutta, in Metallurgical and Material Science Engineering. He has worked as consultant in a European multinational before this joining Concordia University and his areas of interest primarily entail supply chain management, knowledge management and sustainability studies.

Femina Carolin Christopher is working as Junior Research Fellow in SSN college of engineering. She has completed the schooling in St. Mary's Girls Higher Secondary School. Then she has done her UG course (B.Tech- Biotechnology) at Vel Tech High Tech Dr. Rangarajan Dr. Sakunthala Engineering College. Additionally, she has completed PG Course (M.Tech- Environmental Science and Technology) in SSN College of Engineering, Secured Gold Medal in M.Tech Environmental Science And Technology (1st Rank in Anna University, Chennai). Now she has got admission to do Ph.D at the same college. Currently, she is doing her research in the field " Application of enzymatic treatment in industrial wastewater". In this research, she would like to invoke her creativity to utilize the best of her abilities and she will contribute her efforts towards the research growth.

Anirban Ganguly holds a BSc and MBA degrees from the University of Calcutta, and also MS and PhD from Stevens Institute of Technology, USA. He is currently an Associate Professor and Director, Center for Asia Pacific Business Research & Innovation with the Jindal Global School of Business at O. P. Jindal Global University, Haryana, India. His research interest include operations and supply chain management, technology and innovation management, risk analysis and knowledge management. His research has been published in International Journal of Production Economics, International Journal of Operations and Production Management, Industrial Management & Data Systems, The Engineering Economist, International Journal of Knowledge Management, Engineering Management Journal, IEEE Aerospace & Electronics Systems Journal and International Journal of Innovation and Technology Management, among others.

Elumalai Gunasundari was born and has been living in Chennai, Tamilnadu, India since 1992. Currently, she is doing her Ph.D. in Technology in Centre for Research, Anna University, Chennai, Tamilnadu, India. Her research focuses on the biosorption of toxic pollutant using algal biomass. She has an M.Tech in Polymer Science and Engineering (2015) from Anna University and B.Tech in Chemical Engineering (2013) from Adhiparasakthi Engineering College (Anna University affiliated). She has published three research papers in highly reputed International Journals. She has also published one book chapter in the reputed publisher by Springer and three book chapters under revision in the reputed publishers.

Arun Kumar Nageswar is a post-graduate from Visvesvaraya Technological University, Belagavi, India. He has Master of Technology degree in the field of Digital Electronics. He has a Bachelor of Engineering degree in Electronics from B.M.S College of Engineering, Bengaluru, India. Business analytics and Machine

Learning is his main area of interest. Arun has presented research papers in IEEE seminars and has published research papers in IEEE Xplore Digital Library. He has co-authored a book chapter titled 'Disruptive Innovation for Auto Insurance Entrepreneurs' in Springer publication.

Tharwa Najar (PhD, University of Mannouba, Tunisia) is an assistant and a Doctor in Management Sciences in the University of Gafsa, Tunisia. Her researches have been published in management journals and supply chain journals. Her research interests include the supply chain management and information systems use and interorganizational relationships in B2B environment in the automotive industry.

Katarzyna Osiecka-Brzeska is an Assistant Professor in Higher School of Administration and Business in Gdynia, Poland. She graduated from the University of Gdańsk, where in 2014 she defended the PhD thesis "Determinants of use of renewable energy in Poland in the context of sustainable development". Katarzyna Osiecka-Brzeska has a professional experience in the field of process and project management. She has cooperated with Polish corporation in the field of high-tech, telecommunication and renewable energy investment projects. Her main field of research is sustainability at national and corporation levels.

Senthil Kumar Ponnusamy is an Associate Professor in the Department of Chemical Engineering at SSN College of Engineering, Chennai, India. He received his B.Tech. in Chemical Engineering (University of Madras, India), M.E. in Environmental Engineering (Anna University, India) and Ph.D. in Environmental Engineering (Anna University, India). He has 11 years of teaching experience, 10 years of research experience and 1 year of industrial experience. He is a recognized Anna University Research Supervisor to guide Ph.D./ M.S. candidates. Under his guidance, 03 Ph.D Scholars have completed, and 10 Ph.D. scholars are currently doing their active research in the area of Waste Water Treatment and Alternative Fuels. He has published more than 125+ research papers in a highly reputed International Journals (Authors h-index is 22+ with 2013+ citations) and 70 research papers in National/International Conferences. He has also published more than 25 book chapters in the reputed publishers which include Springer and Elsevier. His active research area includes Adsorption Separation Technology, Activated Carbon, Alternative Fuels, Advanced Oxidation Process, CO2 Sequestration, Chemical Reaction Engineering, Environmental Engineering and Nanotechnology. He was a recipient of many outstanding awards from home and abroad.

Yaashikaa Ponnambalam Ragini is pursuing PhD in Department of Chemical Engineering, SSN College of Engineering, Chennai. Her research focus is on wastewater treatment and elimination of heavy metals in industrial effluents. She has published papers in reputed journals and book chapters in Springer and Elsevier. She is a member of the Indian Society for Technical Education and European Federation of Biotechnology (EFB).

Alma Isela Rodriguez Hernandez is a researcher specialized in collaboration in the Mexican pharmaceutical industry and collaboration as a form of strategy of the companies and public organizations.

Anbalagan Saravanan, Assistant Professor in the Department of Biotechnology, Rajalakshmi Engineering College, Chennai, India. He has over 4 years of teaching and 3 years of research experience. His active research area includes Environmental Biotechnology, Waste water Treatment, Enzyme engineering, Pharmaceutical sciences, etc. and published over 38 research papers in various International journals and 18 book chapters in Elsevier and Springer. He also has received a young researcher awards and best researcher award. He has organized/attended many conferences, workshops and seminars at national and international level. Member of professional societies like International Association of Engineers (IAENG) and European Federation of Biotechnology (EFB).

Asim Talukdar is an Associate Professor of Management Practice and Associate Dean (Career Development). He received his Bachelors from University of Calcutta and his PGDM from Indian Institute of Management, Calcutta and Fellow PhD from XLRI, Jamshedpur. Besides academic experiences, Dr. Talukdar also has extensive industry experience having worked in the senior leadership roles at a number of companies in India like NIIT Ltd,, HT Media Ltd., Maruti Suzuki Ltd,, and PepsiCo (India).

José G. Vargas-Hernández, M.B.A., Ph.D., is a member of the National System of Researchers of Mexico and a research professor at University Center for Economic and Managerial Sciences, University of Guadalajara. Professor Vargas-Hernández has a Ph. D. in Public Administration and a Ph.D. in Organizational Economics. He has undertaken studies in Organisational Behaviour and has a Master of Business Administration, published four books and more than 200 papers in international journals and reviews (some translated to English, French, German, Portuguese, Farsi, Chinese, etc.) and more than 300 essays in national journals and reviews. He has obtained several international awards and recognition.

Siva Yellampalli is currently working as a Principal with VTU Extension Centre, UTL Technologies Ltd. He obtained his MS & PhD from Louisiana State University. His area of research is system level design for power optimization. His area of research encompasses different research fields such as VLSI, mixed-signal circuits/systems development, MEMS, and CNT sensors. He has published a book in the area of mixed-signal design and edited two books on carbon nanotubes. He published 70 plus International Journal papers & IEEE Conference papers. In addition, he has delivered keynote speeches at International conferences held in Canada, Dubai & Spain including tutorials at various IEEE International Conferences. He has been a consultant to a variety of industries and acts as a reviewer for technical journals and book publishers.

Index

T

U

www.ingramcontent.com/pod-product-compliance
Lightning Source LLC
LaVergne TN
LVHW080606300926
849162LV00005B/1056
* 9 7 8 1 5 2 2 5 5 9 2 1 4 *